THE SAME ONLY DIFFERENT

MARGARET WEBSTER

THE SAME ONLY DIFFERENT

FIVE GENERATIONS OF A GREAT THEATRE FAMILY

LONDON
VICTOR GOLLANCZ LTD
1969

Printed in Great Britain by
Lowe & Brydone (Printers) Ltd., London

for Pamela

ACKNOWLEDGMENTS

I am greatly indebted to Miss Helen Willard and her assistants at the Theatre Collection of Harvard College Library for their help in obtaining much of the MSS material used in Part I; to the curators and librarians of the Gabrielle Enthoven Collection, Victoria and Albert Museum, London; the British Drama League, London; the Theatre Collection at Lincoln Center, New York; the University of Texas Libraries; the British Museum; the Libraries of Lincoln's Inn, the Inner Temple, and the Garrick Club; Mrs. Anthony Thomas of the Ellen Terry Museum, Small Hythe. Messrs. Mander and Mitchenson supplied me with interesting material from their collection and very kindly agreed to check my typescript. Mrs. Jane Brundred proofread for me and assisted in compiling the index; Miss Vera Ledger did much patient research on the Webster family affairs. My thanks to all of them.

I gratefully acknowledge the permission of the following for the use of copyright material:

Harvard College Library (See above.)
The Public Trustee, the Society of Authors and Professor Dan H.
    Laurence (Letters of George Bernard Shaw.)

Acknowledgments

Mr. W. D'Arcy Hart (Letters of Ellen Terry.)

Professor Charles E. Shattuck ("Bulwer and Macready.")

George Allen and Unwin Ltd. ("The Art of the Actor" by Co-quelin, Tr. Elsie Fogerty.)

Hutchinson Press Publishing Group ("To Tell my Story," Irene Vanbrugh.)

Messrs. Putnam and Co. ("Four Years at the Old Vic," Harcourt Williams.)

Hector Bolitho ("Marie Tempest.")

The Charles Dickens letter on page 63 is from the collection of the Count de Suzannet in Lausanne and is quoted from the transcription in the Nonesuch Press, by permission of the estate of George Macy.

My thanks are due to the following for various items of information and other miscellaneous gleanings: Dame Sybil and Sir Lewis Casson; Mr. Edward Craig; Professor Allan Downer; Mr. Maurice Evans; Miss Freda Gaye; Mr. Ivor Guest; Mr. Peter Henschitz; Mr. Laurence Irving; Sir Alick Jeans and his staff of the *Liverpool Daily Post;* Miss Eva Le Gallienne; Miss Kathleen Lockley; Miss Caroline Ramsden; Mr. Ernest Raymond; Lt. Col. Rudyard Russell; Mr. Leslie Staples and Mrs. M. E. House of the Dickens Society; the public relations staff of the *Daily Telegraph;* and Mr. J. C. Trewin. Also to many actors and people of the theatre who have lent me their memories; to all those who helped me to recover my lost MSS and papers while I was working on this book; and to Pamela Frankau, whose example and encouragement enabled me to write it, though she did not live to read it.

Martha's Vineyard, December 1968

FOREWORD

The family of the Websters was active in the British theatre, with many excursions to America, through four generations—five, if you count the dancing master who began it all. Actors have always tended to marry actors. This was understandable. Until fairly recent times they were "rogues and vagabonds" by law, debarred from "society", and unable, or unwilling, to settle down to the orthodox routines of trade. The Websters were connected by marriage with many other theatre families, among them the Wrights, the Lupinos and the spreading clan of the Broughs. My father married a newcomer to the profession, May Whitty. Three of my four uncles and aunts married actors. All of them were well-known players; one, the Ben Webster the First of this book, was an actor and manager of a type now extinct, a figure of magnitude on the London stage of the nineteenth century, who witnessed its revolutions and helped to shape them. My only first cousin, Jean Webster Brough, was, so far as I know, the last acting member of her family, as I am of mine.

This book covers a period of a hundred and forty years, until two of us, my mother and I, transplanted ourselves to sink new roots

Foreword

in a new world and begin a new cycle of experience. The first part contains the Webster family folklore, as handed down to me. It proved to be colorful, but incomplete. Unknown relatives rose from the depths, known ones sank out of sight. Since I am not obsessively ancestor-minded, I have been concerned only to clear the main channels through which the theatre current ran. In doing so I have used a great deal of unpublished material gleaned from widely scattered sources.

The second part is based on firsthand experiences, as told to me by my mother and father. In the summer of 1939, the last summer they were ever to spend in England, they dictated to me a mass of notes and recollections. Later, my mother collected all her old engagement books, dating back to the middle Eighties, and transcribed their entries. Sometimes she added comments as she went along. The result was not a diary, in the full sense of the word, but it is an invaluable book of reference. After my mother and father died, in 1947 and 1948, I recovered a quantity of their letters from a bombed-out storage house in London. The third part of the book begins when, like Alice, I step back through the Looking Glass and become recognizable to myself as me.

Over this period of time, it could be said that the theatre changed totally. The shapes of buildings; the nature of scenery, costumes, lighting; the quality (and quantity) of audiences, their demands and expectations; the training and employment of actors; the status of the stage as a profession; the economics of the theatre industry and the nature of the men who controlled it; above all, the plays themselves: these things were wholly different in 1937 from what they had been when Ben I was born in 1798. The crafts and skills of acting have remained the same, however, no matter to what material they have been applied or in what sort of building they have been exercised. When Roscius was an actor in Rome he had to prepare himself in much the same ways as an actor does today, though today's actor scorns to think so. Only the jargon has varied and the emphases shifted.

But despite the transformation of circumstance through which the Webster actors lived, the common ground of their experience has remained: the aspiration, the learning and the practice, the

Foreword

endeavors and ideals, the battles and defeats and momentary triumphs. Above all there were, I think, the same compulsions. I would prefer to call it dedication. "The theatre," my mother once said, "is an opportunity for giving, not a machinery for getting." It is a credo almost impossible to sustain under the everyday pressures of earning a living. Nevertheless, a sense of it remained, or so I believe, under all the failures and futilities and vanities, the razzle-dazzle and the transitory fame, so quickly blown away. We were a theatre people in a kind of theatre which will not come again.

CONTENTS

Part One   Old Ben

PROLOGUE *3*

CHAPTER

1   JOURNEY TO LONDON *6*

2   THEATRE ROYAL, DRURY LANE *17*

3   THEATRE ROYAL, HAYMARKET *41*

4   ''WE AT THE HEIGHT'' *55*

5   THE ADELPHI, OLD AND NEW *72*

EPILOGUE *92*

Part Two   Young Ben and May

6   THE INHERITORS *99*

7   PRELUDE IN LIVERPOOL *109*

8   YOUNG AMBITION'S LADDER *127*

9   GREAT STARS IN THE SKY *151*

10   TO AMERICA AND BACK *166*

11   GOLDEN INTERLUDE *193*

12   BRAVE NEW THEATRE *203*

13   SOME ENDINGS . . . *230*

xiii

Contents

Part Three   . . . and Margaret

14   SOME BEGINNINGS 259

15   A TIME TO SOW 282

16   LIVE AND LEARN 304

17   JOURNEY TO PICCADILLY CIRCUS 328

18   JOURNEY TO NEW YORK 353

EPILOGUE AND PROLOGUE 377

GENEALOGY 394

INDEX *following page* 396

ILLUSTRATIONS

following page 76

I   Portrait of Ben Webster I
           "The Reading of a Play in the Green Room of the Adelphi
           Theatre"

II–III   BEN WEBSTER I
           As Tartuffe
           As Joey Ladle in *No Thoroughfare*
           In *Apollo Belvi*
     (*By courtesy of the Theatre Collection of the Houghton Library, Harvard College*)
           As Penn Holder in *One Touch of Nature*
           As Robert Landry in *The Dead Heart*

IV–V   The New Adelphi Theatre, 1858
     (*By courtesy of the Enthoven Collection, the Victoria and Albert Museum*)
           Clara Webster
     (*By courtesy of the Theatre Collection of the Houghton Library, Harvard College*)
           Playbill for the first night of *Money*, December 8, 1840
     (*By courtesy of the Enthoven Collection, the Victoria and Albert Museum*)

VI–VII   MADAME CÉLESTE
           As "Miami, the huntress of the Mississippi," in *Green Bushes*
     (*By courtesy of the Theatre Collection of the Houghton Library, Harvard College*)

Illustrations

VI–VII   M A D A M E   C É L E S T E   (*continued*)

     Dancing the polka with Ben Webster, 1847
     (*By courtesy of the Theatre Collection of the Houghton Library, Harvard College*)
     Herself
     (*By courtesy of the Theatre Collection of the Houghton Library, Harvard College*)

VIII   Program of the benefit given for Ben Webster on his retirement
     Ben in his seventies
     Dedication of a testimonial dinner to Ben Webster, 1864

following page 236

IX   B E N   A N D   M A Y
     Ben
     May
     Ben and May at Woolacombe, 1892

X   T H E   W E B S T E R S
     Ben, Booey, and Lizzie
     Anna Sarah Johnson, mother of Ben III
     William S. Webster, father of Ben III

XI   T H E   W H I T T Y S
     Alfred Whitty, May's father, with Michael
     Mary Louisa Whitty, May's mother
     May
     Gretchen

XII   B E N   W E B S T E R   I I I
     In the first production of *Lady Windermere's Fan*
     As Sir Lancelot in *King Arthur*
     In *The Prince Consort*

Illustrations

XIII   MAY WHITTY
        In *Prince Karl*
        In *The Last of Mrs. Cheney*
                        (*By courtesy of Mander and Mitchenson*)

XIV   BEDFORD STREET DAYS
        Ellen Terry
        Edith Craig
        Marie Tempest
        Ethel Barrymore
        Hilda Trevelyan and Cecilia ("Cissie") Loftus in *Peter Pan*

XV   May Whitty becomes a Dame Commander of the British Empire, 1917
        Annual meeting of the Theatrical Ladies' Guild, 1909

XVI   Ben as the Caliph Abdullah in *Kismet*, 1911

following page 364

XVII   Miss Margaret Webster in fancy dress, 1909

XVIII   May Whitty, Peggy Webster, and Ben Webster in a charity pageant

XIX   Peggy as Puck in a school production, age fourteen
        Margaret Webster in *Medea*, 1929

XX–XXI MARGARET
        As Rosaline
        In *The Devil's Disciple*, 1930
        As Lady Macbeth at the Old Vic, 1932

Illustrations

XXII–XXIII   *Richard II* directed by Margaret Webster

(By courtesy of Geoffrey Landesman)

XXIV   Margaret Webster, director

(By courtesy of Trude Fleischman)

Dame May Whitty in the movie version of *Night Must Fall*

(By courtesy of Metro-Goldwyn-Mayer)

Ben and May in 1942, their Golden Wedding Anniversary

PART ONE

———————— ୪୪୪ ————————

Old Ben

PROLOGUE

My great-grandfather, Ben I, died in 1882. I was born in 1905. Nevertheless, I met him twice; on a strictly professional level.

We called him Old Ben in the family, to distinguish him from other Bens, including Young Ben, my father. A large painting of him hung in our dining room: forty-ish, strong face, dark receding hair, big nose, mobile lips and a lively, grey-blue eye; you could only see one and a half. Underneath was written: "To his grandson, from Squire Bancroft." This confusing inscription meant that Sir Squire Bancroft had presented the portrait to *its* grandson, Young Ben. As a child, I found it a little forbidding. Various engravings of Old Ben were hung around in darkish passages: as Tartuffe, as Triplet, as Apollo Belvi. I liked Apollo Belvi—the airy walk, the swing of the hips, the beribboned pumps, the impertinent cock of the head.

A very splendid silver epergne used to adorn the center of our table on high feasts and holidays, inscribed: "To Benjamin Webster Esq., from the Authors, Actors, Officers and Artizans of the Theatre Royal, Haymarket . . ."; and there was also an impressive salver presented to him when he left the Haymarket for the

3

Adelphi by "all the members of the company and others who have fulfilled engagements with him at the Little Theatre including the band artists and every servant on the establishment, as an affectionate token of regard and respect . . ." I found these rather touching. But I never took very much notice of Old Ben until I met him for myself.

In 1933 British Actors' Equity was struggling to get born. It had reached the point where every member had to undertake, voluntarily, to play only with companies which were one-hundred-per-cent Equity. Fate chose this moment to present me with my first chance to star in the West End of London. The part was Charlotte Brontë. The manager engaged for Emily a young star, far more distinguished than I, who was not a member of Equity and who refused to join it.

I wrote to him, explaining as gently as possible that unless all the Brontës became members, I could not be one of them. He sent for me to come and see him in his little office, tucked away under the roof of the Royalty Theatre. It was full of rolltop desks, old playbills, swivel chairs and tarnished gilt mirrors from bygone drawing-room comedies. The air was charged. He told me what a fool I was; he argued and stormed.

Finally, he dragged from behind one of the desks a framed print, and set it in front of me. "Look at it!" he said. It was Old Ben, as himself, leaning back in an armchair with his legs crossed, very nonchalant. I told the manager that we had a similar print at home. "But it's signed!" he said, triumphantly. "It's signed twice!" Indeed it was, once with a facsimile signature and once by hand; I knew the writing very well, it was almost identical with my father's. "And what," demanded my employer-not-to-be, "what would *he* think if he could hear what his granddaughter—" "*Great-*granddaughter," I murmured. "—*great* granddaughter has been saying to me today?"

I answered that since Old Ben had once sponsored an actors' association in his own day, the first of all such projects so far as I knew, I hoped he might approve of British Equity; but that in any case we would have to sort it out in the hereafter, and Emily Brontë must still become a member. This was his cue to say that I could go. I did so. I knew that I should never see my name in lights outside the Royalty Theatre. As I left the office, I cast a backward glance at Old Ben. I thought he looked pleased.

The second time I met him was more than twenty years later. I had spent most of the intervening time in the United States. My father and mother had died there. It had been a difficult task to dispose of their English possessions by remote control. I had decided to give the portrait of Old Ben to the Haymarket Theatre, since both he and Squire Bancroft, the donor of the picture, had contributed remarkable chapters to its history.

Some time later, after my return to London, I was directing a play there myself. The Haymarket, besides being very handsome, very dignified and full of history, is also extremely inconvenient. To get backstage from the auditorium, the director in a hurry has to climb up to the Dress Circle, change trains, and travel via the management's offices to the first-floor dressing rooms and so down again to the stage.

I was making this trip for the hundredth time; a dispirited trudge, filled with despondency, an awareness of all the things yet to be done and all the might-have-beens. In the management area, which was half dark, I passed a door, partly open. I became conscious of an Eye. I pushed open the door; the office was empty. I looked up at the wall, and there was Old Ben. "It's an arrogant head," I thought, "I hadn't remembered that; an actor's face if ever I saw one; the expression . . . hard to analyze . . . cynical? a little perhaps . . . amused? quizzical? appraising? certainly a challenge."

"How's it going?" said Old Ben. "Still the same as ever?" I was startled. "Well, no," I said, "I mean, everything's changed from what it was in your day. It's all quite different. . . ." He appeared to raise an eyebrow. I paused. Someone came along the passage and turned up the lights. I lifted a hand in salute and trudged on.

CHAPTER ONE

———— ০৪০ ————

Journey to London

The genealogy of the Webster family is not so much a tree as a jungle, swarming with Bens and Harriets and Johns and Williams. They all act, or dance. They appear for a moment on the stage, brilliantly spotlit, strike a dramatic attitude and vanish into obscurity. "For if an actor is to live in men's memories beyond the generation he lives in," wrote Old Ben himself, " 'by'r lady he must build churches', and even that would not much avail him."

The first of the theatre Websters to stride firmly into the limelight is Old Ben's father, Benjamin Nottingham Webster of Bath. Where the Nottingham came from, or why, I have no idea. His eldest son occasionally used it too, though very seldom. Theatre historians cling to it, quite without reason. They also repeat the engaging legend that Benjamin of Bath was descended from a certain Captain John Frederick Webster who was Conductor of Amusements there, died dramatically in a gambling duel, and bequeathed his office to a notable successor, Beau Nash. The legends provide some colorful intervening Websters of Bath; but they are all, alas, irrelevant. Benjamin came, incontrovertibly, from Sheffield. His

6

eldest son, Ben of the Haymarket, the Ben I of this book, gives a perfectly clear-cut account.

"Bath is my birthplace, and my father, a Yorkshireman born, is well known there as a professor of dancing. . . . He was the friend of Cooke, Elliston, Munden, Emery"—famous actors of the London stage—"and first came to Bath by command of the Duke of York to organise the Bath volunteers and met with so kind a reception there that he was induced to leave the army and settle down into a professor of dancing. . . . He had formerly been a composer and actor of pantomime, but it was only for a short while, his parents being violently opposed to it, particularly his mother whose maiden name was Buck and who was the first cousin of the celebrated Captain Cook and descended from the Bucke who wrote a vindication of Richard III during the reign of Henry VII."

It may have been this act of courage which prompted a contemporary to remark: "There has always seemed to me a good deal of the Buck about Ben." The Buck ancestors allegedly include the Sir George Buck who was Master of the Revels at the Court of James I and kept record of the entertainments provided by William Shakespeare, his colleagues and contemporaries. There is also a suggestion of kinship with the great American senator Daniel Webster; but this claim, if not fictitious, is at best remote. The Sheffield branch of Bath Benjamin's family kept in touch with him, however, and were visited from time to time by the Bath clan.

During the London period of his youth, Bath Benjamin trained as a dancer under the finest masters of his day—Gaetano Vestris, Gallini, Louis d'Egville—so, at least, he told the public. He studied further in Aberdeen under Francis Peacock and David Strange. It is a dazzling array of names. But in 1793, under the threat of war with France, he girded on a sword and joined the army. He served in the West Indies, was invalided home, married a Miss Elizabeth Moon of Leeds, and finally, as his son relates, came to Bath—like Captain Absolute—"to recruit." He called himself "Captain," too. The records give only "Sergeant-Major of the Volunteers".

Ben the First was born on September 3rd, 1798. A second son,

Old Ben

Frederick Vestris Webster, was born in 1802. Seven years later their mother died, and shortly afterward Benjamin married again and fathered five more children. In 1819 his second wife also died. The inexhaustible Benjamin married yet a third time. Four more children resulted, the last when he was sixty-eight years old. All of his offspring were taught to dance as soon as they could walk, and most of them to play the fiddle, the piano and the drums as well. They were Benjamin's stock-in-trade. To the end of his life he lived on them, grumbled at them, and wrote them impenetrably illiterate letters demanding not only sustenance but affection.

One of these—a typical instance—complains furiously that his daughter, Mary Anne, will not make him a "goosbery Pye" unless he provides her with the ingredients: they have "a bit of a Flare-up" in consequence. His son Jack is "the greatest scoundrel ever made I can do nothing with him without sending him houte of this whorld, *dam him*. . . . Alfred as got a very bad leg again" and shamefully neglects his duties. Moreover, when old Benjamin finds him sharing "cake plumbs and goosberys" with two of the neighbors, "he never said Father will you take one and then with a great effort he asked me to take a little wisky and then I asked them to give me a bit of cake and a bit it was indeed . . . Mr. Saunders as asked me for the other quarters Rent besides the four Pounds so I think I have enough to make me miserable."

Nevertheless, the dancing establishment prospered for many years. There was a Morning Academy "for Instruction in every novelty of the Fashionable and Elegant Accomplishment of Dancing, and for the Practice of Exercises calculated to improve Personal Deportment" (four guineas per annum). There was also an Evening Academy "for the Practice of Quadrilles, Waltzing, Gallopades etc." Private tuition was given; families were "attended". Successive Mrs. Websters and the Webster young of both sexes adorned the Academy circulars and appeared as dancers at the Bath Theatre Royal. One branch of the family danced its way to Bristol, another to Chester. Benjamin's youngest-but-one daughter, Clara, became the most celebrated English ballerina of her day.

Ben seemed fated to become his father's assistant; but fortune intervened. The Duke and Duchess of York, Benjamin's patrons, came to Bath and the little boy was presented to them. Ben relates what followed: "I was educated at Dr. Barker's Academy for the Navy, in consequence of the Duchess of York having promised my father a commission for me and but for the death of an excellent mother when I was only ten years of age I should probably have been 'seeking the bubble reputation in the cannon's mouth' and gained a page in history." But the succeeding Mrs. Webster, his stepmother, begrudged the money spent on uniforms and equipment for the eldest son, and evidently had an eye to his earning capacity. "I made my first essay on the stage as a principal dancer at the Bath Theatre in 1809, and after having continued some two years longer at school, I was taken thence to assist my father in his profession, very contrary to my wishes, having always a great aversion to it."

He danced frequently at the Theatre Royal, Bath, through the ensuing years; but after December 9th, 1815, his name vanished abruptly from the playbills. He "could endure this sort of life no longer." He packed up his clothes in a bundle, took "all his earthly means, consisting of £10," and left.

"I started for Cheltenham, hearing there was a company performing there, and after an anxious delay of three weeks, was engaged by Watson the Younger at twenty-five shillings a week to play Harlequin, little speaking parts and Second violin, which I did by slipping on a Greatcoat over my stage dress, at Warwick, Lichfield and Walsall races. I commenced my career as an actor on the day of attaining my eighteenth year in the humble part of Thessalus in *Alexander the Great*. The musical and dancing part of my engagement I got on pretty well with, but when I went on to deliver the few words Thessalus has to utter they 'stuck in my throat' and beyond the first line, all was 'inexplicable dumb show.'"

In Warwick he found lodgings with a Methodist couple; they introduced him to Rowland Hill, who offered to make a preacher of him. "How sweet a reflection it would be in after life," said the future postal reformer to the young Harlequin, "to think that you have aided souls instead of damning them." But Harlequin replied by saying that there was "as good a moral in every play, if rightly understood, as there was in any service he ever heard, and that the stage conveyed morality in its most pleasing form by appealing to the heart as well as the feelings."

In Walsall Young Harlequin's career nearly ended before it began; for he took a tremendous flying leap through a paper hoop into the wings, and would have dashed his brains out against the brick wall beyond, if another actor had not sprung forward and caught him in his arms. It was the visiting star, the famous "Young Roscius," Master Betty. After four weeks in the race-course towns, the company broke up without having been paid their final week's salary. Ben continues:

"A portion of them, myself among their number, joined a manager named Irish Wilson in a sharing scheme and fitted up a barn at Brownsgrove, near Birmingham. Before starting for Brownsgrove I purchased at Birmingham a sword à la Kean, that would serve for Richard III or Sir Giles Overreach, these being the two characters I most aspired to act, and as I footed it to join the corps dramatique in its humblest form the hills echoed again with the speeches I expected would electrify the good people we were about to initiate into the mysteries of drama as acted by a strolling company.

"The appearance of the theatre rather damped my ardour; it was nearly outside the town and in a very humble-downish kind of condition; two large stones marked the door of the 'Grand Entrance'; the way to the stage door was through a cow-yard, the door itself was a hole barely three feet square, which led to a trap door that brought you at once to the U.C.R.H. [Up Center Right Hand] of the stage. The dressing rooms, the space between the wings and the walls, were formed by pinning the sheets of the performers' beds against the wings, which rendered them quite secluded and decent except when the naughty little boys bored holes through the wooden walls on the ladies' side."

After a week's work, the actors had converted their barn into a theatre. They borrowed materials on credit and painted four sets: "a splendid modern chamber, on its reverse, a prison; and a Gothic scene, on its reverse, a kitchen. A wood was painted on the walls."

The opening bill consisted of two plays and a variety of singing and dancing turns; there was, however, no orchestra, since all the musicians in the town were Methodists and would not play in A Theatre. Ben Webster wrote his own billing: "From the Theatre Royal, Dublin." He played two parts in the first piece, danced a hornpipe without music between it and the farce, and then appeared as an Old Gentleman "in a modern suit and my head chalked for want of a wig." He also played the music between the acts and the accompaniments to the songs, rendered by one of the actresses "in every key but the right one."

They were a great success all through October. The shares came to twelve or even eighteen shillings a week apiece. Sometimes a member of the audience would whistle a hornpipe for Ben's dancing; and a needle manufacturer's daughter took a fancy to him and kept him supplied with little parcels of tea and sugar. He began to need them, for in November the shares dropped to eighteen-pence each and they lived on "bread and spring water." "In the midst of this misery," an elderly couple in the troupe, a Mr. and Mrs. Jones, contrived to get an engagement with Mr. Talbot who was the manager of a theatre in Belfast and in several other Irish towns. They recommended Ben to him for "little business and Harlequin," and he was engaged at thirty shillings a week. But the job was not to begin till late in January; how to live in the meantime, and how to get to Belfast, remained a problem.

A benefit performance was given for Mr. Jones, but it resulted in a loss. They pinned their hopes to Webster's. He resolved to do everything he could think of; a hornpipe, of course, was included, in which he would go through the additional "manual and platoon exercises." But on the night, when he came to "fix bayonets," he found that the borders and drops were hung so low that the maneuver would have ripped them to pieces. He sang a song, having taught someone to draw a bow across the D-string to give him the note. And then . . . then came the evening's great moment: the last act of *Richard III*. The sword à la Kean leaped from its sheath at last. The stage was so narrow that every inch had to be used for the fight; and "just as Richard was driving Richmond to the extreme upper right corner, some devil opened the trap stage door and Richmond vanished . . . as it were sunk through the earth. In vain did Richard call upon Richmond to come on and kill him. No, Richmond was too much hurt; so Richard, determined not to be cut out of his die, cast himself on his sword and expired amid the groans of the audience." The benefit made no profit and the theatre was locked up for lack of rent, with the scenery inside it. The local squire took pity on Ben and lent him £1. It was a fortune.

At last the Joneses obtained an advance from Talbot and a letter of credit to a Belfast captain trading to Liverpool. The evening before they left, they helped the other actors to retrieve the scenery by "removing a board or two" from the barn, smuggling it to a temporary hiding place among the churchyard tombstones, and getting themselves and it out of town before dawn.

The Irish tour provided good experience, congenial company and the usual quota of hilarious and ridiculous incidents. Among the actors was David Rees, who was to recur in Ben's life at a very crucial moment. Talbot told Ben that low comedy was his forte, "which annoyed my tragic ideas excessively." The tour ended in Dublin, where the management could not pay the company their final week's salary and offered to let them have the theatre rent-free for two weeks instead. With the idiotic optimism of actors, they took it, and lost every farthing they had made.

Back to England went impoverished Ben, barnstorming his way to London via the circuses of Manchester and Liverpool. According to his own account, he married before he was nineteen, "a widow with children of her own"; "a millstone round my neck," he added, with more bitterness than gallantry. In fact, he did not actually marry his widow until more than three years later, for the sufficient reason that she was not, until then, a widow. His brother Frederick, in the course of a flaming family row, accused him of having "lived for two years in open prostitution with the Chaste Mother West" and of having been beaten for it, on one occasion, by the enraged Mr. West. However, he was finally married to "Sophie West, widow" on his twenty-third birthday and she remained with him, faithful, patient and loving, until her death twelve years later.

In London Ben was lucky at first, and got himself a job. It was the littlest of "little business" at a fine new theatre which had just been built south of the Thames. The play was called *Trial by Battle*. He was one of a chorus of Smugglers who had the opening lines, the first ever to be spoken on the new stage. The date was May 11th, 1818. The theatre was the Coburg, later to become famous as the Old Vic.

It was scarcely a fashionable theatre. The neighborhood was squalid, ill-lighted and dangerously infested by footpads. The venturesome playgoer took care to be attended by linkboys. Much of the audience was local. "In the gallery," says Hollingshead, though he speaks of some years later, "were fifteen hundred perspiring creatures, bare-headed and in shirt-sleeves. This 'chickaleary' audience was always thirsty and not ashamed. They would tie their neckerchiefs together and haul up bottles of beer from the Pit. Their likes and dislikes were made deafeningly evident." These traditions lasted until Emma Cons swept them out by main force from the Royal Victorian Hall; and even then, those who knew "the Vic" in its earliest days would testify that the remnants of them died hard.

Not that the theatres across the river in London proper were so very different, even the two Royal houses of Covent Garden and Drury Lane. The Pit covered the whole floor of the house, with the apron stage, though smaller than of old, projecting into it. It was the habitat of a jostling, dictatorial, rough and ruthless crowd of self-appointed judges. The Gallery was often the semi-official preserve of the ladies of the town, who plied their trade quite openly. Lighting was still by oil lamps and candles, which meant that the audience was almost as fully lit as the actors. To hold and tame this exacting, restless monster demanded tremendous power and nerves of steel. Subtlety came later, if you were good enough to manage it.

After nine weeks of tough work at the Coburg, with little to show for it, Ben went as ballet master to a little theatre in Richmond. Other provincial engagements followed, either as ballet master, principal dancer, leader of the band, light comedian or low comedian. The sword à la Kean rusted in its scabbard. Back in London, things went from bad to worse. He pawned the few possessions he had. He got deeper and deeper into debt. He could not seek work in the provinces, for he had no means of getting there. But he walked to all the little towns near London where there was even the shadow of a theatre. At last he heard that Mr. Beverly, manager of the Tottenham Street Theatre, was about to open a brief season in Croydon.

"I applied to him for Walking Gentleman. 'Full.' For little business and utility. 'Full.' For Harlequin and dancing. 'Didn't do pantomime and ballet; besides, didn't like male dancers; *their* legs didn't *draw!*' For the orchestra. 'Well,' said he . . . with a strong expression which need not be repeated, 'why, just now you were a walking gentleman!' 'So I am, sir; but I have had a musical education and necessity sometimes compels me to turn it to account.' 'Well, what's your instrument?' 'Violin, tenor violincello, double bass and double drums.' 'Well, by Nero! He played the fiddle, you know . . .' and I was requested to give a taste of my quality on a borrowed violin. I began Tartini's 'The Devil's Solo' and had not gone far when the old gentleman said that would do and engaged me as his leader at a guinea a week.

"Had a storm of gold fallen on me it could not have delighted Semele more than me. I had others to support, board myself and get out of debt. I resolved to walk to Croydon, ten miles every day, to rehearsal and back to Shoreditch, on twopence a day—one pennyworth of oatmeal and one pennyworth of milk—and I did it for six weeks, Sundays excepted, when I indulged in the luxury of shin of beef and ox-cheek. The gentlemen in the gallery pelted the orchestra with mutton-pies. At first indignation was uppermost, but on reflection we made a virtue of necessity and ate them under the stage . . .

"At the end of the sixth week I had so pleased Mr. Beverly . . . that I was asked to give a specimen of my terpsichorean abilities in a sailor's hornpipe. I essayed the task, buoyed up with hope; dashed on the stage, got through the double-shuffle, the toe and heel, though feeling faint; but at last, despite every effort, I broke down through sheer exhaustion, consequent upon a near approach to starvation, and the curtain dropped on my hopes and I burst into an agony of tears. However, the mourning was soon turned to joy, for Mr. Beverly behaved like a father to me, and engaged me as walking gentleman and Harlequin for his London Theatre, where I made my first appearance as Henry Morland in *The Heir-at-Law*."

Ben had reached London, real London, at last.

But the Tottenham Street Theatre—it later went through a bewildering variety of other names—was an unlucky house. Ben was just beginning to get good parts when Beverly's management came to an end. He succeeded in getting work at the English Opera House in the Strand, reasonable parts for himself and a walk-on for Sophie as well. In September 1819 he actually dared to write a letter to "Winston Esq.," the stage manager of the Theatre Royal, Drury Lane. He applied for "little business, and I would also sustain the characters of Harlequin or Pantaloon in Comic Pantomime. My wife for chorus and figure. My terms are £3 for us both."

No doubt it was one of many hundreds of such applications, and it probably went unanswered. But Ben was in luck again. In June 1820 he played in a benefit performance. Among the stars who took part in it was Robert William Elliston himself, the "Great Lessee" of Drury Lane. Elliston had once, allegedly, been a friend of Bath Benjamin. Probably the recollection was just strong enough to make Ben a person in his eyes instead of a name on a letter.

There was talk of a job for the season of 1820–21. Elliston employed his usual delaying tactics. They are in vogue among managers to this day. Keep the actor in suspense till the last moment, when his hopes have almost gone, and then offer him the contract if he will take less money. It was precisely this maneuver that had once lost Elliston the services of an unknown provincial actor named Edmund Kean. But as a rule it succeeded, and it did so now. Ben accepted half the salary he had originally asked.

Of course he did. In 1820 you were not really an actor until you had penetrated the great fortresses of either Covent Garden or Drury Lane. Ben had done it; and with his wife, too. Thirty shillings a week between them . . . but never mind; they would be within the magic portals. They could bill themselves henceforth as "of the Theatre Royal, Drury Lane." It was the cachet, the passport, the road to fame. It was also the road to a great deal of misery; but they did not know that.

Nor could Elliston know that he had signed a contract with Jack the Giant Killer.

CHAPTER TWO

———— ᎧᎧᎧ ————

Theatre Royal,
Drury Lane

On the back of an English Opera House playbill for August 1820 (Mr. Webster is playing 1st Lord, Mrs. Webster a Lady of the Court), the following announcement appears:

> The WINTER THEATRES. While the Patentees of the Winter Theatres incessantly complain of the encroachments of other Theatres . . . it is time the attention of the Legislature and of the Publick, should be called to the gradual encroachments made by these great establishments on their more limited and more defenceless neighbours. Till within the last ten years, the Winter Theatres never exceeded an average of two hundred nights; opening in the *middle* of September, and closing *early* in June. They have now gradually extended their performances from the *beginning* of September towards the *end of July*, leaving only an interval of six or seven weeks, when the town is comparatively empty (and in the dog-days) for the summer theatres to reap their scanty harvest. The Theatre Royal Drury Lane has now re-opened in the *middle of August*, leaving the summer Theatres *twenty-one*

17

nights only, free from an oppressive covetousness, which it appears can only be bounded by the ruin of more humble rivals.

This was an entirely factual and surprisingly moderate statement of the case against the two "Winter Theatres", so called because they were allowed to remain open during the winter months. Under patents dating back to the reign of Charles II, no London theatre was permitted to set itself up in competition with the two Royal leviathans, Covent Garden and Drury Lane. Not only were the other playhouses restricted as to time, but no "dramas" might be performed in them that would threaten the monopoly of the Patent Houses. Of course, these prohibitions were circumvented in all sorts of ways. Very occasionally a theatre did secure a Royal permit. Samuel Foote managed it for his "Little Theatre in the Hay." The permit was supposed to be for his lifetime only, but once having adopted the title of "Theatre Royal, Haymarket," his successors clung to it like limpets. Even so, the Haymarket playing season was circumscribed like the rest.

Sometimes the little theatres would manage to play beyond the prescribed weeks by not officially selling tickets, and pretending that they were not open at all. It was illegal to take money at the doors, so they would take it through a window. The Strand Theatre suborned an adjoining sweetshop, where you paid four shillings an ounce for rose lozenges (and a box seat), or rather less for peppermints (and the Pit). Ticket-selling by stealth became an art which survived to bedevil the Lord Chamberlain's office throughout its existence.

Plays were disguised by changing their titles, inserting irrelevant song-and-dance turns and calling them "burlettas." The Lord Chamberlain sought in vain for a watertight definition of a "burletta." Even Shakespeare, most jealously guarded by the Patent Houses, was bootlegged onto humbler stages. *Othello* became *The Venetian Moor*, and everybody footed it featly and sang a great deal.

The drama, impossible to eradicate, forced its way through other crevices. Sadler's Wells in North London and Astley's Circus on the Surrey side found their "spectacles" tending toward dialogue, toward plot and acted scenes. The true circus performers were greatly disgusted by these interruptions. Said Ducrow, the horseback rider, in a phrase which has become proverbial: "Cut the cackle and come to the 'osses . . . You say 'Yield thee, Englishman!' Then you answer 'Never!' Then you say 'Obstinate Englishman, you die!' Then you both fight. There, that settles the matter; the audience will understand you a deal better, and the 'osses won't catch cold while you're jawing."

However, the Royal Theatres could do this sort of thing too if they wanted. They were not limited to drama; they could and did alternate it with opera and ballet and even with circuses and performing lions. They did pantomime, of course. This was a staple diet. Every theatre bill of fare, everywhere, had to include a main dish followed by a farce, a pantomime, harlequinade or "extravaganza," and a sketch or operetta, sometimes more than one. The first-comers paid the Full Price and settled down to gorge themselves from six thirty p.m. till midnight. At eight thirty or nine o'clock there was a Second Price for those who were content to skip the roast and settle for the dessert and snacks which followed.

Naturally, only those actors who were employed at Drury Lane or Covent Garden could hope to make a living during the "winter" months. The rest had to find work in the provincial stock companies. In the summer the fortunate members of the Royal Theatres would betake themselves, complete with billing, to the smaller houses, much as Broadway stars patronize summer stock today. The great actors seldom played full seasons at "the Lane" or "the Garden," but gave a series of special performances for which they were paid by the night. Successful plays did not have long, consecutive runs, but were repeated at intervals as often as the traffic would bear, or the stars consented to reappear.

In 1820 Drury Lane was not doing much to justify its privileged position. Garrick and his shining days were a faded memory. Mrs. Siddons had retired. Sheridan's magnificent, new—and far too big—auditorium had burned to the ground. The rebuilt playhouse (much as it is today) had been administered by a committee of noble amateurs, of whom Lord Byron was one. He reported that everyone argued with everyone else on matters of policy, and that the play-reading subcommittee read about five hundred plays of which "not one could be conscientiously tolerated." Gas lighting was introduced in 1817, despite widely expressed fears that it would poison all the actors and half the audience.

From its mounting muddle and declining fortunes Drury Lane was rescued by one miracle—the advent of Edmund Kean. He had fought his way onto its stage, ugly, half starved, despised and rejected. He had made the theatre his own. When he was playing, it was filled; when he wasn't, there was nothing significant to replace him. Five years after his debut, the amateur committee resigned, and the lease was taken over by Robert William Elliston, an experienced and respected manager, and himself a fine comedian.

He engaged well-known actors and generally sound companies. In Ben's first season J. W. Wallack was among the stars—he was later to found a whole dynasty of actors in America—and Fanny Kelly, so beloved by Charles Lamb. Madame Vestris sang charmingly, "wore the breeches" divinely, and was everybody's darling. B. Webster occasionally said a few lines, the first of them as Almagro in *Pizarro*, and carried a lot of spears. Sophie Webster could occasionally be glimpsed in the background.

Christmas came, and the pantomime, and on the second night the Pantaloon was taken ill. "Mr. Webster supplied his place, and succeeded so well as to elicit general praise from Mr. Winston and others, who said that he had saved the pantomime from being damned." This must have raised his hopes.

Sir,

I take the liberty of writing a few lines respecting my playing Pantaloon which I hope you will approve of. You are well aware sir of the great fatigue a person endures in the performance of Pantaloon besides the injury that continued falls and bruises do to the constitution. When these are taken into consideration I hope sir you will not think me too presuming in asking a pound a week extra during the run of the

Theatre Royal, Drury Lane

Pantomime or a raise to my salary (which is only 30 shillings a week) of ten shillings a week for the remainder of the season.

I remain

Sir

Your obedt Servt

B. Webster

The evidence indicates that he got five shillings more a week for the rest of the season. But Elliston liked him well enough to offer him a job in the provinces through the summer layoff months. He then went back on the offer, but promised to release Ben in time for him to take another summer engagement; which he did, with Alfred Bunn in Birmingham. Elliston then went back on that also. Hadn't he promised to let him go? said Ben. "Yes," said Elliston, "to any man but Bunn." Ben replied that he had now signed the contract, and went off to Birmingham.

"Three days had not passed over his head in this button-making town" before he received a lawyer's letter insisting on his return: his absence was "attended with the greatest inconvenience . . . and disappointment to the public. We trust you will see the necessity of complying with this notice and save yourself not only the expense and inconvenience of an action, but the odium necessarily attached to such odious conduct." Big guns for the Drury Lane fortress to train on a thirty-five-shilling-a-week bit player. Ben stuck it out; he thought Bunn would support him. So did Elliston; to spite Bunn, he brought the action. It dragged on for two years and was finally settled out of court. It cost Elliston several hundred pounds and Ben seventy-five, or about seven months' salary. Bunn's support did not extend to paying anything.

Meanwhile came two seasons in the provinces, dispiriting and frustrating in some ways, but instructive. He learned "the low comedy business" in Birmingham; the "melodramatic business" with De Camp in Newcastle, Sheffield and Chester; "the light comedy and singing low comedy, such as Leporello." Back with Bunn again, he and his wife got £2 10s. a week between them, "the Harlequin business and country boys" for Ben, "second chambermaids" for Sophie. In Bath, through the influence of his family, he was offered "general utility." He regarded the offer as "degrading." "I do not," he said, "possess general utility." He told his father that he thought of giving up the stage altogether, and Benjamin began to rejoice in the prospect of a new dancing master. But it all ended in one of the Webster family flare-ups, and Ben went off to Birmingham again. At this point Elliston asked him back.

It was to be a three-year contract: £4 a week for the season of 1823–24, £4 10s. the second season, and £5 the third. Ben accepted. Of course he did. Drury Lane was still the irresistible lodestar. It took him another thirteen years of exasperated struggling before he could free himself wholly from its magnetism and draw his sword à la Kean against it. But this time he was a little less trusting. He protected himself by starting a shop just around the corner from the theatre, at 5 Russell Court. He sold newspapers and secondhand books, "being very well versed," he said, "in old and rare books." He grew increasingly to rely on it, and it was the forerunner of a publishing enterprise, *The Acting National Drama*, which he edited for many years.

At the theatre, he was still kept in the background. The season was chiefly distinguished by Elliston's having secured from his rivals at Covent Garden the services of a rising young actor, William Charles Macready. This talented, self-sufficient, relentless young man was very obviously destined to succeed or supplant Edmund Kean. But they did not meet this season: Kean went on tour, and Macready played only an intermittent series of performances—at £20 a night. At Covent Garden he had been known as "the Cock Grumbler," and his new colleagues saw no reason to discard the soubriquet.

In May there was a new production of *Measure for Measure*, cast without Kean or Macready but with the full strength of the rest of the company, not including Ben. On the opening day, at about three o'clock in the afternoon, a messenger arrived at the shop in Russell Court, posthaste from the theatre. Mr. Harley was ill. There was no one to play Pompey. Somebody had had the bright notion that Webster was a quick study and would be able to do it.

Ben was out on his newspaper rounds; the family were terrified lest he should miss the chance; trembling, they said they were sure he could. At five thirty he got home, "with my blue bag full of periodicals," and they handed him the script. He rushed to the theatre, distraught. No one was there. He sat down and learned the lines; at night he went on and said them. He "was honoured with three rounds of applause at the end of Act II sc 2" and overwhelmed with compliments and protestations of gratitude. The notices the next day were glowing; he copied them all out in his memorandum book. Everyone told him his fortune was made. It wasn't, of course.

He was promoted to the First Green Room, "to which my salary did not entitle me," instead of the lesser one reserved for lesser actors; but he still did not get any parts. There were too many senior claimants. ("For regular big-part performers . . . no doubt the National Theatre does provide the right conditions. But for the large number of Juniors, some twenty-five out of a total strength of sixty-eight, who have been under-employed for the past year, the situation must be miserably frustrating," said the *Times* of London, on March 11th, 1967.) Ben started writing round to other managers; he ran his bookshop and began scribbling plays on odd scraps of paper during his long waits at rehearsals.

He played such parts as came his way with increasing authority. One of them was with Macready as Erni in Sheridan Knowles's new play, *William Tell*. It wasn't until 1826, as the result of a row royal with Elliston, that he began to get anything really good.

In December the *Theatrical Inquisitor* did him the honor of selecting him as the seventh in its series "Actors of the Present Day," under the Shakespearian headline: " 'A worthy gentleman, well-bred and wondrous affable.' " The writer explains that his purpose in choosing a comparatively unknown player is to "foster dawning genius" and to draw attention to one "whose native humour and comic tact deserve to be better known than they are." The Drury Lane management is overtly blamed for stifling a valuable talent; and "we would certainly advise Mr. Webster to leave as soon as possible a situation in which his energies are cramped and his abilities confined as in a dungeon, and choose a wider field for the display of those abilities, where they will be more frequently seen and duly appreciated, and by so doing reap the permanent advantages which his merits undoubtedly deserve, profit and fame."

Elliston, however, had more to worry about than the self-sought publicity of ambitious young actors. His great Moloch of a theatre was driving him to bankruptcy, as it had driven so many of his predecessors. It sapped his health and devoured his energies. He had a stroke and was forced to give up the lease of the theatre. It was bought for £10,000 by an American, Stephen Price. Perhaps he had been impressed by Ben's acting; more probably by the article in the *Theatrical Inquisitor*. At all events, he gave him an increase of salary and some "very considerable and excellent parts." Perhaps it was in an upsurge of hope that Ben began to keep a diary.

Like many another diarist, his enthusiasm was greater than his staying power. It lasted only sixty days; and even within so brief a space there are several entries with "Nothing"; "Ibid"; "No day"; "Naught. Nothing will come of nothing." But when he devotes the diary to his colleagues it comes brilliantly alive. It is a Green Room gossip column.

The name "Green Room" is supposedly derived from its carpet of green baize; or, some authorities maintain, because the green baize floor cloth, traditionally used for all tragic plays, was stored there. Sometimes it was bare except for a few chairs; sometimes elegantly furnished. Its most important equipment was "a large pier and mantel glass and a movable swing glass. . . . This is the first point to attend to on entering the Green-Room, to see if one's dress is in perfect order, well put on by the dresser, hanging well and perfectly comme-il-faut." Then the actor or actress "sits down and enters into conversation with those around, which is interrupted every now and then by the shrill voice of the call boy making his calls." Green Rooms were an essential of every theatre until well into the present century. There was one at the Haymarket when I played there in 1928. At Drury Lane, the Green Room was central to the theatre's life, and an ideal seedbed for the diarist.

Theatre Royal, Drury Lane

The famous actors of Ben's day move in and out of it gossiping and telling funny stories, boasting and borrowing money, dwelling on past triumphs and destroying current reputations. But the towering hero of the diary is Edmund Kean. "I observe he always pronounces his name Cane," says the diarist. Kean is in America when the diary begins—on January 1st, 1827. He sends John Cooper "a curious letter and card," written partly in Indian: "that though he was told he would be a king, he never believed it till now, as he had been chosen king of the Huron tribe of Indians . . ." The card had "an Indian's tatooed head on one side decorated with a tomahawk and bow and arrow and his kingly cognomen . . ."

Jan 2nd Hughes has been at Liverpool a week waiting for Kean I suppose. The Times says he is arrived. Duke of York expected to die every moment . . .

Jan 5th Duke of York died. Kean drunk in White Hart Yard at Smithson & people running from various parts to look at him in that state. He went into the Kean's Head & introduced himself as Captain Smith & his friend . . . as Lieutenant Yankee Doodle. Hudson, the landlord, tried to get him to bed but it was of no use.

Jan 8th Mr. Price said Kean's dress as Chief of the Huron tribe cost 700 guineas . . . The consideration on which Kean was made a Chief was, he was to act as their ambassador in England, & endeavour to obtain of the King of England all the fishing & hunting land which had been taken from them by the British for the last 150 years . . . Miss K said as long as she was able to be carried out she should always go and see Kean play. Dowton walked out of the room . . . The audience on the rise of the curtain called for Kean & would not suffer any of the first scenes of the play to be done; & after two or three efforts Kean came on; nothing can exceed the shout that welcomed him; it lasted exactly three minutes. He bowed gracefully but there was nothing servile in his manner. After the first scene he came into the Green Room & I shook hands with him . . .

Jan 11th Kean again wonderfully received. He has got a sore wound in his left heel which occasions him to limp a little off the stage, but not on. On Price remarking that he was lame, Kean said, "Not when acting". . .

Jan 22nd Auld, the Harlequin, fractured his skull in so violent a manner by a fall . . . that he died the next day. He . . . was the most jemmy jumper and Harlequin I ever saw.

Jan 25th Kean played Sir Giles Overreach [in *A New Way to Pay Old Debts*] in capital style but his leg pained him very much he was afraid it would be perceived from the front, but it was not. He has placed himself under Carpue who has forbidden him drinking brandy, but allows gin, rhum or whiskey, for which he gives the reason—"If we put a man's heart," says Carpue, "into brandy it becomes a mass of worms but if we place it [in] gin, rhum or whiskey it preserves it whole and sound". . .

Jan 27th First night of the new opera. Braham remarked he was a naval officer in more ways than one for he just reached to Bedford's middle . . .

Feb 1st Kean played Hamlet in parts very finely but still suffers greatly from his leg. Mr. Powell told me they could not keep Kean from the Fountains &c. Mr. Price told a friend of his that Kean's nights alone had paid him back all the losses of the previous part of the season, which were considerable . . .

Feb 15th Kean has been [here], since he played at Brighton, said he heard since he had been there they had killed him again. Kean said he thought his death would be a very good vehicle for imitations. The stage to represent the Green Room & the performers entering one after another & he began by giving us a specimen of what he meant. *Braham*—"I hear Kean is dead; poor little fellow, I should have been glad to have been friends with him till his death had he not committed that sad faux pas & rendered the thing impossible"—*Munden* —"Is the dear boy dead? Where is he? Where is he? that I may kiss his toe." Then one of the company was to address Munden & say the company had thought of making a subscription to have gold nails in his coffin instead of brass ones &

should be [happy] to receive his mite towards it. "I'll see him in hell first," hobbling out of the room . . .

Feb 26th Kean played Richard. An apology was obliged to be made for him by Wallack at the end of the first act. Kean was in very low spirits and cried, a circumstance that I believe never occurred before . . .

Feb 27th Sir Giles. We did not begin till a quarter past seven, Kean being taken with a violent fit of vomiting & vomited a great quantity of blood. He was obliged to be quite nursed to get through the part. Waiting between the acts &c he said he could not afford to lay by & had no doubt the country air would do him good. At the end of the play he was called for but I could not hear what he said. He went on in his cloak which is lined with racoon skin. He plays in Manchester Thursday next Shylock as that is the easiest.

The diary, to our loss, ends here. Had it lasted the season, it could only have recorded disaster for Kean. A new play, *Ben Nazir*, was especially written for him, but he was totally unable to learn the lines. The first night was a horrible ignominy. He went over to Covent Garden; and the Drury Lane management, in revenge, presented his son, Charles, as Young Norval. The boy had nothing on his side but youth, a contempt for his father, and, of course, the Eton education his father had given him; but he was received with kindness. It must have seemed that Kean was finished and that the throne was Macready's for the taking; but it wasn't quite as easy as that. There was another six years of fight left in the dying lion.

Macready could wait, though he did it with an ill grace. "That low man," he called his brilliant, battered rival. He was sober, hardworking, socially ambitious, respected and widely disliked. This was not surprising. He had a violent temper; and though he was often filled with remorse afterward, this did not heal the wounds he inflicted. He loathed actors and readily told them so. Critics were "beasts of hell"; a stage manager, typically, "a wooden-headed, incompetent booby, a dull-brained clod." He despised the stage as a profession and longed only for the day when he should have made enough money to retire. But he was insatiable for the excellence of his own work and of the productions in which he appeared. He was dictatorial, but he was also dedicated.

London was divided into two factions, one for the star ascendant, the other for genius in decline. The members of the Green Room at Drury Lane inevitably picked up sides. Though Macready seldom condescended to enter it, the ever-ready telltales must have made sure that he knew who was for whom. There can have been no question as to where Ben's allegiance lay. Nothing could have equaled the first hero worship, when Edmund Kean came into the Green Room "and I shook hands with him." But to take part in the interstellar warfare was dangerous; these could be deadly games; and Ben was a struggling young actor, with other people dependent on him.

Later, when he was an old man, and a famous one, he described the problems that had faced him: "Actors are prone to marry young, and it often mars their advancement in life. The couple cannot always get situations together. If they do, the salary is less for the united pair than if they were two and distinct; but the husband has to fight the battles of two instead of one as to parts etc and consequently is seldom out of hot water and often out of an engagement. Then a large family is the consequence, for actors are very prone to this sort of thing, too: and ambition becomes blunted or blighted in the circumstance of the provision of food, as actors are also prone to sacrifice everything for their children. I was placed in this predicament."

This pronouncement was among the family archives. It has an authentic ring and evoked my sympathy. But as I studied it I began to be puzzled. Certainly Ben carried the burden of his innumerable half brothers and sisters from Bath. But his own three children were not born till he was in his late thirties and already a prosperous actor-manager; at least they were the only three I had ever heard of. What, or who, was responsible for the blunting and blighting of his youthful ambition? In the hushed sanctuary of Harvard Library, as far removed from the turbulent theatrics of Drury Lane as could possibly be imagined, I came upon an answer.

Theatre Royal, Drury Lane

The letter, in an unformed, childish handwriting, is addressed to B. Webster Esq, 78 Drury Lane. It is dated Wednesday, November 9th, 1825, and postmarked from Sheffield.

Dear Parents,

Tomorrow I start for Leicester, where I shall remain for three days, but where I shall go to next I don't know . . . All my relations were very glad to see me particularly *Grandfather* (who is very ill, and I am afraid will soon leave this world for a better, shortly; therefore dear father write to him as soon as you can, for he has complained sadly at your not doing so . . .

There follows a list of Sheffield relatives, including one who had seemed "very cool" toward the writer. He, or she, continues:

. . . Writ soon as y. receive this. Very well mother so you never wrote that letter for Mr. Holland to bring to me but you must write on half the next letter. I was going to be married to Miss Stoker, and Mr. M had taken the lodging for us and Mr. De Camp was to bill our £2. 15. 0 between us but Mr. Stoker said we had better wait a little longer or else Mr. Macready had settled all about it. Don't tell Louisa this or else she may upbraid me with in consteincy. Good Bye. . . .

Once more God bless you believe me
Yours Affectly
J. Webster
Give my *very very very* best love to Miss Baker and Mother
mum   about Miss Stoker.

And who, I said to myself, is J. Webster? J for what? John? "Dear Parents . . ." Could this be one of the blunt-ers and blighters? The Websters certainly had Sheffield relatives and "*Grandfather*" was perfectly in character with old Bath Benjamin, grumbling away as usual; though, contrary to the writer's pious pessimism, he was to live another nine years and father two more children. Mr. De Camp was the local theatre manager, Fanny Kemble's uncle. The marriage part sounds like a theatre joke, though it didn't seem at all in character for Macready. But in all the family legends there had never been any mention of a J. Webster.

I found two more letters:

Monday Nov 21st 1825

Dear Parents,

I am *now* at Newark but start on Thursday for Edinburgh from Edinburgh I go to Plymouth (the distance is 500 miles) from P to Exeter from E to Bristol and from B to Bath. O my dear Father and Mother I am so happy I never hardly go out because I love so to enjoy Mr Macready company at home whenever he has time he is telling me stories and amuses me so that I am almost sorry when ½ past five comes which is the time he goes to the Theatre. He has bought me a *History* of *Rome* and when I've read that I'm to have the *History* of *Greece*. But Father I am sorry to say it but I have lost somehow or other Plutarch Lives. I was sitting reading and Mr. Macready was writing and all of a sudden Mr. M asked me if I had ever seen the Devil I could not help laughing and he asked me what I was laughing for I told him it was because he asked me such a strange question so says he ecod you would not laugh if you was to see him. I have nothing more to say only give my love to Granny and *all* good friends God bless you my dear Parents and believe me

Your affectionate son
J. Webster

Write as soon as you can

[postmarked, Dublin] February 7th 1826

Dear Parents,

I am sorry that I have not written before, but I have been so busy about my journey here that I have not had a minute of time, I started from Liverpool on Thursday last and after a voyage of 4 and 20 hours I arrived in the *City of Dublin*. I stay here a month which is a long time for us. *I am quite Factotum Mr. Macready calls me his Squire.* I came over to Dublin by *myself* with all Mr. Macready baggage for he said he could trust *me* if it were twise as much. My *dear dear* Parents if *my* letter gave you so much joy what must *Mr. Macready* have given you he shewed me the letter before he sent it you and said I deserved it. *Father Father* I have had my *Bells* stolen from me after all my care. I have nothing more to sa only give my best love to Granny Mr. Craddock and *all my pretty ones* "Shakespeare". . . .

Your affectionate and dutiful child
J. Webster

Do Do write a very long letter by return of post.

The remaining item in the sequence was a note to B. Webster from one Thos. Jones, delivered by hand:

Dear Sir,

I am requested by Mrs. Orry to inform you of her having seen Mr. Macready this day (Wednesday) who wished to see you this afternoon at six o'clock or as early as possible tomorrow, to make some arrangements concerning *John* who *must* come with you . . . if John has any things to get ready Mrs. O thinks he had better bring them up with him and she will get them done . . .

So it *was* "John". I followed back along the trail. I found a letter to Ben from Alfred Bunn in the summer of 1823. "I have set you down for £10 per week for yourself and your wife, and whenever I want your son I will give him 2/6 per night." A child actor, then, and Ben's son.

The letters charmed me by their gaiety and innocence; and the picture of Macready is unique, a laughing, watercolor sketch among the heavy portraits in oil. But what was John doing with Macready? It seemed extremely unlikely that so young a boy would be engaged solely as Macready's "Factotum," but even more improbable that he should accompany him as an actor. It was never the practice for a touring star to bring any of his own company with him, not even his leading lady. Surely Macready wouldn't have stooped to include a two-and-sixpenny child actor among his baggage.

But he did; and the reason was revealed by a penciled note which drifted up from the family papers. It is unsigned and unaddressed, but the handwriting is unmistakable:

> Theatre Royal, Drury Lane. May 29th 1827
>
> Sir,
>
> My son having obtained considerable fame by his performance of Albert with Mr. Macready in *William Tell* at Dublin and elsewhere and having myself been equally fortunate in the *Boy of Santillane* and other pieces . . . I propose if I can so arrange it, going with him to a few places during our vacation, my son to perform his characters and myself my original character of Domingo and other comic parts . . .

I read *William Tell*. Albert is a tremendously long part. It requires, moreover, a special skill: in Macready's words, "dexterity in the use of the bow was indispensable to the performance." It would have been impossible to "pick up a child," as the theatre phrase goes, in every different town and risk its shooting arrows into the rest of the company, including Macready himself. Little Albert would have to go with his father.

Macready had first performed the play at Drury Lane in May, 1825, with Clara Fisher, a popular child prodigy, as the boy. Later that year, and again in 1826, he took it on tour as part of his repertoire; and with him went young John. I found the press reviews. "The son is excellently played by a boy of the name of Webster . . . we do not think that [Clara Fisher] could do it any better" (Dublin). ". . . this is really a very fine boy, in elocution perfect, in action graceful and natural; his voice is particularly sweet and clear . . . Young Webster looks a fitting child for such a father" (Edinburgh). Sweet, golden music for the boy and his "Dear Parents"; the skies were his, no doubt, and the sun and the moon and the stars.

Macready left for America and John was taken on at Drury Lane itself. His name appears in the ballet and on other playbills for the season of 1826–27. Macready came back, and *William Tell* was scheduled for revival. One can imagine the confident hopes. But here is the playbill: "Albert . . . Miss Vining." And darkness was upon the face of the earth.

However, a small consolation was in store. In April 1827, Macready went to Paris to star with an English company at the Théâtre Favart. *William Tell* was again in his repertoire, and Webster, not Vining, played Albert. Macready was much admired by the French press and public. Among the tributes is one from Louise d'Orléans, Queen of the Belgians, in a letter to her father. After praising the star, she adds: "Master Webster, son élève, enfant de 14 à 15 ans a très bien rempli aussi, le rôle du fils de Tell." Frederick Webster writes to his brother Ben: "My kind love to John who I daresay will be delighted with his visit to Paris. It appears young Macready can't do without him." This turned out to be a dangerously optimistic pronouncement.

John continued to lead an eventful life. A friend wrote to his parents, who were on tour, to warn them that "a very foolish act of which John has been guilty has found its way into the London papers" though "the names are suppressed." It was apparently a romantic escapade followed by a juvenile attempt at suicide which "was not attended by the result he expected." Good friends took care of him, and Macready, with whom he was about to play a few more performances of *William Tell*, behaved with kindness and understanding. John recovered rapidly, resilient as ever. "I hope I shall be able to shew my gratitude for your forgiveness," he wrote to his parents, adding cheerfully that he would have sent them "some souls from Yarmouth" but he was afraid they would not keep. The following week in Cambridge he was probably restored completely by the local newspaper, which said: "It is not always that early talent is a sure indication of future excellence, or we might safely predict that Master Webster . . . will one day be worthy of his dramatic patron."

Two years later he had graduated to adult parts in the stock company at Colchester. A letter to his mother says that he is counting the days till the Christmas holidays, "though I am very happy here except that I am so teazed by the girls for they won't let me alone at all I am called 'the handsome Captain' from my playing Captain Crosstree in *Black-Eyed Susan* . . . you needn't tell *Mary* this or perhaps she will be *yellow*."

So there was John Webster, fully accounted for and ready for his own career. But a small doubt assailed me. I compared the various dates. I came to the conclusion that he must have been born in 1811 or 1812, when Ben was at most fourteen. I finally realized . . . the "young widow with children of her own"—the "millstone round my neck"—Sophie West. West to Webster is an easy transition and must have simplified the situation. Perhaps John never knew he was not Ben's son.

I have found no record of any brothers and sisters, and if John alone constituted the "millstone" it would seem that Ben was making a great fuss about very little. The child turned rapidly from a liability into an asset. But he never did fulfill the radiant promise of his youth. The Cambridge critic's warning turned out to be justified. Nevertheless, he was the only one of Ben's children or stepchildren who sustained the true Webster tradition. There was, later, a playwright son and a theatre executive; but only John was an actor.

During the Twenties and early Thirties Ben continued to play at Drury Lane, though he managed to fill an increasing number of engagements at other theatres and to work as a playwright and a stage manager. He clung to the security, much as he resented the servitude, of the Theatre Royal. He could not do otherwise. He was still responsible for old Bath Benjamin, who rumbled and grumbled his way through the years, exacting as ever. The third Mrs. Webster did her best to pay her way by taking dancing classes, but she had four young children to look after. Half brothers and sisters, few of them self-supporting, repeatedly descended on Ben and Sophie in London. A letter from Bath Benjamin to his son typifies the family problems. It is dated March 1829.

. . . I have been so perplext and tormented with one thing and another that I have been very unwell all the Winter, and I am afraid I shal loose the use of my Right Arme, the littl and next finger are quite benumbd, and if it had not been for Mrs. Webster exerting herselfe a great deal I do not know wat I should have done and I thank God I am in hopes she will do very well she as fifteen in one Ladies School and eleven in another, business as been very bad and I have very little to do Alfred is very provoking yesterday he took it in his head he would not play for Mrs. Webster and left her in the lurch at a school where she as fifteen so I am never to have anything but truble and at a time when evry exertion should be made to keep me from the Workhouse, he never gets out of bed till nine or ten o'clock I think one thing or another will be too much for me I am now getting old and think I shal not be hear long if you can procure a good tune or two I will thank you all yr family are very well and send love to you all, and believe me your

affectionate Father
B. Webster

P.S. I can hardly old the Pen.

Fortunately, the youngest children, Clara and Arthur, began to show signs of considerable talent. They got engagements in Bath and at other theatres also. Ben the breadwinner must have been considerably relieved; not so poor old Benjamin. Their mother naturally had to accompany the children as their guardian as well as their choreographer, leaving Benjamin alone. He wrote to her in Swansea:

"No-one as called on business Bath is very dull and hot . . . I am quiet lonely solitary and miserable no-one comes to see me and I have no-one to go and see . . . I ashure you I am so miserable I think I shal not live till you come back again."

He does not forget, however, to add a brisk, professional postscript on the outside of the letter: "You cannot get fleshings out of London." Presumably Ben had to supply this necessary equipment. Nevertheless, his burdens lightened as the Bath Websters grew up; and his own star began to rise at last.

Old Ben

Drury Lane was rocking through a period of turbulence under different managers and different stars. In 1832 Macready and Edmund Kean finally played together, or against each other. Kean was not vanquished, but the smell of defeat was in the air. In 1833 the egregious, notorious and much-detested Alfred Bunn became lessee and manager of the great national theatre.

Seldom can anyone have been so inappropriately named. He was a bejeweled, ample man of unquenchable assurance, a flamboyant impresario who fancied himself as a poet. He bounded like a rubber ball between Drury Lane and the Bankruptcy Courts. His various tenures of office were marked by spectacular coups and utter debacles. In the season of 1833 he ran Drury Lane and Covent Garden in tandem. The most famous actors in the world could be seen in all their finery dashing madly across Bow Street in the rain on their frenzied way from an exit in one theatre to an entrance in the other. He made his money out of opera, circuses, even performing lions, all of which he preferred to drama. He subjected his actors to every sort of indignity and annoyance. Macready eventually became so exasperated that he stalked into Bunn's office and knocked him down. It was probably the most popular thing he ever did.

The rule of such a manager at Drury Lane must have made it easier for actors like Ben Webster to free themselves from its clutches. They were beginning to create a world elsewhere. Ben played increasingly important parts at other theatres. One of them had a stage door in Suffolk Street, just off the Haymarket. It led to his future.

"In the year 1829 I made an engagement with Mr. Morris [lessee of the Haymarket Theatre] who is one of the old school of managers who really treats his actors like gentlemen and not like slaves. It is to him I am indebted for everything in the way of name and fame by enabling me to make a stand in first-rate characters and keeping me continually before the public in a prominent light."

Morris was not, in fact, the most brilliant of managers—"a very capricious and unreasonable person," is Macready's typical comment. But his theatre had a fine history, a semi-royal cachet and the chance of becoming a serious rival to the Patent Houses; or at least Ben Webster thought so.

In 1830 and again in 1832 Edmund Kean came to the Haymarket, playing out the last acts of his life's drama, the glory almost gone, the effort more protracted and more painful; but the flashes were still there, the spark that could suddenly enkindle a whole theatre. Ben played with him—Roderigo, Oswald, Lancelot Gobbo. In 1833 Kean dragged himself to Covent Garden, and one night was carried, dying, from its stage; a public, painful, miserable end. Macready, reluctant but correct as always, was one of the pallbearers. It was on this occasion that Macready first met John Forster, who was to become the bane and burden of his future associates.

In 1835 Charles Kemble, the last of the "old school," came to the Haymarket to play Benedick—"too old, a wreck," commented an experienced playgoer; but he praised the Dogberry and Verges of the Haymarket's comedy team, Ben Webster and J. B. Buckstone.

By this time no less than fifteen theatres were in existence, battling the Patentees. They were making herculean efforts to get Parliament to repeal the strangling legislation which upheld the monopoly of the two Houses; so far, however, in vain. Ben was determined to join their ranks. He began to train himself in many ways. In 1832 he took over the old City Theatre by Cripplegate, in company with an experienced actress-manager named Mrs. Waylett. This brave little theatre had tried to outface the Patentees and stay open during the "winter" months by pretending to be an "Academy." Nowadays we are better accustomed to academies pretending to be theatres. Ben's management lasted only one season; but it confirmed his determination not to spend the rest of his life in thralldom to the Giants.

The "minor" theatres and their players were beginning to organize themselves in more ways than one. While he was at the City Theatre, Ben received the following communication from Osbaldiston, then manager of the Surrey Theatre and afterwards of Covent Garden:

Sir,

You will find annexed a copy of the resolution entered into at a Meeting yesterday to which I venture to call your attention and that of the City company.

The next General Meeting will take place at 3 o'clock precisely at Arkley's Museum Tavern Surrey side of Black-friars Bridge . . . where the attendance of *every actor and other dramatic Artist* is particularly requested that a perfect understanding may be established throughout the profession. Resolved unanimously

At a meeting of actors and others held in the saloon of the Surrey Theatre on Tuesday, 29 May 1832.

1. THAT this meeting consider it absolutely necessary to the effectual carrying on of the Cause of the Drama that all the members of the profession interested in this cause zealously co-operate in forwarding it.

2. THAT as the best means of ensuring such effectual co-operation the persons assembled at the present meeting form themselves into a Dramatic union.

3. THAT each member of such union holds himself responsible for his share of the expenses . . . according to his professional emoluments.

4. THAT every member of the Minor Theatres be invited to join the Union.

There follow the appointments of a President and a Secretary, provisions for the election of a Committee and the signatures of twenty-six actors. These names should be recorded on tablets of bronze in the offices of every English-speaking Actors' Union—though I sometimes wonder whether they would recognize their descendants.

Having tasted blood as a manager, Ben added to his practical experience of running a theatre by serving as stage manager for the Osbaldiston regime at Covent Garden. It was a position of authority and responsibility, more like the production manager or general manager of present times. He already knew what it feels like to be a produced dramatist. In 1831 his play *Highways and*

Byways was done at Drury Lane, with Liston in the cast. In 1832 *The Golden Farmer* opened at the Coburg. Four years later it achieved enormous success in New York.

The whole picture of Ben's life was changing. In March 1835 his wife, Sophie, bore him a son, christened Ben, the first of his acknowledged children. In October she died. She had shared poverty and hardship with him, played many wearisome Walking Ladies and Second Chambermaids, endured his angers and, one would guess, his infidelities; for he was never a man of easy temper. Evidently he could not live alone. In July 1836 he married again, Harriet Herbert Ireland, spinster, aged twenty. There were no witnesses from his own family at the wedding. Four months later their first son was born, christened (poor child) William Shakespeare. Two years later there was a daughter, Harriette. Thereafter, Harriet Herbert Ireland disappears from his history, as shadowy as a ghost. In the surviving letters to and from him, nobody mentions her, nobody inquires for her, she might never have existed; though she lived for another twenty-four years.

In 1836 also, old Benjamin died in Bath. The family was on its own dancing feet. Ben was free to take a hard look at his own future. He was playing at Covent Garden, still nominally under Osbaldiston's management, but with Macready, the star, dictating his own terms, his own casting, his own plays, which he also directed. Among Macready's tight little circle of counselors and adorers was a prince among busybodies, John Forster; and among the playwrights was Bulwer-Lytton. Ben and John Webster were both in his new drama, *La Vallière*. Macready demoted Ben to a smaller part than the one for which he had been cast, and described him to the author as "very unmeaning and inefficient." Not that this meant very much; even Helen Faucit, whom Macready admired as much as his nature permitted, was "frequently feeble and monotonous." Forster, who was the critic of the *Examiner* and thereby the voice of Macreadydom, remarked that "Mr. J. Webster whimpered in somewhat too juvenile a fashion as Young Vane." The play was a failure and ran nine nights.

Nevertheless, Ben had the acumen to size up the situation. Bulwer-Lytton was a dramatist to be reckoned with. He was also of noble family, a Member of Parliament, an extremely successful novelist—and a devotee of Macready, who, in turn, was easily the most important star in the English-speaking theatre. Moreover, Covent Garden closed during the summer months. The despised bit-part actor came to Macready's dressing room one night and offered him a job. He announced that he had taken over the lease of the Theatre Royal, Haymarket, and would be happy to have Macready star for him during the summer season, opening as Hamlet.

Macready recovered his breath sufficiently to ask an extremely large salary. Ben agreed to it. He stipulated his plays. Ben said he would do them. He demanded the best actors. Ben undertook to get them—and did so. It was a roster of the finest names in the English theatre, as well as some new discoveries, such as a young provincial actor named Samuel Phelps. There had been no such strength of casting, and no such salary list, on the London stage for years. Macready signed the contract. Ben had got a tiger by the tail.

On June 12th, 1837, the Tiger opened as Hamlet; on the 16th he played Othello; on the 18th, Richard III. It was a dazzling first week for a young and untried manager. On the night of the 18th, old King William died. This meant, of course, that the theatre had to close. It was a bitter blow. But they went on rehearsing the new play, Sheridan Knowles's *The Bridal*, a piece which Macready had cherished for years and nobody else liked very much. Its fate was far more important to the actors, naturally, than the death of kings. It opened a week later to an audience even more brilliant than the cast. Dickens and Browning were among Macready's admirers. The theatre glowed with the aura of success. There was a new feeling in the air and a new monarch on the throne, the young Queen Victoria.

CHAPTER THREE

―――――― ⚬⚬⚬ ――――――

Theatre Royal, Haymarket

Ben had found his real métier at last, and to fulfill it he drew on all his other talents and his twenty years of toughening apprenticeship. He was a type of theatre manager for whom there were few predecessors and have been fewer successors. He was not a "bricks-and-mortar" man; he never owned his theatres or made money out of buildings; nor did he have to devote large slices of the profits to his backers. Later he said: "I did not have the assistance of a single farthing beyond what I had saved by rigid economy out of a very small income." The money he made out of the theatre he plowed back into it.

This has been true of many star actor-managers all through the generations until the present day, when they have practically ceased to exist. But Ben had no intention of trying to make himself a star. This meant he did not have to find plays which were vehicles for himself. He could, and did, pick himself some ripe plums, such as Tartuffe, Bob Acres, or Triplet in *Masks and Faces*. But his choice of plays was completely free. He wanted the best stars he could get.

He understood actors, relied on them, and was a generous

paymaster to them—though he sometimes saved on the scenery. At
the Haymarket he never wavered from the policy with which he
had begun. His flaring, lamp-black posters hurled at you a long
succession of star names, sometimes as many as ten at a time on
the same playbill. They constitute a roster of all the best acting
talent, English and American, for nearly fifty years.

Yet he once said, long after he left the Haymarket: "I have
made all my money by pieces, none by persons, with the exception
of—now stare—David Rees, who drew me more than [Tyrone]
Power ever did, until he got drunk, in the same number of performances." He denied the accusation that he had "relied on great
hits with great stars. My great hits were in pieces without stars—I
mean, money-making hits." Perhaps this was not wholly true. Few
managers are willing to attribute all their successes to the actors.

However, it is certainly true that Ben got on well with authors,
being also an author himself, and, increasingly, a translator,
adapter and carpenter of plays and afterpieces. His letters to writers are firm, purposeful and to the point. Many an author paid
tribute to him in return: Douglas Jerrold, Mark Lemon (of
Punch), Palgrave Simpson and Charles Dickens. Since authors do
not normally care very much for "the management," this is impressive.

Westland Marston said of him: "No manager could have been
more pleasant to deal with. In my own four or five contracts with
him, I never knew him attempt to beat down the price of a piece by
depreciation, by remarking, for instance, that it was risky or that
times were hard. If he really wished to produce your work, his
brief formula was 'Just draw up a memorandum while I write the
cheque.'" He describes how Ben once cheered him up after a
failure and said he was " 'determined to make a stand'; and when
the bad notices made this impossible, he never murmured at his
own loss or disappointment but did all he could to put the baffled
dramatist in heart, spoke of his unshaken faith in him . . . and
showed himself the staunch friend that has been described."

Ben must have had to learn authority and confidence, together
with an even temper which certainly did not come naturally to him.
Like all managers, his problems were multiple and more complex,

in some ways, than those of his successors a hundred, or even fifty, years later. For the manager of the Eighteen-forties had to provide what might be called "total entertainment." There was no other. A theatre had to put on drama, opera, ballet, musical pieces, farces, "spectacles" and acrobatics. It ate up material almost as fast as television does today, and a writer had to turn it out as quickly. Sometimes, so a Haymarket actor testifies, the company played five pieces a night for weeks on end. They had to be multiple performers; and the supply was not unlimited. With the rapid proliferation of new theatres, the available talent was spread very thin.

The Haymarket manager had no scruples about employing the family talent wherever it came in handy. His pretty young half sister, Clara, danced (with Arthur) and played bit parts. Brother Frederick became business manager and then stage manager—indeed, he worked for Ben in various theatres all his life. Frederick's small son George inherited the infant prodigy department. In the odd fashion of the times he played scenes from *Hamlet* or *Richard III* as afterpieces to the main drama.

John's name flits in and out of the playbills. Like so many child actors, he had a hard time graduating to adult parts. By 1838, however, he was doing well. He played Nicholas Nickleby at the Adelphi and several prominent parts at London's newest theatre, the St. James's. There is a print of him as Nickleby in the Garrick Club library, under which some wag has written:

> *Oft has it been my lot to mark*
> *This self-conceited talking spark,*
> *And thought how true the saying ran*
> *That says your tailor makes the man.*
> *No actor he—some mere machine*
> *Crawling about the mimic scene,*
> *Who thinks of naught but well-cut coat*
> *And speaks as parrots do, by rote.*

Fortunately, most London managers do not seem to have shared this jaundiced view.

———

Old Ben

For two seasons Ben and Macready alternated under each other's management, though Macready would have hated to have it put that way. He had taken over the management of the Covent Garden "winter" seasons and Ben "gave in his adhesion"—Macready's phrase. During the summers Macready consented, for an ever-rising salary, to return to the Haymarket.

The contrast between the two theatres could hardly have been greater. Macready's productions were lavish, scenically complex, with elaborate stage machinery and armies of supers drilled by "Sergeant Macready" to within an inch of their lives. The companies were good, but no actor was allowed undue prominence. Young Phelps, for instance, was taken over from the Haymarket and politely smothered.

To Macready's honor, he made a mighty effort to restore the genuine Shakespearian texts and to mount them worthily. He also tried to uncover new poetic drama. But Byron's *The Two Foscari* was a failure and Browning never delivered a satisfactory script. The two successes among the new plays were both by Bulwer-Lytton, *The Lady of Lyons* in the first season and *Richelieu* in the second.

But Macready's running of his company must have been wholly alien to Ben, who was a working actor all his life and respected other actors; not so Macready. At rehearsals he would surround himself with his friends, who applauded their hero and made audible comments on the supporting cast. It is recorded that during the Mrs. Quickly scene from *Henry V* Forster kept jumping up and down, crying: "Put her through it again, Mac, put her through it again!" until the actress declared that she was not a circus horse, and walked out.

At performances Macready encouraged, or allowed, similar practices. Even Helen Faucit, who admired and loved him, seems to have thought this rather too much. Of a Command Performance before Queen Victoria, she says:

"The side scenes were crowded with visitors, Mr. Macready having invited many friends. They were terribly in the way . . . Worse than all, those who knew you insisted on saluting you; those who did not, made you run the gauntlet of a host of curious eyes—and this in a place where, most properly, no strangers had hitherto been allowed."

One can only deduce that Macready was armored in an impenetrable vanity.

Whatever Ben Webster thought, he kept quiet. His own theatre was much too small for the grand type of Macready production, nor was he greatly interested in scenic effects. Plays and actors were his stock-in-trade. Very politely, he established a Bulwer-Lytton bridgehead by asking for the rights to publish *The Lady of Lyons* in his edition of *The Acting National Drama*. He followed this up by: "I confess I am most anxious to produce a drama from your pen at the Haymarket, feeling it to be the only theatre from its size where the legitimate drama and the beauties of poetry can be duly appreciated." He sent a list of his company, which was a fine one, but added, "This is essentially a comedy company and therefore I beg respectfully to suggest that should you honour me so far as to write for the Haymarket, you do so without regard to any particular names, and I will engage efficient persons."

Macready came back to Ben's theatre, grumbling incessantly. "I am in a strange land with such unsympathetic people about me"—no claque in the wings, perhaps. "This dog-hole of a theatre . . . dirt, slovenliness and puffery make up the sum of its character." It wasn't true. Ben conducted his theatres with judgment and liberality, said less prejudiced witnesses. But Ben kept quiet and concentrated on Bulwer. He meekly asked for the chance to give performances of both the existing plays and pursued the idea of a new one. He even enlisted the help of Forster, keystone of the Bulwer-Macready arch; finally he got Bulwer's promise. He immediately paid £600 down for the script, more than Bunn or Macready himself had ever given the author. He waved aside the offer of a receipt for his check as "perfectly unnecessary." He must have enjoyed this lordly gesture.

All the time he was steadily building his theatre as a rival to the Patentees. Bit by bit he got the Lord Chamberlain to allow extensions of the "summer" season over the autumn months. Macready gave up the unequal struggle to remain solvent at Covent Garden. In 1839 he returned to the "dog-hole" for the fully extended season, four nights a week at £25 a performance. He could hardly do otherwise since his own particular playwright was already under contract there. Helpfully, he told Bulwer "of Webster's judgement and penetration I have no opinion whatsoever." He was sure that *Richelieu* couldn't be mounted in so small a theatre and tried to get the author to withdraw *The Lady of Lyons*.

Nevertheless, final contracts for the new play were signed on October 9th, 1839, for an opening on October 31st. It was called *The Sea-Captain*. Bulwer and Macready fussed and worried themselves and everybody else. The leading lady was thought inadequate and poor John Webster, in a small part, very bad. Three days before the opening Bulwer tried to withdraw the play. Then he cheered up and it was Macready's turn to despair. The opening performance, however, was received with much enthusiasm. Macready wrote in his diary: "I am most thankful to God for what I feel a great escape."

It wasn't a good play and it wasn't a success. By December the houses were off an average of £95 a night, "which is not a winning game." Other plays were put into the bill on intervening nights to keep it going. But Ben was determined, at all costs, to keep his actor-author team. He bought another new script from Bulwer; it was eventually entitled *Money*. He also, of course, bought the consequences.

The financial terms were the same as before. But Bulwer added a rider: if at any time during the rehearsals or before the opening night, he should, for any reason whatever, "feel convinced . . . that the play would not be likely to have that success which alone would answer either of us," he would have the absolute right to withdraw it or postpone it. Forster and Macready were empowered to represent his opinions; in effect, to make his decisions. Ben set his teeth and signed.

Forster proved an invaluable casting director. King, Munden, Palmer and Dowton, he said, were the only players worthy of these parts; wonderful actors, indeed, but all dead. A fine cast was, however, assembled. Helen Faucit, "on the urgent representation of Mr. Webster," agreed to play a part quite unworthy of her. There was a good deal of shifting around. Walter Lacy was cast as

Blount; but Macready and Forster un-cast him and gave the part to John Webster. Macready then decided that John was "too fat," and Lacy was brought back again.

Ben had put himself down for a juicy character part, originally called Doleful and ultimately Graves. Indeed, this was Bulwer's casting also. Macready, however, decided differently. Ben should play a much smaller role. He told him so one night as they were waiting to go on in the current play.

For Ben it was the last straw. "He started a long, desultory harangue," wrote Macready in his diary, "about his talent and what he had been and done, of which I have lived in total ignorance." Macready threatened to withdraw the play. They had a violent argument, terminated by the necessity of making their entrances.

Ben sat down next morning and wrote a letter. The surviving draft is crisscrossed with furious amendments and over-strikes. But it emerged approximately as follows:

My dear Sir,

In addressing you I beg you distinctly to understand that I have not the slightest wish to offend you but really (independent of your threat of last evening) your contempt of me as an actor and manager is made so painfully apparent by your words and manner that I must give vent to my feelings on the subject, and as we are both of an irritable temperament, have thought it best to write rather than speak my feelings on the subject. Every man is more or less an egoist, especially in the profession we have adopted, and I am vain enough to suppose that I have some judgment. . . . The pieces introduced by you are always attended with great expense . . . As regards the authors, no allowance is ever made to me for previous failures and you always appear to me to be the last to urge any consideration of the kind indeed rather to encourage a contrary feeling. Secondly an increase of actors . . . then there are extra scene-painters, dresses etc. I know you will say you do not compel me to this, but you also say you will not act with such and such actors and unless such effects are produced by such scenery and such dresses it is of no use to attempt to bring out such and such pieces. Now all these points as far as my means will allow & even beyond, I have always cheerfully acceded to . . . till at last my patience is exhausted as my pocket will soon be, if I do not make a stand against these continued unproductive outlays. Last evening you thought proper . . . to threaten to send [the play] to Covent Garden Theatre—a theatre directly opposed to the one in which you are receiving one hundred pounds per week at the least for ten months of the year. But if you feel justified in doing so, I beg to repeat what I then said, that you are at perfect liberty to act as you please; for however I might regret such decision, no threats shall scare me from delivering an opinion where my own interests are vitally concerned. Now, my dear Sir, I wish you to clearly understand me upon another point—In admiration of your talent I will give in to no man and your great merits I have advocated both in private and in public but unless we work amicably and zealously together in perfect confidence with each other, and I must reluctantly confess my faith in your friendship to me is shaken by last night's threats, I feel that it would be far better for me to jog on comfortably in my old & humble but profitable way, than to endure this continued scene of splendid misery which will probably end in loss. Again assuring you that I mean nothing offensive in what I have written leaving you perfectly free to act either for or against me, I am,

My dear Sir,
Yours most respectfully,
B. Webster.

Macready offered to tear up his contract; Ben refused. Finally, on Bulwer's own recommendation, Macready withdrew his objection to Ben as Graves. They patched up a truce, the honors being clearly with the manager.

After the second rehearsal Macready, who was, of course, directing the play, said that he did not wish to have anything to do with the costumes or scenery; but Ben was too wily to be caught by that one. He replied that "it was not his wish to assume final authority on these matters." Forster wrote Bulwer that "Webster is not at all unwilling to do what is best—only he is for the most part ignorant of what it is. He is going to great expense in furnishing." Macready, however, complained that he was never at rehearsal because he was out chasing up secondhand card tables for the Club scene. Forster was dissatisfied with the scene painter; Ben got another; rehearsals proceeded. You would have thought that the crisis possibilities were exhausted. They had barely begun.

David Rees precipitated the next one. Ben's old comrade from the Irish fit-up days was playing Stout—"just the man for it," said Forster. "I know of no other half so good anywhere." But on the night of November 9th, during a performance of Byron's *Werner*, the unfortunate Rees "exhibited decided signs of drunkenness." Forster heard that this was apt to be a periodical visitation which happened every three months or so and "lasted more than one day." He and Macready were in an uproar and threatened to withdraw the play. Bulwer was not in London, but busy Forster sent him a blow-by-blow account.

Ben brought them a "piteous letter of penitence from Mr. Rees with solemn protestations of amendment." This was not enough. Forster wrote on November 12th: "Mr. Webster has just solemnly engaged himself to me . . . that if Mr. Rees *at any time* between the present date and the production of the comedy, or *at any time on the night of its production* before the whole five acts are over, should present himself *to the audience* in such a condition as to warrant the suspicion of the least drunkenness—the comedy is to be at once withdrawn—Mr. Webster leaving the money in your hands and incurring all the expenses at present gone to and consenting to continue to do so—until he finds a person we can all approve for the part of Stout," even if this meant postponing the production till the following season.

Probably no other manager has ever put himself in such mortal peril for a friend. It is good to record that David Rees got through without a lapse; but sad that he died three years later in Cork "from habits of intemperance." This is also, undeniably, a partial justification of the Forster-Macready attitude. No one who has had to deal with an actor who is a confirmed alcoholic can fail to understand their fears; the rare factor is Ben Webster's courage.

The original opening of *Money* had been announced for November 5th. It was postponed several times; finally, it was to be the 28th. Macready fell out of love with his part and was only a little mollified by a hat selected and ordered for him by the Count D'Orsay and a waistcoat with broad purple stripes designed by that famous dandy—"a remarkable and precious waistcoat," said its admirer, Charles Dickens.

After mid-November everyone became increasingly depressed. Two of Macready's children, his son Henry and his daughter Harriet Joanna (aged three and a half), were ill and he was desperately worried. Bulwer got very nervous, "quite ill-tempered," so Macready wrote in his diary, and "spoke harshly to the actors . . . Haughtily, I should say, certainly unphilosophically," even to Helen Faucit herself.

On Monday, November 23rd, Bulwer and Forster wanted to withdraw the play; Ben said he would be bankrupted and "insisted on his confidence of the play's *success*."

On the 24th all looked golden with promise. Bulwer brought in a new ending for Act IV and apologized to Miss Faucit. Macready's little boy was better, and he himself in such good humor that he agreed to renew his contract with Webster for the following season. On the 25th they rehearsed the new scene. On the 26th Harriet Joanna died. Macready was prostrate. So was the production.

Forster wrote to Bulwer: "Webster was with me yesterday in the highest sorrow, as may well be supposed, on his own account. He was quite sensible of the proprieties of the case . . . and issued a placard saying that 'a severe affliction in Mr. Macready's family would prevent his appearance that night' and that the comedy was necessarily deferred."

Forster issued instructions that the actors were to be kept rehearsing by Ben or the stage manager; every actor knows what that must have been like. Wallack and Phelps agreed to play some extra performances of their plays until the bereaved father could recover himself. On December 3rd the boy was pronounced out of danger; but Bulwer insisted that "Webster must not wish any indelicate or inconsiderate hurry"; the father's feelings must be consulted above all things; he added shrewdly that if the play opened and the child then died, it would be an "irrecoverable blow."

Everything depended on little Henry. He was worse—he was better—he was worse again—at last definitely better. Macready returned to the fray and Forster was left with nothing much to do but "distrust Webster as 'Graves'."

The curtain finally rose on December 8th, 1840, "after a series of procrastinations which, however annoying to the management, seem but to have whetted the curiosity of the public, the house being in a state of perfect 'cram,' and the strongest indications of impatience for the drawing-up of the curtain displaying themselves in all directions." It proved an immense, triumphant success. Ironically, the reviews were not particularly good, especially for the play. Rereading it, one can understand why. But the acting and production were loudly praised. "Mr. Webster has done everything possible to render the piece attractive—we do not believe the Haymarket boards were ever so adorned before."

Money ran for eighty peformances, which was phenomenal in those days. Most important of all, Ben was able to announce that "that high-minded and liberal nobleman, the present Lord Chamberlain, having taken into consideration the strict devotion of this theatre to the interests of the legitimate drama, has kindly granted a special license of two months in addition to the present season." Henceforth it could stay open from June until March, a very great achievement for its manager and the direct result of having a long-running show. Macready, characteristically, was furious. He was planning to take over Drury Lane the following season, and the Haymarket playing weeks would overlap his own.

Nearly forty years later, Old—by then very old—Ben made his last appearance at a Drury Lane benefit performance in "his famous character of Graves"; and in 1880, when the Bancrofts took over the Haymarket, completely rebuilt it and inaugurated a wholly new regime, the play they chose to open with was *Money*.

The kind of hurricane which everyone connected with the

production had endured is not unknown to theatre people today, though perhaps the winds seldom reach such gale force. Sometimes everybody settles down to a new comradeship, like the survivors of a battle. Ben had no quarrel with Bulwer-Lytton; he later presented several of his other plays. He also took full advantage of Bulwer's political influence in Parliament and at Court in the campaign for the repeal of the Patent Acts.

But with Macready there were abiding grievances. It is hard to tell whether there was a tiny echo of resentment from the days of the Edmund Kean rivalry, or whether Macready was temperamentally incapable of working in harmony with any manager whatsoever, or whether he and Ben were especially alien to one another. Certainly they had nothing in common, except, perhaps, that they were both superstitious. It is recorded that they once met to sign an agreed contract and went away again because it was a Friday. They served the theatre in diametrically different ways: Macready never reconciled himself to being an actor; Ben could not have breathed in any other element; Macready, however insufferable, was an artist; Ben, however admirable, an artisan.

Marston tells a story, which he evidently believes, of how Ben once grew so exasperated that he wrote Macready a letter challenging him to a duel. The Eminent Tragedian replied that he would accept the challenge "when his correspondent had taken rank as a tragedian by a successful performance of Hamlet." A sandbag carefully dropped from the grid would have been the only fitting reply to this. But Ben, more subtly, formed an alliance with the rival Macready most feared, young Charles Kean. Meantime, as a manager, he knew a box-office attraction when he had one; and he had amply proved that he was not going to be deflected by vanity from his fundamental purpose.

His bitterness against Macready, however, did not abate with the years. In 1848 he wrote to a friend:

"Is it not too bad that Her Majesty should have been humbugged into a Command at Drury Lane for Macready's *exclusive* benefit and under the idea that by such patronage she is serving the English Drama? You know as well as I do that the exorbitant terms of this lump of egotism and his only condescending to act in plays when *he* only has a chance—written by his *particular* friends, has been the bane of the profession and the serious injury of all Theatrical speculation."

Nevertheless, both men had something to gain from their association; even Macready knew it. When, in 1849, he decided to retire from the profession he had always detested, it was to the Haymarket that he returned for his series of farewell performances. Since he had long before eschewed the cares of management, he was a wealthy man. He had always yearned for the day when he could afford to say goodbye; now it had come. The farewells were protracted: *Hamlet, Othello, Macbeth, Henry IV;* "Last Appearance but One," "Last Appearance," "Positively Last Appearance," "Last Appearance for Ever.". . . All London flocked to see him, headed by the Queen and the Prince Consort. Ben, grimly gleeful one imagines, nursed the box office as long as he possibly could. He arranged to buy the star's costumes as soon as they were truly discarded "for ever." "He has a very excellent bargain," said Macready, "but he met me in a very gentlemanly way."

Naturally, he described the Haymarket company as "an incompetent mass of incapacity . . . the usual number of dolts and imbeciles"; but since there were, in fact, no better actors in London, he took most of them with him to Drury Lane for the Final-est Farewell of all, *King Lear.* The enthusiasm was overwhelming. When the tumult and shouting had finally died he drove quietly home in his carriage and wrote in his diary: "Thank God." Others may have echoed him.

Yet his contributions to the theatre of his time were immense. His standards were unrelentingly high, his taste in drama lofty, if fallible. His use of scenery, costumes and even lighting were much ahead of his time, his handling of crowds imaginative and precise. He was the first "director" in the sense which we now attach to the word. He saw a play as a whole and neglected no part of it.

As an actor he was unremittingly self-analytical, to an extent which must entirely have banished spontaneity or any impulse of the heart rather than the head. Even Helen Faucit, despite her enormous respect for him, found him petrifying to play with.

Old Ben

Fanny Kemble complained that he growled and prowled and roamed and foamed around the stage like a tiger, and she never knew when she was to be allowed to speak.

Perhaps he was not a woman's actor. Charlotte Brontë remarked, in her usual candid manner: "It is the fashion to rave about his splendid acting. Anything more false and artificial, less genuinely impressive than his whole style, I could scarcely have imagined . . . I said so, and by saying so produced a blank silence, a mute consternation."

From the point of view of his managers, his colleagues and his fellow actors he was quite simply intolerable. Yet there are a few pictures of him which stay in the mind colored with warmth and affection. One is of the Eminent Tragedian who told funny stories to amuse a little boy and read to him so absorbingly from *The History of Rome* that the child was "almost sorry when half-past five came" and his friend turned back into the Terrible Tiger and marched off to the theatre to devour his prey.

CHAPTER FOUR

ठ०ठ

"We at the Height"

The Patent Theatres were falling into decline. Inch by inch the Haymarket overhauled them. Ben Webster got the finest stars to play for him, sometimes for a whole season, more often for a series of performances. They appeared either in their own vehicles, in the Haymarket repertoire of plays, or in "new and original" productions. "Mr. Webster, the really honourable and enterprising manager of the Haymarket [is] ever on the alert to produce novelty and strengthen his company with all available talent."

Charles Kean and his wife came often, he growing more pompous as he grew more assured. Like Macready before him, he took over his own physical productions, mistrusting Ben's supposedly slapdash methods. He inaugurated a style which eventually made him famous as "not merely the upholder but the upholsterer of the English drama." Madame Vestris, for whom Ben had often carried a spear, came from Covent Garden with her husband, Charles Mathews; they had been battered into bankruptcy by their efforts to stage Shakespeare for the Moloch House with the same care and elegance as had been their trademark at the Olympic.

Ben's closest friend and oldest comrade was J. B. Buckstone, author of innumerable popular farces and melodramas, and an ebullient actor as well. "I think I have bothered their quiet style of acting here," he wrote Ben from Edinburgh. "They have never seen any comedian scarcely but Murray and his second, both chaste actors. Lord help them if they expect much chastity from me." Buckstone's "partner" was Mrs. Fitzwilliam, who "wore the breeches" like Vestris, and would nowadays be cast almost exclusively in musicals. John Oxberry, the universal biographer, thus describes her: "There are a certain number of persons in the dramatic world, admitted on all hands to possess great talents, whom everybody is delighted to see upon the stage, and yet who never draw one shilling to any theatre whatever." This chilling pronouncement is still regularly validated in the theatres of London and New York.

Buckstone and "Mrs. Fitz" played regularly at the Haymarket between their own tours of the provinces and the United States. From New Orleans, in March 1842, Buckstone wrote:

My dear Webster,

I received your reply to mine, in which I named the time of my return, I have just concluded an engagement here, and in spite of the times (Banks breaking—fires etc—in every direction—Caldwell's Great St. Charles caught fire on Sunday night, a theatre as large as Drury Lane, and is now a heap of ruins . . .)—have still been doing well, indeed everyone says greatly, for the bankrupt state of everything in this and other cities, in this country.

. . . I have been delighted with Havana . . . and the Spaniards were in an excess of delight with Madame [Mrs. Fitz] and her singing and changes of dress . . .

There are sad fears for the safety of the last Boston Boat she is now 23 days out and no account of her. I hope and trust there is not another steamer gone. The people in New York seem *Boz* mad, and *I* think have been making great apes of themselves and of Dickens too . . .

I expect you have had to fight a hard battle with the two great houses opposed to you—but I have every faith in your foresight and pluck, and am sure you will fight your battle well. What a selfish canting piece of humbug all that Macready management business is—the revival of the drama!!! —they should write the upholding of Mr. Macready and his clique of newspaper toadies!

As soon as I get over the excitement of my return I shall go to work hard and fast . . . for I am in great hopes the international copyright law will pass in this country . . .

Transatlantic traffic in actors and plays was, by this time, brisk in both directions, greatly facilitated by the advent of the new steamships. Many English stars toured the States, even though the distances were great and the risks considerable once the Eastern seaboard cities were left behind. One of the Haymarket stars published a vivid account of his travels by embryo railroad, tumble-down coach, on horseback and afoot through the semi-wilderness of the Middle West.

He was an Irishman by birth, brought up in Wales, who had gone to an Irish teacher to correct his Welsh accent and made a career out of the result. He was Tyrone Power the First. In September 1840 he wrote to Ben: "I acted last week in Boston just 3 weeks after making my bow of adieu at *Haymarket*, this is worth a paragraph, and when one thinks of the distance is almost incredible." He was full of triumphs, full of plans and full of expert advice about stocks. "Sell USS by all means and buy Illinois or Indiana *State* stock—sell, man, sell!"

He planned to be back at the Haymarket by the end of the year, but delayed his sailing. Bulwer-Lytton, after the opening of *Money*, suggested that the following season he might "alter 'Sir John' for an Irish blarneying fellow to be played by Tyrone Power." Macready, for obvious reasons, was against it. He need not have worried. Power never came back to the Haymarket.

As an old man, Ben Webster used to tell his grandchildren a ghost story. His great-granddaughter heard it, and repeated it in turn to Tyrone Power's great-grandson. "One night," Old Ben would say, "it was a windy night in March, as I was reading in my study . . ." There was a ring at the front door. His manservant went downstairs to answer it. Presently he returned, visibly shaken. "Please come down, sir," he said, "Mr. Power is at the door." "Nonsense," Old Ben replied. "He only left Boston a few days ago, he can't possibly have got here yet." "But he's there, sir, all the same," the man insisted, "he's outside the door, all drenched with rain . . . his coat—it's dripping wet . . . and he won't speak and he won't come in . . ." Ben went downstairs. The front door stood open. There was no one. The street outside was perfectly empty; and perfectly dry. Days later, the news came. The steamship *President* had foundered in a storm; Tyrone Power had been drowned.

To A. Bunn Esq.

Mr. Webster wishes to play "The Child of the Werck" [Wreck] next week. will you oblige me with the loan of the Orchestral parts and MSS as the no arrieve of the Président leaves me without aeither.

I am, my Sir

tout à vous

Céleste.

The sight of this letter took me back vividly to an incident of my childhood. I could see the picture on our dining-room wall, a very large affair, imposingly framed: *The Reading of a Play in the Green Room of the Adelphi Theatre*, said the plaque underneath. My mother explained it to me. There were the actors, some thirty of them, standing respectfully around in their Sunday best; the plaque had a little chart with their names. On the walls were painted various prints and lithographs which now hung in our house. The man behind the table, with a script in his hand, was, naturally, Old Ben. And the elegant lady in white, draped in an armchair stage center front? "That," said my mother with an acid edge of amusement in her voice, "that, of course, is Madame Céleste." It did not take me long to discover that she was the great love of Old Ben's life.

58

"We at the Height"

She was born in Paris, in 1814 by her own account, though 1811 is the likelier date. She was trained principally as a dancer. In 1827 she went to America with a ballet troupe and performed a *pas seul* at the Bowery Theatre as an afterpiece to *The School for Scandal*. The following year, in Baltimore, she married a Mr. Elliott. A chivalrous reporter in *The Gentleman's Magazine* gives an account of the sequel: Mr. Elliott was "a festive young gentleman . . . who had almost succeeded in squandering the whole of the handsome fortune which the deceased livery-stable-keeper, his father, had left him." Céleste bore him a child and for some years "supported him in affluence." Then, "finding the yoke galling beyond endurance, [she] abandoned him for good. There were those who did not hesitate to throw dirt at her." Elliott died, and the daughter, who had remained with him, was supposed never to have seen her mother again. In fact, she married in Baltimore and both she and her husband became Céleste's good friends.

But there was something about Céleste which provoked romantic flights, especially among American reporters. There is, supposedly, a "soi-disant Count" who robs her of a fortune and disappears. There is another dastardly Frenchman, who robs her of another fortune, treats her with great brutality, and has to be paid £2000 to go back to France, where he is "kindly led by a merciful Providence to an open window in the Rue St. Honoré, Paris, and [is] further prompted by the same Providence to tumble out of the window and break his d—d neck."

I suspect that there was more romantic fiction than fact in these accounts. Certainly she kept her married name of Elliott throughout her private life. A letter from Dickens in March 1869 refers to her "daughters." By far the most probable candidate for fatherhood is Old Ben. One of them was with her when she died, tactfully referred to in an obituary notice as "Mrs. V. E. Elliott."

Her professional career is easier to follow. She returned to Europe from the United States in 1830, danced successfully in Paris, and was urged—reputedly by Chateaubriand—"to make higher pretensions and tread the boards as an actress." She danced (under the management of Bunn) in Manchester, Liverpool and Dublin, where a crowd, led by Daniel O'Connell, collected under her window and gave "Three cheers for Madame Céleste and the French Revolution." She finally made her first London appearance at the Queen's Theatre in the ballet of *La Bayadère* and subsequently "gained applause" at Drury Lane in mime parts such as Fenella, the blind girl, in *Masaniello*, and others written specially for her, such as *Child of the Wreck*.

Between 1834 and 1838 she made several American tours; she was enormously popular, rivaling Fanny Elssler, Jenny Lind or Fanny Kemble. A British reporter describes the phenomenon with some amazement:

"In the period of three years she realised upwards of £40,000. Her popularity with our Transatlantic neighbours exceeded anything that we in England can form any idea of. Saluted by the soldiery, cheered by the populace whenever she made her appearance and elected a free citizen of the United States, she was the goddess of American idolatry . . . In Washington the late General Jackson introduced her to his Cabinet, who offered her congratulations due to her attaining this honour."

In 1838 she came back to London a wealthy woman, and set about making herself into an actress. Like Vestris and Mrs. Fitzwilliam, she excelled in "breeches parts," dancing and singing with tremendous effect as all sorts of dashingly clad officers, Arab boys and prancing Turkish characters. She spoke her first line at the Adelphi Theatre in *St. Mary's Eve*. It was "My shee–ild! My shee–ild!" Throughout the forty years of her English career she never lost her French accent; perhaps she didn't try very hard. It may have limited her range, but it endeared her to English audiences, as, in a much later day, Yvonne Arnaud's accent did to hers.

Céleste first came to the Haymarket in 1838, though Ben must certainly have known her long before, for she was gregarious and very well liked. Said Mark Lemon: "One more kind, amiable, considerate and generous does not adorn any class of society." She was also, professionally, a good businesswoman and an able director of her own type of material. Edmund Yates summed up her partnership with Ben: "Full of natural energy and resource—full of French excitement and élan . . . she obtained a great influence over Ben Webster which, during the long years of its duration was never exercised, I believe, save for his good." They must have been deeply and gaily in love.

Probably the dancing began it. Colman relates: "My earliest recollection of him [Webster] takes me back to the Haymarket ever so many years ago where I saw him dance the polka (divinely, I thought) with Mme. Celeste in a little piece called *The Trumpeter's Daughter*." All Ben's correspondents defer to her. They send their respects, wishes or regards to "Madame," or "Madame Céleste." Only the jovial and privileged Buckstone calls her "Céleste." He and his "Fitz," Ben and Céleste must have been a lively and charming quartette. I have yet to meet any mention whatever, in any letter sent or received by Ben, of "Mrs. Webster."

"Madame" seems to have occupied a settled, family position in his life. She was particularly devoted to his eldest (official) son, Ben II. On March 14th, 1852, she writes him a charming letter from Mobile, Alabama, during the course of an American tour:

Mon cher petit ami,

Combien de fois aurai-je la félicité de te renouveler en ce jour mes voeux les plus ardans [ardents] pour ton bonheur present et future [sic], de loing [sic] comme de prêt, prières te suiverons [sic] partout ou [sic] Dieu guidera tes pas. Mon cher Ben, quand même mon affection est bien grande pour toi, je t'envoie un bien petit souvenir . . . ne regarde pas la petitesse de l'objet comme preuve de la grandeur de notre amitié . . .

(My dear little friend,

How many times shall I have the pleasure of sending you, once again on this day, my most fervent wishes for your present and future happiness? Whether I am close to you or far away, my prayers will follow you wherever God may direct your path. Dear Ben, my affection for you is very great, but the present I am sending you is dreadfully small. I hope you will not think of its size as any indication of the strength of our friendship . . .)

She is bringing back with her "une foule de jolies choses" for his "museum"—a bullet found on the battlefield of New Orleans and a leather pouch which belonged "au Grand *Chef Black Fox*" and other "petites curiosités." She sends him once more "mes voeux les plus sincères pour ton bonheur et la prosperité de tes jeunes années en t'embrassant de tout mon coeur."

The friendship evidently subsisted. From Ben I to Ben II there is a letter of October 1855 full of loving pleasure because the boy has passed his examination into Trinity College, Cambridge. It ends: "Madame sends her congratulations to you and to say she never doubted you could pass or do anything you like."

Society seems to have made up its mind to accept her relationship with Ben. Perhaps the final accolade was the naming of a horse which later won the Manchester Gold Cup "Ben Webster" and of the filly foal which he (the horse) sired out of "Excitement", "Madame Céleste." The only sign of disapprobation I have found sounds a professional rather than a moral note. In 1844 Ben was running two theatres in London and a third in Liverpool; "they demanded his constant care and personal attention," writes a Liverpool reporter. "But the polka epidemic having broken out, he was tempted to neglect his duties and went dancing about the country with Madame Céleste."

By 1842 the Haymarket was acknowledged the social equal of Covent Garden or Drury Lane. Ben had the interior completely remodeled. He put backs onto the benches of the Pit and introduced gas "for the fee of £500 a year and the presentation of the centre chandelier to the Proprietors." This munificence may have been precipitated by the rising cost of oil. The bill for five nights, oil and candles together, was already £16 13s. 4d.; the contractor had further urged upon him the necessity of "removing the whole of the lamps at present in use; everything has been done to them, but 'tis of no use—they are worn out." New lamps must be built for the whole of the stage, "Solar Burners on the Float Lights and also Prompter's Wings and O.P. Wings, new patent reflectors for all the lamps on the stage, Brackets for the Green Room consoles, lanterns for the Pit and Gallery, chandeliers for the Saloon." No wonder Ben thought it the right moment to introduce gas.

He made a virtue of necessity. Gas gets star billing on all the playbills for the season of 1843–44. Buckstone wrote to him: "With the coming in of gas and all your constellations in your company it will be hard if you do not have a brilliant season."

Ben later claimed that he had spent £12,000 on improvements to the theatre, all of which reverted to the advantage of its owners, not to himself. Over the years he remodeled the auditorium, widened the proscenium, and improved the stage to the limit of its capacity.

But there remained the perennial problem: where were the plays? A building is worth no more than what goes on inside it. Ben tried everywhere for new scripts. In 1843 he offered the extremely handsome sum of £500 for a new English play. A distinguished panel of experts undertook to judge the manuscripts; ninety-eight were submitted, and there was considerable excitement.

An aspiring dramatist named Charles Dickens wrote to his friend Douglas Jerrold:

My dear Jerrold,

Yes, you have anticipated my occupation. Chuzzlewit be damned—High Comedy and five hundred pounds are the only matters I can think of. I call it "The One Thing Needful, or a Part is better than the Whole." Here are the characters:

Old Febrile	Mr. Farren
Young Febrile (his son)	Mr. Howe
Jack Hessians (his friend)	Mr. W. Lacy
Chalks (a landlord)	Mr. Gough
Hon. Harry Staggers	Mr. Mellon
Sir Thomas Top	Mr. Buckstone
Swig	Mr. Webster
The Duke of Leeds	Mr. Coutts
Sir Smivin Growler	Mr. Macready

Old Ben

Servants, Gamblers, visitors etc.

Mrs. Febrile	Mrs. Gallot
Lady Tip	Mrs. Humby
Mrs. Sour	Miss V. Clifford
Fanny	Miss F. A. Smith

. . . the fine days are over, I think. The horrible misery of London in this weather with never a fire to make it cheerful is hideous.

But I have my comedy to fly to. My only comfort! I walk up and down the street at the back of the theatre every night and peep in at the Green Room window—thinking of the time when "Dick—INS" will be called for by excited hundreds, and won't come—till Mr. Webster (half Swig and half himself) shall enter from his dressing-room and quell the tempest with a smile, beseech the wizard if he be in the house (here he looks up at my box) to accept the congratulations of the audience, and indulge them with a sight of the man who has got five hundred pounds in money and it is impossible to say how much in laurels. Then I shall come forward and bow once—twice—thrice—roars of approbation—Brayvo—brarvo—Hooray—hoorar—hooroar—one cheer more—and asking Webster home to supper shall declare eternal friendship for that public-spirited individual . . .

I am always, my dear Jerrold,—Faithfully your friend,
The Congreve of the 19th century,
(which I mean to be called in the Sunday papers.)

In prosaic fact, the prize was awarded by unanimous vote to a comedy called *Quid Pro Quo* by a Mrs. Gore. It was then proudly presented on the Haymarket stage; and laughed, hissed, booed and hooted off again. "An egregious failure," commented Ben, and went on to the next thing.

Nevertheless, 1843 was his year of triumph; for in that year Parliament at last repealed the Patent Acts. The reign of Drury Lane and Covent Garden was at an end. Ben leaped into action; he mustered all the plays he could find and all the actors he could get and prepared to go on forever.

"We at the Height"

"Feeling that patronage was not confined to period and place, I endeavoured to take John Bull by the horns and persevered till the leviathans gave way, and this favoured spot became the only constant home of drama for three years without closing once a night, and I should have continued to pursue that course had not the principal performers complained of want of relaxation; consequently I have since made what are termed seasons, averaging about ten months each."

The silver epergne which so impressed me in my childhood commemorated this "season of 1843–44 which extended through his firm encouragement of the English Drama and English Talent to Four Hundred nights, an event unprecedented in the history of the British Theatre." In the speech of presentation it was stressed that "the Haymarket has been English from top to toe"—one cannot help reserving Madame Céleste's toe—"and, to crown all, ever a full and joyful English audience."

But these triumphs were marred by a shocking tragedy. Ben's young half sister Clara was at Drury Lane, which was once more in the hands of the irrepressible Bunn. She was rapidly winning recognition as the most brilliant of the new British dancers and a rival to the French and Italian ballerinas. On December 14th, 1844, she was to dance one of her finest roles, Zelika the Slave in *The Revolt of the Harem*. The back of the stage was lighted by a sunken trough of oil-burning lamps, unguarded. Clara's flimsy ballet dress touched one of the naked flames and started to burn. The other dancers recoiled from her to save themselves. Panic-stricken, she rushed toward the front of the stage, and her dress blazed up about her like a torch. A carpenter dashed from the wings, pulled her to the ground and beat at the flames with his hands; another threw his coat over her and extinguished them. They got her to the Green Room. She was horribly, appallingly burned. After two days of excruciating agony, she died.

In 1844 Ben took over the lease of the Adelphi Theatre and installed Madame Céleste as directress. For nine years he ran both theatres and went on several provincial tours with her. Buckstone wrote for her the melodrama of *The Green Bushes*, in which she played Miami, the Huntress of the Mississippi, in Act II, and Madame de St. Aubert in Act III ("The Atonement"). It was a vast success on both sides of the Atlantic and became her great starring vehicle throughout her life.

But the Haymarket remained Ben's prestige theatre. He was an established manager now, and something of a martinet. During an absence on tour he wrote to his stage manager: "I hope you fined Mr. Adams for the falling down of the flats in *Used Up*." In another letter he directs: "If the underlings do as they like they shall do it elsewhere upon my knowing their names. The conduct of Mr. Shaw I think unpardonable also the grumbling of Mr. Worth. Miss Kendal shall not enter the theatre again." Shades of Macready, the Great Bashaw!

But the actors of rising greatness came eagerly to Ben's theatre: Mrs. Stirling, for instance, and a young man, Irish-born like Tyrone Power, Barry Sullivan. The trade across the Atlantic, now a two-way affair, brought E. L. Davenport, and the younger Wallacks. Ben had a row with James Junior, and threatened to fire him for continuing to wear his own mustache as Sir Benjamin Backbite. This, too, has a Macreadian ring.

Charlotte Cushman, who really did "wear the breeches" in classic parts, played her famous Romeo at the Haymarket to her sister's Juliet. Ben wanted her to return there, but she replied:

"Take my word for it, all old parts are bad for me in consequence of *comparison*. I cannot stand this test well. I know myself perfectly . . . As I look on Viola now—it is *weak* for me, and my sister does not wish to do Olivia in London . . . All the novelty of my acting Romeo and Ion is rubbed off. I do in honesty think that a new play would pay you better than anything else could . . . I should be so glad to make a hit in a new play, for indeed I need it . . ." This poignant cry has been echoed down the years.

But Ben couldn't find her a new play and she did appear as Viola, with her sister as Olivia and Ben as Feste. In another revival of *Twelfth Night* he played Malvolio, very finely by all accounts. He liked playing Shakespeare. Once, greatly daring, he put on a

66

production of *The Taming of the Shrew* as it had never been presented since Shakespeare's day and never was again for a century or so. It was entirely devoid of scenery, except for one drop "representing Hollar's London in Shakespeare's age . . . a very pleasing view." Placards were hung up to indicate locality. The text was rescued from the distortions of the eighteenth century, and the Christopher Sly scenes, long banished, were restored. Ben rewarded himself by playing Petruchio; it does not seem to have been very good casting.

The Haymarket was essentially a comedy theatre and had not the facilities for playing much Shakespeare, except when Charles Kean came to the theatre. But Ben loved the plays, and his memorandum books are full of little jottings about them. He inveighs against the "insanity" of the Baconians; he proclaims that "Shakespeare is easily understood if simple measures taken . . . There is [no] mystifying sentences about him. He wrote for the million and is worth a million of other writers." But there is an interesting manager's-eye view: "The indifference of Shakespeare for the world and its outward shew is marvellous though evidenced in his writings. He seems to have written but for money and that obtained never to have penned another line and retired from life in London and all his companions without the least care. He was one of the most mercantile managers (*vide* Macready's speech) that ever lived in my opinion." Ben certainly cannot have said this when he attended the Birthday celebrations in Stratford, and proposed the toast to The Immortal Memory. The Bard of Avon—mercantile!

"From time immemorial mankind has delegated to the affluent, the educated and the powerful the province of directing taste and opinion on all subjects connected with happiness and mental improvement . . . in the SOVEREIGN LADY of these realms the people of England happily possess an example which their own approval . . . must ever incline them to follow . . . By all ranks it was esteemed a graceful and becoming act in the Ruler of a civilised and intellectual people to set the example of patronizing a class of entertainment that, when directed to the improvement of the heart and mind, becomes a valuable adjunct to education in its highest aims, and only when neglected sinks into a coarse and demoralising amusement." (Reigning Sovereigns, Presidents and Heads of State, please note.)

Thus pontificates the preface to the Royal Dramatic Record of the Court performances at Windsor in December 1849. One does not habitually associate the name of Queen Victoria with theatrical prosperity, but in this case she deserved well of the British stage. She was the first sovereign to command performances at Court for a hundred and fifty years.

Charles Kean and Ben Webster were appointed to arrange them. To represent "the pure English drama" they chose *Hamlet* and *The Merchant of Venice*. Then came a Haymarket item called *Used Up*, adapted by Boucicault from a French farce, and on the fourth night a translation of Kotzebue's *The Stranger;* this rather odd choice was either out of compliment to the Prince Consort, or because "the sparkling French *vaudeville* having sent its representative to Court, it would scarcely be just to exclude the sombre but respectable ambassador of the German drama."

In *Hamlet*, "the necessity of adapting the stage business to the capacity of the little theatre, occasioned some alterations to be made in the usual acting copy of the tragedy. The Ghost's part was somewhat curtailed, and owing to the insufficiency of the space for the requirements of the funeral ceremony, the whole of the Grave-diggers' scene was omitted."

The little auditorium at Windsor nearly burst with distinction. In addition to the Queen and the Prince Consort, there was the Royal Mother, the Royal Husband's Royal German and Belgian Relatives, the four Royal Children, "occupying"—one can hardly evade capital letters—"the Seats on the Steps." There was also imposing support from selected members of the British nobility. After the performances, "a handsome entertainment"—meaning food—"was provided at the Royal Residence" and "a Special Train was placed at the command of the professionals, who were conveyed to town at a comparatively early hour."

Ben was quick to cash in on the splendid publicity—no doubt,

Charles Kean also. "The brightest anticipations were formed of the beneficial influence our Gracious Sovereign's patronage would exercise upon the future fortunes of the stage." And it actually turned out to be so, not only in terms of immediate box office, but in the whole status and dignity of the theatre. The Drama had been received at Court; it began to be accepted by society. After the long interregnum of her widowhood and retirement from public life, Queen Victoria renewed the Command Performances. At Windsor the accolade of knighthood was conferred on Henry Irving, the first ever to be bestowed on an actor. It has proliferated since, even under a Sovereign Lady whose interest in the theatre has been amiably nonexistent.

In 1851 it was hoped that the International Exhibition at the Crystal Palace would have a similar effect. Theatre managers were sure they would make a fortune; and indeed everybody came to London; but nobody came to the theatre. This phenomenon has been repeated regularly ever since. It happened again, exactly as before, in 1964 at the New York World's Fair; and every theatre manager on Broadway was astounded.

Ben's last big success at the Haymarket was *Masks and Faces* by Tom Taylor and Charles Reade. It was preceded by almost as many gale warnings as *Money* and was as big a triumph. Charles Reade, who had vigorously hated everybody, rushed around, embraced them all, took a call, received an ovation, cried for joy. The play did endure for several generations. Triplet was played by many well-known actors, none of them, it was said, so good as Ben. In 1920 it was made into a silent film, with Sir Johnston Forbes-Robertson. The villain was played, with supreme elegance, by Ben Webster III.

About this time, when he was in his early fifties, the Haymarket manager was faced with a choice. He had vanquished the leviathans, and he was probably the most powerful man in the London theatre. "We have now but one national theatre," wrote a fervent lady journalist, "and that is THE HAYMARKET." Since Macready's retirement the heritage of Shakespeare had been up for bids, and with it could have gone the unchallenged leadership of the British stage. Charles Kean was a strong contender; but for all his careful, well-studied productions he was no great actor. Phelps had set up a brave and shining little kingdom at Sadler's Wells, as much a theatre apart then as it has been an opera house apart in recent years. He did not seem disposed to storm the metropolis.

Ben, with his veneration of Shakespeare, must have been tempted to try for the nomination; but he would have had to find a great actor to play Hamlet and Othello and Macbeth. He must have realized that he could not compete with Phelps and Kean by playing Gratiano and the First Gravedigger. Not until the Nineteen-fifties has anyone tried to sustain a classic repertory by starring the management or the director or the building. It remains to be seen whether such experiments will prove lasting. At all events, Ben could not find his great actor. He turned up twenty years later. His name was Henry Irving.

It is more difficult to understand why Ben did not try to add luster to the comedy reputation of his house and to assume the kind of leadership which later fell to the Bancrofts, Charles Wyndham and Gerald du Maurier. Perhaps the reason was simply "mercantile." He had long before stated that the Haymarket bills were paid by the Adelphi, with its popular melodramas and farces and extravaganzas. Perhaps Céleste, "directress" of the Adelphi, got tired of paying them. Buckstone was ready to take over the Haymarket, which must have made it seem to Ben like handing over his child to an affectionate uncle. At all events, he decided to leave it and devote his energies to the Adelphi.

During the final series of performances he gave himself a present and played Falstaff for the first and last time. On March 14th, 1853, he made his farewell. The company presented him with a silver loving cup and the salver of my youthful memory, with its inscribed "token of regard and respect." Many eloquent speeches were made. Allowing for the hyperbole of leave-taking, they have a genuine ring of warmth and affection. So does Ben's own farewell, despite a pardonable nobility both of style and sentiment:

"We at the Height"

". . . During the sixteen years I have held power here, the longest lesseeship in London on record, I have had many trying political and other not dramatic influences to contend with; but no person employed by me has ever felt them, either in manner or money; and I can conscientiously state, in all my transactions as man and manager, I can leave an honourable and honest name to my children . . .

"A manager's life, ladies and gentlemen, is not a bed of roses. With the mind ever on the stretch for your pleasure, and his physical powers endlessly employed in carrying out the mental efforts of others, who would induce the thoughtless to laugh at scars who never felt the wounds of such a position? . . . 'Tis said 'uneasy lies the head that wears a crown,' but far more uneasily lies the head begirt with the tinsel crown of theatrical sovereignty, where every popular favourite is a viceroy over him."

Finally, he has a dig at the ingratitude of the theatre owners and hopes, though he obviously doubts it, that they will behave better toward Buckstone. There are the usual gracious expressions of thanks to the public, to his actors and other colleagues and—as tersely as possible—to the press. He wishes his audience all happiness and prosperity and hopes he will "have the gratification of seeing many old and familiar faces" when the curtain, having fallen at the Haymarket, rises again at the Adelphi.

In that theatre there remained for him almost twenty-five years of active life.

CHAPTER FIVE

―――――― ∞∞∞ ――――――

The Adelphi,
Old and New

I have often wondered what letters people keep and why; what governs their survival or destruction? Most of Ben's business correspondence was probably destroyed when he retired and many of his private letters when he left his Brompton house in 1870. A sale of papers and valuable books was held soon after his death, and naturally the famous autographs were snapped up—Dickens and Thackeray, Wilkie Collins, Rachel and Edmund Kean, Tenniel, Macready and so on. A number traveled to Harvard, via Mr. Samuel Woodward of Cape Cod. A few descended to my family, but were scattered by the vicissitudes of London bombings and transatlantic journeys. A few more drifted back into my hands. But I have wondered why such a very odd selection was ever kept at all.

For instance, among the survivals are an astonishing number of requests for free seats—or rather, free "boxes"; for in Ben's time the first two balconies of any theatre were divided into boxes. The gentry would have scorned to sit anywhere else. Some of these requests are peremptory; some grumble at a delay or announce testily that they weren't able to use the box after all and want another for next week.

The "free list" in Ben's day was an accepted thing; the Patent Theatres in particular found it a serious incubus, since everyone who had ever owned a share in the company had the right to be on it. It diminished rapidly in the later years of the century; but in the Nineties I find a letter of my mother's saying that she has succeeded in "biting a man's ear." This was theatre slang for asking for free seats and getting them. In my own youth, actors provided themselves with little visiting cards, inscribed with the name of the company they were, or had been, working for. We pushed them across box-office windows with nervous smiles and varying results. "House seats" today are a very different matter; you pay a fortune for them if you can get them at all. But I cannot imagine that anyone would keep the applications.

Someone—the same person?—also seems to have kept an "actors' complaints" file; it runs haphazard through the years and includes many familiar items. Mrs. Nisbett declines to play a part "without a line of comedy in it." J. L. Toole hurriedly scrawls, "My dear Gov, For God's sake don't cast me as 'Trip' as it is right out of my way keep me to Moses as you said—." E. L. Davenport complains that he is being "sacrificed on the altar of the Wallacks' greatness" while, almost simultaneously, J. W. Wallack is furious because "the part in Mr. Norton's farce is merely a 'walking gentleman.'"

John Billington—but in an affectionate and charming letter—says that Ben has "dealt a death-blow to my hopes" by giving his line of parts to another actor; but, he adds, Ben Webster "being, although a manager, still more eminently an actor . . . will appreciate an actor's feelings" and is "bound to treat brother-artists with more delicate consideration than they expect to meet from a mere trading manager."

Most touching of all, an old actor who has been many times "turned empty away" concludes that there must be some special and personal reason for this: "when I hear you extolled, (as I very often do) for extreme kindness and goodness of Heart I can only regret that I should appear to be a Solitary being, debarred from entering into a just appreciation of your Sympathy for Old Friendship or Fellow Craftsmen which you must be aware I am, or I should not have offered my services at so trifling a Sal' to what I have heretofore been in the habit of commanding. I would even have *accepted less* if you had offered it, as the respectability of being attached to your theatre was more my object than emolument . . . I conclude by reminding you that in 1818 you asked and I gave! in 1844 I solicit and you refuse! I still remain, with the greatest respect . . ." We have all, in our time, received this heart-tearing letter; the writer is always a kind, sweet man and a dreadful actor. But why did Ben keep it? Was it, perhaps, a hair shirt?

Indeed, Ben had a reputation for being as generous to his fellow players in private as he was indefatigable for their public well-being. This did not prevent him from having constant and furious quarrels with them. The storms subsided almost as soon as they had blown up. He and Keeley will never speak to each other again because Keeley has deserted him and gone off to another theatre; and in no time at all Keeley is writing: "You had better make it Thursday for Madame and less enfants as all the boxes are gone for tomorrow night." Ben hurls insults at Charles Mathews and before you know it, they are gay and affectionate colleagues once more.

In this random mailbag there are naturally some oddities of the kind which one keeps because they are funny and one never knows how to file them. One of Ben's is from A Father:

My dear Sir,

It is with pain that I am obliged to say that I cannot allow my daughter to go on the stage in the sailor's dress. If it was possible that her own tunic would do for the part I should have no objection, but as it is I regret to say that it is a style of dress that I cannot allow her to wear . . .

There are a scattering of social notes. For instance:

The Adelphi, Old and New

Dear Webster,

An idea in the nature of an inspiration has occurred to me this morning . . .

I was contemplating my dismantled study with the carpet in the corner like an immense roly-poly pudding, and all the chairs upside down as if they had turned over like birds and died with their legs in the air, when it flashed upon me why should I bring you and the ladies so far to a dreary house when there is the Household Words office on your way home? I instantly changed the venue, sent down certain bottles to Wellington Street, and shall expect you there. Please tell Madame Céleste so, with my kind regards . . .

Faithfully yours always
Charles Dickens.

There is a note from a manager friend in New York thanking Ben for the recommendation of various plays, but, much more warmly, for an excellent recipe for cider cup. He continues: "We have had a regular flare-up with the musicians, who have struck for 20 dollars a week, and some get it!!!"

I treasure the copy of a contract between Ben and two of his most valued stars, the Keeleys. It is written on a single sheet of blue notepaper. It sets forth briefly salary, dates, parts, billing, in that order, and is signed by both parties and one witness. So simple a disposal of the problems, which are timeless, seems to date from a golden age of innocence—and good faith.

When Old Ben moved to the Adelphi, the whole theatre system was beginning to change. There were fewer visiting stars, and the emphasis shifted toward companies. The Haymarket was the first company ever to tour the provinces as a unit. The actors went at their own risk, but Ben "was so pleased with the effort of his company to fill their vacation, that he played with us the first night in all the towns we went to without charge, not even accepting his railway fare." The time was coming when stars and company touring together would take over the provincial theatre, forcing the stock companies into bankruptcy.

There were signs of change in the audience, too. Royal patronage, which continued at the Adelphi, had its effect. The raffish, roaring fellows of earlier years were now little in evidence. They went over to the burlesque houses or the "three-penny theatres" and were replaced by the respectable middle class. When the Lord Chamberlain inquired stiffly about the admission of prostitutes without payment, and required the manager to "state in writing whether any such practice exists at the Adelphi Theatre," I feel sure that Ben answered with a righteous negative.

Most curious of all, a theatre revolution was rapidly taking place owing to the change in London's dinner hour. As people began to eat at six or seven o'clock in the evening instead of at three o'clock in the afternoon, theatre programs were inevitably shortened. The three- and four-play marathons went out of fashion; Charles Kean started a new routine of one play and a curtain raiser; the Bancrofts were to make it one play alone.

Melodrama and farce had been the trademark of the Adelphi, and the tradition, though modified, continued. Its most regular house author was Dion Boucicault—Dionysius Lardner Boursiquot, to be exact—who bestrode the stages of England and America like the colossus of his day. Some of his finest melodramas had their first, or first English, production at the Adelphi; *The Colleen Bawn*, *Arragh-na-Pogue* and *The Octoroon* were notable among them. There was also a high standard in afterpieces supplied by writers such as Mark Lemon or "those quaint species of mortal Aristophanes," the brothers Robert and William Brough.

Boucicault's *Janet Pride* was a fine vehicle for Webster and Madame Céleste and was hugely popular. Dickens relates that she was much offended because he hadn't seen it, "and says with a very tight cheek 'M. Dickens est artiste, mais il n'a jamais vue [sic] *Janet Pride!'* " There was a dramatization of Scott's *Guy Mannering*, in which her Franco-Scottish Meg Merrilies challenges the ear of imagination; and in a revival of *Masks and Faces* her Peg Woffington must have appeared to come from the Paris boulevards rather than from Covent Garden.

To his Grandson
from Squire Bancroft

Portrait of Ben Webster I
(now at the Haymarket Theatre)

"The Reading of a Play
in the Green Room of the
Adelphi Theatre"—Ben I seated
at the table, May Whitty standing
beside the painting

Ben Webster I

As Robert Landry in *The Dead Heart*

posite page: As Tartuffe   As Joey Ladle in *No Thoroughfare*
In *Apollo Belvi*   As Penn Holder in *One Touch of Nature*

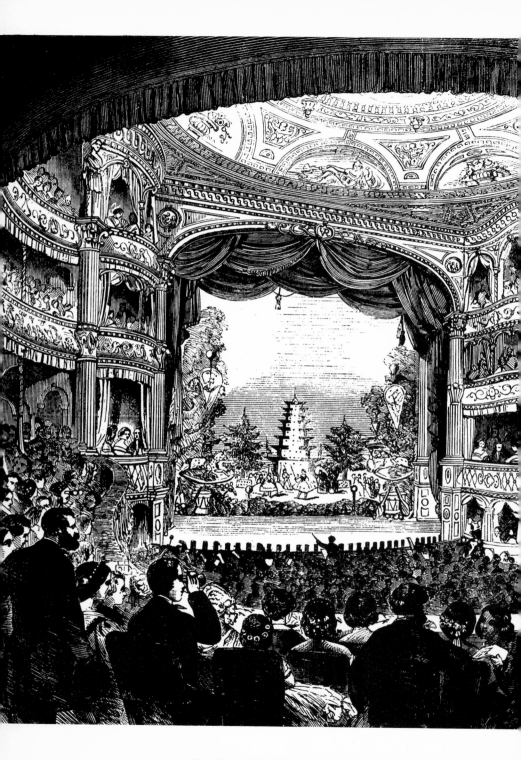

The New Adelphi Theatre, 1858

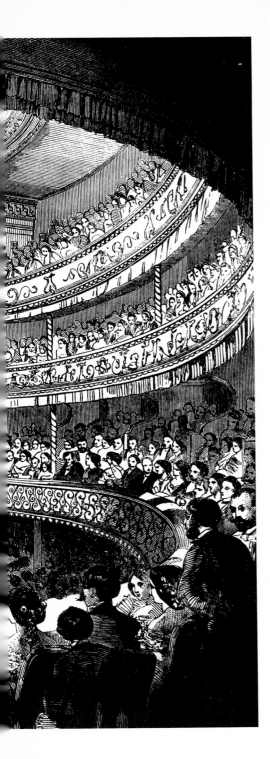

Clara Webster—"From a Sketch taken previous to her Death, and in the dreſs she wore on the evening of her melancholy and fatal accident. The Drawing is considered by Mrs Webster and her Son, a most striking Likeneſs of their beloved and lamented relative"

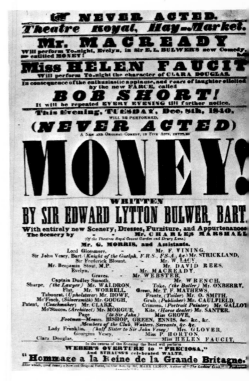

Playbill for the first night of *Money*, December 1840

Madame Céleste

Opposite page: As "Miami, the huntress of the Mississippi," in *Green Bushes*

Dancing the polka with Ben Webster, 1847

Program of the benefit given
for Ben Webster on his retirement

Ben in his seventies

Dedication of a testimonial dinner
to Ben Webster, 1864

III

In 1855 Céleste created a sensation by appearing as Harlequin —the first time a woman had ever played it in England, despite Vestris and all the "breeches" actresses. She dressed it à la Watteau, with powdered wig, three-cornered hat and half-mask. The traditionalists were outraged, and ardent partisans sprang to her defense. "I never saw anything more graceful"; "nothing more delicate and graceful can be conceived." However, it seems to have been Madame's custom to give herself occasional nights off. She trained an understudy so carefully that not even her most devoted admirers could tell the difference; much virtue in a half-mask.

The quality of plays presented at the Adelphi was not as high as it had been at the Haymarket, nor were the casts quite as brilliant, though there were many fine actors among them. By now there were far more theatres to compete for the available talent. John Webster does not appear on the playbills. In fact, he vanishes from the records after playing at Sadler's Wells in 1844–45. This was Phelps's first season and he was obviously trying to build a fine, permanent company. John started with important parts, such as Gratiano, Roderigo, and the Dauphin in *King John*. Had he been good enough he could have made an excellent place for himself in what turned into a memorable regime. It seems unavoidably clear that he wasn't. He had made, although precariously, the transition from child actor to juvenile, but he does not seem to have developed either into a leading man or a character actor. If he did, recording fame keeps silence.

Ben and Céleste managed the Adelphi together for six years. He was over sixty, prosperous and powerful. He read new scripts as avidly as ever and commissioned or bought many that were never produced. He spread his energies to occasional seasons at other theatres, for he was growing restive in the cramped conditions of his own. He began consulting his friends about a project for rebuilding it in accordance with the new audiences and the new customs. It is doubtful whether Céleste approved. Dickens certainly didn't; he thought the plans "wrong from beginning to end." The Queen, however, gave her blessing to the new accommodations designed for Royalty, and all went grandly forward.

The last night of the old theatre was on June 2nd, 1858, and the last play to be done on its stage was a Webster-Céleste duologue. The whole company received tremendous cheering and Ben made a speech, to a "special and hearty ovation . . .

"He had no sooner retired and the curtain descended than the name of *Mme. Céleste* was ejaculated from all parts of the house, and when she made her appearance the cheering and waving of handkerchiefs was a sight seldom witnessed . . . one more cheer, and the audience retired for the last time from the present building, which was the worst-constructed, badly-ventilated and most uncomfortably-seated theatre in London."

The new theatre reopened the following season with new everything, including a new Act-drop painted by Clarkson Stanfield and presented by Ben Webster. It was rechristened "The Royal Adelphi." There were new prices for the new seating: Orchestra Stalls, Dress Circle Stalls, Pit Stalls (with Elbows and Cushions, 2/–); Amphitheatre Stalls (also with Elbows and Cushions, 1/–); Gallery, 6d. "NO SECOND PRICE." The pattern of the English and American auditorium was set; it would not change for almost a century.

Ben had made a laudable effort to eliminate the "fees" which had hitherto been insinuated by front-of-house staff, and tacitly allowed by theatre managements, into the price of seat reservations, programs, refreshments and anything else they could think of. (The word "ice" had not yet been made applicable.) It was later reported that the support he received in carrying out this policy was something less than unanimous.

The playbills also offered a most convenient service in the form of "Lost Property" announcements:

"Lady's Golosh, 2 Handkerchiefs, Gloves, Fan, Tobacco Stopper, Lorgnette Case, 3 Umbrellas, Walking Cane, Head-dress, 2 Keys, Shawl, Bracelet, Cigar-holder, Gauntlets, Cigar-case and cigars, Scarf, Smelling-bottle, Hat, Pen-knife, Lady's bag, Brooch, Stick, Muff, Victorine—can be had on application at the Stage Door without any fee or reward."

Further down the playbill the actors' names were impressive: Paul Bedford, J. L. Toole, The Wigans, Mrs. Mellon, Edward Wright and so on; but no Madame Céleste. Her name was to be seen a few yards up the street outside a rival theatre. The directress of the Adelphi had become the manager of the Lyceum. The Webster-Céleste partnership was at an end. Whether the decision had been professional or personal, amicable or bitter, I do not know. In any case, something happened very shortly afterward which exacerbated and publicized whatever differences lay between them.

In Ben Webster's memorandum book occurs this scribbled note: "I wonder if anyone has ever been haunted by a name as I have been and that name associated more or less with evil—that name is Charles and almost as fatal to me as to England—from Charles, a treacherous boy I placed confidence in to Charles Macready—Charles Marshall—Charles Mathews—to the unkindest cut of all Charles Dickens. Jan' 30/60 Ist night of 'A Tale of Two Cities' of which I could write a tale." He then, exasperatingly, doesn't.

The first night in question had taken place at the Lyceum Theatre under the management of Madame Céleste. The dramatization of Dickens's novel was by Tom Taylor and the author himself. Céleste made a great hit as Madame Defarge. Behind these simple circumstances lay a very murky tale.

Two years earlier, the dramatist Watts Phillips had sent Ben a play called *The Dead Heart*. Ben bought it but never produced it, though he put on two of the author's other plays. In April 1859 *A Tale of Two Cities* began to appear as a serial in *All the Year Round*. After the first three or four numbers Watts Phillips began to get understandably agitated. He brought unremitting pressure to bear on Ben, and on November 10th, 1859, while the Dickens serial was still unfinished, *The Dead Heart* opened at the Adelphi with Ben himself as the hero.

It was, said the papers, "a most unprecedented hit. The life-like pictures of the French Revolution have never before been equalled, even on the Parisian stage, for correctness of detail and costume, and the acting of the principal characters has received the universal stamp of praise." But it was the plot which caused the real sensation. Robert Landry is a man unjustly condemned to the Bastille and rescued after many years. There is a big "Return to

Life" scene. In the end Landry forgoes his chance of vengeance for the sake of the woman he has always loved, and, by a trick, takes her son's place on the scaffold.

There was, naturally, considerable uproar in literary and theatre circles. Tom Taylor and Dickens made their own version of *A Tale of Two Cities*, Céleste produced it, and seven weeks later Sydney Carton, on their behalf, followed Robert Landry to the guillotine. London was divided into "Websterites and Phillipsites" versus "Célestites and Dickensites." There was much recrimination; accusations and counteraccusations darkened the air. Both box offices did a roaring trade. But it seems unlikely that there was much harmony between the rival managers.

The Dickens factions made a straight charge of plagiarism. Phillips replied that the script had been in Webster's office for over two years and that he had repeatedly urged its production before *A Tale of Two Cities* even began to appear. Ben added that he had once taken the manuscript down to Brighton to read to some friends, and that Dickens had been among them. The plagiarism charge bounced back. Men of good will then and since have inclined to a perfectly honest "common origin" theory. There was plenty of source material: an episode in Carlyle's *French Revolution;* a book of Bulwer-Lytton's called *Zanoni* (1842); a play by Dumas, *Le Chevalier de la Maison Rouge* (1847). Ben excused his own delay in producing *The Dead Heart* on the grounds that he had presented the Dumas play, adapted by Boucicault as *Geneviève; or the Reign of Terror*, only six years before, and hadn't wanted to repeat the same theme too soon. He and Céleste had both played in it. Indeed, they had done a one-act play called *The Bastille* at the Haymarket many years earlier still. Revolution themes were in the air, the Bastille was a fortress much beloved of melodramatists; as for the "substitution-sacrifice" theme, it was probably acted out by primeval cavemen.

After the smoke of battle had drifted away, both plays survived. Irving played *The Dead Heart;* and forty years after the first Lyceum *Tale of Two Cities* it reappeared on the same stage, with Martin Harvey, as *The Only Way*. Ben Webster III was in both of them as an aristocrat, blue-blooded and foredoomed.

However, the controversy certainly drove a deeper division between Ben and Céleste. In 1862 she went over to Drury Lane with the Adelphi's bestselling dramatist, Dion Boucicault, and played there the Adelphi's most popular play, *The Colleen Bawn*. She went on tour in the provinces, to America and even to Australia; it was many years before she appeared at the Adelphi again.

The breach between Ben and Dickens was quickly healed; indeed, Dickens himself behaved with impeccable calm throughout the controversy. He later described Ben Webster as one of the most "honourable and generous" men in his profession and felt that he ought to be at the head of "anything good allied to it." Ben cannot have taken very kindly to Dickens in the Macready days, when the young and vastly successful "Boz" was a member of the Inner Circle and sat with Forster at rehearsals making uncalled-for comment. But in their later years they were close colleagues.

Dickens was always extraordinarily philosophical about the pirated dramatization of his novels and stories. Since there was no copyright law to stop the pirates, he made the best of what he could not help. Ben himself dramatized several of the short stories and did a version of the Sarah Gamp scenes from *Martin Chuzzlewit*. It is unlikely that he paid the author for any of them, even when he was doing *The Cricket on the Hearth* at both the Adelphi and the Haymarket simultaneously.

A Christmas Carol became standard Christmas fare at the Adelphi. J. L. Toole, a famous comedian in the making, habitually played Bob Cratchet. He recounted that "Every night at 8 o'clock for forty nights I had to serve a goose and plum pudding. Mr. Webster provided a real goose and a real plum pudding, which were served smoking hot for the Cratchets' Christmas dinner." It became apparent that Tiny Tim, an ethereal, skin-and-bones little girl, was accounting for about three man-sized helpings every night, as she sat huddled on her little stool on the hearth. Watchers were strategically placed to try and solve the puzzle. They at last discovered that she was smuggling the food to a relay of small brothers and sisters, children of one of the stagehands, who were carefully concealed behind the fireplace.

But it was in working together for a diversity of theatrical charities that Dickens and Ben Webster learned to know each other best. It was said of Ben, and with very good reason, that he "deserved well of his profession"; at least, he never ceased to work for its welfare.

He and Dickens were associated in an effort to get an allocation from the Edward Alleyn funds of Dulwich College, "the actors' college", to help indigent actors instead of residents of local parishes. But the charity commissioners refused them.

Their most important undertaking, and, as it turned out, the most controversial, was the formation of the Royal Dramatic College. The name is misleading. The purpose of the fund was defined by Charles Kean at an inaugural meeting in July 1858: "To provide an asylum for some of those who, having long administered to your amusement, seek rest and comfort in the evening of their lives, for the brief space allotted to them after years of toil and trouble, before the dark shadow descends upon the dial of life." There was later to be a collegiate school attached to the institution, but it was a subsidiary project which was never fulfilled.

It was announced that the Queen had promised her patronage as soon as the enterprise should be "sufficiently advanced." "That," said Ben Webster in his speech, "is the highest honour that could be conferred on us; and so deeply am I interested in this cause, that without any attempt at ostentation I will give, from large masses of stone I have in Wales—approved, good stone—sufficient to face the whole of the twenty tenements, and the whole of the stone required for the collegiate school. But the vitality of the entire building is in your hands . . . in the shape of pounds, shillings and pence." These were forthcoming, in the shape of capital and annual subscriptions; Charles Kean, Charles Dickens, Ben Webster and William Makepeace Thackeray were elected trustees.

All of it, however, was predicated upon the offer of a munificent gift—five acres of land at Langley, near Windsor—by a Mr. Henry Dodd, a wealthy philanthropist who had made his money from the collection and disposition of "dust". Unfortunately, he and the Committee immediately began to quarrel; Dodd made conditions and restrictions; the Committee disputed them; there was much public controversy. Dodd suggested that Dickens should be asked to arbitrate; Dickens said, or Ben said he said: "Have nothing more to do with Mr. Dodd." They didn't. But it is a fair deduction that an idea had lodged in Dickens's head which was later embodied as "the Golden Dustman" and christened Boffin.

Indefatigable Ben rose above Mr. Dodd and got the grant of some land from the London Necropolis Company, near Woking. The obvious jokes were, of course, forthcoming; to which Ben stiffly replied that the College would be four and a half miles away from the cemetery; and in April 1860 he himself laid the first brick. "A pretty large company was assembled and the new institution was founded amidst the pleasant jingle of glasses and fizz of champagne." This seems to have been about the pleasantest thing that ever happened to it. But it did get built, and for a brief time numbered Ben's dying brother Frederick among its inmates. This, no doubt, caused accusations of "undue influence."

The College continued to arouse ill will, though it is hard to discover just why. "False in principle and useless in practice," said one critic. "One of Webster's mistakes," said another. Probably it was mismanaged; and there may well have been jealousies and quarrels about, and among, the inmates. Certainly there were disagreements as to its value as an institution; but, added one of its critics: "No-one can question the good intentions of the founders, nor can they deny the self-devotion with which Mr. Webster has struggled to carry out the originally determined plan . . . No man has been a more loyal friend to the 'poor player'."

The Dramatic College faded away; but other similar institutions took its place. The stage was and still remains an extremely precarious profession. Even since the coming of the welfare state it has been faced with the necessity of looking after its old and indigent members. Ben Webster's Dramatic College was the forerunner of a number of highly diversified institutions, from the Actors' Orphanage to the Royal Academy of Dramatic Art.

Old Ben

Ben himself undoubtedly contributed to the controversies aroused by the College. He was "a good hater and a staunch friend"; but as he grew older he grew increasingly quarrelsome and addicted to litigation. Perhaps it was as well that his elder son had become a lawyer. He had been accepted as a member of the Inner Temple, and finally, in 1859, been called to the Bar. He became more interested in writing plays for the Adelphi than he was in practicing law. But litigious Ben needed the services of his son. Once a cab driver charged him five shillings for the fare between Old Brompton and Victoria Station, although the statutory fee was only four; he had had to pay it or miss the boat train; but he told the cabman he would bring him to court, and he did and won the case. He was often within an inch of lawsuits with the press, and he got himself into a legal action with Dion Boucicault when the latter was his tenant at the Adelphi. It was a confusion of who was supposed to announce the forthcoming bills and who was empowered to change them. Neither man took kindly to shared authority.

This particular quarrel very nearly had disastrous consequences. The protagonists worked themselves up into such a state of rage that they would neither write nor speak to one another; and when, just at this point, a famous American actor arrived to appear in a new production at the Adelphi, neither the manager nor the author-director appeared at the first rehearsal. Boucicault finally arrived and began by delivering a tirade against Webster, who, as it turned out, was concealed at the back of one of the boxes. The actor almost left in despair. However, a truce was finally patched up between them and the production went on; which was fortunate, since the actor was Joe Jefferson and the play *Rip Van Winkle*, and it made a great deal of money for everybody concerned.

Ben remained as full of energy as ever. He leased other theatres and ran them concurrently with the Adelphi. He continued to act and to write or adapt a large number of afterpieces and even full-length plays. Ben II became one of his house authors. But the work at the Adelphi began to vary in quality, to lack rhythm and consistency. The front-of-house staff had never fulfilled the stand-

ards Ben had tried to set. Old colleagues like Mark Lemon began
to complain of imprecision in the business and stage management
of their plays. Manuscripts, to the fury of their authors, were left
unread or unreturned. The walk-ons and supers were sometimes so
hastily assembled that the term "Adelphi guests" came into the
theatrical vocabulary.

Ben suffered increasingly from an old failing—"a certain loose-
ness in the text." The young man who had learned Pompey in two
hours was many years behind him, and now, "whether from care-
lessness or too much occupation he was seldom perfect in the text
when he appeared in a new part. A 'fishing' for words and dragging delivery took away from his effects till he warmed into his
part, recovered his memory or supplied the loss of it impromptu."
In 1867 he had a severe illness but immediately afterward he
made a noble comeback as Joey Ladle in *No Thoroughfare*, by
Dickens and Wilkie Collins. Dickens reaffirmed his old comradeship by writing: "Tell Webster, with my regard, that I think his
proposal honest and fair; that I think it, in a word, like himself;
and that I have perfect confidence in his good faith and liberality."
But Ben was now seventy years old; he must have missed many of
his old comrades, his brother Frederick and, of course, Céleste.
The whole pattern had changed.

He had always, since his first successes at the Haymarket, lived
a prosperous country-gentleman sort of life in what was then the
semi-rural district of the Old Brompton Road. Douglas Jerrold
pictured him "rolling home as on a cushion with your sparkling
greys" from some shared festivity. Bulwer-Lytton, failing to find
him at the theatre, wrote: "I suppose you were busy watering your
flowers in that brilliant sunshine at Brompton." He himself wrote
to Ben II: "We have a supply of eggs every day for breakfast but I
have ordered some to be kept over for sitting. The hen you left
sitting had two chicks but the Turkey egg was spoiled because the
moment the chicks were hatched they left the nest."

He lived there for more than twenty years. But the changes
came suddenly, as they so often do. In 1862 the ghostly Harriet,
his wife for twenty-six years, died at Brighton "after a long ill-

ness." Both his sons got married: Ben II to Charlotte Frances
Wright, daughter of the Adelphi comedian Edward Wright; the
younger son, William, to the daughter of W. S. Johnson, who
printed the Adelphi playbills. They moved into homes of their
own. Will had three children in fairly rapid succession. The
youngest was Ben's first grandson: Ben III, my father.

When he was over seventy, with retirement looming inexorably on the horizon, Old Ben moved to Kennington on the south
side of the river, where he already owned some property. It was
still a countrified area, popular with actors as they grew older. His
picture collection was sold; it included a scattering of alleged
Titians, Rubenses, Poussins and Hogarths, some of which would
probably have failed to withstand modern methods of verification.
There was also a good deal of "Dead Game" and "Mountain
Landscapes."

As a child, I used to envisage him in splendid retirement at
Kennington, with spacious gardens, impressive butlers and heavy
mahogany furniture. It was a shock to read, later, about his "de-
cayed old cottage" behind the church. The truth lay between the
two. "At the back of Kennington Church," says a reporter from
The World, "in a position which may fairly be described as 'round
the corner from everywhere,' is a house of fair size . . . a square,
uncompromising edifice of what may be called the Hideous Period
of Architecture." An American visitor thought it "a beautiful cottage." In any case, it was a modest one.

Forty years of management had not left Ben a wealthy man.
"The secret of what will and what will not be a theatrical success,"
he observed, "is as far from being discovered as ever." "When my
theatre was dirty and old and uncomfortable it was always
crowded. The public made me rich and I tore down the old hovel
and built them an elegant theatre to show my gratitude. Confound
them! They won't come into it!"

Some ill-advised investments had lost him money. Among them
were some Welsh quarries, from which he had generously offered
the stone to build the Royal Dramatic College. Robert Brough,
however, dubiously remarked of them:

The Adelphi, Old and New

'Tis said that Webster's mines of lead
Existed only in his head.

He and Céleste were reconciled. She came back from time to time and gave a long series of Farewell performances. Some of them, it was said, were designed to help her old friend Ben. They are variously reported. One observer says of *The Green Bushes*, when she was in her middle sixties, "Few old actresses have stood so many re-appearances so well. I shall ever be proud of having been at that performance." But another comment makes chilly reading: "She re-appeared on the scene of her former triumphs only to sadden old playgoers by comparison with the past . . . and to incite the incredulity of the younger ones."

From Céleste herself there is a flash of warmth. When she was almost seventy she came over from Paris to appear at Drury Lane in a benefit for Mrs. Mellon. The theatre was crammed to see her. To Mrs. Mellon's letter of thanks she replied:

My dear friend,

You owe me nothing. I am happy to have had it in my power to serve you and your dear children . . . it was simply a pleasant Christian act of affection and love. I assure you I was happy on the morning of your benefit to see that I was still living in the hearts of the people—that I was not entirely obliterated from their memory . . .

Every day of the year brings many things to one's mind, and not the least of its recollections are the dear, true old friends that distance separates us from . . .

God bless you, *friend of my youth*,
Céleste Elliott.

Unlike Macready, Ben fought off retirement as long as he could. In 1872 he was still active in the management of the Adelphi. They called him "the Nestor of the stage." He took in Chatterton as a partner, but it proved disastrous. Chatterton "energetically endeavoured to revive the glories of the Adelphi and ended by

87

swamping it and Webster." Ben emerged in print from time to time to protest furiously against the unauthorized debts contracted in his name. There is a touching description of him in his room at the Adelphi, surrounded by heaps and piles of manuscripts, all plays that he had bought at one time or another. Some bore only the cover, the title page and some blank sheets of paper. They had been bought on trust and the trust betrayed. But Ben seemed to know by instinct which toppling heap contained what; asked for an old play of Boucicault's, produced and then forgotten many years before, he shuffled off to a dark corner of the room and laid his hand on it at once.

In 1873 he played his last new part, the old Jesuit in an adaptation of *The Wandering Jew*. His performance was very moving; but the physical effort and the strain involved in learning the lines were apparent. The following year he gave in and announced his official retirement.

Of course they gave him a farewell benefit at Drury Lane. It was a generous custom which often became a tyranny. The play was—it very frequently was—*The School for Scandal*. "These monster gatherings," sighed poor Helen Faucit, "must be unsatisfactory for all concerned." But she agreed to play Lady Teazle. She had a very bad cold, was agonizingly nervous, and had to have new dresses made for the occasion; but she came out of retirement for the sake of her old manager, who was, besides, "an actor whom [she] admired and regarded as a true artist." The rest of the cast dazzled the eye. "Valete et Plaudite," said the program cover.

There must have been an all-star cast of ghosts in the Green Room, too; not Macready, since he never went there, but all the laughing, full-blooded giants of Ben Webster's youth; and Kean, the little man, dominating them all; and maybe even the patient Sophie, if she was not too humble for admittance; and Clara Webster, who had lain, perhaps, on that very couch in her smoldering, blackened rags, burned to the bones.

At the end of the play a recitation was given by the new star from the Lyceum, Henry Irving, and Mrs. Keeley presented a check; it was for £2000, the largest sum, it was said, ever raised by a Drury Lane benefit. Charles Mathews observed that it exactly equaled the combined ages of the principal players. Ben Webster spoke, "eloquently and briefly," and then drove away for the last time from the stage door of so many crowding memories.

In fact, it wasn't quite the last time. He appeared in another benefit, for Buckstone, and then once again, Squire Bancroft says, on March 1st, 1877. The play was *Money*, and Ben was to play one scene from his original part of Graves.

"When the sad wreck of the once famous, handsome actor came to the wings dressed for the performance, I saw plainly how feeble he was. As his cue approached he suddenly clung to me in a terror-stricken way and said with emotion, 'Oh, my dear boy, where am I? I'm very frightened; I don't remember what I have to do.' Fortunately he had but a few words to say. I endeavoured to cheer him, and putting my arm around him, said gently, 'It's all right, Mr. Webster; you remember Mrs. Bancroft, don't you?' 'Remember Marie? Of course I do!' 'Then, Sir, you've nothing to fear; she will look after you directly you step on the stage.'

"His cue came nearer and nearer. I told him how and when to start; he gave me a last wistful look, and then obeyed me like a little child. After the applause which welcomed the great comedian of days gone by had died away, he stood as if in a dream—Mrs. Bancroft gently took her place by the old man's side and helped him through the lines he had to speak."

It is a touching picture of an old man, fallen in health and fortune, tottering to his decline.

Six months later, on his seventy-ninth birthday, Old Ben got married. The bride's name was Eleanor Phillips. She was twenty-six years old, and a few months previously she had borne him a son. Once again, as in his marriage to Harriet, there were no Webster witnesses at the shotgun wedding. It was evidently kept as secret as possible. It is not referred to in the biographies or obituaries. My father never said a word of it; I doubt very much whether he knew. It seems, however, to have engendered considerable ill will between Old Ben and his children.

Old Ben

Nevertheless, his daughter Harriette, who had always been his favorite, continued to look after him. She was now married to Edward Lawson, editor and part-owner of *The Daily Telegraph*, a prosperous and generous man. She may, perhaps, have been glad that Old Ben had found someone to look after him; but it seems more probable that she and her brothers thought Eleanor Phillips a designing hussy and were slightly ashamed of the old man for presenting them with a new half brother, belatedly legitimized, forty years younger than themselves.

Ben, however, lived, vigorously, for several more years. Edmund Yates describes him as "the halest and heartiest of octogenarians":

"His hands tremble as they trembled twenty years ago, neither more nor less; but there is no tremolo in the voice and the blue eye is strangely bright. From the shoulders of a man still strong hangs a bright-blue dressing-gown, turned over with facings of vivid scarlet; above the face, kept clean-shaven as of old, is a smart smoking-cap. Still speaking in the strong, measured tones which produced such an electrical effect in . . . *The Dead Heart*, Mr. Benjamin Webster continues the conversation. 'They killed me the other day, my very dear friends. They took a snycope for death and covered me with a sheet. When I came to, I could not think what was choking me; but when I found out what it was, I saw the situation at once. As I came to my door here I heard a well-known voice exclaim, "Well, here's to his memory! Poor old Ben! He's gone at last!" "Not yet!" I roared, for I was enraged to see two fellows drinking whisky-and-water in my room under my supposed corpse, and—confound them—*my* whisky!' "

Later he elaborated the story to include a foray to the local pub, where the doctor sat, "eating tripe-and-onions with a gin bottle by his side, quite comfortable. 'A pretty fellow you are, to send me out of the world before my time!'" said Old Ben. "He started up as though he were shot." This sounds suspiciously like an echo from one of the Adelphi afterpieces. Perhaps it was.

Ben still went to his clubs, preferring the Green Room to the Garrick. In the Albion Bar they found him "genial and gentlemanly . . . the youngest of us welcomed his companionship." But he went to the theatre very rarely, "fearing to encounter the night air." In February 1882, Céleste died in Paris; on July 8th, Ben Webster, in London. "The name," wrote Palgrave Simpson, "will carry back the memories of old playgoers to a very remote period; and his death severs a link between the far past and present of the British stage."

EPILOGUE

"He enters into the very soul of a character as Landseer into the life of a dog." The comments on Ben Webster's acting nearly all tend to this homely conclusion. He was not one of the very few great actors whose names enduringly survive their generation; but he was an extremely able one, the kind that distinguishes a company or a theatre at the height of its power and is God's gift to authors and directors.

He is credited, even in old age, with the "unflagging vitality" which is the essence of all fine actors. It was said of him that he had no marked personal mannerisms and was not of any "school". "He could adapt himself to practically whatever character he chose to study"; "he always thought out his subject in detail and when he had filled in the picture, it was perfect." His playing was said to have "the refinement, delicacy and finish of French acting," which he studied and admired; and he is frequently compared to the great French *comédiens*, Got, Régnier and Lemaître.

His evident versatility is the more to be admired within the framework of his period, when the "lines" of an actor's "business" were precisely laid down and he was not expected to cross them. If

Epilogue

Old Ben had not been his own manager it is very unlikely that he would have had the chance of playing both Bob Acres and Robert Landry, let alone Triplet, Feste and Tartuffe. Sometimes, as in Petruchio, they thought that he miscast himself terribly. But this happened remarkably seldom, considering his opportunities.

Marston believed that he never lost his yearning to play tragedy and once brought him a play which had a tragic part for him; but the manager triumphed over the actor and he rather sadly declined it. The sword à la Kean was never drawn save in a comic battle. But a vein of tragedy is invaluable to a comedian; without it Ben could not have played Triplet or Malvolio nor earned, as Robert Landrӯ, favorable comparisons with his successor, Henry Irving.

Coquelin, who was perhaps the greatest of the French actors in Ben's genre, bases his Art of Acting on the duality of the actor. Number One "conceives the character to be created . . . sees it as the author has drawn it . . . steeps himself in the intention of the author . . . realises his plane of action in the plot, sees him as he must be."

Number One then "adapts" Number Two to express every element in the personality required. "He pictures Tartuffe in a certain costume and he assumes it. He endows him with a certain gait, and adopts it . . . He controls his own face, his own body, cutting and stitching at his own skin until the critic within him, Number One, declares himself satisfied. But . . . so far he has achieved only a superficial likeness, the exterior, not the personality itself; he has got to make Tartuffe speak as he hears him speak . . . move, act, gesticulate, listen, think from the very soul of Tartuffe himself . . . Then the public will not exclaim as he makes his entrance 'Ah! here comes [Coquelin] . . . or [Webster] . . .' They will cry out, 'Here is Tartuffe!' Otherwise you have failed in your job."

I do not suppose that Ben Webster ever reached the level of Coquelin; but I think he must have been that kind of an actor. I wish there were more of them.

As a manager, his career speaks for itself. It covered a period of many changes—the decline and fall of the two Patent Theatres, which was partly his doing; the establishment of working companies, long-term units, which he had exemplified and fostered; the beginning of touring companies at the expense of the resident stock theatres.

In his day the shapes of theatres had changed. The Pit had retreated close to the back wall; when the Bancrofts rebuilt the Haymarket in 1880 it was altogether Pit-less. The apron stage had diminished to a fraction, and it, too, was about to go; the Bancrofts (again) introduced a picture frame all around the stage. The boxes were driven to the side lines and the corners of the auditorium. Overhanging balconies, unknown till 1820, seated the reputable middle-price public. The Orchestra stalls were becoming the arbiters of artistic excellence and the dictators of economic success. The roaring boys and the prostitutes had gone. Society was moving in.

Scenery had changed. The green floor cloth, which for generations had been the ritual accompaniment of serious drama, had departed; so had "grooves" and sliding wings, or nearly so. Fechter had experimented with sectional stages; Boucicault with complex stage machinery for moving heavy, realistic, wood-and-canvas sets. Realism had become the rage, from the Bancrofts' real bedrooms to Charles Reade's real pigs.

Lighting had changed totally, from oil and candles to gas, and so to "limes". Macready had started to experiment with them and Charles Kean had perfected them. A stick of lime burned in a gas jet gave a brilliant, controllable beam, which could be varied by the use of colored glass. The limelight man up on his wooden perch became an artist. A few months before Ben's death, the first London stage was lighted by electricity.

The Haymarket was a small stage, not well adapted to scenic effects, nor did it normally present the sort of play which calls for them. But throughout Ben's lifetime there was still great emphasis on "spectacle". It lasted well into the twentieth century; indeed, until the cinema came along to do it better. But the "dioramas", the "Pepper's Ghost" tricks, the blood-chilling perils by flood and fire were becoming the limited province of melodrama. It is a tenable theory that the theatre lost some excitement with their passing. Ben dabbled in them at the Adelphi, and seems to have done them

very well when he wanted to; but I do not think he was deeply
interested in them. He cared about acting; and plays.

He put together wonderful companies. His record at the Haymarket has probably never been bettered. For the dramatic repertoire, he did the best he knew—the best there was. "He sought to
bring to light new dramatic ability by offers which, if they now
seem moderate, were then liberality itself." So testifies Marston,
himself an author. "To authors I find I have paid £30,000 if not
more," boasted the manager of the Haymarket in his farewell
speech.

Bulwer-Lytton, Sheridan Knowles, Douglas Jerrold, Tom
Taylor and Charles Reade, Planché, Mark Lemon and the Brothers Brough—not to mention the towering Boucicault with his
hundred and fifty plays and adaptations—these were the finest
playwrights of their day. It is a sobering thought that of the
hundreds, perhaps thousands, of "dramatic pieces" produced by
Ben Webster, not one now remains in the repertoire of the English-speaking theatre.

Yet he had kept the lamps alight. He saw the new plays
coming; the Tom Robertson comedies began to appear more than
ten years before his death. They had an immediate impact on the
fashionable, acceptable style of acting. Ben was essentially a
"prose" actor, despite all his poetic leanings, and he might very
well have thrived on the new, realistic, quieter methods. It was his
misfortune that they came just too late.

The long night of the drama was nearly over; great revolutions
were already in the making, of which he never knew. Arthur
Pinero had written his first play; Bernard Shaw had written his
first column as a drama critic; in Russia, Dr. Chekhov was beginning to try his hand at authorship. The year after Ben Webster
was born, Sheridan wrote his last play, *Pizarro*. The year before
Ben Webster died, Ibsen was writing *Ghosts*.

PART TWO

Young Ben and May

CHAPTER SIX

———— ◊◊◊ ————

The Inheritors

BEN WEBSTER'S WIDOW

Admirers of the late Benjamin Webster will regret to hear that his young widow is not in comfortable circumstances, and if my information is correct, she has recently been deprived of her furniture under a bill of sale held by a relative of her late husband. Mrs. Webster is one of the most admirable of women, as she is a devoted mother and as she was an affectionate wife, and the mainstay of the declining days of the eminent comedian whose loss we all deplore. I believe Mr. Henry Irving, with the generosity which usually distinguishes him, has behaved in the kindest possible manner to the almost friendless widow, and I am sure that if Mr. Irving were to appeal to the public on her behalf, his appeal would meet with a liberal response. If the Editor of the *Daily Telegraph* were to second the appeal nothing would be wanting to enlist the sympathies of an appreciative public in the relict of a very able and remarkable actor.

Young Ben and May

This clipping, from the *Daily Telegraph* of August 26th, 1883, was actually my first introduction to Ben's third wife. It evokes speculation. The request to the paper's editor has an overtone of reproach, since this was Edward Lawson, Ben's son-in-law, who should have known all about the situation anyway. And who was the wicked relative menacing the friendless widow with a bill of sale? Surely not Harriette Lawson. Her benevolence toward her father may not have extended to his widow and born-out-of-wedlock son but it is impossible to picture her sending the bailiffs to take possession of the furniture.

The eldest son, perhaps? Céleste's "cher petit Ben," my great-uncle? Would it have been in character for him to do so? I found that I knew very little about him. He was never referred to in my hearing except cursorily: "barrister—wrote plays—did some stuff for the *Daily Telegraph*." He must have withdrawn from public life some time in the late Seventies, for I could find no trace of his practicing law or writing plays beyond that date. I assumed that he died young and had no children. I was quite wrong.

He died, as I eventually discovered, in Bognor, on the Sussex coast, where he had lived at a quiet little lodging house with his wife and daughter. The inscription on his tombstone is touching:

"In cherished memory of my fondly-loved husband Benjamin Webster B.A., Barrister-at-Law. A devoted husband and father who passed from his dear ones on November 16th 1895. Greatly missed and sadly mourned by his sorrowing wife and daughter and by all who knew his worth."

There is a perceptible note of reproach in the last phrase. Below his name is that of his wife, who lived till 1914, with an inscription of equal tenderness, devised by their daughter, Charlotte Frances.

In 1939 my parents and I were staying at a friend's house in Sussex while they told me "the story of their lives" as biographical material. At this same time, only a few miles away, Charlotte Frances Webster was living in loneliness and considerable poverty. I am sure my father never knew that she was still alive. I never heard him speak of her; he may never even have known of her existence, though she was one of his very few close relatives. She must have known of him since his name (her father's name) was often in the papers; but she made no attempt ever to get in touch with him or with any of the family. She lived till 1956, unmarried, "domestic housekeeper retired," says the certificate, and gives her age as ninety-five.

Ben II and his wife and daughter took shape for me as a gentle, sad and loving trio. I do not know what happened to estrange him from his brother, Will, to whom he had once been very close. He may even have quarreled with Old Ben, for he was not present at the funeral. Perhaps it had something to do with the third wife. Certainly the rift was deep and lasting. But I still could not picture Ben II as a man who would descend on the young widow in her pitiful, black rags and make off with the dining-room table.

The remaining candidate is, of course, the second son, William S-for-Shakespeare, my grandfather. Reluctantly, I have to concede that this is a possibility. According to his children he was a Micawberish character of marked financial instability, always waiting for something to turn up. Perhaps the furniture did.

My grandfather's youth is less well documented than that of Ben II. The only letter I have found is a charming one written by Old Ben on Will's fifteenth birthday, proffering both pocket money and advice. It ends: "God bless you! let me see you the envy of the ignorant, the respected of the just and wise, and you will be the pride and happiness of my old age." It was a hope doomed to disappointment.

William followed the law, like his brother, but as a solicitor, not a barrister. He must also have done some work, soon after he left college, among the front-of-house staff at the Adelphi. A small square of lace-edged satin records that the ushers and ticket takers are offering him a "trifling testimonial . . . in acknowledgement of his uniform consideration and gracious kindness" to them. It was probably on the announcement of his engagement. He married a delicately pretty young girl named Anne Sarah Johnson. Her father, W. S. Johnson, was proprietor of the Nassau Steam Press, which printed, among lesser things, playbills for the theatres and other fascinating items such as *Dick's Penny Plays*. They had three children, Annie, Lizzie and—presumably the old man's first grandson—Ben, Young Ben or Ben III, born on June 2nd, 1864, who was my father.

Annie rapidly became a masterful young lady. She had christened herself "Booey," something to do with the color of her eyes. Her birth coincided with the death of the Prince Consort and was designed, she later asserted, to console the nation for that sad event. Eliza, the second daughter, had inherited her mother's delicate features and blond hair, soft as silk, together with an enormous bass voice. Ben, as a child, a youth and right through to his old age, justified, better than any other man I have seen, the adjective "beautiful."

Soon after his birth the family moved to an old Georgian house in Brunswick Square, Bloomsbury. It was quiet there, tree-shaded, foggy in the winters, disturbed by nothing louder than the clip-clop of horses' hooves on the wooden-paved road, the mournful bell of the muffin man or an occasional barrel organ, with its flat, tinkly tunes. The children were free to use the big garden which ran the length of the square; they could also use other neighboring gardens, belonging to the squares where their friends lived.

It was a peaceful house, but not a happy one. Father William indulged in long, unexplained absences. At the age of ten Young Ben, on a visit to some cousins, wrote to his sister: "I am very glad to hear you have been so gay; I suppose you liked *The Bohemian Girl* very much. I was not at all surprised to hear that Papa had not been home nor that he would not be home before Sunday and I expect we shall receive news to say that he will not be home then." Their mother was gentle, timid, and an almost chronic invalid. She would lie on a chaise-longue by the drawing-room windows, gazing out over the gardens, and the children would be told to keep very quiet. Sometimes large men with large boots and bowler hats would march into the house, and she would whisper to Ben to fetch her jewel case quickly and put it under her pillow. He would sit on the stairs outside her door like a guardian cherub, admitting no one. Afterwards he would ask Booey who the men were. "Bailiffs," she would reply darkly, vouchsafing nothing more.

He never remembered very much about his famous grandfather, and if he ever saw him act, as he well might have done, it left no impression. He would tell me of being taken with his sisters to visit the old man in Kennington—this was when I still envisaged mahogany and butlers—at Christmas or New Year's Day or someone's birthday. Old Ben would tell theatre stories in his resonant actor's voice: the Tyrone Power ghost story; or the one about lighting Queen Victoria to her box at the new Royal Adelphi, walking backward ahead of her with the candelabra held proudly —and falling down two unaccustomed steps to land on his back at his Sovereign's feet, still holding the candelabra. But whatever were the mysterious rifts in the Webster family, they did not permit much contact between Old and Young Ben.

It has not been possible to establish the year in which the program shown on page 104 was printed, or rather handwritten in a tiny, painstaking script; but the beneficiary cannot have been more than eight years old.

Indeed, Mr. B. Webster had not long been admitted to the august company of his elder sisters. When very small indeed he had been taken to see a play about the Hunchback of Notre Dame; this had so terrified him that for years afterward he would dream of it and wake screaming. It was perhaps because of "Ben's Quasimodo fits" that he had reached the advanced age of five before he was allowed to join the performances which took place, two or three times a week, in the back drawing room of number 9 Brunswick Square. He didn't particularly want to; he was corralled into it because they found it so difficult to play the Balcony Scene from *Romeo and Juliet* without the crucial interruption of "Madam! Madam!" from the offstage Nurse. So Ben, in his nightshirt, was stationed outside the door with his ear pressed close against it. When he heard his sister Lizzie say: "The more I give to thee the more I have," raising her voice perceptibly, "for both are *Infinite*," he yelled, "Madam! Madam!" with all his might. After a couple more "Madams" he was allowed to go to bed. They were his first lines off any stage.

The repertoire of the Webster Sisters progressed from Scott-Gattie's children's plays to all the popular pieces to be found in *Dick's Penny Plays*, such as *The Hunchback* and *The Lady of Lyons*, and thence to Sheridan and Shakespeare. Booey directed,

Young Ben and May

~

Theatre Royal Brunswick

~~   ~~

━━━━━

~ Mr. B. Webster's Benefit ~

*Mr. B. Webster begs to announce that his
benefit will take place, tonight,
Thursday, March 24ᵗʰ
when he will appear, supported by the
entire company in selections from*

━━━━━

Julius Caesar
Act IV Scene III

Brutus   Mʳ B. Webster
Cassius   Miss Webster

━━━━━

Macbeth
Act I Scene VII

Macbeth   Miss L. Webster
Lady Macbeth   Miss Webster

━━━━━

Recitation
"The Charge of the Light Brigade" (Tennyson)
Miss L. Webster

━━━━━

Ruy Blas
Act IV Scene I

Don Salluste   Mr. B. Webster
Ruy Blas   Miss Webster
Queen   Miss L. Webster

104

frequently cursing her sister for looking at the audience instead of at her. She was (and remained) a vigorous and capable actress, especially remarkable for her Sir Peter Teazle. The addition of young Ben enormously enlarged the potential of the troupe, and he was rapidly promoted, first to the Widow Melnotte, then to the title role in *Froggy Would a-Wooing Go*, and at last to the full repertory. A particular favorite was a one-act play called *Our Bitterest Foe*, in which all three performers engaged in mortal combat. Sometimes William S. would come home late at night to find his three children fast asleep on the floor from sheer exhaustion, still clutching their several trusty swords: one property dagger (Booey), one wooden ruler (Ben), and (Lizzie) the silver skewer which, on humbler occasions, served to hold together the boiled beef.

Despite the amenities of the double drawing room as a combined stage and auditorium for their productions, the children sometimes felt that their real home was with their grandmother, their mother's mother, in St. Martin's Lane. This was both a home and a workshop; for in the warehouse in the back, close to the attics where Chippendale had once worked, stood Grandpa Johnson's great steam presses. On Sundays they were silent and made a wonderful setting for games of hide-and-seek; but on weekdays the house shook with the whirr and clang of machinery. Sometimes the children were allowed to hold the sheets, still damp and curling, of the *Family Herald*, or the latest of *Dick's Penny Plays*, or the London playbills for the week. They would be shown some of the old ones from the files: *The Merchant of Venice:* Shylock . . . Charles Kean, Gratiano . . . Ben Webster. Years later the Nassau Press would be printing Shylock . . . Henry Irving, Gratiano . . . Ben Webster.

Granny's brother was Joseph Moses Levy, known affectionately to the children as "Jo-Mo"; he would come puffing up the stairs, immensely fat, sink down in an armchair and invite little Ben to sit on his knee; this was difficult, since there was very little knee to sit on. Jo-Mo was also a printer, who had once taken over the *Daily Telegraph* as payment for a bad debt; he and his son, Edward, had turned it into one of the most influential papers in

England. Edward had added a Lawson to the Levy and subsequently became the first Lord Burnham. He had many friends in the theatre, such as Bancroft and Hare and Irving; and he had married Old Ben's daughter, Harriette. The families were therefore doubly related, and Granny's house swarmed with their friends.

As the children grew older, they were admitted to the adult suppers which took place every Wednesday evening. It was a free-for-all; anybody's friend was welcome, and after a preliminary tryout was accepted as a member of the circle. There was grown-up talk of the theatre and literature and politics, and the ranging interest of a lively group of people widely engaged in the activities of their day. Naturally, there was homemade music; Aunt Harriette noticed that young Ben had a singularly pure and sweet boy's voice, besides looking like everybody's casting for a choirboy. She sent him to Dr. Stegal, choirmaster of Lincoln's Inn, who agreed. Soon a small cherub with golden hair and blue eyes appeared in the front row on the Decani side, singing as loud as he could and surreptitiously flicking orange pips at his opposite number on Cantoris.

Lincoln's Inn was and still is one of the several fraternities known as the Inns of Court, composed of students and practitioners of law. They have not changed much since Shakespeare's day. Barristers and solicitors have their offices or "chambers" in secluded courts and buildings of collegiate appearance. The community had its own chapel, complete with choir, as well as its own hall and kitchens. In other respects the monastic comparison is deceptive.

In Ben's day, the boys of the choir received a free education from the Stationers' Company, one of the oldest of the City of London guilds, as well as a small payment for their services; which made him a wage earner at twelve years old. On weekdays he would travel down Gray's Inn Road by horsebus and then trudge along Fleet Street to school. Sundays were spent at the Inn. He would bring his own lunch and cook it, with the other boys, in the great vaulted kitchens below the Hall. They taught him how to beat his piece of steak with an umbrella to make it tender. Dr.

Stegal was a stern master; strict, also, to visiting preachers. If the sermon went on too long he would pull out a big "hunter" watch, snap the lid open, and look at the time, snap the lid shut again, and repeat the process until the sermon petered out in an intimidated "and now to God the Father . . ."

On special Sundays and high holidays the finest choirs in London—Lincoln's Inn, the Temple, the Chapel Royal, the Abbey —would join the boys of St. Paul's Cathedral for the massed services; no flicking of orange pips or snapping watches here; all the cherubs in red or black, white surplices, starched ruffs, brushed hair, singing their innocent hearts out.

Ben's schooldays brought three tragedies, small in themselves, which, however, he never forgot. I think he came to feel that they represented a pattern in his life—the pattern of never quite managing to win. As an amateur track runner he lost by one place the championship of the Bloomsbury Square fraternities; as a schoolboy he lost by one point the "top of the school" position, because he had left at home a drawing which should have earned him marks in the qualifying examination. As a choirboy he had waited in patient agony for the chief soloist's voice to break. At last it did, and he was to sing "Oh, for the Wings of a Dove" the following Sunday; as he soared into the second phrase, his own voice broke too.

As he grew older, the choice of a profession became imperative. The stage seemed obvious; but his family, led by Aunt Harriette, seems to have undergone one of those attacks of good sense which beset all theatre families. At such times they passionately assure their children that the theatre is of all professions the most insecure, the most degrading, the most heartbreaking, the most detestable. The child is to abjure the stage forever; far better to be a postman. Naturally the children don't believe a word of it. But when Granny and Aunt Harriette assured Ben that it would be much better to be a barrister ("a gentleman's profession," said Granny), he was quite ready to acquiesce. He didn't much care for the stage.

His sisters played very frequently with amateur groups, some of high quality, and with one of these he had made his grown-up debut. It was a melodrama, and his first line was supposed to be: "I am Green, the detective." Just before he went on he forgot his name; clutching at the scenery in anguish, he pulled a door down. It didn't seem auspicious. He settled down peacefully to study law. At this point, his mother died. The family finances were found to be in a deplorable condition. Aunt Harriette, who had often helped her brother with unpaid loans and the girls with clothes and pocket money, offered some vigorous advice. Booey took it.

She moved the family to a smaller home in Guilford Street. She marched around to the local tradesmen and promised them that all outstanding debts would shortly be paid as she was about to get a theatrical engagement. She heard that Hare and Kendal were going to produce a new play called *Young Folks' Ways*, and that there was an ingenue part in it. She went to see them and got it. She made her debut with aplomb and success and settled down at the St. James's Theatre as to the manner born.

At first she was extremely annoyed to find that her understudy, playing a tiny part in the afterpiece, was to share her dressing room. This was a little girl from Liverpool called May Whitty. "A quaint little thing," Booey told her brother and sister, with a strong North Country accent, who had no experience except in operetta. Gradually she began to patronize her and instruct her in theatre history and protocol. Booey's approbation was apt to come suddenly and to subside as rapidly. Ben and Lizzie were inured to welcoming her new protégées with glad smiles, only to see them cast into outer darkness shortly afterward without ever knowing how they had offended. They realized, with some apprehension, that the little understudy was about to be cast in this role.

CHAPTER SEVEN

Prelude in Liverpool

The symposium that night, in 1952, was to be on The Irish Theatre. The distinguished panelists assembled by the University of Virginia were Elizabeth Bowen, Dennis Johnson and Padraic Colum. Mr. Colum, they told me, was the self-effacing little man in the corner of the Faculty Lounge, where I was being given tea.

I got myself introduced to him. I told him that I hated having to miss the symposium, but I was lecturing myself that evening. "I'm particularly interested," I said, "because my mother played *The Countess Cathleen* in the special performance when Yeats and Lady Gregory inaugurated what afterward became the Abbey Theatre." He was very faintly interested and asked her name. "May Whitty," I replied. He disapproved. "It's not an Irish name." I bristled somewhat. "There are records of the Whittys in County Wexford in the twelfth century; sometimes sheriffs and sometimes horse thieves; but there." "Oh," he answered, nonchalant but firm, "they may have come over with the Normans, but they're not Irish." I could hear the ghost of Michael James Whitty come screaming over the white-pillared portico calling upon his great-granddaughter to do something with fire and sword.

Young Ben and May

The family folklore of Michael James Whitty is always colorful. It depicts him as a barefoot boy from Ballyteigue arriving in Liverpool with nothing but his Irish wits, a pen and a totally unsubstantiated claim to the Earldom of Shrewsbury. As an old man, he himself gave a more factual account: He was born in 1798, the same year as Old Ben Webster, at the farmhouse of Nichoree, parish of Duncormick, outside Wexford.

His father was a farmer and a shipowner in the modest port of Wexford. His eldest brother was destined for the church and had a private tutor in Greek and Latin. Michael James was allowed to share the lessons. "At a very early age" he became his father's business assistant, but the business failed. When he was twenty-three he went to London and began to write.

"I contributed articles (bad ones of course) to the literary periodicals of the day and in 1822 I wrote 'Tales of Irish Life,' a production . . . which was recommended beyond precedent by illustrations from the pencil of my friend George Cruikshank."

His belief in his work was already formulated:

"I was very ambitious and I had a very exalted opinion of myself. I almost looked down on Homer and thought very little of Dr. Johnson. At an early age I devoted myself to the press . . . and I now find that the pursuit was a noble one, a great one and a proud one." He maintained all his life that the press was "the instrument of liberty, freedom and progress all over the world." He believed that everyone connected with a newspaper, from the editor to the messenger boys, should combine to "use the press for the public good." Having made a name in the journalistic world of London, he was offered the editorship of a projected paper in Liverpool, the *Journal*. He brought out the first number in 1830. He comments: "It was entirely successful."

Liverpool was a great city. It was the home of the British shipping industry in the golden age of shipping. Up the river to the docks of the River Mersey came the produce of the world, and most especially American cotton for the mills of Lancashire; downstream with the tide flowed all the manufactured goods of the Midlands and the industrial North. It was a city of advancement, ferment, questioning.

When Michael James arrived there it was seething with the upheavals of Catholic Emancipation and the Reform Bill. He flung himself into the fray. Even his enemies called him incorruptible. "Unsqueezable in the hands of mob or ministerialists; defiant of cant, no matter by whom sanctioned . . . For great men he had great veneration; for mediocrities none whatever and when twitted on this score he was wont pleasantly to defend himself by quoting the saying that 'scorn of pismires did not imply irreverence for lions.' "

In 1836 he accepted the office of Chief Constable of the city. Like his sheriff ancestors, he could enforce the law. Legend has it that during the Chartist riots he would ride out alone among the mob armed picturesquely with a shelalagh. He eliminated the chronic gang warfare of the Liverpool docks by arming the police, for the first time, with night sticks. He formed a new fire brigade within the police force to fight the cotton depot fires. After twelve years, he accepted a check for £1,000 from his grateful fellow citizens and retired. With it he bought his own paper, *The Journal*.

Unlike his horse-thief ancestors, he understood that if you disapproved of the law you need not break it; you could bend it. His weapon was the pen. A justice of Preston County Court was overbearing and tyrannical; Whitty attacked him in a searing editorial. He was summoned by two bailiffs to appear before the judge. He got two of his old police boys to arrest the bailiffs for not having a warrant. After a sensational trial, he was fined. He refused to pay the fine. He was escorted to Lancaster jail by a cheering mob; his fine was paid by his friends and the mob escorted him home again. The judge was removed from office.

He campaigned vigorously for the removal of the crippling Stamp Duty from newspapers. He promised that if it were abolished, he would found the first daily penny paper in England, and he did. On June 11th, 1855, the *Liverpool Daily Post* was born. He made it one of the most respected papers in England. He was the first provincial editor to take advantage of the new telegraph wire and to give his readers every morning an account of the preceding night's parliamentary debates. His eldest son, Edward, reported them in a new style, with light, satiric comment and vivid snap-shots of men and events.

Michael James wrote the leaders. He was for Gladstone in moderation and idolized Garibaldi. During the American Civil War he was for the North, while Liverpool was passionately for cotton and the South. In 1873 his successor wrote of him:

"It is scarcely possible now to realise the courage demanded of such a man in the focus of that pro-Southern virus which so fiercely fermented in press, parliament and public.

"Unmoved by any save the purest motive, he not only main-tained the abstract right of the North, but contended in the face of continuous catastrophe that the North would and should triumph, as it ought, in arms as in justice . . . Some of Mr. Whitty's friends apprehended an affection of the brain. Others recoiled as from an outlawed social enemy with whom it would be criminal to dis-course forbearingly . . .

"At last 'the world's dread laugh' gave way to laughter at the scoffers . . . The drama played out, the curtain descended. He never drew it up; never took credit either for his extraordinary disinterestedness or extraordinary discernment."

The friends he won in America often urged him to go there; but he never moved far from the editorial chair; and from it he retired most reluctantly when his failing eyesight made it impera-tive. The paper missed him. "He was a journalist of distinguished gifts and a leader-writer rarely excelled." He wrote "like a gentle-man, ere spasmodic slop and grandiloquent drivel passed for fine writing . . . and he especially ignored the dismal acrobatics of comic duncedom."

In fact, he was a tremendous man in public life. As the father of a family, he was intolerable.

He had fourteen sons and daughters, who inherited his obstinacy, his determination and much of his writing ability. The sons scat-tered, probably to escape from home. The two elder daughters,

Anna and Sarah, remained the guardians of their father's old age.
They were emancipated and intelligent women, talented in music
and literature. Anna wrote a novel and many short stories. But to
the rest of the family they were jealous monsters, barring all access
to Michael James. Such, at least, was the view of his youngest son,
Alfred.

Alfred was the only one who stayed at home and worked on the
paper. He married a quiet, unassuming, graceful young woman of
solid Lancashire stock named Ashton—Mary by baptism,
Bonny by universal nickname. They had three children: the
eldest a son, Michael; then a girl, Gertrude alias Gretchen; and
the youngest, born on June 19th, 1865, Mary Louise, if anyone
ever remembered; but no one ever did except income-tax officials
and passport authorities. To the rest of the world she was May.
Alfred was to be heir to "the Paper"; he was to pass it on, in turn,
to his son.

Alfred was a sociable, generous young man—"improvident,"
said his formidable sisters. He was tall and stooping, with curly
hair and a very wide, disarming smile. He was a gregarious fellow,
loving music and the theatre. He lost, cheerfully, quite a lot of
money collaborating with H. J. Byron, the dramatist, on the management of the Court Theatre, Liverpool. He disagreed with his
juggernaut father about practically everything; and however liberal Michael James may have been in public life, he knew where
autocracy began; which was at home.

The three little Whittys were taken on regular visits to the
family home, known as the Big House. It was a punctual and
inescapable duty and they detested it. All of them feared their
grandfather. Michael couldn't admit it, of course, being a boy; and
May scorned to be less brave than he; but Gretchen did, for she
was simple and without guile and later christened herself "the fool
in the middle." May secretly shrank from her turn to be led up to
the tall, gaunt old man, ensconced deep in his wing chair by the
fire; she dreaded, but dared not evade, the moment when he would
fix his fierce, blue, empty eyes just a trifle above her head and pass
his fingers all over her face. More than anything else, she feared
and hated his blindness.

Young Ben and May

Aunt Anna and Aunt Sarah bought suitable toys for them to play with during their visits. The toys were taken from a locked cupboard when they arrived, placed in an upstairs bedroom and locked up again when they left. Once, unobserved, they tried to vary this amusement by borrowing the plaster bust of Garibaldi, which, on a black pedestal, towered over the half-landing. But in trying to lift him down, Michael dropped him; the Father of Italian Freedom lay in pieces on the floor. Appalled, they crept downstairs and distributed him among the footstools under the dining-room table. But at tea, a meal of great formality, Aunt Sarah's foot, questing for a stool, bumped into his left ear. Trembling explanations followed. Michael James turned his sightless eyes toward the culprits. Then he laughed. The criminals almost fainted with relief; but their father looked uneasy, and the aunts remained grim.

Alfred and his father were quarreling incessantly over everything, his clothes, his politics, his friends, his theatre interests. The old man clung to the control of the paper and would not let his son have the authority he needed. Anna and Sarah always seemed to stand in the way of reasonable discussion. Soon afterwards the children were taken to the Big House for a visit they never forgot. As they came downstairs to say goodbye the drawing-room door burst open and their father rushed out. Aunt Anna followed and stood in the doorway; behind her, they could just see Michael James, standing with his back to the fire, his hands clenched on the knob of his stick, his eyes glaring. Alfred turned and cried: "You can't do it! You can't do it! I'll go to law about it!" "You'll regret it if you do," replied Aunt Anna grimly. Alfred looked at her for a moment and then walked out of the house. Mrs. Whitty hurried the children after him. They clambered into the waiting four-wheeler and drove home in silence. Alfred Whitty never entered his father's house again.

Later, the children learned why. The paper was to be sold outright; Edward Russell was to be its editor. There was no mention of Alfred in the transfer. His services would no longer be required. Anna told him that the old man would pay Mrs. Whitty a hundred pounds a year toward the children's upbringing and would continue it as an annuity under his will; but on one condi-

tion: the sale of the paper was not to be contested. Alfred wanted
to fight, but his wife's father refused to let the precarious hundred
a year be endangered; Alfred had to give way. He left his wife and
children in Grandpa Ashton's care and went off to London to earn
his living.

Michael James had been true to the paper; he had chosen a
great editor, the future Lord Russell of Liverpool, but the effect on
Alfred's family was cataclysmic. The children rarely went to the
Big House again, except to have reluctant music lessons with Aunt
Sarah. Soon afterward, Michael James died. Young Michael was
allowed to attend the funeral in a black top hat with a "weeper"
hanging almost to his feet. He felt very sick in the coach and
couldn't understand why May envied him.

Mrs. Whitty and the children settled down in Grandpa Ashton's
house, along with other Ashton relatives. May grew quite fond of
the benevolent old tyrant who occupied the best armchair and was
waited on by all the females of the family. Secretly, however, she
thought the Whittys a far more romantic clan. She was encouraged to discover an Ashton relation named Thomas Holcroft, who
had written a very successful play, *The Road to Ruin*, still in the
repertoire of London theatres.

The best thing about the Ashton house was its huge glassed-in
bookshelves, from which she pulled down everything she could
reach. She had demolished Dumas by the time she was six and
devoured *Household Words* and *All the Year Round*, with the
Dickens novels embedded in them. Once, to her mother's horror,
she was discovered reading Ouida, the most avant-garde novelist of
the day. Grandpa only laughed. "Let her read whatever she likes,"
said he. "It won't hurt her"; and he continued to toss her his own
books, like bones to a voracious puppy.

Sometimes, too, there was music in the evenings. Friends
would come in, and almost all of them sang something or played
something; even Grandpa would "Refuse," in a gruff baritone, "to
Plant in That Bosom a Thorn." Mrs. Whitty had a charming light

soprano voice. Once, she told her children wistfully, she had actually sung in public, in the Great Ballroom at Margate; not under her own name, naturally—Grandpa would never have allowed that —but as "Miss Holcroft," after the *Road to Ruin* relative. Carl Rosa had heard her and been impressed and even offered to train her for his opera company. But of course Grandpa had instantly put a stop to *that*, and the concert-giving had abruptly ceased.

The Ashton relatives were agreeable enough. The chief excitement of the household was provided by Cousin Nellie, who was an entrancing redhead of seventeen, a central attraction for the youth of the neighborhood. There were courtships and quarrels and bouquets and broken hearts, and at every moment of romantic crisis Nellie would go into hysterics. The first time May saw this happen she was fascinated. She rushed to the stairs and called up to Gretchen: "Quick—come quick! Nellie's having hystics!" Then she rushed back to study and remember the phenomenon.

For all his good will, however, Grandpa Ashton could only supply the Whitty family with a home. They were dependent for their food and clothing on the money Alfred sent from London. But he had never been happy and never prospered there. Once he tried his luck in America, but came back, disheartened, to his bachelor lodgings in London, where nobody looked after him and he could not be bothered to look after himself. When he was only thirty-eight and his youngest daughter ten, he caught pneumonia and died. His widow was left with the problem of how to feed, clothe and educate their three children.

An old friend of the family, "Uncle" Joe Nightingale, promised to look after Michael's schooling, and took him away to London. He also proffered the capital to enable Mrs. Whitty to start earning something for herself. She decided to open a little school, the last resort of many "distressed gentlewomen" who had, themselves, only the sketchiest of schooling. Grandpa gave a rather reluctant consent. The family moved to an old house in Newby Terrace, where Mrs. Whitty bought the "goodwill" of a little school which was going out of business; it consisted of one family of three sisters. The house, however, was a big, pleasant place, looking out over fields and gardens; there were gleaming brass bedsteads and a real bath which had a room all to itself.

"Young Ladies," a select few, were to be instructed in English, Calisthenics and Free-hand Drawing, for eight guineas per annum, the Day pupils. Boarders could be fed, housed and instructed too for forty-five guineas. Music, Singing, Dancing and French were extra. The teaching staff consisted of a rather vague female cousin, a visiting French master with the engaging habit of wiping his pen in his hair, and an arithmetic master who arrived all too often in a rather glazed condition, pleading that he had had "an unfortunate experience" on the preceding night. Mrs. Whitty herself taught the music and singing.

Her pupils were never numerous. She had a deplorable tendency to take the children of friends for half price; and despite her gentle blandishments, she never succeeded in obtaining the patronage of the neighboring family, "The Four Misses and Eight Masters Overton," a jackpot for any school. It was not surprising that the establishment never really prospered and eventually dwindled out. But it was the only formal education May and Gretchen ever had. They continued it in their own ways. Gretchen was domesticated and a musician; she became an accompanist much in demand. May pursued her voracious reading.

She had long been accepted as chief storyteller to the community. Sometimes she wrote the stories down; one was even published in a Liverpool weekly, the *Porcupine*. In a subheading the editor stated that the author, "a child of nine years, had written the story hoping that it might in some shape interest and amuse the poor little sufferers at the Children's Infirmary." As in all good stories, the best bit came at the end: not only did the Prince marry the Very Poor Woodcutter's Daughter, but he arranged for his brother to marry her Very Poor Sister too. "They shall not be bothered with poverty any more," said the Prince. "That will be nice," replied the heroine; as well she might.

But the stories May liked best were the ones which she acted out for herself beside the drawing-room fire, with Gretchen supplying sympathetic chords and trills on the piano when required. They

E*

involved a lot of emotion and a frequent dose of "Nellie's hystics" and ended, more often than not, with a dying fall on the hearth rug. Since there was only one character, there were few other solutions.

The first time May was ever taken to the theatre she was so terrified that she screamed loudly till she was carried out. The piece was a pantomime called *The Three Bears*. Further visits to other pantomimes taught her that everything always came right in the end, and terror was replaced by enchantment. The pantomimes of 1870 were opulent affairs, with such diverse side issues as "Grand Maypole Merrymaking," "Grand Pageant of the Statues into Living Legions," "The Demon Chase, Terrific Combat between Flop, Flappity and Mrs. Grumblegriffin" and, to finish up with, "Grand Entry of the Allied Armies from both Hemispheres Commanded by their Royal Leaders." But magic began long before any of that. It began with the green-baize curtain blanking the proscenium arch; with the squawky, purposeful dissonance of the orchestra tuning up; with the heavy curtain roller beginning to move—turning—going up, up out of sight, and the beautiful painted drop behind it, with its bright-blue lake and bosky trees and fat clouds and fat cupids and fairylike figures in gauzy skirts, wafting you through into the never-never land. After that, May believed everything, implicitly. "Mother! I can see fairies!" she cried out, once, going home. "Can she, mother?" inquired Gretchen, honestly wanting to know.

Uncle Joe Nightingale knew all the bigwigs of the London stage, such as Marie Litton and Lionel Brough and Mrs. Kendal and even old Ben Webster. Through Uncle Joe's influence the manager of the Prince of Wales Theatre was persuaded to allow May to stand in the wings at one performance and watch the harlequinade with which all good pantomimes concluded. This was a new kind of magic. May was awed by the sight of the men on the light platform tending their hissing "limes," the enchanted woodland stacked up against the wall in a pile of two-dimensional painted canvas and the ethereal Columbine in her floating tulle skirt sneezing as she waited for her entrance and clutching to her throat a piece of red flannel. It did not damage the previous illusion; it simply lent it depth.

At the very end a white sheet was lowered in front of Harlequin and Pantaloon, and a huge lamp set on the floor behind it to create the shadow show which brought down the curtain. Suddenly the clown dashed up to May, red nose and all, and seized her hand. "Want to come on?" he said; and before she knew what he meant he had rushed her onto the stage with him and jumped with her clear over the lamp. A thousand people, she reflected breathlessly, had seen her leaping shadow. She had been on the stage.

The theatre visits were rare as the girls grew older, unless Uncle Joe were around to get them free seats, but they were none the less treasured. Uncle Joe had lodgings with their mother's sister, Lally, in London. Sometimes, when they went to stay with her on a visit they would catch glimpses of his friends, the giants of the theatre world. It was natural, therefore, that May should turn to him when, at sixteen years old, she reached her great decision. She was going On the Stage. She and Gretchen were growing up; the family finances were more strained than ever; somebody would have to do something; and this, she announced, was the obvious thing to do.

Fortunately for her, Mr. and Mrs. Kendal were at this moment playing their annual autumn engagement in Liverpool. Uncle Joe offered a letter of introduction. The Kendals were so eminent, and such pillars of respectability, that Grandpa Ashton could hardly forbid May to use it. In due course she presented herself to Mrs. Kendal at her hotel.

Mrs. Kendal inspected her with peering, gimlet eyes. "You're very small," she said. "I shall grow," May answered. "Can you dance?" "No." "Never mind. Say you can. Sing?" "Er . . . a little." "Say you can, say you can." She wrote a note to Captain Bainbridge, then running a season of light opera at the Court Theatre; delivered a speech on the mission of the stage to reform the world; nodded briskly to cut short the stammered thanks; and dismissed the applicant.

Young Ben and May

Accompanied by her mother, May waited upon Captain Bainbridge. He read the letter without really bothering to look at the bearer. "All right," he said, "you can start tonight. In *The Mountain Sylph*." "Tonight?" gasped May. "Wh-what as?" "A sylph, of course. Just follow the others and do what they do. Be at the theatre half an hour before the show. They'll give you some clothes in the wardrobe." May and her mother, both quite dazed, sought out a theatrical make-up shop and bought such grease paint as the man behind the counter assured them would be necessary. May had no idea how to put it on.

At seven o'clock Mrs. Whitty took her daughter to the stage door and there left her, to rejoin Grandpa Ashton, who, rumbling a little, had consented to this wild procedure as a one-night experiment. He had even decided to come and watch, exuding the certainty that No Good Would Come of It. May, alone and trembling, couldn't find anyone who had time to bother with her. The wardrobe mistress flung her a graying ballet dress and told her to put it on. She discovered that Captain Bainbridge had put Mrs. Kendal's protégée in a dressing room with one of the principals, who was openly enraged that a new chorus girl had been foisted on her. May was every bit as dismayed; she wanted no favors. She took her make-up box and the ballet skirt and climbed up to the chorus room at the top of the theatre. As she pinned the voluminous folds of tired tulle about her, bitterly regretting her inability to fill them out as the previous wearer had apparently done, the other girls tried to explain what was required of her, but it was too complicated. The stage manager was far too busy to answer her questions. "Just do what the others do," he said.

The first act seemed to take place outside some sort of peasant's hut; the chorus were Mountain Sylphs in support of the Prima Donna Sylph, who was engaged in luring the Young Peasant away to her haunts in the Fairy Forest. To appropriate music, the line of ballet-skirted figures tripped onto the stage, gesticulating and pirouetting in concert—or almost in concert. For at the end of the line came a distinctly smaller sylph with agonized eyes fixed on her next-door neighbor, faithfully performing these motions about half

a beat behind the others and perceptibly in trouble when the
movement of a turn forced her to lose sight of them for a moment.
What happened after that was never very clear to May; but she
was a huge success with Grandpa Ashton, who lay back in his seat
and shook the theatre with his laughter. "If that's what she wants
to do," he gasped, "let her do it!"

The Mountain Sylph, which May recognized many years later
in ballet form as *Les Sylphides*, gave place to *Faust and Marguerite*, in which May functioned as a Merry Peasant and a Spirit from
Hell. Then preparations for the pantomime began. Bainbridge
offered her a voice test; she assiduously studied "Scenes That Are
Brightest" and passed it. But at this point Uncle Joe intervened.
His friend Marie Litton had said that the pantomime was neither
suitable nor necessary as a road to dramatic excellence. The pantomime was vetoed and May's heart was broken. To be forced into
retirement at sixteen!

The seclusion was not for long. Uncle Joe Nightingale was
taken seriously ill. Mrs. Whitty and her daughters rushed to
London, to Aunt Lally's house; but they were only just in time to
see him alive. Almost at once they were peremptorily summoned
back to Liverpool. Within a few days Grandpa Ashton, too, was
dead. The little cluster of women was left entirely without male
protection. Mrs. Whitty and Aunt Lally decided to pool their
resources and take a house in London where they would try to let
lodgings. Michael, who was working as a shipping clerk, must be
left behind in Liverpool. Gretchen would help with the house. But
it was undeniably imperative that someone else should do some
breadwinning. "I shall return," said May, "to the stage."

In the year of old Ben Webster's death, 1882, she prepared to
storm the fortress of the London theatre. It had changed a great
deal during the last decade of his life and was set, now, in the mold
which was to frame it for the next ten or fifteen years. The glory of
Covent Garden and Drury Lane had vanished; one had become an

opera house, the other housed only pantomime and melodrama. The reigning monarchs were the Bancrofts at the Haymarket, the Kendals at the St. James's, followed by Wyndham at the Criterion. Irving, at the Lyceum, had put on the mantle of Shakespeare in all its glory. At the Princess's, Wilson Barrett was playing melodramas which May came to know very well, *The Lights o' London* and *Hoodman Blind*. The Gilbert and Sullivan operas had just become the "Savoy" operas; the Gaiety was in its witty, dashing, "naughty" prime. All in all, London was a splendid, if rather frightening, theatre town.

Of course, little May Whitty from Liverpool could not aspire to heights like these. But she got an introduction to Alexander Henderson, once a Liverpool manager himself, now running a season of light opera at the Comedy Theatre. Once again she was given a job in the chorus; the operetta was *La Mascotte*. She made her first appearance on the London stage, unrehearsed as before, on April 11th, 1882. She was a Merry Peasant in Act I —she felt quite familiar with this role—and a Lady of the Court in the ball scene. Among the principals was Uncle Joe's friend Lionel Brough. As he waltzed past the new little Court Lady, sitting on a sofa and "watching" as if her life depended on it, he murmured gently: "Keep your feet together." She did so, then and thereafter.

Boccaccio followed *La Mascotte*, and *Rip Van Winkle*, hugely successful, came after that. The chorus was, among other things, a crew of ghostly spirits who came up trap doors in the stage floor. Usually they participated in the story with concerted comment, gesture or advice; or else they appeared in scenes of general merry-making or woe in which the local populace was supposed to share. No more than a minimal competence in song or dance was required of them. Little Whitty, however, soon became a "character" among them. She didn't sing very well, but she was always the first to learn a new routine or a piece of business, and was quite often given a solo line, such as: "Come, girls, let's away!" She was a good listener off the stage as well as on, and many confidences were poured out to her. She and her mother would discuss them earnestly as they rode home on top of the horsebus. Mrs. Whitty thought Grandpa would have been greatly reassured could he have seen how respectable and hardworking the girls really were.

As soon as the soft glow of the gas footlights dimmed, they would hurry up to the big dressing room at the top of the theatre where a bevy of mamas awaited them. The clothes would be carefully hung up, under the watchful eye of the chorus mistress, and the make-up assiduously cleaned off; no one would be allowed out on the streets with a trace of rouge on her lips. The girls, heavily chaperoned, would go directly home to unimpeachable domesticity. There were, of course, occasional exceptions. May and her mother were once invited to the home of a girl who was not married to the father of her child. May hoped there would be at least a whiff of sinful glamor about this; but it turned out as dull and suburban as could be imagined. The stars of the line-up were the tall, handsome beauties, the "show-girls," set apart from their humdrum companions, well dressed and well paid. They brought Gilded Youth to the front rows, and caused the stage door to be besieged after a performance by Mashers and Stage Door Johnnies. Several of May's contemporaries graduated to the peerage through a preliminary lane of chaperones, bouquets and diamonds.

Such triumphs were not for hardworking Little Whitty; indeed, she scorned them. Once she was lured into the Green Room by an Important Person in the theatre, through whom possible advancement lay. But when she realized that his attentions were neither pure nor professional, she repulsed him with fury. He cried at her, "You're nothing but a cad! A female cad! And I have no use for female cads!" May was secretly oppressed by a fear that the accusation might be true.

The lodging house in Seymour Street was not proving a great success. The Whitty ladies were terrified of the gentlemen guests and most reluctant to demand the rent. Gretchen began to feel that she could no longer be kept by her family. She persuaded herself into an engagement with a man twenty years older than herself, "something in the city," red-faced, aggressive. May hated him. She tried as hard as she could to prevent the marriage. The night before the wedding Gretchen became panic-stricken and very nearly yielded. But there was the trousseau—the wedding breakfast—the presents—so much money spent out of the household's scrimped savings . . . The marriage took place. May never forgot Gretchen's face as she and her bridegroom drove away for their honeymoon.

What followed was not uncommon in the days when mothers told their daughters nothing and men were often brutal and demanded everything. "I will never forgive you," Gretchen wrote to her mother a few days later. She was in fact physically harmed for life. The bridegroom brought her syphilis as a wedding present. She, who was so full of loving-kindness, was never able to bear children. May was so deeply shocked that it was many years before she overcame her revulsion to anything that came within the area of sex, even when it was called "love."

After a year and a half at the Comedy, she began to be restless. She was earning a living, but it hardly squared with her ambitions. She wanted to act, not jig up and down with twenty other girls and laugh merrily on cue. She decided to try and get a "real" job; she applied for an audition with the Hare and Kendal management at the St. James's; rather surprisingly, she was given an appointment.

This was starting at the top, indeed. The St. James's led the way in the new styles of acting, playwrighting and directing. Much of the revolution which had given birth to them had been due to Mrs. Kendal's brother, the playwright and director Tom Robertson. W. S. Gilbert, who was once a stage manager for him, has described what his new "method" meant: "Formerly, in a conversation scene, you simply brought down two or three chairs from the flat and placed them in a row in the middle of the stage and then people sat down and talked and when the conversation was ended the chairs were replaced. Robertson showed how to give life and variety and nature to the scene by breaking it up with all sorts of little incidents and delicate by-play." Robertson fought stereotype and exaggeration. "No tears, no tragedy, no pocket-handkerchief," he would exhort. Before he died, still a young man, he had founded the school of English comedic acting which lasted till the Nineteen-thirties and perhaps is not quite dead yet.

John Hare had learned his business with the Bancrofts, who first produced the Robertson plays. He was a volatile character actor, swift and authoritative, who, as a young man, had always played old ones. He directed most of the St. James's productions. Kendal was the rather dull, solid-worth type of leading man; Mrs. Kendal was then accounted one of London's finest actresses, sound in tragedy, adept in comedy, highly experienced, fluent and versatile. As a management they had a distinguished record; and they had just acquired the services of a new young playwright, Arthur Pinero.

The group which confronted May on the stage of the St. James's when she went for her audition was going to become almost as distinguished. There was Dion Boucicault, son of Boucicault the Great and himself an aspiring director; the "juvenile," George Alexander, and his understudy Herbert Waring. There was also a gentle young man named Brandon, who asked her whether she knew what the scene she was going to read was about. "If not, I'll try and explain, if you like . . ." said the future author of *Charley's Aunt*. She read the scene and got the job; it was to understudy the ingenue and play a maid in the afterpiece, *A Scrap of Paper*. The actress whom she was to cover was making her professional debut and there was quite a fuss about it. May thought enviously that this inexperienced newcomer would never have got the job except on the strength of her inherited family name, which was Webster.

She found herself sharing a dressing room with Miss Webster, who took no trouble to conceal her dislike of the arrangement. She teased May about her accent—May decided to profit from this— about her reading (Swinburne and Meredith and Browning), about her provincial ways. Gradually, however, May became aware that the dislike had turned to patronage, almost to benevolence.

Booey—she had been promoted to the use of the nickname— would sometimes take her to one of the rare matinees which other theatres gave on special occasions. They saw Irving's Hamlet together and agreed that it was extraordinary. May thought privately that the most moving thing in the production was Ellen Terry's Ophelia, but she didn't dare say so. They went to see Salvini's Othello, also at the Lyceum. May was overwhelmed by it, swept away by the actor's tragic power. When it was over, she blundered out onto the steps of the theatre, blinking in the daylight and still mopping up her tears. Dimly she became aware that a golden-haired young man with blue eyes was standing smiling at her and that Booey was shaking her arm and saying, "This is my brother, Ben."

CHAPTER EIGHT

———— ᕷᕷ ————

Young Ambition's Ladder

Little Whitty was not having a very easy time at the St. James's. When she first met Mrs. Kendal in the theatre she proffered a timid "How do you do?" Ma K, as she was called, glared at her and said, "So you got here at last, did you?" She was not spoken to again. She was perfectly prepared to accept this. Above all things she was eager to study and learn. She would crouch behind fireplaces and peer through cracks to watch the star. Bit by bit, like learning a language by mastering the dictionary, she came to appreciate what she saw: the smooth, flawless, technical accomplishment, the experienced ease. But she was never tempted to laugh, only to smile; not to cry, only to admire.

John Hare was similarly expert; livelier, perhaps. "The Meissonier among theatre artists," Ellen Terry called him. As a director he was less a stickler for truth than his master, Tom Robertson, had been, but meticulous as to stage business, timing, detail. He was impatient of slowness or stupidity. If he lost his temper he expressed it vigorously but without malice by throwing his top hat on the floor. Once, when a group of actors had to make a general entrance, he cried furiously from the auditorium, "There's a man that isn't there!" and smashed his hat to pieces on the orchestra rail. He then looked at it in surprise, threw it into the pit, and went on rehearsing.

Like many other London theatres of its time, the St. James's did not stick to the same bill for very long. There were revivals of old successes interchanged with new plays. A grand production of *As You Like It* was announced, quite a daring departure for a management generally devoted to "modern" plays. Booey was to play Phoebe. May understudied her and was a Court Lady and a Wedding Guest. "Practically a Merry Peasant," she thought bitterly. At rehearsal she was bold enough to find Rosalind a trifle corseted and Orlando made of wood. Hare did not feel at all in his element as Touchstone. "How like you this life, Master Touchstone?" asked Corin one morning. He answered, "I don't like it at all and I won't rehearse," and he flung down the hat and walked out. But of course he walked back again after lunch.

At the first dress rehearsal the assembled Court found a beautiful canopied pavilion where Duke Frederick and his entourage were to watch the wrestling. In it, to May's surprise, was a dazzlingly dressed young man, much bowed to by everybody. "Who," she asked, "is that?" "The Duke's son and heir, of course," was the reply. "But," said the little understudy, rather too loudly, "Celia says, 'Thou knowest my father hath no child but I.' " A silence fell. Mrs. Kendal turned and looked at her. Managerial discussion ensued. But it was decided not to waste such a beautiful costume, and the line was cut instead.

For nearly two years May stayed at the St. James's, understudying and playing little bits. At home, life was precarious and her salary essential. The lodging house had been given up; brother Michael came to London; he contributed to the household budget but needed a lot of waiting on. Gretchen tried to leave her dreadful husband and come home; but there was no legal way by which she could do it. He appeared on the doorstep accompanied by a policeman and demanded "his conjugal rights." She was forced to go back with him.

May saw an increasing amount of the Webster family. She was given the freedom of Granny's Wednesday evenings at St.

Young Ambition's Ladder

Martin's Lane. She was graciously allowed to play with Booey in some pastoral scenes organized and directed by an outdoor-Shakespeare fanatic named Ben Greet—his first attempt in what became a lifelong career. Once, indoors, she played Lucetta to Booey's Julia in *The Two Gentlemen of Verona*. She was determined this time to prove to the lofty Websters that she really could act. But a bad notice in the *Era* shattered these hopes and induced thoughts of suicide. There were moments, quite a few, when the "outer darkness" look came into Booey's eye; but Ben would turn his back firmly on Booey and invite May to supper next Sunday.

He had been admitted as a member of the Inner Temple and was studying for his law finals; but he found time to sing at concerts and was increasingly in demand by the Irving Amateur Dramatic Club. He made a great success as Biron in *Love's Labour's Lost*. In June 1885 the Webster household was *en fête* to celebrate the double event of his passing the law examinations and attaining his twenty-first birthday. Two weeks later the Whittys, rather more modestly, saluted May's twentieth. Ben gave her twelve pairs of shoulder-length suède gloves in pastel shades, which he couldn't possibly afford, and sang at the party. Mrs. Whitty was charmed. Booey and Lizzie were not. The atmosphere was strained. He afterwards recorded: "There was unwarrantable interference on the part of my sisters."

He was called to the Bar; but there was a gap of some months before the Michaelmas term began. John Hare invited him to join the St. James's company on its annual autumn safari into the provinces, to play Le Beau and a small part in *A Scrap of Paper*. Since a barrister was not permitted to follow any other profession under his own name, Ben made his debut as Mr. B. Nottingham.

Lizzie decided to come too; and May was invited, presumably at Ben's insistence, to share the Webster lodgings. None of them had been on tour before, and in spite of the undercurrents they couldn't help enjoying themselves. They learned the routines of arrival. The landlady, "Ma," would view them with an appraising eye; she would either clasp them to her ample bosom, call them "ducky," and put some more coal on the fire, or she would repel them with a flat glare, jerk her head toward the door on the left

129

and say "In 'ere." They grew to evaluate these portents. At the end of the week they would sign the guest book, finding a good deal of agreement among those who had come before. It would be: "Stay but a little I will come again . . ."; or "Quoth the Raven . . ."; or, in the more plant-infested living rooms, "Per ardua ad aspidistra."

Once they had a week-long feud with a landlady whose sitting room was so thickly encrusted with plants and ornaments and knickknacks that it was impossible to move. Each morning before they went out they would pack everything away in a cupboard; and each afternoon when they returned the ornaments would be back, every one in its allotted niche. Not a word was ever said on either side.

They learned the meals so that they could have prompted them: cold meat and salad on arrival on Sunday; weekdays, dinner at three p.m., hot on Monday, cold on Tuesday, hashed on Wednesday; fish-and-chips on Friday; Thursday more flexible, usually something to do with sausages; Saturday, finish up the bits or a lamb chop. They learned to feel the beds cautiously. "Be sure they are dry," wrote Ben to May a few tours later, "put a mirror between the sheets and wear flannel."

But even the discomforts were new and funny and adventurous. They were seeing "the world." They learned about the drizzly, empty Manchester streets on a Sunday night when you got off the train; and the roaring pub life of Glasgow on a Saturday. They fell in love with Edinburgh, Holyrood Palace and Princes Street. In Liverpool May rediscovered the Aunts and found them, now that she was free, capable and entertaining women. She was hardly frightened at all, not even when she dropped a crumb on the carpet and Aunt Sarah, without a word, fetched a dustpan and brush and silently removed the offending object.

The Webster sisters were great excursionists, and they made expeditions up the Pentland Hills or down the River Clyde or, from Birmingham, to Stratford-on-Avon, where the Memorial Theatre had only recently been built and there were still few visitors. In short, they did all the things that British touring actors went on doing for the next sixty or seventy years, till touring became almost a vanished occupation. In spite of Booey's fits of the

sulks, May's touchiness and Lizzie's tactlessness, which was phenomenal, they thought of it, later, as a happy time. Back in London, Mr. B. Nottingham vanished; Ben put on his white barrister's
wig, in which he looked all of fourteen, and "went into Chambers"
with Montague Williams, one of the great defense counsels of the
day. Booey pursued her career, which, as one critic put it, "afforded
her plenty of practice and praise"; and May came to a decision.

She had had enough of being patronized and snubbed by the
Webster sisters, with their airs and their ancestry and their Royal
Theatre ways; Ben was sweet and she knew he wanted to marry
her; but she hadn't the least intention of getting engaged or having
anything to do with men, ever. She was tired of creeping about the
St. James's being glared at by Ma K. She wanted experience. She
had read that Squire Bancroft had played three hundred and forty
different parts during a three-year apprenticeship with stock companies, and Irving, so it was said, nearly a thousand before he made
his first London success. She wanted to learn and she wanted to be
somebody in her own right. Surreptitiously, she began to look for
another job.

When it came, she was amazed at her own temerity in taking
it. A small-time stock manager named William Neebe was getting
together a company to play two weeks in the London suburb of
Edmonton, followed by a short tour of "the smalls" not far away.
The repertoire consisted of the Sheridan-Boucicault axis with a
farce or two thrown in. They would do twelve plays in the first two
weeks and May would play the lead in eleven of them: Lady
Teazle, Lydia Languish, Kate Hardcastle, the heroines of *London
Assurance* and *The Shaughraun*, not to mention *East Lynne*. She
would be paid £2 a week. Since almost all the company were
veterans of this kind of thing, there would be no preliminary
rehearsals. Each play would be rehearsed once and played that
night. May took a deep breath and said she would do it.

First, she went to Mrs. Kendal and asked to be released. Ma K,
unexpectedly gracious, said she would talk to "the gentlemen," and

they agreed. Then came the matter of clothes. Every actor had to provide his own, whether modern or period. Each of them would acquire a "theatre basket," a large wicker affair lined with canvas and fastened with rod and padlock, in which they accumulated the costume tools of their trade. "Lines of business" still subsisted in the small stock companies, not very different from what they had been in Old Ben's day, and the characters tended to wear a kind of uniform.

Lionel Brough, as a younger man, described the mandatory outfit for a low comedian: "*very* large plaid trousers, spats or gaiters, a scarlet vest of plush, ferocious tie, short cut-away coat of any hue, always provided it was not human! And a white hat with a black band. The wig was ALWAYS red." Young actors with tragic leanings saved up for a sword, like Irving and Old Ben before them; but it was no longer the essential weapon it had once been. The "heroines" accumulated bits of lace, fans, feathers, petticoats, two or three "basic" dresses convertible to almost any period, jelly-like pieces of colored-glass "jewelry" sewn onto gold braid, and a wig of white cotton wool for the Sheridan or Goldsmith parts.

May had to accumulate this wardrobe from scratch, and could never have done it but for the devotion of her mother, who was ready to accompany her to Edmonton and sew day and night. Gretchen got occasional leave from her monster to come and help. A member of the St. James's company volunteered the loan of a riding habit for Lady Gay Spanker and Claire Ffolliot. Booey and Lizzie contributed hand props and advice. Edmonton gleamed like Eldorado. Independence Day had dawned.

But it was not entirely golden.

"My dear Ben," wrote May on January 29th, 1886,

I am stealing a few moments from my study of "May Edwards" in *The Ticket-of-Leave Man* to thank you for your most satirical of epistles if I may judge by the congratulations contained therein . . . and to tell you how delighted we shall be to see you on Sat. afternoon—please try to be here by half-past three—at the latest—as we take a frugal meal at that time. As regards your staying for the performance . . . my vanity is such that I'd rather you didn't see me in that part as I haven't time to think what to do with it and I can't touch it, I shall be too vile for words! I am glad Gertie happened to see my one little success out of a list of failures but certainly she deserved it after having witnessed the murder of Miss Hard-castle, and she will be again cast down if she sees Lady Teazle tonight. I can't describe to you how frightened I am of it—if I'd only seen the play!! Please excuse this shaky writing but my hand is trembling so I can hardly hold the pen . . . I had a funny adventure last night, I didn't give my fool of a young man the right cue (not Elmore but a much greater idiot). I couldn't think of it, so whispered to him to go on, but he was so overwhelmed that he walked right off the stage—it was a front scene and we were alone—I gathered my scattered senses and made a few remarks, being in the greatest passion I was ever in in my life . . .

Gertie is quite right, we are *starved* with cold, my nose has assumed a scarlet appearance that I fear will never leave it more—

Good-bye, pity your unfortunate, miserable friend,

May

Not because of my red nose but Lady Teazle and Claire.

Her letters continued daily, chronicles of desperation; one cannot imagine how she found time to write them. The following Wednesday the end is at least in sight:

". . . I am feeling horribly seedy today . . . I've been rehearsing 2 parts for tonight. I don't know either of them and feel too ill and tired to learn. I have still Lady Gay and Lady Isabel [in *East Lynne*] to study for Friday and Saturday night. Mon. night went off pretty well—I almost knew my part and so tried to act a little and made passionate love to Elmore, who didn't know his and in consequence didn't return it."

On her one night off, someone was ill and she had to deputize for them; she was told the plot of the scene and improvised the lines as they came along.

The season was vastly appreciated. The local critic reported: "We ourselves almost forgot we were in Edmonton, so cleverly was all arranged." May Whitty came in for a variety of commendations, culminating in "her rendition of the character [of Lydia Languish] was perfect, and she won a perfect furore of applause." These were certainly the first good press notices she ever received and I suppose that none were ever more precious to her.

From Edmonton the company went on to another London suburb and thence to Banbury, where they encountered deep snow and terrible business. May studied the leads in three new plays, including *The Octoroon*, in which she did a back fall off a table— quite a usual practice for Boucicault's heroines; but no one showed her the trick of it; she just had to find out by hurting herself how not to hurt herself. She reported to Ben that she was "in the last stages of hump . . . Don't be surprised if I turn up in town next week. I am getting desperate and cannot go on assisting at the murders of these pieces much longer. I have come to the conclusion that I would rather make a dash at new parts than go on getting into worse faults with old ones . . . It is bitterly cold . . . If only some kind friend would leave me ten thousand a year!" Ben got very worried and sent her ten shillings.

The following week the company tottered on to Hungerford. "An awful week is before me, with a quite new version of *East Lynne* . . . and we are totally destitute of ladies so I have several farces to study and I am simply in despair and worried to death. I do nothing but try to get away, and then Mr. Neebe and the gentlemen look at me reproachfully and tell me I should smash up the whole affair and ruin them all." Business was terrible and they heard that Neebe hadn't enough money to pay their fare to the next town. Gleefully, May went off to her "dreary lodgings" to pack; but there was a last-minute reprieve. A few days later, however, the end came. The final week's salary was not forthcoming, so the company pooled the resources of its theatre baskets, the paste buckles and the worn velvet waistcoats, and pawned its way back to London. Nevertheless, May cherished in her heart a tiny gleam of glory.

She started the rounds of the agents. Blackmore's was the most powerful. His outer office was always crowded with actors sitting on hard chairs under the dirty, uncurtained windows, or leaning against the wooden rail behind which a secretary sat at bay. Some were silent and wistful and waited patiently for hours on end; some were belligerent and aggressive. Mr. Blackmore himself rarely appeared, except at lunchtime, when the door of the inner sanctum would swing open and he would push his way through the besieging group. "Can't see you today—can't see anybody today!" he would exclaim, waving a pudgy hand with a gold ring on the little finger. "Come back later—nothing doing today—yes, yes—next week perhaps—very busy today . . ." and he would vanish importantly down the dark stairs.

Neebe reappeared, with an offer to play a week in Bath. He would do *The School for Scandal*, especially for May. She wired an acceptance; and the very same day Blackmore got her the offer of a small part in a tour of *The Candidate* with Charles Wyndham, star and manager of the Criterion Theatre. She was torn between her desire to accept it and her loyalty to Neebe, fortified by her love of Lady Teazle. Mrs. Whitty reminded her of the Hungerford episode; and Michael took matters into his own hands and wrote two telegrams, one accepting Wyndham's offer and the other explaining matters to Neebe. Neebe behaved magnificently. He wired back: "Have spent two pounds on printing but no matter."

Afterwards May was grateful for her family's firmness. Although the Wyndham tour was short, she learned some valuable lessons: clarity, precision, pace; which does not consist in gabbling, but in shortening pauses and picking up cues. Wyndham played comedy with mathematical exactness, but his smooth, light dexterity made what he said seem no more than the natural and spontaneous expression of his thought. He did not teach much by direct instruction; you watched and tried it out and became a little better at it. People thought of Wyndham as an easygoing light comedian. They seldom remembered that, in addition to his Criterion successes, he had produced over three hundred plays for special matinees at the Crystal Palace, including some Greek tragedy. Moreover, said May, "I like him so much—he is so kind and not a bit like a manager."

This was the first time she had been allowed to travel unaccompanied by her mother or Aunt Lally. She shared digs with another member of the company. "I loathe housekeeping," she wrote, "perhaps because I know nothing about it." Still, she felt very grown-up, with her fashionable hair style and her nineteen-inch waist and her sophisticated ball dress for the second act. It was a shock to be told that she looked fifteen. But there is no pleasing actors and never will be. She began to look back wistfully to those few brief weeks as a leading lady. "I shall soon become 'umble once more," she wrote to Ben, and added, needing contradiction: "You know your family don't believe in me and I'm never sure you don't agree with them." For this she later apologized, as well she might. Still, "I look back with pity on the poor little dismal understudy at the St. James's. It is such a comfort to play some kind of part, however small, one feels so much more important."

She spent the next two years on tour, much of the time as Dora, heroine of *The Harbour Lights*, a melodrama which ran for over five hundred performances with William Terriss and Jessie Millward at the Adelphi. All London successes now had touring duplicates and an actor could make himself a solid and permanent livelihood without ever appearing in the West End. Popular actor-managers, both in England and America, would spend three quarters of their time on the road. There was much to be said for the system. It brought the theatre to everyone all over the country and it kept actors flexible enough to meet and cope with different audiences in different theatres. Or, in theory, it should have done. In practice, touring companies were apt to become ingrowing, squabbling, shop-talking closed communities leading a very dull life.

So, at least, May began to think. Her heroines of melodrama were not a source of inexhaustible delight. "Dora is such an active young woman," she wrote wearily, "always on the trot . . . it's no use, I hate melodrama—with a painfully virtuous hero and a painfully wicked villain—the hero is so stupid I think . . . and then Dora is painfully good and it's such a long and tiring piece, five long—and to me dreary acts. I feel as if I'd been all my life on this tour."

The old stock companies had been driven from the field by the touring industry (they were eventually to come back again and claim their revenge); but there were still occasional stock seasons, especially at Christmas, of which May was able to take advantage. Then there would be the usual frantic changes of bill and lack of rehearsal and fears and frenzies and fresh costumes—"five gowns for the five acts including a ball-dress," she groaned. And still more melodrama. "My next part is very thankless . . . principally to weep or perhaps vary the monotony with a little screaming. I am knocked down by the villain twice and my elbows are fearfully bruised already from last week."

Back on tour again, she was constantly ill with colds, head-aches, neuralgia, ulcerated throats. There was also a persistent internal pain which she thought was a legacy from the *Octoroon* back falls. Ben got very worried about her. He suggested she might like to try coming back to the St. James's but the Whitty spine stiffened at this. "I don't scorn your suggestion, but in the first place I don't believe in the practice one gets and I feel I would rather go on working in the provinces and gaining my experience with playing good parts before attempting a town engagement, and in the second, I don't care to risk the humiliation of a certain refusal from my former manageress. They don't believe in me and Mrs. K would be delighted to snub me." Sometimes she despaired utterly and was convinced there was a curse following her. "There are no hopes for me in the histrionic line—your family are right." She almost gave up; "but then I thought of my debts and shuddered and of all my hopes and yearnings . . ." She was just twenty-one.

Poor Ben must have known only too well that this belligerent inferiority was largely the result of contrasting herself with the "easy-way Websters." "I'm sorry that Boo's part [in the new St. James's play] is so bad. But she can't always have Paulines and Phyllises and must have a little of the rough with the extreme smooth of her theatrical existence. Please don't think I'm envious

Young Ben and May

. . . I think it's done me good to have roughed it, it rubs the edges off. My present tour is a liberal education of the unpleasant side."

She did try to lighten the touring routine, or even to galvanize it into some sort of activity. "Let's rehearse some scenes from Shakespeare," she would say to the company; and there would be a brief flare of enthusiasm, which would trickle away into lethargy from all those who were not playing the best parts. They would relapse into their old habits of sleeping late in the mornings, eating a huge meal at three in the afternoon and (the men) taking their exercise in the billiard saloons. There were, as yet, few golf courses and none for women; lawn tennis had only recently been, quite literally, invented. If you wanted exercise, you took a tram to its terminus and walked; more often May stayed at home and read. In the grimy mill towns of northern England during the winter, it was not a surprising choice.

She grew to hate the sight of her theatre basket, waiting inexorably to be packed every Saturday night and unpacked every Monday. The Sunday train-calls offered at least a slight diversion. Trains carrying touring companies would crisscross at Derby Junction with a great chuffing and shunting of their special coaches; the actors would get out and dash along the platform to snatch a cup of tea from the buffet and greet each other in transit. Once a member of the company completely mislaid her own carriage. "Where's the *Harbour Lights?*" she frantically demanded of a porter. "Couldn't say, miss. Where's it going?" he answered. She looked utterly taken aback. "I don't know! Last week we were in Leicester!" But the Sunday-evening arrival, which had once been full of excitement and promise, now became drearily repetitive. The same empty station yard, the same rain, the same dreary little street with its identical houses; the same overcooked cold meat, undercooked cold potatoes, beetroot bled white and cheese which would be rejected by even a novice mouse. The same smell of "onion" gas; the same smoke without fire in the living-room grate; the same lumpy bed. You tried to get the rooms with good beds, but it couldn't always be managed. I find a penciled postcard to "Mrs. M. Whitty" from a landlady in Scarborough: "Dear

138

Madam i resived your post card and i have seven fether beds but i have them all full so i carnt do with you i sorry."

Her loneliness was increased by a pathological dislike of nearly all the men in the companies. Her mother had stressed the perils surrounding a young actress touring alone; the woods seemed full of dragons. The new "villain" in the *Harbour Lights* is "a soulless brute." The rest are generally "cads." But (characteristically): "The new 'Dave' is so difficult to act with, but off the stage he is very nice and most gentlemanly . . . I am at present pondering whether I'd rather have a horrid man with whom I can act or a nice one with whom I can't. I think the former, as off stage it doesn't matter." No wonder they called her "our prude" and told her she had no heart at all, only a lump of ice. It took patient Ben seven years to melt it.

She had woven for herself a cocoon of misery and ill health, and he was quite evidently her life line. Although there is to be no talk of love or anything like that, a perceptible astringency creeps into her letters when he confesses to being "mashed on Marie Tempest in *Dorothy*" (as who was not?), or to seeing little Possy Something several times at Granny's parties. His own letters are filled with a loving selflessness astonishing in a boy of twenty-three, the spoiled darling of his family—except that he completely lacked the capacity to be spoiled. His career at the bar was not flourishing. In his wig and gown he looked like a schoolboy Sir Galahad, but it didn't bring in the briefs. Once the judge called upon him to defend a burly Bill Sikes ruffian accused—rightly, Ben thought—of robbery with violence. He did his eloquent best. When he sat down the prisoner demanded of his warden: " 'Oo the 'ell's this bloody kid talkin' abaht, me?"

His performances for the Irving Amateur Dramatic Club were more successful. The *Era* applauded his Prince Hal as "the incarnation of bright manhood." He veered toward the stage again. John Hare offered him a part in *The Hobby-Horse*. He hesitated. Granny and Aunt Harriette were against it; so, oddly enough, was May. She agreed with them about a barrister's superior social position and endorsed their view that "the stage is such a nasty profession for a man." She predicted that he would have a hard time "unless you are as exceptionally lucky as Boo has been." More revealingly, she feared that the stage would engross him and she would lose him. But she understood that he needed to earn money; and when his senior at the bar, Montague Williams, decided to retire, she realized the battle was all but lost. Hare and Kendal held out the bait of yet another part, and that clinched it. She wrote: "I wish you success with all my heart—why, we shall have another Benjamin Webster before we know it!"

He made his official debut at the St. James's on March 3rd, 1887, as Lord Woodstock in *Clancarty*. It was not incandescent. He had had only one really good scene, and it was cut at the dress rehearsal to facilitate a scene change. "What a wicked shame!" wrote May. "Will it ever be put in, I mean if the scenery is arranged?" (She still had much to learn.) The *Chronicle*, which had urged him to go on the stage, promptly gave him a bad notice. "The Chronicle," wrote May, "is a fool."

Nevertheless, his career proceeded easily and he fell easily into its ways. When the Hare-and-Kendal autumn tour came round May offered him veteran advice about digs, and once, in Brighton, left him her own rooms plus a legacy of cheese and cold veal pie. He didn't have to do much touring at first, though plenty of it was to come later on. After a couple of London engagements, he received one morning the following letter, written in a thin, sloping hand:

Queen's Hotel

Manchester.

11 Oct. 1888

Dear Mr. Webster,

If you are free in December I would be very glad to offer you an engagement.

I would want you to play Malcolm and would engage you for the run of the play. Engagement to commence 22 Dec.

Should you be disengaged and will send terms that you would accept, I will answer by return.

Faithfully yours,

H. Irving.

Young Ambition's Ladder

A second letter was dated October 14th:

Dear Mr. Webster,

  I am glad that you are able to join us and I hope that you'll be happy and stay for a long while.

  As you have been receiving £7 I offer you £8—that you may feel yourself advancing. Will that be satisfactory? . . .

May could easily have thought—she almost certainly did—that this was another example of the luck of the "easy-way Websters." To enter the stage door of the Lyceum was nearly as great an achievement for Young Ben as it had been for Old Ben to cross the threshold of Drury Lane; and he was to play an important part in a new production—not Irving's first *Macbeth*, but Ellen Terry's first Lady Macbeth, and the first time they had played it together.

They were at the zenith of their powers, he a man of fifty, she just over forty. They were the darlings of fashionable London; moreover, they had made Shakespeare fashionable too. Since the days of Charles Kean he had been "box-office poison"; only Phelps at Sadler's Wells had succeeded in keeping him theatrically alive. But Irving's Hamlet at the Lyceum in 1874 had inaugurated a new era; and when Ellen Terry joined him in 1878, the poison turned to gold.

Ben was suitably impressed with his good fortune. He entered the Green Room for the first time with fear and trembling. The company was sitting in a circle, waiting for Irving. An old man with white hair got up from a far corner and came over to him. "Are you the young man, Webster?" he asked. "My name is Howe—'Daddy' Howe. I played with your grandfather for thirty years. Sit down."

The production aroused violent controversy. Irving, the critics said, was not a "great soldier." (They are always saying this about Macbeths; great soldiers, it seems, must be powerful, burly creatures, not a bit like Alexander or Napoleon or Montgomery or Eisenhower.) Irving himself thought he did his finest work in the part. Ellen Terry said of him: "His conception of Macbeth . . .

seemed to me as clear as daylight. But the carrying-out of the conception was unequal. Henry's imagination was sometimes his worst enemy. It tempted him to try and do more than any actor can do." His finest moment, she thought, was at the end when, looking like "a great, famished wolf," he faced Macduff with the line:

Of all men else I have avoided thee . . .

"He suggested, as only he could suggest, the power of fate. He seemed to envisage a power against which no man can fight, to hear the beat of its inexorable wing."

She adds that, with his great gift for the uncanny, he would have played the Sleepwalking Scene much better than she did herself. But May, who later played in it with her, would have denied this hotly. Ellen Terry's flaming Norse Queen was also an ardent woman, not at all in the "fiend-like" Siddons tradition, and she aroused furious argument. It is easy to visualize how she looked from Sargent's flaming picture of her in the glittering beetles'-wing dress. Oscar Wilde drily remarked: "Lady Macbeth seems an economical housekeeper, and evidently patronised local industries for her husband's clothes and the servants' liveries; but she takes care to do her own shopping in Byzantium."

Her performance is illuminated for us by two of her own annotated prompt copies, one for the production of 1888 and one two years later. Lady Macbeth is "a woman"—"every inch a woman"—she has "only a woman's strength"—she faints, really faints, because Macbeth is safe. In Comyns Carr's prefatory essay she underlines "It is natural to a man to anticipate, in a woman to remember." At the end of the Banquet Scene ("that damned party in a parlour," she calls it), she is frightened, her reason has begun to be shaken *because* "now . . . she knows him . . . he is a brave soldier but a weakling and she has only now found out the full extent of this."

The emphasis on Macbeth's weakness grows in the second set of notes; because of Irving, one wonders, or in spite of him? Her notes about him stress her own love of speed, as against his slowness and deliberation: *"Please* quickly" . . . *"Please* at once" . . .

"a look please like lightning will help me here." There is an abundance of technical notes, fascinating to an actor, matters of breath, phrasing, gesture, "don't use a music-hall voice." There are protestations against cuts, often not in her own speeches; in his "light thickens" etc., "much of this shld be restored—so *very* good for acting." Many of these lines are, in fact, restored in the second version. There are also, in the first prompt copy, a great many notes on scenes she herself was not in, indicating that she must have been "eyes" for Irving; some of them do not concern either of them, as, for instance, the first Witches scene, and the one between Malcolm and Macduff in England. Against the line "Stands Scotland where it did?" comes the extremely characteristic comment "*Love* in the word Scotland."

One hopes young Malcolm took notice of this. Indeed, the entire production must have been a liberal education for him. The Macduff, who became extremely important to him in his later career, was George Alexander.

If May envied Ben's success, she must also have rejoiced for him; and the envy was lessened by the fact that she herself was playing in the West End at last. While Irving was on his autumn tour, before the *Macbeth* production, he lent his theatre to Richard Mansfield, the American actor-manager. When he came back, Mansfield continued his season at another theatre with *Prince Karl*, *Richard III*, *She Stoops to Conquer* and *The School for Scandal*. May joined the company, which was a mixed Anglo-American cast, a rarity in those days as it is still. In the first two plays she only understudied ("I! a leading lady!"); but then came two good parts, Constance Neville, and Lady Sneerwell, a very juvenile Sneerwell, ten years younger than the Lady Teazle. Lionel Brough was in the company, playing Tony Lumpkin, at fifty, with all the infectious high spirits of a boy.

May was fascinated to watch Mansfield, especially as Richard. She found him, personally, an irascible little tyrant with a fiery temper and great charm. For example, he would become infuriated with the callboy. "Out with him!" he would cry. "Out! out!" and everyone would busily bundle the poor boy out. But the next night he would be back again, smiling, and Mansfield would be charming to him, having completely forgotten the incident. For *Richard III* walk-ons were required; Mansfield specified that they must be tall, good-looking, athletic, well-educated gentlemen. "How much is he paying them?" May inquired of the stage manager. "One shilling and sixpence a night" was the reply. At the end of the season Mansfield invited her to come to America with his company, but she refused. When he asked her why, she said: "If you throw me out of your theatre in London, I can go home to my family. But what should I do far away on the prairies in the middle of all those Indians?"

Instead, she started on the agency round once more; but she was hastily summoned to take over the lead at the Standard Theatre in the revival of a melodrama called *Lost in London*, one of Old Ben's Adelphi successes. She had one rehearsal. She was, of course, the heroine, the wife of a rugged Cornish miner, who was seduced by the villain and the lure of the Great City. At the end of Act II she was rescued from him and it by the faithful miner, who had walked from Cornwall in time to invade the respectably dissolute ball she was attending and stand, a fateful figure, announcing in his simple, Cornish way: "Ah want mah wahf." In Act III she died, of shame, in a garret. The finale of the ballroom scene was complicated by the fact that the management possessed a hansom cab which, in the tradition of Vincent Crummles's pump, had to be worked in somehow.

The scene was therefore rearranged to take place outside the house. Rugged Hero arrived in hansom cab. Heroine fainted (back fall down steps of house), was lifted into cab and driven off to tremendous applause. May did the fall, unrehearsed, without concern. She had to revive a little, since it is all but impossible to get into a hansom cab while unconscious. She felt a twist of pain; but had no time to do anything but rush off to change for the Death Scene.

She had been much perplexed as to what dress she could reasonably die in. The grand ball dress in which she had driven away was whaleboned and unsympathetic; on the other hand there had been no evidence of a valise with spare clothing in the hansom cab. With no time to shop before the opening night, she had finally settled on an amorphous grey garment which seemed to reconcile the demands of realism and romance. But the elderly character actress who had immemorially played Tilly, the Faithful Maid, surveyed her sternly. "Aren't you going to die in white?" she demanded. May explained, nervously. Tilly listened without comment and remarked at last, "I never knew a Nelly that didn't die in white." May went shopping the next morning and died in white for the rest of the run.

From the sorrows of Nellie, she went to join the great farce actor Willie Edouin in a play called *Our Flat*, which he had acquired, rather halfheartedly, for the lump sum of £25. The leading lady was Fanny Brough, Lionel's niece, and perhaps the most gifted of all the numerous Broughs. May's part was a small one; she did not know that fate was about to deal her the ace of trumps. Rehearsals were brief and she was much occupied with preparations for Booey's wedding, at which she was to be a bridesmaid. She never saw the play through and didn't know whether the very "moderate" notices were justified or not. Before the end of the first week, Fanny Brough lost her voice. It was obvious that she wouldn't be able to play the Saturday matinee; there was no understudy; May supposed, drearily, that they would close. But just as she was leaving the theatre, the stage manager came up to her with a script in his hands. "Take this home and learn it," he said. "You've got to play it tomorrow afternoon."

She went home, asked for black coffee, and worked till six a.m., slept for an hour and worked again; at nine thirty she left the house, pausing dramatically on the steps to turn to her mother: "I am going to my ruin," she announced firmly. At the theatre, Edouin was walking up and down with a cigar between his lips; he didn't smoke it or even chew it, he just held it in his mouth and never said a word. At the end of the first act he took it out. "You know it!" he said. "I know the words," she replied sulkily. The worst was yet to come.

In the second act May and the Poor Young Husband had their flat entirely stripped by bailiffs, who removed everything except a pair of curtains. The home had then to be refurnished immediately to make it presentable for a visit from The Prosperous Employer upon whom All Depended. Husband, naturally, was Out. May and Faithful Maid had to fill the bare stage with settees made out of packing cases, screens from clotheshorses draped with shawls, armchairs out of hip-baths, and a variety of other furnishings, all contrived in full view of the audience, at high speed, and timed to fit in with a flow of quick-fire dialogue. It was as precise as a ballet and as breathless as a trapeze act. May had never seen it. Edouin took her through it, lucidly, once. At the matinee, when the scene came, she resigned herself to prayer and knew no more till she found herself standing with her back to the footlights, surveying a perfectly appointed stage, with her heart thudding as if she had been running a quarter-mile race. There was a roar of applause from behind her.

Fanny Brough returned to the cast briefly and then left it for good. The play ran into a success, and May played in it for nearly two years. It afforded her wonderful training with the expert and irrepressible Edouin, who was a music-hall type of comedian with all the tricks of the trade at his command—juggler, conjurer, pantomimist. It was, moreover, his pride and delight to "break up" the other actors. He would invite his children to sit in a box and have bets with them about how often he could make the others laugh. It became May's pride to keep a straight face, no matter how outrageous the tricks he played on her. Laughing on the stage can be a perfectly dreadful compulsion. From the days of *Our Flat*, May was able to preserve an unruffled composure in the face of practically anything and to glare with disapproval at many weaker brethren.

Most important of all, it brought her success, which she desperately needed. She had been spiky, arid and afraid; now she blossomed and flourished. Some people are spoiled by success when it comes to them too young, and May was only twenty-four. But in her case it was the cure for many things; her health improved, at least for a time, and many of the self-inflicted torments vanished. She was no longer overshadowed by the Websters. Booey was married and had left the stage; and in a newspaper popularity poll she, humble Little Whitty, was voted London's favorite young actress.

Young Ambition's Ladder

She still lived with her mother and Aunt Lally; she began to feel a little restive, but she was no longer tied. In fact, the family had already begun to split up. Her brother, Michael, had decided that there was no future for him in England and had gone off to try sheep farming in Australia. In 1890, after years of battle, the English law had finally consented to recognize minimal rights for married women. It became possible for Gretchen to seek a divorce. Mrs. Whitty, trembling with horror, was prevailed upon to face the ordeal of the witness box. Gretchen won her freedom. For a year or two she made a desultory living on the stage and by "Women's Page" journalism. Then she too made up her mind to leave England, not to follow Michael, but to head west across the Atlantic. The next time the three little Whittys met was many years later, in New York.

May began to make friends outside the theatre, where she found several young men who were not "cads." One of them was Justin Huntly McCarthy, son of Parnell's chief lieutenant. He brought her artistic education up to date by introducing her to young writers and painters who were to distinguish the imminent Nineties. He was horrified to discover that to May "lunch" meant a Bath bun in a tea shop. He took her to restaurants in Soho, showed her how to make sense of a French menu and how to choose a wine to go with it.

He took her to the House of Commons to listen to the Irish debates. During the weeks of excitement and tension which followed the O'Shea divorce case he would call for her at the theatre, straight from the melodrama of Committee Room 15. One night he arrived with a torn coat and no collar. The vote had gone against Parnell; the Irish members had literally fought each other in a scuffling mass all down the stairs into the lobby of the House. The Parnell drama was over. It was May's first introduction to politics, and she never recovered from the inoculation.

A pleasurable "river" life was beginning. Actors would hire a skiff or, more often, a flat-bottomed punt at Staines or Maidenhead and go down by train every Sunday morning armed with picnic baskets to spend the day on the Thames. Ben and May, Herbert Waring and his wife, shared these expeditions. During the *Our*

147

Young Ben and May

Flat summer she stayed at Taplow and commuted every night by train and four-wheeler cab. Neither motorcars nor motor launches had yet intruded on the water-lapped peace of the river bank; but a great extension of its activity was about to take place; the day of the bicycle had dawned. In May's diary there are a few discordant notes: a mention of the income tax at the monstrous figure of sixpence in the pound; some grumbling at crowds and traffic; many mentions of doctors. "Mostly ill" is the record for December 1890. But when she was persuaded to take two weeks' holiday from the play, she was utterly miserable.

She never neglected her theatrical education. It was the age of "special matinees," and she played in many of them. There were no union restrictions nor any prohibitions against the mingling of professional actors with the dedicated and often talented amateurs who, in the Dickens tradition, made the stage their avocation. London companies also played "flying matinees" at suburban theatres, or even at Brighton or Southsea. For some reason they were only paid half salary for these excursions. A favorite venue was the Crystal Palace, once the glory of the 1851 Exhibition. It had been transplanted to South London, where it housed, impartially and simultaneously, poultry and opera, actors and dog shows. The competition was audible and tremendous.

There were many things to be seen, too, between engagements or in spite of them: all the way from Fred Leslie and Nellie Farren at the Gaiety (*Faust Up to Date*, a lampoon on Irving and Ellen Terry; she vastly amused by it, he furious) to that difficult Norwegian, Ibsen. May's diary records *A Doll's House* in June 1889, with Janet Achurch, and *The Pillars of Society* a month later. There were several London visits from Sarah Bernhardt, whom May admired extravagantly, and from Augustin Daly's American company, with Ada Rehan as Viola and as Katharine, the Shrew. Just as May had always thought Ellen Terry the greatest Ophelia she ever saw ("I've never seen Ophelia really played since—it has always seemed like such a small part"), so she thought Ada Rehan's Viola the most melting and her Katharine the most tempestuous and flaming. A couple of years later came Duse, whom she thought the greatest of them all. Night after night (May was fortunately out of work at the time) she would sit on the hard Gallery benches watching that wonderful face that mirrored every thought even before it was spoken. "There have been only two faces in the theatre in my life-time," said Ellen Terry, "Irving's and Duse's." What a fortunate generation, who could see these four actresses, all quite different, each of genuine greatness!

It is the way of the theatre not to let one hit constitute a career, and a series of mediocre engagements followed *Our Flat*. The one May remembered best was *Linda Grey*, starring the beautiful Lily Langtry. The Prince of Wales came to the opening night; but he only lasted one act. After that he vanished from the Royal Box and spent the rest of the evening in Mrs. Langtry's dressing room, thereby creating alarm and despondency among the cast. The critics next day endorsed his opinion. Somehow, May didn't think it mattered. Life was sliding by so much more easily, softly, gently. In March 1892 comes a note in her diary: "Ben and I bought punt at Thames Ditton. Great event." It was the outward and visible sign of a greater event. She had at last agreed to marry him. "Of course he's much too good for her," said tactful Lizzie Webster to Mrs. Whitty, who was not pleased. But May agreed, and remained all her life of the same opinion.

She spent the summer at a cottage near Marlow with Gretchen, about to leave for America, and Florrie Waring. It could only be reached by pony trap, that is if the pony hadn't run away or shied and wrapped the wheel round a lamp post in the High Street. Ben, who was playing at the St. James's, would come down by train on Sunday mornings, bringing his bicycle, and ride over to join the empunted party at Cookham or Hurley. In July there are notes of visits to dressmakers and to a friendly antique dealer who would give Ben and May lunch in the garden of his old manor house before selling them lovely Sheraton and Hepplewhite furniture for a fantastically low price.

They were married in the usual embarrassed flurry of mishaps and orange blossoms. The bridal veil didn't come, and the bride-groom went flying around to the shop to fetch it. They were both much more nervous than on an opening night, Ben nearly dropped the ring, and Mrs. Whitty cried a good deal. At the reception, the best man, upon whom they had relied to shepherd the guests, was nowhere to be seen. It transpired that he had gone around to the Websters' house to have a bath. "Bobby" Brough, Lal's son, about to marry Lizzie, deputized nobly. Gretchen did her social best, which, since she didn't know many of the people present, included shaking hands warmly with the detectives. At last the bride and groom drove off thankfully to Waterloo Station, slightly spattered with confetti.

Their destination was Woolacombe, a tiny village on the North Devon coast. Someone had told them it was quiet and they would like it; but Mortehoe Station revealed nothing except flat fields and a squat, boxlike hotel. Their hearts sank. Woolacombe, however, proved to be two miles away, "down-over the hill." The solitary station fly with its shiny, cracked leather seats and plodding horse set off down the lane between the overhanging hedges. Suddenly there was a tang of the sea, "like a hand stretched out to welcome you," May thought. The road got steeper; the driver stopped and put a drag on the wheel; it scraped gently against the surface of the road. The blackberry leaves growing up the banks were powdered with dust; the fern and bracken had a surface of whiteness. The smell of the sea grew unmistakable.

At last they came to a bend of the road where the enfolding hills sloped down to meet each other. There, between them, a triangle of blue, was the sea itself and the narrow outline of Lundy Island at anchor on the horizon. "I think we're going to like this place," said Ben.

They came back to it, summer after summer, for over thirty years. For them, as later for their child, there was always magic at the end of the Woolacombe road.

CHAPTER NINE

Great Stars in the Sky

Young Ben and May could reasonably have looked forward to a period of some security, though I doubt that they ever did. With a little bit of talent and a little bit of luck the London actor of those years could lead an enviable life. He was generally engaged by the season, often for several seasons. This would mean seven or eight months in London and two on tour, with a holiday in between. He was seldom tied to a long run, nor was he terrified of a short one, for if a play was a failure and came off, an earlier success would be brought back for revival while a new production was being prepared. This meant that the repertory system, though much weakened, had not altogether vanished. An actor's "line of business" had ostensibly vanished. Insidiously, however, a worse evil was creeping in to replace it, tighter and more limiting, which eventually became known as "type-casting."

The profession was not nearly so overcrowded as it later became. To enter it was still a bold decision for a respectable young man and of course much more difficult for a young woman. There was plenty of touring employment and enough stock or repertory for training purposes, though this type of theatre had dangerously diminished. But London dominated the British stage, and was itself dominated by the star actor-managers.

They were men of genuine accomplishment themselves and therefore generally respected by their companies; which did not mean that they never abused their privileges, nor that actors ever stopped grumbling, for I am sure they never did. There was envy, resentment, conflict of many kinds; but not the gulf which later separated the performer from the "bricks-and-mortar" manager and the business tycoon. Actor and manager shared a craft; they played scenes together, and met at the Garrick or the Green Room Club.

They were Establishment men, most of them, only recently admitted to society and preoccupied in becoming its pillars. But they esteemed their profession and caused it to be esteemed. They ran their theatres like a benevolent feudal hierarchy. They were certainly not iconoclastic nor avant-garde; their choice of plays was limited in taste and range. But they placed at the service of the playwright well-run theatres, handsome productions, skilled, experienced actors, and a stability of plan and purpose. An age of stars is supposed to be lethal to dramatists; but this one saw the emergence of Pinero, Barrie, Wilde, Maugham and Galsworthy, even if it favored Henry Arthur Jones and others, less talented, whose work has already perished. Even Ibsen and Shaw managed to get onto the London stage, though it was more in spite of the actor-managers than because of them.

My mother and father knew and played with almost all these men in England, and many of them in America, from the Eighties until after the First World War, when the tradition weakened and finally vanished. It was an unbroken succession, from Irving, Bancroft and the Kendals to Gerald du Maurier, who, in England, was perhaps the last. Toward the end of this period I myself caught glimpses of some of its now-vanished giants. The earlier of them are shadowy figures, moving in mist. Sometimes they come sharply into focus, the image in my memory matching the reports and the records without disparity. I have, for instance, vivid snapshots of Sir Squire Bancroft at eighty walking down Garrick Street, tall, lean, with shining silver hair, a monocle on a broad ribbon, morning coat and top hat, stiff-backed and courteous. My father would describe him, on arrival at the Garrick Club, sitting down to bridge with his old friend Sir John Hare; Hare volatile, impatient, testy, playing quickly and then snapping his fingers and crying "Come on B., come on, come on!" Bancroft considering, dignified, not to be bustled. All this fits the actors I have read about, the fine but unexciting leading character man and the quick-witted chameleon-comedian. Lady Bancroft I met—was presented to —once: a tiny, Dresden-china old lady who left me with a memory of lace ruffles and pale-pink powder and dancing, mischievous eyes. It was not in the least difficult to translate her into Lady Teazle or Polly Eccles or even the Marie Wilton who had once charmed all hearts as Cupid in Old Ben's Adelphi pantomimes.

Sometimes, however, I am bothered by a kind of triple vision; and this is the case with Mrs. Kendal. There is the ogre of Little Whitty's youth, disagreeable and dictatorial as a manager, as an actress an efficient machine. I was startled when I first realized that this formidable figure was, at the time, a young woman less than forty years old, described by contemporary observers as an actress of fullness and warmth. Superimposed on these images is my own picture of an old woman of eighty in button boots and a Victorian bonnet trimmed with violets whom I used to meet when I was seventeen or thereabouts.

She had a flattish, rather merry face, the eyes very bright and with the ghost of a twinkle. She was a Dame by this time; but then so was my mother, and they were on terms of "dear May" and "dear Madge." I was, however, prepared to be intimidated; I sat at her feet metaphorically and sometimes literally, and asked humble questions. "What is necessary, do you think, Dame Madge, to become a great actress?" She answered: "The courage of a lion, the strength of an elephant and the hide of a rhinoceros." I asked her about some of the great actresses—the *other* great actresses, I hastily amended—of her day. Ellen Terry? Charming, charming; all the men loved her; never knew her words; turned to you with a delightful smile and made it look as if it were your fault. Sarah Bernhardt? Yes, indeed a great actress; from the waist down.

She asked me if I had a latchkey of my own and shook her head to hear that I did. "I never had a latchkey till I was sixty-nine, when my husband died. Why should I have needed it? Mr. Kendal had one." She was given to aphorisms. "There is no heat," she said, "in burnt love-letters." I later discovered that this is not a fact; also that the line is a quote from one of her famous roles. Nevertheless, I began to feel that I had vicariously misjudged Ma K. No doubt she had been a bully in her time; mellowed, and no longer "the party in power," she remained respected and allowed herself to be amusing.

The great ones of the next generation, who were in power at the turn of the century, begin to be more vivid to me. Many of them I later saw on the stage. Beerbohm Tree's Fagin in *Oliver Twist* gave me my first experience of terror in a theatre. I saw George Alexander too, several times, but my memory of him is strangely dim. Yet in the Nineties and Nineteen Hundreds, when the epoch of the star-manager was at its zenith, he was probably the most important of them all.

May had known him as a juvenile in the Kendal company, and Ben had played Malcolm to his Macduff. He moved surely and steadily toward his objective, which was to go into management for himself. In 1890 he took over the Avenue Theatre. Ben went with him. There he did three new productions, all strongly cast, all moderately successful. Ben had somehow got shifted from his handsome, romantic parts to a series of "silly ass" types, and was forever fixing a monocle into one blue eye and resisting attempts to make him put on a mustache. At the Avenue, he distinguished himself by accidentally touching one of the new electric-light sockets with the ferrule of his walking stick and thereby plunging the whole Charing Cross district—or such of it as was electrically lit—into darkness.

In January 1891 Alexander moved to the St. James's, where he ruled in great glory and considerable wealth until his death in 1918. During his reign he made it the Establishment theatre par excellence. Here the feudal system worked to perfection. The productions were faultlessly mounted; money was spent generously but wisely. His wife, Florence, supervised the costumes and also the furniture and props, which were all genuine of the genuine. Everything was in place from the very first rehearsal. The department heads were like beneficent butlers, even including that newcomer the electrician, who practiced a parvenu skill. The housekeeper, Mrs. Evans, ruled backstage with an iron hand. Occasionally she would decide to confiscate all the little stubs of candle over which everybody melted black grease paint for their eyelashes. There would be screams of fury and refusals to go on; but Mrs. Evans would be adamant: the fire laws. Naturally, the candle ends sneaked back again within a few days and remained until the next raid.

There would be tea in the Green Room on matinee days, cake and sandwiches and a silver tea service. One of the ladies of the company would preside, under the watchful eye of Mrs. Evans. She once reproved my mother for wasting tea by brewing it too strong. Everything was conducted with the utmost decorum, and there were separate staircases for the ladies' and gentlemen's dressing rooms. All this respectability sometimes made the St. James's seem a trifle airless to its inhabitants; some of them took pleasure in detecting feet of clay; mischief intruded. It was reported of Bobby Brough ("Sydney" officially, but never called so) that he wrecked the opening night of *Rupert of Hentzau*. The curtain was supposed to fall on a tableau of Alexander lying in state on a catafalque in full Ruritanian uniform, head upstage, gleaming cuirass, beautifully polished jack-boots; on their soles Bobby had chalked the price, 17/11.

Nevertheless, the organization, backstage and front of the house, was undeniably perfect. It has been said that in a profession which operates almost wholly in an atmosphere of frenzied lunacy, the St. James's remained calm, orderly, aloof. Tempers were not lost; authors were not argued with—at least, not publicly; actors were not harassed or bullied; difficulties were anticipated and not left to wreck the dress rehearsal and imperil the opening night. As a director "Alec" was neither finicky nor dictatorial. He arranged and controlled the traffic; he made suggestions; he pointed things out; he tactfully translated the authors' views; he relied on the tested skills and hand-picked personal qualities of his actors. It was said of him that he was the last man to whom you would go for sympathy, the first to whom you would turn for advice.

He himself was not a great actor, but he was an extremely sound one. "He does not act, he behaves," said Oscar Wilde, very ungratefully, for Alexander's performance as John Worthing was said to be flawless; and he had the range to cover such romantic heroes as François Villon, and Rudolf in *The Prisoner of Zenda* as well. The star-managers were not expected to be the slaves of any "line of business." The St. James's leading ladies were women of magnetism and accomplishment, such as Marion Terry and Irene Vanbrugh; the character actors, men and women, were of the highest class. Alexander was not greedy and was very willing to share the limelight and the applause. It was easy to be funny about the St. James's; it is easier still now, when its glittering society audiences, respectful Pit-ites and socially stuffy plays belong to a vanished era. But no theatre has ever offered its artists and its staff a greater sense of confidence and security in which to do their work. Ben stayed there three years the first time, very happily despite some thwarted ambitions, and returned to it many times thereafter.

Almost as soon as he became a manager in his own right, Alexander started trying to get Oscar Wilde to write a play for him. Toward the end of 1891, after much procrastination, a good deal of fuss and a sizable advance, Wilde delivered *Lady Windermere's Fan.* The plot was an extremely orthodox woman-with-a-past affair, very St. James's indeed; but the dialogue crackled with impudence and wit. At first, it threw the company off balance. They had never had to speak that sort of dialogue. They tried to sparkle like anything, and found themselves sounding flatly artificial. Irene Vanbrugh has recorded that she had the same problem as Gwendolyn in *The Importance of Being Earnest;* at last her sister said to her, "Perhaps the lines will seem natural to you if you think them first." And lo and behold, it was so. (I thought of this recently, when a London company played a revival of *Lady Win-*

dermere as if they had been embalmed and were terrified of cracking.)

Wilde had stipulated that for the part of the "green carnation"
young man he must have "someone beautiful"; it was agreed that
Ben Webster merited the description. Ben was not wholly pleased.
He would have preferred to play Lord Darlington, and later did so;
but Cecil Graham, though a part without substance, is a Roman
candle of brilliant epigrams. Oscar was charming to the company,
interfered very little, allowed "Alec" to persuade him to cut some
of the wordier speeches, even though he complained that one of
them had cost him "a piece of infinite labour," on which he had
spent all of ten minutes. Wilde was at his best when he was
working, alone with those whom the theatre made his collabora-
tors. He learned quickly how to place a piece of business, how to
turn a spoken, as against a written, line.

"Dear Mr. Webster," he wrote to Ben, " 'What should we men
do going about with purity and innocence? *A carefully thought-out
button hole* is much more effective!' Of course arrange your but-
ton-hole as you talk."

Later, while *Lady Windermere* was on tour, Ben wrote to
May: "They still seem unable to see the humour of my role. Oscar
told us we were going to educate the provincial masses with his
work, but I fear I don't enjoy the scholastic employment he has
given us." And from Liverpool: "The play went exceedingly well
. . . I actually got some laughs; though my remark that 'the
devotion of a married woman is a thing no married man knows
anything about' is still received with the stony silence of moral
disapprobation."

No such dull-witted puritanism afflicted the white ties and kid
gloves, the titles and tiaras that flocked to the London opening
night. They received the iconoclasm with acclaim and misquoted
the epigrams with relish. Oscar took a curtain call to huge applause, leaning negligently against the proscenium arch and
smoking a cigarette. The mighty critic Clement Scott almost had
apoplexy at this effrontery. For a hundred and fifty-six performances the St. James's was packed to its dignified portals.

Young Ben and May

Three years later Oscar Wilde's finest play, *The Importance of Being Earnest*, opened there. The Queensberry scandal was at bursting point; many of the first-night audience, Ben and May among them, knew of the frantic efforts which were being made to prevent Lord Queensberry from getting into the theatre and fulfilling his threat to present Oscar with a bouquet of carrots and onions. Excitement was at fever heat; but the play was a crashing success. A few weeks later, when the scandal broke openly and Wilde sued Queensberry for libel, a violent revulsion of feeling took place. Oscar's name was hurriedly removed from the billboards outside the theatre. This, however, was not enough to pacify enraged society, and the play itself was withdrawn. Fifteen years passed before Alexander dared to revive it. Then it ran a year.

At the end of the second trial, on the night when the news of Wilde's conviction was announced, Ben happened to be presiding at the Green Room Club dinner. The very actors who had flattered Oscar and begged from him, rose to their feet and cheered, yelling venomous and ribald comment. Ben, a pacific character by nature, found himself standing on a chair, shouting them into silence, telling them they were a set of self-righteous hypocrites, refusing to stay and witness such indecent exultation. He jumped down and ran out of the building, hearing, not the hubbub in the room behind him, but the roar of cheering as Oscar Wilde leaned against the proscenium arch at the St. James's, smoking his impertinent cigarette.

In 1893 a new kind of play came to that theatre, and a wholly new kind of leading lady. She rocked it to its solid foundations. Pinero sent Alexander a script called *The Second Mrs. Tanqueray*. Since he was the most famous and successful dramatist of the day, this amounted to a royal command for its production. Alexander began reading with keen anticipation; he continued with growing horror. The heroine was a fallen woman, very fallen indeed, and the play was on her side; she was a rebel, and it rebelled with her. People would think it an attack on the purity of English womanhood;

there might easily be a riot. Alec paced his room; he gave the script to his wife; he went for an agitated walk in Hyde Park; he wondered if Pinero would let him do it just for special matinees; he thought this unlikely; he came home, he consulted his friends, he hesitated and agonized. Finally he decided to take the plunge.

Another difficulty arose instantly: the leading lady. His established woman star was Marion Terry, Ellen's younger sister, gracious, witty, sophisticated, charming; capable of suggesting a past peccadillo, as she had done to admiration as Mrs. Erlynne in *Lady Windermere*, but surely she could sin no further; as the tempestuous Paula Tanqueray she couldn't be said to "do." But then no established actress that either Alec or Pinero could think of would do either.

What followed has been several times recounted in several different versions. I retell the story as I heard it from my mother and father, who participated in it. May attended the opening night of a new melodrama at the Adelphi Theatre, *The Trumpet Call*. There was an unknown actress in it, a handsome, gypsy creature with an odd name, Mrs. Patrick Campbell. May didn't think much of either the play or the acting: "awful rubbish—vilely acted all round," she wrote. But in the last act Mrs. P. Campbell's skirt fell off. Any actress might have been excused for rushing off the stage overwhelmed with shame and confusion; not Mrs. P. Campbell. She gathered it up, wrapped it around her with all the dignity of a Roman empress investing herself with the purple, and calmly went on with the scene. The tittering audience was hushed and held; a ripple of admiration widened through theatrical London.

It reached Pinero and Alexander; this woman sounded as if she were the type they needed; they went to see her and decided that she was. "No name," said Alexander gloomily; but Pinero thought Paula Tanqueray was name enough. She was engaged. The rest of the casting went easily and well; Ben played the very difficult and crucial part of Captain Ardale. Rehearsals began.

They were a great change from Alexander's easygoing surveillance. Pinero was a martinet. He knew precisely what he wanted from every line; he dictated every move, every inflection. Irene Vanbrugh, who created so many of his heroines, has left this description of him: ". . . nearly six feet tall, rather thick-set, with a highly-coloured complexion, dome-like bald head, which was inclined to jerk forward when he wanted to accentuate what he was saying. He would walk back and forth along the stalls, the front row being removed for the purpose. Hands clasped behind his back, concentration personified, each step taken in complete measure with what he was thinking, each word carrying its full weight so that everything he said seemed to pierce through to your brain."

The company was intimidated; all except the newcomer. She appeared to regard the St. James's hierarchy with irreverence. She did not treat her august—and amiable—manager with becoming respect at all; on the contrary, she kept flicking him with innocent little remarks, feathered, but also barbed. She was not even awed by Pinero. At one point he took particular pains to demonstrate a scene of passion for her: she would, he said, storm across the stage and sweep everything off the top of the grand piano in ungovernable fury. Mrs. P. Campbell listened; she stormed on cue; she reached the grand piano; she picked up a very small ornament: "Here," she said, in tones of black ice, "I knock something over," and dropped it delicately onto the carpet. The company were scandalized but also secretly amused. Everyone, however, dreaded the opening night. The success of the play depended on Paula Tanqueray, and she needed authority and experience, not just impudence, looks and luck.

Ben, whose first entrance came late in the play, arrived at the theatre during the first act. He found Pinero pacing up and down the alleyway outside the stage door. "How's she doing?" said Ben. "Haven't heard a word," replied Pinero. "Alec says she'll be all right if she doesn't crumble." When the interval was called, Pinero knocked on Alec's door. "How is she?" he asked. Alec replied morosely that he feared she was crumbling. Pinero went straight to her dressing room. "Magnificent," he told her, "you're being magnificent!" And she was, to the end of the play. The next morning *The Second Mrs. Tanqueray* and the only Mrs. Campbell were safely ensconced in theatre history. Paula bequeathed her sin-stained past and tortured present to numberless heroine-descendants. "Mrs. Pat," perhaps fortunately for the happiness of mankind, remained unrepeatable and unique.

The autumn tour that year consisted of *Tanqueray*, *Lady Windermere* and two other plays; both Marion Terry and Mrs. Pat were in the company. The atmosphere was not exactly harmonious. During the tour Ben was promoted to play Lord Darlington, with Mrs. Pat as Lady Windermere. "Heaven knows what she is!" he wrote to May after his first performance. "I should say drunk; but as she fooled the entire evening and made remarks to me when her back was to the audience, she kept me completely self-conscious and nearly dried me up once—that she wasn't a genius, that she had no dramatic instinct I knew, but that she hadn't one throb of artistic feeling which might have led her to approach her task seriously or at least have a little consideration for the possible nervousness of others, I only learned last night . . . I pray that I may never have to act another scene with her as long as I live."

Of course, he knew perfectly well that Mrs. Pat did not drink. This was just a small example of the hell and havoc she loved to create around her. It was the kind of thing that reduced Alec to gibbering fury. Years later Bernard Shaw sent him the script of *Pygmalion* for himself and Mrs. Pat. He is reported to have told Shaw that he would get any other actress in the world and pay any salary she asked—give the author any terms he cared to name— "but go on for another play with Mrs. Campbell I will *not* . . . I'd rather die."

Posterity, viewing her largely through the perspective of the Shaw-Campbell letters, is apt to dismiss her shenanigans as the pranks of genius, but there were many who suffered under the mischief without seeing much of the genius. Nevertheless, it was there; and even with Ben the impression of it must have endured, for fifteen years later he was lured back to be her leading man on a long tour of the United States. Most theatre people are optimists; they always think it won't be so bad this time; softening, deceptive veils swirl over the horrors of the past; and Ben could never remember to cherish a grudge. He was later reminded.

Young Ben and May

A random dip into my mother's diaries for the years following her marriage reveal a kaleidoscope of people and events. The former begin to predominate. A long run of *Our Boys* is notable chiefly for the friendship it engendered between the Websters and the Esmonds, Eva (Moore) and Harry, the playwright and actor; there is "seeing much of Fred Terry"; "Ailsa [Edy] Craig"; and many others. There is, apparently, a reconciliation with Booey and much Wagner-visiting together to hear Jean de Reszke. There are the things she saw: *The Master Builder* and *The Wild Duck* when they were first done; Barrie's first play, *Walker, London;* the visiting Comédie Française; and all the Duse productions. In August 1894, back from Woolacombe, there is the note: "Reh tour F-R Profligate Dip."

Johnston Forbes-Robertson was a charming man to work for, treating his companies as courteously as Alexander, and much more human and accessible. May admired his acting and capitulated, as everyone did, to his grave beauty and that modulated, brushed-velvet voice; admiration warmed into lasting friendship. She enjoyed playing in *The Profligate* and being the villainess in *Diplomacy*. She was pleased when the Liverpool Aunts were impressed with her performance, her foreign accent, her chic Parisian "get-up" and the general air of prestige which surrounded her. She found herself being quite kind to them.

But she was not yet proof against those plunges into black despair which had once afflicted her. Forbes-Robertson planned a revival of *Caste*, and May, for some obscure reason, had set her heart on playing the very filleted heroine, Esther. When he gave the part to someone else, she wrote to Ben, "Mr. Forbes has given me my death-blow"; further progress in the theatre was "hopeless." It was only to be done for one trial week in Islington; and in the end she did play the part. Neither the production nor her performance stirred so much as a ripple.

Another friendship begun during the tour was of immeasurably greater importance. There was a young man in the company whom she had met once before when he was playing as an amateur with the Old Stagers. He turned out to be a heaven-sent companion on Sunday train-calls; they read the same books and laughed at the same jokes and spoke the same language. He was playing the small part of Algy in *Diplomacy*, and on the opening night he was so nervous that everyone forgot their own troubles in a fever of anxiety for him. They prayed that he would be all right. They needn't have worried. Gerald du Maurier was going to be quite all right.

The following spring Ben received an offer from Henry Irving which was flattering, but extremely confusing. It was to replace Forbes-Robertson as Sir Lancelot in the new production of *King Arthur* in London, followed by various revivals; Ben was to play Gratiano, Claudio in *Much Ado*, Malcolm once more, and the "romantic juveniles" in a number of non-Shakespearian plays; after a month's layoff the company would sail for the United States, where they were booked for a ten-month tour; and Ben would have the option of playing a further season in England if he so wished. All of this was magnificent from the point of view of the actor; but what about the married man?

During the two and a half years since their marriage he and May had been separated by their work for much of the time; but May felt she could not possibly let him go away alone for ten months; especially to that country of beautiful women and wealthy but violent men, not to mention the cowboys and Indians. Yet if she went with him she would lose, or so she felt, all she had worked for. Her hard-won position, now to be advanced and consolidated, would slip away. The British public in those days had a long and faithful memory for its favorites; but theatre managers, then as now, were incapable of remembering anyone whose name wasn't in plain sight outside the theatre next door, or who wasn't at that moment waiting in the outer office to be interviewed. Moreover, there was the financial hazard. May would not be earning money for herself, and if she went along as a camp follower there would be very little left of Ben's salary by the end of the tour.

These agonizing decisions have always to be faced by young married couples in the theatre. Many marriages, or, alternatively, many careers, have been broken by the immediate consequences, or by the delayed effect of thwarted ambition, frustrations, obligations, regrets and resentments. In the Websters' case, there was much tortured appraisal. In the end May decided that Ben must accept the offer and that she would go with him. I think that she would always have made the same choice, could she have had it over again; but that is not to say that she never regretted it. Until the day she died she remained convinced that the upward curve of her career was cut short when she left for America with the Irving company and did not recover its momentum until she was over seventy years old.

Irving, however, with a percipience which he often showed, though never ostentatiously, eased the situation. He made a place for her in some of the ingenue parts in the repertory and put her on the salary list. She joined the company in London for the final performances which preceded its departure. She never rehearsed more than twice: once to be shown the business and positions by the stage manager, and once to run through the lines.

Her first part was as Irving's daughter in *The Lyons Mail;* and in one scene she had to be dragged sobbing from his arms, leaving him in his prison cell, condemned to die. When they reached this point, May indicated that here some sobbing occurred and turned to ask where the exit was supposed to be. Irving raised a sardonic eyebrow. "Can't scream?" he said. "Voice bad? Pity. Ought to be able to scream." "Of course I can scream," retorted the old heroine of *East Lynne* indignantly, and forthwith split the rafters. Irving appeared satisfied. But on the opening night, as she clung in his arms sobbing distractedly, she became aware that he was thumping her head and muttering furiously in her ear, "Box! Dammit, box!" She stole a quick look and realized her crime: she had inadvertently obscured his face from the line of sight of the right-hand box.

Her first appearance in *Louis XI* was even more disconcerting. She had a scene with the Dauphin (Martin Harvey) while Irving as the King was lying "dead" on a couch at the back of the stage. In the middle of it he began to swear, at first softly and then more loudly, with bloodcurdling intensity. "Christ! Blast them! God damn 'em! Christ almighty . . ." she distinguished, coming from the dead monarch. "What's the matter?" she whispered to Harvey, in terror. "Don't worry," Harvey whispered back, "he always does it." She learned later that this was true. The curses were routine; they meant nothing whatever, not even, as far as she could gather, to Irving.

Her third part was in *The Corsican Brothers;* she had to go on hurriedly to replace an actress who had sprained her ankle, and she had no rehearsal at all since this was the day that Irving went to Windsor to be invested by Queen Victoria with the order of knighthood. (It was also, incidentally, the day on which Oscar Wilde was condemned at the Old Bailey.) When he came back from the great occasion, Irving was in so amiable a humor that he did not curse, even once, throughout the entire performance. May almost forgot her lines.

On August 31st, 1895, the company sailed for the United States.

CHAPTER TEN

———— ⁂ ————

To America and Back

Oscar Wilde might express himself as "disappointed with the Atlantic Ocean"; cynics might refer to it as "the Herring Pond"; but the Irving company felt like pioneers—or at least the newcomers did. They traveled a hundred strong, actors, executives, stage and wardrobe staff as well as innumerable wives, children, minions and appendages. They were going to live together for almost a year, as close a community as any caravan of circus wagons.

Irving and Ellen Terry had made their first American tour in 1883, and this was the fourth since that time. They had been the first English stars to bring so large a company and the entire physical production of each play, just as it had been done at the Lyceum. Americans, audience and critics alike, responded with enthusiasm. The success of *Faust*, for instance, was probably due as much to its extraordinary lighting effects as to Irving's Mephistopheles. Later, in 1905, Ellen Terry wrote: "In 1883 there was no living American drama as there is now . . . such productions of romantic plays and Shakespeare as Henry and I brought over from England were unknown; the extraordinary success of our first tours would be impossible now . . . we were *new*. To be new is everything in America . . ." They found the audiences "splendid —discriminating and appreciative" (this did not change); and the critics exhorted their own managers to emulate Irving's "brains and artistic intelligence" in the way he mounted his plays.

On their first tour they had tried to take the entire set of huge productions with them. This involved the use of eight railroad cars, two sixty-foot boxcars and a huge "gondola" carrying the vast impedimenta of scenery and 150 stage baskets. From Philadelphia, their first date, they had to send back eighty flats, twenty-seven cloths, sixty wings, twenty set pieces and twelve framed drops. This list of rejects alone would cause a present-day touring manager (if any) to faint dead away. By the tour of 1895 the trusties of the Lyceum crew knew more or less what problems to expect and how to handle them. The trio of Loveday (Eng.: "general manager"; U.S.: "stage director"), Arnott, master carpenter, and Bram Stoker, company manager and press agent, were armed and well prepared. So were some of the company; but for the rest it was a safari into the jungle. Indeed, the tour was to go much farther afield, travel faster and last longer than any of its predecessors.

Among the veterans was "Daddy" Howe, now over eighty. Irving called him "the agricultural actor" because he grew vegetables in his garden on the Thames and walked ten miles every day from his house to the Lyceum. He had been on all the previous American tours, but had insisted on coming again because he wanted to see New Orleans before he died. Then there were Jack and Nell Martin Harvey, he already a delicate and sensitive actor with a surprising amount of power in reserve. With Nell Harvey, May had had a dramatic first meeting: On the night of her own first appearance at the Lyceum she had practically fallen over a disconsolate figure sitting on the stone floor of one of the corridors, surrounded by all the appurtenances of costume repertory—grease paint, powder, fake jewelry, draperies, belts—and weeping bitterly. It was Nell Harvey; she was only walking on in this particular production and had been relegated to an upstairs dressing room with the other "Lyceum Ladies"; she felt the degradation keenly.

May picked her up, rescued the scattered props and installed them in her own dressing room. A few years later Martin Harvey produced *The Only Way* at the Lyceum, and his wife and leading lady occupied the room which usually belonged to Ellen Terry.

There were many others: Sydney Valentine, a fine character actor who later gave his life to the creation of the first actors' trade union in England; Mary Rorke; handsome Frank Cooper; Edy (no longer Ailsa) Craig, Ellen Terry's daughter; the famous dancer Edward Espinosa, accompanied by a whole raft of brothers and sisters and sons and dancing daughters; gruff old Tom Meade, who once distinguished himself by missing his entrance as the Ghost in *Hamlet*, hurling himself onto the stage on the wrong side and hissing a stentorian "Here, Guv'nor" at Irving's frantic back.

The voyage was horrible and it lasted eleven days. The ship was old, dirty and insufficiently provisioned. Toward the end, when the food shortage became really acute, there would be an undignified scrimmage of famished actors around the door of the dining saloon the moment the gong sounded. Daddy Howe was reduced to prowling round the ship in search of scraps, and once returned in triumph with a whole packet of biscuits which he had unashamedly filched from somebody's cabin.

At last they passed Ambrose Light; all of them crowded on deck, straining their eyes for what they would see: the Statue of Liberty, still in her early youth, and the famous Manhattan skyline. The photographs of it look practically flat to modern eyes but already one building—the Manhattan Life Insurance—had overtopped the spire of Trinity Church, and articles were being written about "the age of skyscrapers." It looked quite awe-inspiring to the English, who also began hungrily to plan what they would eat for their first decent meal. But when they reached quarantine, officials refused to make their inspection because the captain had not been on the bridge to meet them, and the infuriated company had to spend another night on board, enlivened by a tremendous thunderstorm.

Next morning, May and Ben found Gretchen waiting for them on the dock; suddenly America no longer seemed an alien country. It was even then, however, a land of contrasts. The fairylike view from the ship's deck turned to a reality of muddy sidewalks, cobbled streets with cavernous holes in them and singularly dilapidated carriages which jolted them to their hotel. They had very little time to see the sights, as they had to leave early in the morning for Montreal, where the tour was to open. But they visited Broadway, a mere downtown embryo of its later self, but already a Great White Way to London eyes. Cable-haulage trams screeched along it, though elsewhere the beautiful brownstone houses still kept their ancient peace, and the appearance of an automobile was an occasion for public demonstration. Nevertheless, you could not be an hour in New York without sensing its teeming life; the pace was even then a little breathless for a newcomer.

A seasonal heat wave happened to be in progress, so Ben and May dragged from their suitcases the thinnest clothes they possessed and found, even then, that walking along the streets was like being in an overheated orchid house. In the train the heat was unbearable; but when they arrived in Montreal the temperature was thirty degrees lower, resulting in a fine crop of colds all round. The Canadian fall was magnificent, and the trip back to Buffalo kept everyone gazing out of the train windows at an extravagance of color such as they had never seen before. They visited Niagara. They spent a charmed month in Boston, where Gretchen joined them, and then came back to New York for a five-week season. Gretchen went on to Cleveland to be married; her husband was a well-known and well-loved American actor, Tom Wise.

The Websters established themselves in the Marlborough Hotel, where they had enormous rooms with vast closets and a bathroom full of cockroaches. The novelty of the city wore off a little, but never its excitement. They began to get acclimatized ("acclimated"), and to accept more readily than many English visitors the fact that though the two languages bore a spurious resemblance to one another, everything else about America was totally different and must be accepted and appreciated from that standpoint. They quickly learned to hope for nothing they could recognize as tea, but to buy a kettle and make their own. They also realized that they had never tasted coffee before. They learned and enjoyed new foods and new phrases, though May was British enough to feel slightly affronted when the shop assistant who was serving her turned to her neighbor and said in tones of withering contempt, "If there's anything I despise, it's that English accent." She found the prevalence of chewing gum and spittoons a little disconcerting, though she admired the dexterity with which the former could be propelled from a great distance into the latter. The Ladies' Entrance at the hotel was often a necessity, the ordinary entrance being impassable. May and Ellen Terry came back one night armed with huge bunches of flowers and filled all the spittoons to the brim.

New York treated its visitors with generous and unstinting hospitality. The Websters made many friends, writers and theatre people, and laid the foundations of an Anglo-American fellowship, loving citizens, through the years to come, of both London and New York. As actors, they were gratefully aware of the international freemasonry of the stage; walking through any stage door in the world, an actor is suddenly at home. Since there were many nights when she herself was not playing, May was able to see many other shows: *Shore Acres* with James Hearn, Wilton Lackaye in *Trilby*, Mansfield as Beau Brummel, and E. H. Sothern in *The Prisoner of Zenda*—"enchanting," says her note.

In New York she added to her repertoire the tiny part of the Gentlewoman in *Macbeth*. Ellen Terry had asked her to do it, as a personal favor, in order to create the mood and maintain the pitch and tempo which she needed for the Sleepwalking Scene. May accepted with pride and felt rewarded every time she played it. One night the flame of the tiny lamp Ellen Terry carried caught the end of her hair and leaped up the length of it. May stepped forward quietly and brushed it out with her heavy cloak. Lady Macbeth's eyes never flickered; she did not seem to know that anything had happened. Afterward she said, "Thank you, darling —that was a narrow squeak!" She gave May a picture of herself, standing with this same lamp at the foot of a small flight of steps, her arms lifted to one side in the double gesture that was characteristic of her. On the back she wrote: "This way to Mrs. Gaze's party. Three steps up and fall over your drapery." May and Ben were promoted to the intimacy of her friends, who called her "Nell".

There were nights, not infrequent, when she would be distracted by the vagaries of the limelight man and would sleepwalk in pursuit of him. Once, in *King Arthur*, she disengaged herself from Ben's arms and lay down flat on the couch beside him so that the intensity of the light might catch her face. And there were other nights, far more of them, when everybody played a kind of merry-go-round with the lines while the erratic Nell chased some speech that had eluded her.

The tour began just before Christmas in Philadelphia. Going into the bathroom, just after Ben left for the theatre, May found a huge rat calmly sitting on the edge of the bath. Since she was always terrified of "the smallest monstrous mouse that creeps on floor," she lurked in the passage for the rest of the evening waiting for Ben to come home and rescue her. Christmas Day bears the note "With Richard Harding Davis, searching for rat-less rooms."

After Baltimore and Washington, they started through the South, playing mostly one- and two-night stands with night train journeys in between. Since there were seldom any arrangements for meals on the trains, except in Irving's special car, the company took to feeding itself; their cars were gay with the clinking of enamel picnic cups and redolent with the smell of kerosene and frying sausage. Ben shared his upper berth with a specially fitted picnic basket. One night when the train gave an unusually violent lurch, the whole thing plunged overboard with a deafening crash of knives and plates and cups and kettles. "Oh dear!" exclaimed an affrighted female voice from the opposite berth, "did you fall out?"

The journeys were sometimes adventurous. One night they crossed a flooded river where the trestles were so low that the water almost reached up to the engine fires. Edy Craig rushed to her mother's compartment to see whether she was all right and found her completely dressed, gloves neatly buttoned, tying her veil. "Edy darling!" she said, "hurry and dress yourself properly; we shall probably have to swim!"

They fell in love with the beautiful cities of the South, though the effects of the war were still plainly apparent in some of them.

Young Ben and May

The theatres were larger than in England, and much dirtier. A jingle current in American theatreland ran:

> *Way down South in the land of cotton,*
> *Hotels bad and business rotten . . .*

Not only Daddy Howe but the whole company looked forward to reaching New Orleans, about which they had heard so much. From there May wrote to her sister-in-law, Lizzie Brough.

My dearest Liz,

Ben's last letter was written one hot afternoon in Charleston, last Wednesday, a week ago today my diary tells me, but to us it seems years ago! oh! the length of last week—we thought it would go quickly but we were vastly mistaken—each day in a fresh place seemed like a week. Then we looked forward to our week here, but we detest it. We left Atlanta after the show and travelled all the night and all day Sunday —the scenery was gorgeous . . . with magnolia trees and huge firs against a gorgeous blue sky—palms growing wild, like bracken, and occasionally lovely lakes, which we crossed on perilously low bridges. In one lake we saw the remains of a train that had been wrecked three weeks before. We reached New Orleans about 7 o'clock and were dumped down (a favourite expression here) right on the track in the midst of mud many inches deep—after tremendous trouble and long waiting we got a cab, in company with the Valentines, we drove to the Pickwick Hotel, to which we had been recommended. There they had only one room with bath, for which they asked $10 per day, European plan, which means no food only rooms. Fancy £2 a day for your room—that we couldn't stand, and then began a dreary time, we drove from place to place, jolting over the most awful pavement in the world, and eventually had to settle to stay the night at a horrid hotel, but we were all so tired and ill we could go no further. Ben had one of his feverish chills, and I was something of a wreck, so we were glad to get to bed . . . We're rehearsing that filthy leper play every day, takes up all our time, and it's in such a muddle owing to the erratic Nell's stage management.

Oh, this is a vile town, full of smells and dirt, the sewers are open ditches running along the sides of the pavements, and the odour, well . . .

Alas for poor Daddy Howe, who had traveled so far just to see the fabled city! The only consolation the Websters found was that Paderewski was playing a concert there, and they went with Nell to hear him. The "filthy leper play" was *Godefroi and Yolande*, a one-act play by Laurence Irving, Henry's younger son. Irving thought little of it and refused to be concerned with it. But he agreed to have it put on as the first item of a triple bill, reinforced by two of his old stand-bys, provided that Ellen Terry, who had persuaded him into it, would undertake full responsibility. This she did, with more enthusiasm than solid concentration.

As they began to play northward again, through Kentucky and Missouri, everyone's nerves were getting a little frayed. In Cincinnati Daddy Howe was taken seriously ill. May would spend her "off" nights sitting with him. He would talk by the hour of the theatre of his youth, in Old Ben's heyday; he would describe how, if a lamp or a candle began to smoke, a servant of the theatre would walk on in the middle of a scene and snuff it or trim the wick; he would talk of the bewitching Madame Céleste and even of Macready, the Great Bashaw. Hour after hour he would ramble on, clinging to May's hand, while the nurse slept and May grew stiff and cold but dared not move. Once he began to explain to her, very lucidly, the difference between Irving's Shylock and Edmund Kean's. Illustrating it, he suddenly half rose in the bed, pointed at May, and cried out, "and presently thou shalt become a Christian!" The nurse woke with a guilty start and rushed to hold him down. "There, there!" she said, soothing him. "It's quite all right—we'll see that she becomes a Christian in the morning." They had to leave him alone when they moved on to Chicago. A few days later, he died.

G

Young Ben and May

26.2.1896

The Virginia Hotel,
Chicago

Dearest Liz,

. . . All our days are spent in rehearsing the filthy leper play. It is a most involved and difficult piece of work—H.I. has taken it in hand now and even he gets hopelessly mixed at times. He is working us pretty hard at it, but we derive some slight amusement from his remarks—notably today when he said to Miss Rorke, known as "Blowsabella" throughout the Co., "You know you'll have to sweat like billy-ho at this part— you've no idea of it yet." Our placid, solemn Blowsabella sweating like billy-ho at anything . . . ! She plays a fine part, as also does Valentine, a weird, mystical old doctor—it's a part after H.I.'s own heart and he's giving Val some spendid lessons as to how to play it . . .

We are glad to be settled here for a month, a great relief after so much traveling—but it is a most unlovely city, and oh! the mud, rivers of it. It's always bad here, I believe, but just now it's worse than usual owing to melted snow . . .

Edy Craig devised the scenery, the effects, the clothes. It had to be done with very little expenditure. She gathered odd bits of scenery from other plays. She seemed to transform them into something quite different. Ernest Milton later described a revival of it as "an exciting jumble of a production in which one had never before (or since) seen mediaeval representation and atmosphere rescued from the bookish and the dead-as-mutton." Ellen Terry had to make her first entrance along a balcony, looking magnificent as the leper-courtesan in a bright scarlet dress trimmed with poppy leaves (it was adapted from Portia's) and a huge wreath of poppies in her flaming red hair. "I, as a lady-in-waiting, had to follow," wrote May, "but I stood there for a moment transfixed by her strange loveliness and the scene itself, so rich, so beautifully composed."

As usual, Miss Terry worried about the lights. May managed to get offstage for a moment and rushed to the stage manager. "For God's sake get that lime on her," she said, "or she'll go mad!"

There was a soft little chuckle from the darkness and a voice remarked drily: "Better get it right, Loveday. Don't want her to go mad, y'know. Pity." It was Irving. The play went wonderfully, Ellen Terry made a speech of thanks and promised that it should be presented again, which it was, both in America and London. Young Laurence Irving belatedly recognized the generosity of her gesture. Irving and his wife had parted when the boys were infants and had never seen each other again. The boys had been brought up to hate their father and to refer to Ellen Terry—who had come into his life much later—as the Woman, the Creature, the Wench. Their hostility must have been apparent. But she never ceased to try and further their reconciliation with their father, or, in Laurence's case, to promote his plays.

She and Edy were living in the same hotel as the Websters. May and Ben learned to penetrate Edy's brusque manner and to value the qualities behind it, knowledge and judgment, humor and loyalty. She was talented in a determined, almost belligerent way, passionately and possessively devoted to her mother, beset by all the problems which surround the daughter of a famous actress and a beautiful woman, especially when she herself is illegitimate. She and her brother, Gordon Craig, never saw their father after they were small children, though Ellen Terry loved him till the day she died. If Edy was deeply conscious of the situation, she met it proudly. As a girl, she was something of an ugly duckling. Later, as an old woman, she grew extremely like her mother—"her fine head with its abundant white hair, like some great lady of the eighteenth century, beauty of a very remarkable kind, softening the asperities and bringing out all the nobility of her face." She eschewed, almost on principle, the family endowment of easy charm, on which her brother traded so extensively. Later she developed considerable magnetism. During this tour something happened which probably had a decisive influence on the rest of her life.

She fell deeply and passionately in love with Sydney Valentine, who was married. When Ellen Terry found out, she reacted with violence. She crushed the incipient romance as mercilessly as if she had been Father Moulton-Barrett in person. She threatened to send

Edy home to England at once. It was an understandable way for a mother to behave, especially for this particular mother; but it did nothing to help Edy. With extraordinary lack of perception, she proceeded to make matters worse. She was, at this time, carrying on a mild flirtation with Frank Cooper, the handsome if slightly wooden actor who played such parts as Bassanio and Macduff. She would bring him back to supper after the performance and insist that Edy should stay up—or get up, if she had not been playing herself that night—in order to chaperone her. Mother and daughter both talked to Ben and May, who were, of course, powerless to help. Edy remained in the company and did as she was told. No one ever spoke of the episode again.

A problem of another kind faced Ben and May. The Chicago doctors told her that if she did not have an immediate operation she would probably be an invalid for the rest of her life. On the other hand, they didn't seem very sure as to what the trouble really was and whether the operation could actually cure it. She decided against it.

The company started on its way east again, a little weary of the tour and of itself. In Cleveland the Websters met their new brother-in-law, Tom Wise, and loved him instantly, both as a man and as an actor. It is much easier when the two go together. Playing down through New England in April, the insular English realized with surprise that the miracle of the first daffodils and the first blossom is not confined to old England. The final two weeks in New York were a frenzy of seeing friends, shopping, packing. At last came the closing night and a gracious speech from Irving thanking the audience and the United States in general on behalf of himself and his "merry little band," who by this time could hardly stand the sight of each other. On May 16th they sailed home on the S.S. *Etruria* and slept almost the whole way to Liverpool.

There was a bare week for everyone to catch his breath and then a five-week tour before the summer layoff. May left the company, but Ben and many of the others had signed on for the following season. From Liverpool, where the tour opened, he wrote:

To America and Back

We had quite a merry meeting this morning and for some inexplicable reason everybody seemed most pleased at meeting everybody else again . . . it really was quite a refreshing sight with an unjustifiable ring of sincerity about it. Dear Nell was quite delightful to me and enquired most anxiously about you . . . even H.I. shook hands with me with effusion and added his enquiries to the others.

After some futile consultations with the London doctors, May joined the company in Scotland and saw much of Nell. Once she came to visit the Websters' rooms in Edinburgh, which greatly impressed their landlady. She later asked which chair Miss Terry had sat in, as she would like to keep it sacred forever after. The Websters answered that Miss Terry had sat on the table, the piano, the floor, every chair in the room and a stool on the landing. It seemed as if the place would have to be turned into a museum.

There was a too-brief but glorious interlude—taking the punt upriver for Henley Regatta, Woolacombe, a week with Nell at Winchelsea—and they were back in London for rehearsals of the new Lyceum production, *Cymbeline*.

"Stop the train! stop the train! I'm Ellen Terry's little boy!" This, according to Edy, had been young Teddy's furious reaction to the sight of a train leaving Winchelsea station just as the children arrived there. The Gordon Craig who now rejoined the Lyceum company was not unrecognizably changed. Ellen Terry thought both her children brilliant actors, especially Teddy; he had a good deal of her charm and his own good looks. He and Ben played the two young princes in *Cymbeline*, looking very much alike in blond wigs and a good deal of fur-and-leather forest wear. They spoke together the lovely dirge "Fear no more the heat o' the sun," over the body of Imogen. It was not always easy, for Nell was seldom ready to be carried on, and when Teddy did manage to pick her up would go off into fits of giggles and proclaim, as they laid her tenderly on the green grass-matting, that they were tickling her.

Craig was never noted for his modesty and he was not the most popular actor in the theatre, especially with the "supers." In the battle scene he and Ben had to fight their way, shoulder to shoulder, through serried ranks of embattled walk-ons. One night Ben became aware that he was being prodded from behind with a spear, bashed on the head with an ax, pushed and jostled by the troops at his rear beyond the call of duty. At last he turned around and hissed furiously, "What the hell do you think you're doing?" The army wavered and stopped. "Very sorry, sir," whispered one of them. "We thought you was Mr. Craig."

Cymbeline was the last of Irving's important new productions of Shakespeare, and both stars were at their best. The Terry-Shaw letters give a full and revealing picture of it. Even Shaw, who hated Irving and was at that moment engaged in a fierce quarrel with him, wrote in his review: "Irving's Iachimo was no vulgar bagful of 'points' but a true impersonation, unbroken in its life-current from end to end, varied on the surface with the finest comedy and without a single lapse in the sustained beauty of its execution. It is only after such work that an artist can, with perfect naturalness and dignity, address himself to the audience as their faithful and loving servant."

Ellen Terry's Imogen was wholly enchanting, gay, tender, moving. "And her looks!" my mother wrote, "like a girl of eighteen . . . that beautiful mouth that so easily took on the square lines of the tragic mask . . ." The photographs attest it. Her prompt-copy notes, not nearly as full as those on *Macbeth*, reveal again her search for human truth, the refusal to resort to tricks such as "a Bill-Terriss voice," the emphasis on speed, the practical use of the imagination: "*Try* and remove something from a sleeping person and you'll find your heart beating and fear the noise, you'll feel faint and have to sit down—good business." On the flyleaf is a note headed "*Lesson* (to myself) and Specimens = Emphasis: 'I care for somebody that isn't *worthy* of me, because *nobody* that's *worth* me *cares* for me.'" The improvised sentence is perhaps revealing.

In a letter to Shaw she gives a list of the actors in the cast with a brief comment on each. Against the name of Ben Webster she has put: "Shouts but has a sweet face."

To America and Back

Following *Cymbeline* came a revival of *Richard III*, with Ben, who had not played in it before, as Hastings. It is a good, smallish part, redeemed by one very fine speech just before he is taken off to be executed. Ben thought he was playing this really well. So, apparently, did Irving. At the first dress rehearsal it seemed to strike him suddenly that it was odd for Richard to leave the stage at this particular moment while Hastings made his speech. "No reason for it, eh, Loveday?" "No, Guv'nor." "Mm . . . yes . . . silly, eh?" Irving decided to stay onstage and gloat in a corner. Ben knew then that he was beaten; you couldn't compete with Irving's gloat. But he cherished hopes of his speech all the same.

At the second dress rehearsal, Irving had another idea. "Going to execution, isn't he, to the Tower, hm?" "Yes, Guv'nor." "Better bring on some soldiers, Loveday . . . during the speech . . . about forty would do . . . ready to take him off at the end, y'see, won't waste time. And there'd better be some cannon . . . important fellow, Hastings . . . a salvo of cannon from the Tower . . . cue it as the soldiers come on . . . effective, eh?" Ben wrapped his beautiful scarlet cloak around his splendid, glittering armor, made some harmless lip movements and walked off to be executed. Well might the *Times* report of Irving's Richard: "In the presence of this colossal Plantagenet villain all the other dramatis personae are dwarfed to nothingness."

Ben felt rueful rather than bitter. Irving was ruthless, but he was also dedicated. He had complained, at this same rehearsal, that there was something wrong about the drums—rhythm? vibration?—he couldn't define it. Very late, when it finally finished, Ben was crossing the darkened stage as he left the theatre, and there was Irving, talking to the drummer. He had the drum slung over his shoulder and was staring, fascinated, at the sticks in his hand. "Hold them this way, eh? Ha! Odd. Should have thought it would be the other way round." He tried a few taps—a few rolls. "Like this, eh? Mm . . . no . . . better, eh? Like this . . ." Tall hat on one side, eyelids half shut, happy and intent, he marched up and down the empty stage, drumming to himself among the shadows.

Young Ben and May

Ellen Terry was not in *Richard III*. She was studying for the next play, *Madame Sans-Gêne*, one of the few productions which Irving did for her and not for himself. She had always been notorious for her inability to learn lines, as well as for the generous and impulsive charm with which she would turn to another actor as if she were saying, "The stage is all yours, my dear fellow, do please go on, I'm listening . . ." She decided to go down to Margate to study the part which Réjane had made famous; she asked May to come and help her. Unfortunately, she much preferred to talk, eagerly, inconsequentially, of everything under the sun—except the lines of *Sans-Gêne*. One day as they walked along the beach she said, "Let's do the last act. Oh, no we can't—we haven't got the book." "That doesn't matter," said May, "I can prompt you from memory." "Oh!" said Nell, "how abominable!" and she started to work in earnest.

However, she never did learn the lines. On the opening night there were prompters concealed at every entrance, behind the window curtains and in the fireplace; the moment she paused a volley of mutters and hisses would come from every part of the stage at once. Finally, in complete bewilderment, she stopped dead, clapped her hands together, and said in ringing tones, "Will *nobody* give me the word?" The play was a moderate success, notwithstanding. "It's *not* a good play, is it?" she wrote to May, "and to my amazement I find it is a very hard-working part!!!—but I like the woman—she is so *unusual*—"

She and the Websters were good friends by then—"beautiful, bountiful Benny" she would call my father. There are a score of little notes to my mother, written in that bold, graphic script which is so like herself. "Dear Duchess," one of them begins, "(Ben is *sure* to be made a Duke some day—and he would 'look the part' so well) . . ." An array of different signatures includes "Eleanora Alicia Terry," "Granny Nell" and "Muddle-pated Ellen." From Margate, after May had left, she wrote: "Henry comes down on Sunday and then I'll only stop a few days longer. I see the papers say he and I have 'quarrelled'—the blithering idiots! Aint they clever? It takes two to make a quarrel and *he wont!!* I've tried for 19 years and he just *won't*."

Her letters are full of solicitude: May is to *eat*—to keep her feet up—and "*next* time live on the *ground floor* instead of barely under the roof . . . I've heard nothing further about that *lift*." The liftlessness of the Websters' flat in Bedford Street plagued Ellen Terry herself for twenty-five years, because Edy came to live, equally liftless, in the one underneath it.

The season of 1896–97 was a bad one for Irving. He fell one night, damaging his knee, and could not play for several weeks. The handicap came at a difficult time; expenses were increasing, the Lyceum was just past the height of its triumphs, and he was in mounting financial difficulties. Moreover, he no longer had the virtual monopoly of Shakespeare in London. In the same season, Herbert Beerbohm Tree began his management of His Majesty's Theatre. There was a rival in the field. As an actor he was not in the same world as Irving, and his productions were nothing like as imaginative, but they were lavish and spectacular and enormously popular.

Ben's letters from the autumn tour of 1897 reflect the stresses and strains of the time. Actors seldom realize the problems of the management; they see only their own grievances. Also, an actor-manager, even of Irving's stature, is seldom a hero to his company —or at least not all the time. Grievances began to multiply. A new play was being rehearsed, *Peter the Great*, by young Laurence Irving. Ellen Terry had worked hard to persuade Irving to do it. This was a self-denying ordinance. "I've such a part in the new play!!" she wrote to May. "Ye gods! but what does it matter?"

Irving had imported three American actors, which infuriated the Lyceum company. One was a "red-haired jade" (Ben's phrase) with flaming hair, green eyes and a complexion of milk named Suzanne Sheldon. May showed slight signs of being jealous. The second was Robert Taber, whose part both Ben and Frank Cooper were sure they could have played better; and the third was a tall, thin young woman with a husky voice and enormous eyes, bearing the famous theatre name of Barrymore. She dutifully called Ben (aged thirty-three) "Uncle." She had met him the preceding season, while she was playing in London with William Gillette in *Secret Service*. Laurence Irving had insisted that she should play the ingenue in *Peter the Great;* he had fallen madly in love with her, and no wonder. Ethel Barrymore was greatly fallen-in-love-with.

Neither of the young women had as yet attained any eminence on the American stage, and just why Irving wanted Americans to represent the eighteenth-century nobility of Russia was obscure to his "merry little band." There was much resentment, and mutterings involving the Actors' Association. (Coming Equitys cast their shadows before.) Everyone grew restive and sprouted a crop of complaints. The theatre at Cardiff, where the company had never played before, was "a pestilential den and a death-trap in case of fire"; this time the company did complain to the Actors' Association. At a farewell luncheon, the stars made fulsome speeches expressing their gratitude and desire to return as soon as possible; this disgusted everybody. The journey from Cardiff to Edinburgh took five hours and Nell cheerfully kept the train waiting, both before it started and at intermediate stops, with the same insouciance as she was used to displaying during a scene change.

The following morning Ben wrote that there had been a rehearsal call "for the usual Monday tomfoolery and we found Henry in his usual chatty and convivial humour so left him to his quips and his cranks . . . Miss Sheldon seems to think we ought to be in a state of perpetual enthusiasm over the Lyceum and its stars, which is so silly. Henry bores me, as you know, with his nonsensical fidgeting over nothing." They rehearsed *Peter the Great* interminably, as it seemed to them. ("Henry keeps them at it," wrote Nell.) They were evidently stale and tired, and Irving, far more worried than any of them knew, was at his most pernickety and unreasonable.

May was on tour herself with the provincial company of *Secret Service*, a melodrama of the Civil War, which was a tremendous hit at the Adelphi as played by Jessie Millward and "Breezy Bill" Terriss, the handsome and beloved matinee idol of his day. She was playing in Manchester while the Lyceum company were not far away, in Sheffield. Ben wanted to join her over the weekend. He wrote: "There was a call for the second act today, and as H.I. had dried up twice last night and was hurling directions and maledictions about wholesale to cover his discomfiture, I didn't deem it advisable to ask for leave of absence." Two days later he wrote in evident anxiety about whether he would be able to catch the Saturday-night train: "If dear Nell keeps the curtain down too long, as she generally does, I shall make a cut in my scene and make up time that way—she wouldn't know, and if she did I should say it was her fault, which she would never doubt for a moment, bless her . . ."

He adds a lighter note: "It's so funny—Mellish has been getting receptions in *Sans Gêne*, as I suppose the paraphernalia of the entrance makes them think it must be the boss coming on, and H.I. has been vexed in spirit; so last night orders came for moustachios and whiskers instead of clean-shaven . . . and when Nell turned to greet Mellish, not knowing of the change, she went off into shrieks and could only ejaculate 'Oh lor, Colonel, how you've changed!!' that set the whole lot off, which must have been a bit mysterious to the audience."

Ben shared lodgings with Frank Cooper, with whom Nell had begun a mild flirtation during the American tour. He realized that it was assuming more serious dimensions. Presents would arrive for Cooper, with a card "from an admirer" in that unmistakable handwriting. The landlady would come to tell him that "a lady" was waiting downstairs in a carriage. Nell would "drop in" to look at an oil painting Cooper was doing, or he would announce casually that he was going out after the show "to see a friend." Nell took a childish delight in all this transparent intrigue. But Ben, who loved her, resented the jokes in the company, the sidelong smiles and what he felt to be the cheapening of her stature. "Degrading," he called it.

The morale of the company was not improved, and even Irving grew angry. "She called H.I. 'Frank' the other evening all through some supper till he got perfectly furious." But you could never tell whether she was being mischievous or merely absent-minded. "She's been so funny tonight. She's immensely keen on a fly she saved from drowning in the water-bottle and which she insists follows her about from her sitting-room to her bedroom and has written to Sir John Lubbock about it and means to capture it

tomorrow and take it on to Manchester! But she was very fascinating and most entertaining." In Manchester everybody relaxed a
little, partly because there was more room to lose each other and
partly because the theatre had been newly done up in their honor.
"It's the only advantage of travelling with the Lyceum," Ben
wrote, "that they doss up the dressing-rooms and bring out pails
and scrubbing-brushes that are housed for the rest of the year."

The grievances were, of course, inevitable. They never fail to
arise in a company which has worked together for a long time,
when the glamour has worn off and only the hardships and discomforts remain in the foreground. The basic situation at the Lyceum
was just what it had been in Old Ben's day at Drury Lane and is
reputed to be in the National Theatre in England today. An ambitious young actor joins the company, full of enthusiasm and confidence, and then finds himself playing, season after season, the
same small parts, with the road to advancement blocked by a lot of
frozen priorities among those who joined the company before him.
The stars, if there are stars, can't be on their best behavior all the
time. If there aren't any, the company is apt to lack leadership and
example. Inevitably, in the Lyceum company, the young men with
talent, Alexander, Martin Harvey, Frank Benson—even Gordon
Craig—had to get away. It happened, not many years later, to
Ellen Terry herself.

In December, May's tour of *Secret Service* finished and she
joined Ben at Wolverhampton. Late on the evening of the 17th she
got a telegram. William Terriss had been shot outside the Royal
stage door of the Adelphi; would she come back immediately and
be prepared to play for Miss Millward the following night. Of
course, no telephone yet existed. The telegram did not say whether
Terriss was alive or dead. No one else knew that anything had
happened. She caught a train in the small hours; at a stop just
outside London she got a morning paper. Terriss was dead. The
murderer was Richard Price, a walk-on recently dismissed, who
had a grudge against him. It was incredible that anyone could bear
a grudge against Bill Terriss, who was as generous as the sun.

May arrived in London, left her baggage and went straight on to the theatre. The company were standing silently about the stage. Herbert Waring had been called to play for Terriss, but no one knew what was going to happen or what to do. May and Bertie Waring felt it would be almost indecent to ask if they could please rehearse, in case. May was nagged by the callous thought that if she were going to play that night she would have to do something about her clothes. Time went on. She wandered to the stage door. There were crowds in Maiden Lane, standing and staring. "It's too terrible," she thought. "There's nothing to see."

At this moment a cab drew up. A long, lean figure in a tall hat got out and pushed his way into the theatre. It was Irving. "Heard the news early this morning," he said to her. "Thought I'd better come and see if there was anything I could do."

Later he did a great deal. Victorian etiquette dictated that Miss Millward should not even be present at Terriss's funeral, since, though she had lived with him for many years, they were not married. Irving got in touch with one of his friends at Windsor and secured a telegram of condolence to her from the Queen herself. Armed with this certificate of approbation, he proudly escorted her to the front pew. The run of *Secret Service* was resumed with Waring and May Whitty, but it was a heavyhearted exercise.

The season of 1898 was another bitter one for Irving. *Peter the Great* was not much of a success, *The Medicine Man* an undoubted failure. In February a disastrous fire burned the Lyceum storehouse and destroyed the scenery of forty-four of its finest productions. Various revivals filled out the balance of the season; it was Ben's last with the company, though he played with them again on a few isolated occasions.

The following year, Irving, under great pressure and financial strain, agreed to turn the Lyceum into a limited company, controlled by a syndicate. His actors, those who loved him and those who didn't alike, were appalled to see him asking permission to do this or that, unable to spend money as he wanted, when he wanted, giving reasons and balancing accounts—he, who in his own theatre had been a king.

Young Ben and May

He and Ellen Terry drifted apart. She did not "leave" him, as legend has it, but there were no more parts for her. In 1902 she agreed, with his consent, to play in *The Merry Wives of Windsor* for Tree at His Majesty's. Both her son, who adored Irving, and Bernard Shaw, who adored her, urged her ceaselessly to leave the Lyceum and either go into management for herself and produce Ibsen's *The Vikings* (Craig), or stay out of management and play in *Captain Brassbound's Conversion* (Shaw). She did both, to her great loss.

The Lyceum company went bankrupt. It could no longer sustain the past grandeur of the theatre, and there was now far more competition; no less than fourteen or fifteen London theatres were offering good "legitimate" drama, where there had once been no more than half a dozen. Many of them were in the hands of Irving's young men. He went on tour, he played once at Drury Lane in *Dante*, he toured again. On Wednesday, October 13th, 1905, in Bradford, Henry Irving died.

All over the country flags were flown at half-mast; the pillars of the Lyceum portico were hung with crêpe; every cabby in London tied a black bow onto his whip. The funeral was in Westminster Abbey, crowded to the doors with all the notabilities of the kingdom. The coffin was draped with a pall of real laurel leaves which his friend Eliza Aria had made with her own hands. Ellen Terry wrote of it to May, who was in America: "The hubbub is glorious to me. He would have loved it, and I do for him."

Much has been written about Irving, both at first and second hand. He was the giant actor of his age and he is still the yardstick of greatness in the British theatre. But at the present time we do not really seem to want giants so much as regiments, and so we do not grow them. Irving's mannerisms have been copiously described: the dragging gait, the peculiar vowel sounds—to some, like Gordon Craig, they became a balletic dance, a precious example of pure Chaucerian English; to others they were false and absurd. An actor of 1967 gave a supposed "rendering" of Irving's performance in *A Story of Waterloo;* he had never seen Irving, but he had carefully studied the written accounts. Every external, it seems, was there and absolutely nothing of the informing essence. An elder statesman who saw both of them thought the result impertinent and absurd.

A secondary actor is not always a good judge of the star in whose company he plays; but he does have a particular and unique viewpoint. If he is himself a man of sensibility and truth he may well contribute a valuable opinion once the ardors have subsided and the resentments dwindled within the perspective of time. My father admired Irving hugely, both as an actor and as a man; my mother less so. She had suffered, as all his company did, from the eccentricities and selfishness which grew on him in his late years; she had watched his sardonic cruelty to some wretched bit player who couldn't get the line right. Ben, however, would point out that this same actor had been a pensioner in the company for years, kept in it only because Irving knew him to be penniless and unlikely to get another job. He would concede the withering sarcasms, but he would add: "I remember always the extreme sweetness of his smile. Like all big actors, he had a beautiful smile."

Once, a friend of Irving's had recommended a "deserving" actor who was accordingly given a job. He joined the company on tour, drew his first salary, and instantly disappeared. He turned up again three days later, much the worse for wear. Irving sighed gently. "Dear me!" he said. "Don't know what to do with the poor fellow. Can't act, y'know. D'ye think I might perhaps set him up in a little shop?" If one of his company fell sick, Irving would keep him on salary, pay his doctors' bills, and visit him in the hospital, which often demands more genuine kindness. Sometimes, my father would say, the kindness was not unmixed with foresight. When the city of St. Louis was hit by a hurricane, the first message over the wires, once communication was re-established, was from Irving, offering a contribution to the distress fund. The next time he visited St. Louis its people remembered his prompt generosity.

Some thirty years after the "quips and cranks" and petty tyrannies of the Lyceum had gone by, my father wrote this description of "the Guv'nor":

"A man of extraordinary kindness, wonderful dignity, a strange mixture of the good business man and the bad business man, an astonishing worker and intolerant of anybody who didn't work.

"As a director Irving was very careful, but he did not teach one how to say a line unless he thought one's reading of it wrong. Some have said that his productions were over-elaborate. I never thought that. They were very beautiful and he had an unerring sense of drama; his whole life was wrapped up in the theatre.

"At the Lyceum, Irving was very extravagant—he had, indeed, no sense of money when he was striving for his effects. A big set he once devised involved a wait of twelve minutes in 'striking' and subsequent re-setting. At rehearsal Irving said to the master carpenter: 'You must manage that change in seven minutes, Arnott.'

" 'I'm afraid it can't be done, Mr. Irving.'

" 'Little deaf this morning, Arnott, eh?'

" 'No sir, only it can't be done with the men I've got.'

" 'I didn't ask you how many men you had, Arnott. That change must be done in seven minutes.'

"And something like fifteen extra stage-hands were engaged for that change alone . . .

"One of my last appearances with him was at Sandringham House when he was commanded to play *A Story of Waterloo* before King Edward and the Kaiser. He was on tour at the time, and I had to be borrowed from the Lyric Theatre where I was playing. *Waterloo* had been much in demand at charity matinées; but at this time we hadn't done it for five years.

"Irving arrived from Belfast at about 6 p.m., having travelled by the night boat and the train from Liverpool. I went to his bedroom, where I found him much fatigued after the long journey. I suggested that we should go through the words and he agreed. He missed a cue. 'Your line, Sir Henry,' I said.

" 'Oh, is it?' he answered sleepily. 'What do I say?' I told him. In a few lines the same thing happened.

" 'Look here, my dear fellow,' Irving said, 'you seem to know it better than I do—let's leave it.'

"He knew it perfectly, of course, and that night—in November 1902—he gave, as always, a wonderful performance."

People sometimes ask the silly question: What should we think of Irving nowadays? Mother's answer to this used to be that the mannerisms would certainly have changed in accordance with the change in clothes, in customs and above all in plays; but that they would still be there in one form or another because he was an extremely individual genius. They might even seem more apparent, because acting since his time had been, she thought, progressively tamed, planed, cut down to size. Genius, however, would still be the operative word.

About the acting of Ellen Terry neither my father nor my mother had any such reservations. She would be spontaneous and contemporary, whether she had been born in 1847 or 1897 or 1947. "She spoke her lines," my mother wrote, "with exquisite purity, rhythm and simplicity, not ever trying to make an effect, but getting her effects because she translated her thoughts, which were true and real."

Gordon Craig, who was perhaps the last person in the world to assess Ellen Terry dispassionately, pronounced that "she could play only one part, herself." His picture of the charming scatter-brain, the "great dear", the natural actress who didn't really have to try, who was all magnetism and no brains, has gained credence. Fortunately, her own memoirs and lectures, the Terry-Shaw letters and her annotated prompt books have blown this nonsense to the winds.

My mother would certainly have quarreled violently with the "only one part" theory, except, of course, that the innermost essence of an actor is absorbed into every part he plays. The first time she ever saw Ellen Terry was as Ophelia; she recorded her memory of the Mad Scene: "the tall, slight, graceful figure—the short, fair hair like an aureole—the light, greenish eyes with a strange, heart-breaking, bewildered look . . . Ophelia in clinging, white draperies, her arms full of flowers—I always regret that modern directors have abolished the flowers—made them imaginary—they wouldn't have if they'd seen Ellen Terry." This may sound like a very literal and Victorian point of view. I suspect it may also be what the author would have wanted.

There was also her flaming Lady Macbeth, and her Beatrice, all champagne and dazzle. I saw her play some of it when she was nearly seventy; she still "ran like a lap-wing close to the ground," still miraculously embodied the line: ". . . a star danced, and under that I was born." Which of these parts, my mother would have demanded, was the only one she could play?

She was never able to demonstrate whether she had the range of Bernhardt or Duse because she never had the opportunity of playing a repertoire like theirs, plays written for them or chosen by them for their own fulfillment. Throughout her partnership with Irving, his demands, not hers, predominated. Even she, more generous to him than any of her partisans, confided to my mother that she had never quite forgiven him for not letting her play Rosalind. It was a part which might have been created for her special gifts. During their later years together she was forced to content herself with being "useful".

But their association was actually extraordinarily "useful" to her as well as to him. She was not by nature a director or a manager. Shaw, having continually urged her to leave the Lyceum, had little to offer her when she did. Craig simply harnessed her gift to his own purposes and she was content to have it so; but an expensive failure was the only result. Irving's genius as a director, his ordering of the whole, the steel in him, perfectly complemented her own radiance and the outgoing zest for life which streamed from her. She loved people and they loved her back. But in addition, as her own writings reveal, she was hardworking and hardheaded, an extremely able analyst with a discerning eye, trained by painters and artists to observe and select. Her gifts and his formed a unique combination of talents; it is improbable that it will ever be repeated.

It has been asked many times whether she and Irving were lovers. The speculation is not impertinent in that it asks: Was this part of the phenomenon? It has never been answered conclusively, and probably never will be. Gordon Craig for many years vehemently maintained that they were not, and eventually disgorged some letters of Irving's which can only be read as the letters of a man deeply in love. Edy, on this as on other issues, opposed a public silence to her brother's written views; but in private she maintained quite certainly that the two were lovers in the fullest sense. Society took it for granted; but then society regarded Ellen Terry as a "fallen woman", though it thought her more sinned against than sinning, and loved and forgave her. Nevertheless, even Lewis Carroll, who was devoted to her, would not introduce a young girl to her without the permission of the girl's mother.

By the time my parents joined the Lyceum company, and during the years when they grew to know Ellen Terry well, the earlier ardors had cooled. But they would both have been greatly surprised by the notion there had never been more between her and Irving than good-comradeship and professional association. "Though of course," my mother would have added crisply, "no one was actually under the bed." She herself never had the slightest doubt.

Biographers argue the matter back and forth, according to their bias and the nature of their chief informants. Much depends on the image of Irving, more elusive than that of Ellen Terry and more profound. The Craig-derived image is that of an Olympian creature who—perhaps because of the disaster of his own marriage—became remote, self-sufficient, forging the weapons of his own genius alone. Yet the women in his life, not only Ellen, were warm, vital, merry, loving. It is hard to believe that so great an actor can have been so chilling as a man. Some biographers adduce the Victorian proprieties and Irving's concern for the dignity of the theatrical profession, to support their point of view. They claim an equally frigid, platonic status for Eliza Aria, the dear and close friend of Irving's last years. This has greatly astonished her family who, while devoted to "Aunt Eliza", never thought of her as a platonic type. Her niece, Pamela Frankau, went to see her aunt on the day of Ellen Terry's death and found her in floods of tears; understandable indeed, she thought, on the passing of so old a friend. But her proffered condolences were swept aside. "Oh no, it isn't *that!*" wailed Aunt Eliza, "but she'll get to Irving first!"

Young Ben and May

It will never be surely known, the truth as to whether they were lovers, and of course it doesn't really matter. But the imagination, mine anyway, finds it hard to revitalize the glorious Irving-Terry collaboration as if they were partners in a law firm. Certainly they created magic for others. Surely they must have shared in it.

CHAPTER ELEVEN

———— ⚬⚬⚬ ————

Golden Interlude

31 Bedford Street, Strand, London. To a whole generation of English and American actors that would have been a very familiar address; two generations, in fact, for many of my own contemporaries came to know it equally well and look upon it as home.

It was a remarkable flat to find right in the middle of the theatre district within five minutes of any stage door in the West End. "London has a garden," wrote Clemence Dane, and she meant Covent Garden, of which Bedford Street forms a boundary. The Websters lived there for forty-seven years. I remember it well in the days when there were very few trucks. The noise, which was even then tremendous, was still handmade. But the rhythm of the market hasn't changed very much. Its traffic never wholly subsides, as it used to do, and its rush hours begin earlier. If you are rash enough to leave your car within the purlieus of the market while you go to the theatre and perhaps on to supper, you will find it (if you *can* find it) on your return totally engulfed by trucks and bales and flares and shouting men.

In my youth you could walk quietly home at midnight or so through the echoing colonnades before the rush began; but by three in the morning the market and all the little streets and alleys around it would be jammed with trucks and carts and barrows, all heaped high with cases, baskets, open piles of vegetables and fruit. A little later it grew loud with the shouts of contending buyers and sellers, porters and carriers, owners of great wholesale concerns, little country gardeners come to sell their produce in the city. You could hear the richest cockney in town; and the most vivid wealth of epithet, as a donkey with a barrow moved into the path of a towering truck. The market porters, carrying a dozen round baskets piled on their heads like steeples, wove miraculously among the jostling crowds. There were great splashes of color from the flower stalls, and the pavements were treacherous with spilled potatoes and squashed cabbage leaves.

The aftermath of this activity subsided rapidly during the morning, leaving the neighborhood to the humdrum affairs of adjacent offices; booksellers and publishers predominated. As the market cleared you became aware, once again, of the spacious structure at its core, a colonnaded building, more than a hundred years old; and bounding the market square on the west side, the portico of a little church, St. Paul's, Covent Garden. Once it was famous because Inigo Jones had been commissioned to build it very plainly, like a barn, and said he would make it "the most beautiful barn in England" and probably fulfilled his boast. Now it has attained a far wider notoriety because it is there, taking shelter under the same portico, that Professor Higgins first hears the immortal accents of Eliza Doolittle.

On the other side of the church—it is quite easy to miss—there is an enclosed space of grass and trees. The surrounding houses shield it, and quiet reigns there, even now. I remember it as a deeper quiet. You could hear the birds and the church bells; old men sat dozing on the benches and nurses wheeled their perambulators up the paved central walk, decorously, over the worn gravestones. The nannies have vanished now, but it is otherwise little changed. There are iron gates on the far side, between the enclosing buildings, and a smaller paved yard leads through into Bedford Street.

Number 31 runs the length of this smaller yard, a Victorian

building of red brick under its coating of London grime. The top flat had the charm of spacious, low-ceilinged rooms and dormer windows, deeply recessed, looking out over chimney pots and trees and the churchyard. When the Websters first decided to take the flat their friends and relatives were horrified—eighty-four steps to reach this attic! May said she preferred attics to basements and that if people wanted to come and see them, they'd come. They did.

It wasn't till after the American tour that she and Ben were really able to settle down; one or the other of them had always seemed to be away on tour. But they had already installed the guardian spirit of their home. Her name was Frances; she had been a chambermaid at the Woolacombe Hotel; they had met her on their honeymoon. When asked if she would like to come and work in London she said that she might try. She was obstinate, unimpressible, faithful, almost literally unto death. Occasionally she would decide to leave, and leave she did. Presently, however, she would decide to come back again, ruthlessly displacing her successor.

In a series of different capacities, including that of despot, she stayed in Bedford Street until 1940, when it was declared unsafe after one of the bombings. Taking her huge cat with her—she always had huge cats, which ate their enormous way through the rationing of two world wars—she left for the supposedly safer territory of Brixton. A week later she died.

When May and Ben came back from the United States they installed electric light, a small fox terrier named Tuff and a second maid. This last sounds to us as if it indicated great wealth and almost unimaginable good fortune. It didn't; in the Nineties you had a cook and a housemaid as a matter of course. You could even pick and choose. No wonder May afterward thought of it as the golden age. But for her it really was a flowering of happiness, of friendships, of security and fulfillment. For Ben the years brought work, varied and sufficiently satisfying. For May they were clouded by illness and pain, migraine headaches that immobilized her for days together, fruitless visits to doctors, useless and expensive "cures". She could still work, and was always better when she was working. But the tide of managerial favor had receded, just as she had feared it would, leaving her stranded in one of those backwaters that are the despair of every actor. She hated not working.

But later, in recollection, it didn't seem to matter. She wrote: "There were so many compensations, friendships of dear people who have made so much of my life, whose kindness, and the joy and fun of them, are happy memories." The gatherings which later made Bedford Street so well known began with decorous formality. May wrote of it later with some astonishment: "We used to give 'little dinners' for 12 or 14 people which fill me with wonder now. How did we? A dinner meant hors d'oeuvres, soup, fish, entree, joint or 'bird', sweet, savories, dessert. Even then we weren't as formal as was the custom; sometimes greatly daring, I would leave out the joint. I find a menu for one of our 'little suppers'—soup, fillets of sole mushroom sauce, kidneys on toast, hot ham port wine sauce, corn fritters, new potatoes, lemon soufflé, coffee." The circle of friends grew, especially with the growing contingent of Americans who would signalize their approach by peremptory cables: "Arrive Saturday have party."

The suppers became less formal but more frequent; people would drift in after the theatre for cold meat and salads, fruit and cheese, beer, wine—even whisky, at three shillings and sixpence a bottle. Suzanne Sheldon grew worried, on the Websters' behalf, about all this expense. "Well," she decided, "I wouldn't give them butter."

Curiously, it was Suzanne, and Ethel Barrymore, so coolly received by the Irving company, who became the centrifugal force of "the gang". They took a flat across the street, over Heinemann's publishing office, and made of it the Left Bank of Bedford Street. Suzanne had a spirit which flamed no less ardently than her hair. Her sympathies were warm and wide, her partisanship intense, her feeling for drama unquenchable, her regard for the conventions nonexistent. And "Ethel at eighteen—eager young face and beautiful line of jaw . . . her hair blond cendrée, swept back in wings . . . low, throaty voice and gurgling laugh . . ." so my mother remembered her.

The Left Bank gloried in a theatrical poverty. At one time its inhabitants possessed only a single evening dress between them. By the addition of a lace neckpiece and undersleeves it could be made equally resplendent in the afternoon. Ethel complained bitterly that Suzie would go out in it to a tea party and return too late for her to use it in the evening. Suzanne would retaliate by accusing Ethel of monopolizing the only pair of long kid gloves. She would also tell mischievous stories about the romantic heroine of the hour: how she had woken in the middle of the night, flung her arms to heaven in a gesture of despair, cried out in her famous contralto: "God! How bored I am!" and instantly gone off to sleep again.

Ethel acquired, without trying, brilliant young men who adored her, from Laurence Irving and Gerald du Maurier to Winston Churchill, who called her "my harp with the golden sling." Gerald was playing at the Court Theatre in *Trelawny of the Wells*. So, also, was Sam Sothern, younger brother of the famous American actor E. H. "The gang" could never quite make up their minds whether Sam's vague and solemn innocence was a mask for guile or just vague and solemn innocence; but he became a charter member.

Justin McCarthy came back, with his wife, Cissie Loftus: "a wonder-child, fresh from a convent, who had set the little world of London on fire by her impersonations and imitations of great actors and singers. A little, simple figure in a white dress, dark hair hanging to her waist, she would advance very shyly to the footlights and say softly: 'Ladies and gentlemen, if you'll allow me, I would like to give a few imitations . . .'" and, in a moment, the electrifying voice of Bernhardt would come ringing forth in all its splendor, or Yvette Guilbert or Ethel Barrymore, or Mrs. Pat, or even a great operatic tenor such as Caruso. "Imitations" have gone out, with vaudeville and the music halls; they once caused a great deal of innocent merriment, and evoked, as in the case of Cecilia Loftus, really remarkable talent.

There were American actors, such as William Faversham and his wife, Julie, and writers, such as Harrison Rhodes and Richard Harding Davis, who collected wars as lesser men collect butterflies and was always off to cover something in Constantinople or Ecua-

dor. There was Peter Dunne, "Mr. Dooley", who had cried out
delightedly on first talking to May, "Why, you're a Mick!" and
remained her friend forever. There were English writers and playwrights, the two young Irvings and H. V. Esmond and, most loved
of all, the author of the best-selling *Prisoner of Zenda*, Anthony
Hope Hawkins. Anthony believed profoundly in the art of conversation; he would irradiate it with his dry, ironic wit and give it
substance from a mind stored with knowledge. But May loved
him best for the lonely evenings when Ben was at the theatre and
she lay on the sofa, tormented by pain, while he talked gently
". . . of many things: of shoes—and ships—and sealing-wax—of
cabbages—and kings—" till she forgot the pain, or slept.

Others came and went as honorary members of the Bedford
Street "club". Rivalries were intense, hearts would be broken and
mended again, romances—marriages even—would blossom and
then change with startling rapidity. May was forever breaking
something to somebody or proffering a sympathetic shoulder to be
cried on. She spent several hours with Gerald, explaining, as
instructed, just why Ethel couldn't really marry him after all;
Gerald strode around the room, beating his forehead and calling
upon God, while Ben and Cissie, back from the theatre, kept
coughing discreetly outside the door to indicate that they wanted to
come in and have supper. A week or so later Ethel informed May
blandly that she was going off to Ireland with the Esmonds—and
Gerald.

Somehow, despite all the emotional entanglements, the solidar-
ity of "the gang" was never broken. "We prided ourselves," said
May, "on a sense of humour. I defined it as 'an ironical appreciation of the weaknesses of others; if well developed, of one's own.' "

The circle enlarged with the years, as its members made new
contacts and drew in other friends. Ben played with Marie Tempest in her first straight play, *English Nell*. He began by reporting
cautiously that he thought she might be a "flirt"; she had sent him
sandwiches, via the callboy, at rehearsal. Perhaps May remembered that he had once confessed to being "mashed on Marie
Tempest in *Dorothy*." At all events she welcomed "Mary" into the
circle with the very greatest warmth. Ben played later in *Mice and*

Men, which ran a year, with Johnston Forbes-Robertson; he and his wife and her sister, Maxine Elliott, were added to the membership. Gretchen's husband, Tom Wise, came over to play in London, and brought his leading lady, Constance Collier.

Occasionally Ethel would introduce, more formally, one of her illustrious relatives, Maurice Barrymore or John Drew; and one summer she left behind her in England her young brother, Jack, to "finish his education." The fraternity found it hard to understand what further education was supposed to be acquired by a youth whose extensive knowledge of life left them gasping. But May rather nervously accepted the guardianship of the pocket-money which Ethel left to be doled out to him at suitable intervals. He became, in consequence, a frequent caller. He would sit for hours, rising from time to time to announce "I must e'en fly," and then sitting down again.

Once May received from Ethel the usual form of cable—"arrive such-and-such date have party"—and Jack insisted on going to Southampton to meet the boat. But when the rest of her friends gathered at Waterloo Station to welcome her, her first inquiry was for Jack. He had never turned up at Southampton at all. Two days later he appeared, slightly disheveled, and explained that he had, indeed, got as far as the dock, but there he had "met some sailors," who had invited him to play billiards with them. The intervening period was, by tacit consent, left wrapped in mystery.

Suzanne brought her bridegroom, Henry Ainley, the matinee idol of *Paolo and Francesca*, the most beautiful young man in London. Harry came back to Bedford Street all his life, long after Suzanne was dead and many of the others were scattered and gone. Within a few years of his own death he wrote to May: " 'How far that little candle throws his beams . . .' Your window, Mayden darling, is a lighthouse to your friends, the Beacon that leads to your hospitality, a privilege beyond the winning of ordinary spurs and laurels . . . My love and gratitude . . ."

In the summer one or other of the fraternity always took a cottage on the River Thames, somewhere between Maidenhead and Henley, and everyone would visit there or commute by train and bicycle or pony cart. The newcomers learned the art of punting, which isn't as easy as it looks; almost all of them fell in at least once, usually by clinging too long to the top of the pole while the boat shot forward without them. Jack Barrymore performed a heroic rescue, when a lady of the party overbalanced in this way, by diving, with dauntless courage, into fully three feet of water. She walked ashore heartlessly and laughed at him. Punts, indeed, seemed adverse to him. Once, in a secluded pool, he left all his clothes with Sam Sothern in the boat while he went swimming. Sam absent-mindedly drifted off to fish and forgot to come back. Jack walked home through Cookham village quite unperturbed, which was more than could be said of the village.

For the ladies, a costume of white serge skirt and white "shirtwaist" was mandatory; a straw "boater" hat was the prescribed headgear, except for the gala event of the season, Henley Regatta, when muslin hats and dresses were worn. The first time May fell in she discovered that though the straw hat was a fine, independent sailor, the serge skirt was ill-adapted to swimming. The bicycling skirt was allowed to be a little shorter; under it, indeed, could be concealed a modest but determined pair of knickerbockers. Locomotion, as well as dress, was beginning to change. Harry Esmond actually acquired an automobile and would come puffing precariously across Maidenhead Thicket, with Eva perched up beside him on the cylindrical tank that held the gasoline, looking, someone said, as if she were "sitting on a stove."

They learned to know and love all the reaches of the winding, quiet river, the windy stretch by Bourne End and the deep one above Marlowe. They knew each lock, where the little boats paddled in while the lock was empty, its dripping, slime-covered walls towering high above them, and waited till the gates were shut and the water rushed through the sluices and lifted them to towpath level once more. They knew the tree-covered slopes which enfold the river, Quarry Woods and Cliveden. One summer Melba took a house there, near the water's edge; sometimes, in the evening, they could hear her singing, and the river craft would glide in under the overhanging branches, clustering silently to listen, as the golden

Golden Interlude

notes soared into the air. Most of all they loved the backwater at Cookham, where the willows trailed their pointed leaves in the water. Sam Sothern had a picture-postcard cottage there, complete with oak beams and climbing roses, and filled to much more than its capacity with "the gang". Ethel would come down from London by the late train, still in the gala satin she had worn for a supper party. Tom Wise was introduced to the English countryside and was more amazed by the pint-size railway than by anything else he saw. They took him up to Henley Regatta and punted home again through the night. Tom slept peacefully most of the way, waking once when the boat was at the bottom of Marlowe lock; he blinked up in astonishment at the lock keeper, standing in the dark sky high above his head, waved "hulloh" in affable bewilderment, and slept again. They got home at dawn; the men's shoulders ached from punting, the women's muslin hats dripped with dew like sodden rags, the birds shouted an accolade; everyone was blissfully happy.

Looking back, May sometimes wondered why the pattern of those years, the close of the old century and the beginning of the new, seemed so serene and anchored. Anthony Hope remarked, many years later, that people seemed to think of the Nineties as being "all Oscar Wilde or all Queen Victoria," adding justly that "they were not all of either of these remarkable personages." There were turbulent winds of change, not least in the world of the arts. For a time everything was "new": the New Drama, the New Realism, the New Humor, and of course the New Woman.

At the beginning of the decade theatrical newness consisted in being daring about fallen women like Paula Tanqueray, and timid in almost every other direction. But the newness of the middle Nineteen Hundreds meant attacking slum landlords, speaking openly of venereal disease, questioning the sanctity of marriage. In 1895 Wilde was convicted; in 1905 Granville Barker began producing the "social" plays of George Bernard Shaw. The early Nineties shone with a cluster of lyric poets like Richard Le Gallienne; the laureate of 1905 was Rudyard Kipling. The songs people sang were no longer the *Geisha* ditties and "Ta-ra-ra Boom-de-ay," but the patriotic Tommy Atkins ballads of the Boer

Young Ben and May

War. The suffragettes arrived, and the telephone and the Tuppenny Tube. In 1897 came the flaring pageantry of Queen Victoria's Diamond Jubilee, with everyone waving flags and cheering and feeling splendidly unconquerable. Four years later she died.

Ben's first reaction to this event was one of extreme annoyance, because all the theatres had to be closed and *English Nell* received its death blow. May was inconsequentially amazed at the swift adaptability of women. She lunched with Marie Tempest on the very morning of the Queen's death. Every member of the party had already managed to clothe herself in solid black, hat, veil, gloves, stockings and every last accessory. She herself had hurriedly adapted an evening dress and felt rather self-conscious about the neckline.

The pageantry of the funeral almost equaled that of the Jubilee. Here were the troops once more, in their scarlet and gold, the drums (muffled this time) and trumpets, the horses and carriages, the foreign kings, the glittering Indian princes. Here were the crowds, not cheering now, but silent, dense, impenetrable. Ben and May went to view the procession from the house of a friend; but when they emerged from the Underground station, not fifty yards away, the crowd was completely solid. Inch by inch they forged their way through, May clinging to the belt of a helpful policeman, Ben behind with his arms around her waist. At the porch steps the crowd absolutely refused to make way for them. "Why didn't you sleep here?" someone yelled. "Because I wasn't asked," May gasped back. The crowd roared with laughter, parted and let them through.

It wasn't the End of an Epoch, though the journalists never stopped saying so; the old one had finished, or the new one begun, long before. The cataclysmic Twentieth Century was already on its way. The dismal and senseless little Boer War had still to be finished, and that, everyone thought, would be the last of the wars. No one, they said, could be so silly as to fight another. There would be golden years of peace to come. So there were; but not very many of them.

CHAPTER TWELVE

Brave New Theatre

As the brave new century came in there still seemed to be a good deal of old fustian about the theatre. Despite the avant-garde, Shaw and Ibsen, the popular plays were *Monsieur Beaucaire*, in which Lewis Waller entranced all female hearts, revivals of *David Garrick*, with Charles Wyndham, and *Paolo and Francesca*, whose author, Stephen Phillips, was hailed as the greatest dramatic poet since Shakespeare. Costume plays were still in the ascendant and the techniques of play production remained much as ever.

Ben's letters about *English Nell* reveal a haphazard rehearsal scheme which was quite typical. Plays were seldom read to the actors, who were never given a script, merely their own parts, or "sides". This practice had been routine since Shakespeare's day and remained so until the Second World War. The sides contained only the stage directions that directly affected the character, the lines he or she actually spoke, and the last three or four words of the cue line—sometimes only one word—preceded by a row of dots, thus:

I love you, my darling, and shall love you till I die.
. . . .*very much.*
Ah! (*he shoots himself*)

In American scripts the stage direction would be couched in the second person: "(you shoot yourself)." Actors tended to judge a part by the number of its sides. Hamlet, for instance, was well over a hundred; Lady Macbeth, on the other hand, was exactly twelve, so this wasn't a very reliable yardstick. But they hadn't any other. It is not surprising that they were not very good judges. They seldom are, even now, but for different reasons.

Ben wrote of *English Nell:* "Rehearsal was not particularly inspiring. Cartwright is good, I think, but expects you to do everything at once. He was a little grieved that I was smiling at one moment in the middle of Miss Tempest's speeches, since it appeared that she was about to continue, 'Why so glum?' I glummed with lightning rapidity . . . Also he didn't explain the scene at all, or what various chairs and stools represented, and I found, after plucking some flowers, as per the stage direction, that I had really uprooted an old sundial and the porch of the vicar's house."

Ben added that Marie Tempest was very nervous of this, her first "legitimate" part, and that sometimes her Nell Gwynne became startlingly modern. "I felt that at any moment she might give vent to a couplet such as 'And now that mention has been made of France, I think we ought to have a song and dance.' " This was the comedienne who became the embodiment, in the English-speaking theatre, of chic and precision (the precision of a machine gun, I used to think) and a disciplined playing of comedy that was almost unique. She looked like the most fragile, Dresden-china, French marquise; she was really a captain of Storm Troopers. I have read about eyes "snapping". Marie Tempest's actually did; you could hear them from the balcony. I am, of course, unfair to her; she had thousands of admirers and many adorers; and I think I admire her much more now, when technical accomplishment has ceased to be a bore and become a precious rarity.

In the Nineteen Hundreds the membership or "club" societies began to come into their own, replacing the special matinees and Crystal Palace picnics of earlier years. Being immune from the Lord Chamberlain's censorship of publicly performed plays, they could, and did, present the avant-garde. J. T. Grein and his Independent Theatre, with other similar organizations, had almost inured theatregoers to Ibsen; he was no longer regarded as "the Master-Bewilderer". Shaw, though not yet a "commercial" dramatist, had contrived to entertain some people and affront many more.

In Ireland there was already a new stirring. George Moore, Edward Martyn and W. B. Yeats decided that Dublin needed a theatre of its own and playwrights who were Irish, not English importations. In 1899 they hired Dublin's Ancient Concert Rooms for the inaugural productions, Martyn's *The Heather Field* and Yeats's beautiful Irish myth *The Countess Cathleen*. Everyone approached the venture with towering enthusiasm and the innocence of newborn babes.

The actors had to be recruited in London, since there were as yet no resident Irish ones. The responsibility of finding and rehearsing them was at first left to Yeats. The poet, however, did little but wander vaguely about in a long, black cloak, accompanied by a drifting lady in a long, green one; he would discourse on the value of quarter tones in verse-speaking while she plucked at a psaltery throughout the "recitations", muttering, "Cover it up with a lonely tune." The lady's niece, aged fifteen, was to act, or rather recite, the long and difficult part of the Countess.

A week before the opening George Moore felt impelled to intervene. From his ivory tower in Notting Hill he dashed to Bedford Street at top hansom-cab speed. He arrived at the summit of the eighty-four steps breathless but resolute. He rushed May down the stairs and into the hansom cab before he even started to explain. By the time they reached the rehearsal rooms, she found she had agreed to act in both plays and to get Ben to help stage them. There was some difficulty at first in dislodging the lady in the green cloak; she insisted on lying flat on the ground and murmuring into the floor boards to show the new Countess how to invoke the powers of hell in verse. But eventually George Moore had his will; Yeats departed, flapping his cloak in a melancholy way, and the green lady left the field to Ben.

The transformed company arrived in Dublin, but without Ben, who was playing in London. They found the whole city in an uproar because of the supposedly anti-Catholic nature of the Yeats play; there were rumors that the hall would be wrecked and the

actors lynched at the first performance. May was further troubled
by a dreadful cough, which made the speaking of verse in quarter
or any other tones almost impossible. When the curtain rose,
everyone's worst fears were realized; a large section of the audience were determined that the play should not be heard; they kept
up a steady, rhythmic stamping to drown it out. The actors faltered, then steadied, then grew both angry and determined. They
played with their souls, pitting themselves against the hostility in
the house. Gradually the stamping slackened, stopped; complete
silence reigned for the rest of the play. But for the last ten minutes
May had to lie "dead" on a bier in the center of the stage; and then
her cough became unendurable. She grew scarlet in the face with
the effort to suppress it; she thought she would really die. She was
on the point of shattering all illusion and wrecking the play, when
the actress who was playing Oona realized what was happening.
With a great cry of grief, she flung herself over the Countess's
dead body, and May burst into a rapture of coughing beneath her
outspread cloak. The curtain fell to roaring applause.

The rest of the week was a triumphant round of festivity.
George Moore or Max Beerbohm would take May to lunch or
supper, joined by all the rank and fashion of the town. Dublin was
as wildly enthusiastic as it had been furiously inimical. The great
renaissance of the Irish theatre had begun. Yeats and Lady Gregory carried it on from this point to found the Abbey Theatre.

Ben encountered both the old and new currents in the theatre.
With Forbes-Robertson he played Cassio and Laertes. In 1903 he
appeared as Cashel Byron in Shaw's blank-verse farce *The Admirable Bashville*. It was only for a special matinee and meant the
usual disproportionate amount of work. But there were two wonderful actresses in the cast, Fanny Brough and Henrietta Watson,
and Ben was vastly impressed by the author. Directing farce is
no job for an amateur; but Shaw seemed to know just as much
about it as the old pros. He had an inexhaustible fund of invention,
and his sense of timing was flawless.

The following year, Somerset Maugham's first play was produced, *A Man of Honour*. Ben was enormously interested by the
challenge it presented. He realized that the dialogue demanded a

new kind of technical approach and that the characters were not at all the two-dimensional creatures he had so often encountered. He made a success and was, he reported, "a little lionised"; but he wasn't satisfied with himself. Sister Booey, formidable as ever, came with her second husband, A. E. George, also an actor, and a good one. She was thus able to reinforce her usual censorious note with a plural pronoun. "Of course," she said, "we agreed that there is something costumey about you." Ben recognized that, as was so often the case, she had hammered the poor little nail on its wretched, flattened head.

Nevertheless, he was trying; and when he went into the costume play which was his next engagement, he felt the difference acutely. This may have been sharpened by the fact that he found himself wearing the splendid Highland uniform that had originally been designed for Kendal in *Clancarty*—"funny," he wrote, "wearing the garments of my manager of sixteen years ago! . . . It's such a leap from the realism and humanity of *A Man of Honour* to this inhuman drivel with its inverted sentences to represent period—'To my mother's house I dared not go!' is a specimen —it makes me feel like an amateur."

The next costume he wore was briefer, the lines longer, the whole experiment a unique blend of ancient and modern. A young and largely unknown producer was doing some matinees at the Lyric Theatre of Euripides' *Hippolytus* in a new translation by Gilbert Murray. The Murray versions shortly afterward turned Euripides into a fashionable contemporary dramatist, and Granville Barker became the prophet of the new theatre age; both, in this earliest production, were innovators. Ben was ideally cast as Hippolytus; but he was worried, as always, by a feeling of his own inadequacy. He got claustrophobia from rehearsing behind the lowered iron safety curtain, "while workmen on the theatre roof pelt you with wood, plaster and nails," and he was haunted by the perpetual fear, in the cramped conditions, "of falling over a Chorus . . . They are inclined to be, like the steeds of Hippolytus, a little out of control—but I trust they will not gash or wreck our efforts when the day comes." He worked very hard and was a little encouraged; at last he reported that he himself had "no serious complaints" of his own performance, that Murray and Barker and the audience all seemed very pleased with it and that even the much-feared critic William Archer had been complimentary, "tho' not carried away, you understand." I judge that it was actually one of the finest and most moving performances he ever gave. Afterwards he felt tired and dispirited. Virtue had gone out of him. All good actors have felt like this; it is an emptied, lonely sensation after the effort, the stimulus and the achievement.

On Christmas Day, 1903, May's first child, a son, was born and died, owing to the reluctance of a London doctor to be torn away from his family festivities and the incompetence of an inexperienced nurse. May was warned that she should have no more children; but the following summer she discovered that she was going to. It was the worst possible moment, since she was playing the maidenly Miss Susan in *Quality Street* and the costumes of the period do not easily disguise pregnancy. Ben was terrified on her behalf and everything possible was done to discourage the impending child. Nothing had the slightest effect. In January 1905 Ben had an offer to go to America with Ellis Jeffreys in *The Prince Consort*. It was a good part; appropriate too, Ben thought, since in the last act he had to receive news of the birth of his son. "To go or not to go" became once more the question. Once more they decided to go. The day before they sailed, Peter Dunne and his wife arrived in London and generously offered the loan of their New York apartment on the south side of Central Park. The Websters accepted happily.

It was a wretched voyage and they were thankful to see the New York skyline again, now many buildings taller than before, the tip of the island thick with towers. Tom and Gretchen were there to meet them, and also Michael Whitty with the small son whom May had never seen. Michael had discovered that sheep farming in Australia was by no means a paradise; he had come to America, where he took up chicken farming with equal enthusiasm and just as little success.

Brave New Theatre

New York no longer seemed a strange city to Ben and May, despite the transformations of the past ten years. The elevated railroads had appeared; Broadway was much Greater and Whiter than the Way they had known, the theatre district was moving rapidly uptown, and the theatre-building boom had begun. The playbills seemed very familiar; a play of Harry Esmond's was being done, Forbes-Robertson was due to open shortly, Marie Tempest soon after. It was a brilliant season: Mrs. Fiske as Leah Kleschna, Arnold Daly in *You Never Can Tell*, Maude Adams in *The Little Minister*, Ethel Barrymore in some special matinees of *A Doll's House*.

The Prince Consort was a hit, and so was Ben; "the handsomest actor England has sent us for years," said the *Stage*. "If he does not become the hero of the year . . . our eyes have lost their shrewdness." May felt better; the child was not due till mid-April, and meanwhile she saw much of her friends. One night in March she went to see Forbes-Robertson as Hamlet and on to supper at Delmonico's. The following day it became apparent that the child had decided not to wait any longer. There was a terrifying repetition of the previous routine: the doctor had gone out of town on a case, the nurse was young and very frightened. Suzanne's mother, Mrs. Sheldon, arrived full of knowledge and comfort and confidence. Ben, at last, had to leave for the theatre, ineffectual and anguished. During the last scene, the actor who had to announce the birth of the Prince Consort's child made it clear that he was doing just that. "The only thing is, Sir," he added, grinning, "I'm afraid tonight it's a girl."

They vacillated between the names of Elizabeth and Patricia, the latter due to the Wexford Whittys and the imminence of St. Patrick's Day. In the end they decided to christen the infant Margaret and call it Peggy. A newspaper reporter later recorded: "Margaret Webster was born in New York City while her mother was touring the United States."

An elderly Irish nurse named Mrs. Beck ("disguised," May said, "as Queen Victoria") was acquired, and apparently adored by the baby. Ben and May felt that their troubles were over. They had barely begun. The medical warnings were justified. May became so seriously ill that the postponed operation had to be performed immediately. In the home-surgery manner of the times, it was done at the apartment; and when May was scarcely out of the ether, Ben received a cable from the Peter Dunnes saying that they were on their way home and would be glad if they could return to their apartment when they arrived.

Ben was frantic. The play was closing in New York and he had to go on tour with it. He did not dare tell May the news, for she was still dangerously ill. He spent long hours searching for a place in which he could safely install an invalid, a baby and a nurse for each of them; May complained weakly that he never seemed to be at home. Friends joined in the vain hunt for an apartment, but he had to leave for Philadelphia with everything still unsettled. In the end Cissie Loftus offered her own rooms at the Ansonia, Ethel Barrymore arrived with a full complement of equipment for kitchen and nursery and Will Faversham appointed himself mover-in-chief. Under the benign influence of these theatrical stars the baby throve and the mother grew slowly better.

Even this was not the end of Ben's troubles. The tour moved on to Washington; two days after it opened there the National Theatre was condemned as unsafe, owing to some building operations next door, and the company was closed down without salary till the Boston opening two weeks later. Ben protested furiously, but the American actors seemed to think it quite in order. They had hardly reopened in Boston when he read in his morning paper that the bank in which all the Webster savings were invested had "closed its doors." All these tragedies were as nothing to the fact that the Irish Queen Victoria decided to leave and her inconsolable charge screamed without stopping from grief and rage.

The morning after the bank failure arrived a shoal of letters from the Websters' friends containing blank checks for their use. The checks never had to be used, for another bank offered to take over the deposits. The Irish Queen consented to return to her post; and when the hot weather came, the Dunnes rescued the whole family and took them off to Long Island. But the baby had not yet exhausted her capacity for being difficult. She became alarmingly ill and could take no nourishment of any kind until someone discovered a patent food called Imperial Granum. Peter Dunne, parodying Hamlet, remarked:

> *Imperial Granum, cook'd and turned to whey,*
> *Might feed a babe and keep the wind away.*

In subsequent bouts with the play of *Hamlet*, whenever "Imperious Caesar" comes along, the babe in question thinks gratefully of the patent food.

In the fall the Websters moved back to New York. Ben started rehearsing with William Brady and Grace George for a play based on the life of Byron, called *The Marriage of William Asche.* The Favershams returned from their English summer home at Chiddingfold ("much joy," wrote May), he to play in *The Squaw Man*, one of his greatest successes, and she to produce her first son, Billy. This infant was one day to become the discoverer and manager of champion heavyweight and Black Muslim Cassius Clay. William might have been proud of this, I fancy; what Julie would have thought I dare not guess.

The New York theatre was again having a brilliant season. English actors never quite got used to the fact that the power lay in the hands of the great impresarios, Belasco and the Frohman brothers, rather than with the actor stars. But England had never, as yet, evolved their counterpart, because the problems were simpler and could be dealt with by an actor-manager working almost entirely in London. In America the importance of "the road" made this impossible. New York was still only one city among others, not the be-all and end-all of a play's existence. Nevertheless, the Broadway boom was beginning. Theatres were multiplying. Belasco and the Frohmans mustered all the talents of the American stage. The hit of the season was *The Girl of the Golden West.* Belasco's second-act blizzard was a sensation, "needing the services of thirty-two trained artizans, a kind of mechanical orchestra."

The Brady–Grace George play opened in Philadelphia for its tryout weeks, and Ben began to learn several theatrical customs

which had not yet reached England. One was "rewriting the play",
an exercise which survived and was brought to the peak of perfection many years later by the Theatre Guild. Under the rules of this
game, the author's script is treated as if it were a very tame bull in
the tryout bull ring, where everyone is welcome to enlist as picador
or matador and no weapons are barred. The laurels of victory go to
him who can ultimately stab the poor, bleeding creature to the
heart. The routine of cutting, transposing, inserting, altering and
rewriting was already flourishing in 1905. Ben wrote in some
bewilderment from Philadelphia: "We went on rehearsing till
after 6 p.m.; Tuesday, the new Fourth Act; Wednesday the same,
and tonight more cuts . . . and the scene with 'Kitty', composed of
a bit of the original Fourth Act, a portion of the new one and three
or four speeches which I had never seen before. It's rather exhausting." On Friday he asked Grace George which version she intended to play; she replied, wearily, "Whichever I can remember
when I get to it." Some extraordinary dramatic masterpieces
might be evolved from the fragments of plays discarded in Boston,
New Haven and Philadelphia.

Ben wrote, too, of struggles with mechanical problems. Various members of the cast were required to enter or exit, visibly, in
gondolas. These vehicles either rumbled thunderously over the
Venetian canal, protesting with every wheel, or got stuck in the
middle of the stage in the approved manner of Lohengrin's Swan.
The wretched gondolier would sweat and strain to get his craft on
the move again; the audience would watch him, absorbed, while
Brady would dance up and down in the wings shouting furiously,
"Stop it! Lie down . . . ! DIE!"

In New York the play lasted only a month, which was then
considered quite a respectable run. Road booking was where the
money lay. This was still in the all-powerful hands of the Klaw
and Erlanger syndicate. At this time an average of over three
hundred companies went on the road every year; by the late
Twenties it had shrunk to sixty-eight. Now I suppose that six or
eight might be an overstatement. For the great road-booking rivalry had begun; the challengers were the three boys from Syra-
cuse, Sam, Lee and Jake Shubert. They declared war on the

syndicate; they built more theatres; there was competitive bidding for every attraction; there was a great boom; and twenty years later, a great bust.

May decided to travel with Ben when his play set out on tour, and for nearly four months, except for three weeks in Chicago, they played the Middle West and the South, mostly on split weeks or one-night stands. They visited smaller towns than the Irving caravanserai had ever reached. "Cincinnati, Springfield, Hamilton, Fort Wayne, Rockford, Janesville, Madison," runs a stretch in January. Duluth, Mankato, Sioux City, Omaha, St. Joseph, Lincoln, Des Moines, Clinton, Davenport, a similar fortnight during February. March took them to towns of much the same size in the South, where the theatres had not noticeably improved since the Irving tour.

At one particularly derelict house they found these words painted on the back of the asbestos curtain: "We know the theatre's terrible. How's the show?" There was the classic gag about arriving actors who invariably remarked: "What a godawful theatre! Where's the mail?" and its companion piece about the notice underneath the mailboxes which said: "After you've read your mail please tear it up and throw it on the floor. We have nothing to do but pick it up."

In Chattanooga there had been a lynching the day before they arrived and there were rumors that the theatre would be blown up that night. All the liquor stores were closed, all the hardware stores crammed with men buying guns, the box office besieged by a crowd of people returning their tickets, no stagehands to be found. The company got the scenery in place and the curtain up by ten p.m. There were a dozen people in the house and two or three backstage. Suddenly a revolver shot was heard, and everybody left. The actors got the scenery down again and walked back to their hotel through pitch-dark streets in solid formation. The next morning they entrained thankfully for the next town.

They did other plays besides *William Asche*. One of them was about Indians. Ben, who didn't think he looked much like an Indian, went to his dressing room to try on the costume, and found that it consisted of a string of beads. Since the rehearsals had been a little inadequate, May helped by concealing herself inside a wigwam and prompting. They loved the Bradys, though neither was looked upon as the easiest of colleagues. He was an extremely vital director, with an explosive, Irish temper which never concealed his warmth and kindness; she, a comedienne a little on the Marie Tempest line—they were always being bracketed and both of them detested it—but with more humanity. They remained good friends to the Websters.

Passing through New York again in the early summer, Ben and May picked up their baby, now hopelessly spoiled by its Aunt Gretchen, and took it to Boston with them. There, I am told, I learned to say "Bem" and "Peppebby". My earliest snapshot of memory dates from Boston. In June, after a farewell round of parties in New York, the family sailed for home. The newcomer was greeted with a fury of unappeasable barking jealousy by the terrier, Tuff.

After a Woolacombe interlude, Ben went to work at the Court Theatre, under the Vedrenne-Barker management, in a play by Bernard Shaw. Ben was pleased and proud—especially so because he had already had to turn down two similar offers. One had been to play Larry in *John Bull's Other Island* just before he went to America, and the other had been while he was still there. Shaw had written to him:

4th March 1905

Dear Webster,

Do you feel inclined to act for the Stage Society again? You know the conditions: infinite worry and unbusinesslikeness, and three guineas a week for cabs. My reason for asking is that *Man and Superman* is announced for Sunday April 9th (evening) and the afternoons of the 10th and 11th. Now *Man and Superman* at full length would last 7½ hours and kill the performers shortly after they had killed the audience. But I can cut the enclosed comedy out of it. Will you look

214

through it and see whether the part of Tanner attracts you at all?

You dealt me a cruel blow with your confounded American engagement over John Bull. But I will forgive you if you take a proper view of Tanner.

Yrs ever

G. Bernard Shaw

Whether John Tanner attracted him! But of course he was three thousand miles too far away to accept and in the midst of hideous preoccupations which, let us hope, crowded out the disappointment. In September 1906 *John Bull* was revived at the Court, and Larry was the first part Ben played there.

The record of the Granville Barker management at the Court Theatre is still something at which to marvel. It has not, I think, been bettered by any English-speaking theatre since. During the four short years of its existence it did eleven plays by Shaw, some of them original productions, the others for the first time in a public theatre. These were its mainstay. But there were also distinguished new plays by eleven English playwrights, including Galsworthy and Masefield, and translations—mostly for the first time in England—of European dramatists from Euripides to Maeterlinck. Ibsen was represented by *Hedda Gabler* and *The Wild Duck*. It was a wonderfully rich period in the drama of the world; the only notable missing name from the Court Theatre roster is that of Chekhov. It is a remarkable omission, since Barker's later methods were very similar to those which Stanislavsky had evolved in Moscow. *The Cherry Orchard* was produced in Russia the year before Barker's management of the Court began; but no English translations had yet appeared. Lewis Casson has told me, however, that Barker did go to Moscow during 1906; he was probably the only English producer to whom it had occurred to make the journey. He returned much impressed by Stanislavsky and "the name of Chekhov was mentioned"; but Barker does not seem to have got past the language barrier to the treasure that lay beyond.

The plays at the Court were not done in true repertory. For

one thing, the physical conditions precluded it, in a theatre with a proscenium only twenty-one feet wide, a stage twenty-four feet deep and a seating capacity of under six hundred. But the repertory ideal governed Barker's thinking. Each play was done for a brief run, then it gave way to another, and if it had been successful it was revived several times, often with changed casts. His directorial methods, including the Stanislavsky ingredient, were new and different, though he was still feeling his way toward the full expression of them. The repertoire of plays was completely different from anything to be seen in the West End.

While Ben was still playing Larry in *John Bull*, Shaw wrote to him from Ireland:

My dear Webster,

Will you please handle Larry with as strong a hand as possible, and take an inch or two off your make-up, so as to reveal your interesting and sensitive countenance at its full age. Do not soften him or lighten him: on the contrary, make his temper and his political convictions as fierce as you can. The object of this is not to improve on Larry as a work of art, but to impress the management with your capacity for heavies and fifties. Both Vedrenne and Barker protest that you are too light, and too determined to make up like the Angel Gabriel in *The Pilgrim's Progress*, to tackle the part I spoke to you of. I want you to use Larry to educate them in this matter. . . .

His strategy had the desired effect, both on Ben and on the management. A few months later Ben created the part of Sir Colenso Ridgeon in *The Doctor's Dilemma*. Shaw was delighted with the middle-aged character actor who appeared from behind the no-longer-quite-so-juvenile façade. It is a precarious bridge to cross, and Ben might have found it much more difficult but for Shaw's dislike of type-casting and pride in discerning unexpected facets of an actor's talent. "To the oridgeonal Ridgeon," the author wrote in a presentation copy of the play.

Three months later, however, Ben had shed a few years and resumed a little glamour as Charteris in *The Philanderer*. Though it was one of Shaw's earliest plays, it had never been performed professionally before.

Feb 7th 1907

My dear Webster,

I wish you would get as nice notices for your author as you do for yourself. I am seriously thinking of writing round to the press to demand that in future a criticism by a woman should be printed in parallel column to the ordinary masculine notice. Probably that would end in your being more admired than ever; but at least I should get a chance.

The Philanderer will come much easier after a few more performances. The dangerous point in your part is still the scene in the Second Act with the two fathers . . .

As far as the general atmosphere of the part is concerned, your sense of humour and your charm are invaluable; but in this particular scene . . . you must look to your speed and your grip to keep the upper hand. It all depends on the start you give it when you say: "That's right. I am earlier than I intended. The fact is, I have something rather pressing to say to Cuthbertson." If you run all that into one string, you are done for. The first part of it may be as off-hand as you please; but after the word "intended" you must make a distinct break, so as to make the audience feel that something new is coming, and then announce the "something rather pressing" with considerable intensity and perplexity . . .

I don't think there are any other spots on the sun. I think you are all inclined to bother too much about the audience. If they don't like it they must lump it; and you'll find that if you treat them that way they always will lump it. It is really a mere waste of nerves to be anxious when you have so much in hand as your impersonation of Charteris.

Yrs ever
G.B.S.

Six years later, Ben was asked to play Larry again, in an emergency, at only a few hours' notice. He tried to relearn the enormously long speeches as best he could in the time available, praying that they would come back to him when it got to the clinch. Halfway through Larry's first embittered diatribe on Ireland, a voice yelled from the Gallery: "You're a liar!" Floundering for a moment, he managed to recover momentum when he was interrupted by an even angrier shout: "You're a *damned* liar! I'm an Irishwoman meself and I know!" Fortunately, the opposition was then hustled out. Shaw wrote:

1st Jan. 1913

My dear Webster,

Larry was wonderful at such short notice. I am enormously obliged to you for mastering it in so short a time.

. Here are some notes I took on Tuesday:

On entering, if you can possibly keep hanging up your hat, or otherwise turned away from Haffigan until he is introduced by name, and then turn sharply and look at him, all the better.

In the long speech in the first act, pile up the agony after the first *Andante Pastorale*. Make it go faster and faster and fiercer and fiercer until when you come to the eternal fouling and starving and degrading you are quite frantic. You will find this easy when you are familiar with the words, and it will bear it.

Exaggerate the burst of temper . . . You must considerably overdo the modesty of English nature before you approach the Irish limit . . .

Remember "economic incompetence." I forget what you said: Barker exclaimed "A jolly good shot"; and I agreed; but it wasn't incompetence . . .

Don't lift yourself onto the table until the line "Here I am (bounce) none the worse." You anticipated it.

Larry would keep his hat on in the last scene with Nora. It is difficult to contemplate that scenery and believe oneself in the open air; but don't insult the poor old heap of rags . . .

No other spots on the sun, and *they* don't matter. Again, many thanks . . .

All of this was admirably deft, sure direction, an author's realization of character backed by expert technique and knowledge of an actor's psychology. It is never worrying or undermining, always good-tempered and helpful. At rehearsals Shaw was always willing to listen to suggestions and even to embody them if, by any unlikely chance, they were an improvement on his own ideas. He would demonstrate—not tiresomely, but revealing what he wanted. Ben often thought him the best actor in the company. Lewis Casson and Sybil Thorndike have told me the same thing. I don't suppose Shaw would have disagreed.

How or why Ben allowed himself to be lured back to the United States to play a thirty-week tour with Stella Patrick Campbell is something I shall never know. It can only be accepted as another tribute to the extraordinary magnetism which she could always exercise when she chose. People completely forgot how abominably she had behaved to them the last time; or else they began to feel that they had misjudged her, that circumstances, not she, had been responsible, that the true Mrs. Pat was the beautiful, witty, warm and generous woman who was now offering them the enormous privilege of being associated with her. She did this constantly with Bernard Shaw; she has done it retroactively with critics and biographers; who was Ben that he, a very vulnerable and loving creature, should be better armored than they?

She had an amazing capacity for retaining friendships, even when she had driven her friends to the verge of madness. She never afterwards remembered that her relationship with them had been anything but delightful. Consequently, she induces in me—as Mrs. Kendal did—an onset of triple vision. There is the Mrs. Pat whom my father knew, and presently will describe. There is the Stella, adored by countless writers and critics, from Bernard Shaw to Alan Dent, and condoned by countless actors, down (chronologically speaking) to the tenderhearted John Gielgud. And there is the Mrs. Pat whom I met, though I never worked with her.

When I was nineteen or so I went with my mother to a fashionable London dressmaker's where she was having a fitting—for a play, I need hardly add. Mrs. Pat was there, having just finished a similar errand. She sat down and entertained me with a stream of scintillating conversation. Suddenly she stopped and looked at me. She rose, very regal, her little dog clasped in her arms. The deep, throaty voice dropped two full tones. "I can't imagine why I'm doing all this for *you*," she said, and swept out. I met her again, much later, in New York; but this was the old—still stinging—Stella, who belongs to another story.

Even on the American tour of 1908, when she seems to have been ridden by that destructive demon which so often possessed her, she showed another side. Thirty years later I got into conversation with a stagehand at the Shubert Theatre in New Haven. He had known my father; and his friends had been stagehands for Mrs. Pat. He told me that they "spoke of her in a jolly sort of way—she must have been what we call a good fellow sort of a woman." In San Francisco, they said, she engaged the finest doctors to attend an electrician who was ill. Years later, in London, this same man met her, walking along Piccadilly; she recognized him instantly, and embraced him. The men in her company were forever falling in love with her, suffering tortures, loathing her, forgiving her and worshipping her once again. Ben was proof against this cycle of destruction; he was simply and consistently miserable. Her manager, George Tyler, wiser and more impersonal, contented himself with calling her "the Royal Tigerine".

May, though she bitterly resented the torments inflicted on her darling Ben, could never manage to dislike Mrs. Pat with conviction. Stella made her laugh; and in any interchange of wits May could give as good as she got, and generally better. Like most bullies, the Royal Tigerine appreciated people who stood up to her. My mother never thought her a great actress, or even consistently a very good one; but she conceded the personality and the intermittent flashes of genius. Even I, at second hand, can see the Hedda Gabler my mother used to describe; the dreadful sense of being trapped, the resentment, the banked-down passion, the incredulous desperation of the last scene; I can hear, vicariously, the torrent of sound from the piano—Mrs. Pat was her own executant—the wild crescendo of mockery and anguish to which the pistol shot provided the only conceivable climax.

Brave New Theatre

Presumably the parts Ben was to play were what really tempted him, for they were fine ones, and out of his usual line: Aubrey in *Tanqueray*, Lövborg in *Hedda*, von Keller in *Magda*, Lucas in *The Notorious Mrs. Ebbsmith*. Later, Hofmannsthal's *Electra* was to be added, with Ben as Orestes, and a Japanese play which Cissie Loftus termed "a play for mice" and a severe member of the press called "a cause for war." During the tryout weeks in England Ben was nervous about his own performances and apprehensive because there was "no stage manager to arrange things." Mrs. Pat semi-directed herself. "She says I have such a sweet smile and such a good face that she looks ridiculous refusing to go off with me"— this was in *Ebbsmith*—". . . I am not downcast and am going to make an effort towards repulsiveness on Friday."

The company sailed for the United States in November 1907, Ben accompanied by May, Peggy and nurse. The expense was horrific: £10 11s. (about $53) each for May and the nurse, half price for Peggy; outside cabins on the saloon deck. They were apprehensive, too, about their expenses in America. They had reluctantly decided that it would be impossible for the whole family to go on the road. Ben would have to travel alone.

Mrs. Pat had already been acclaimed in New York and was at the summit of her fame; the repertoire of plays was of the highest standard; there was every reason to suppose that the tour would be immensely successful, or so the actors thought. Tyler was less sanguine; he complained from the beginning that it was hard to book week stands with a lot of old plays done in repertory. "They don't want repertory," he said, "they want a new play." Ben wrote from the Middle West: "They won't take unpleasant or serious plays any more—it is an age of the Merry Widow waltz." Apparently it always is.

The critics were apt to be put off by the company's Englishness, even in the matter of dress. "We shall be extremely annoyed with Mr. Ben Webster," wrote one of them, "if he continues to wear that waistcoat." Ben remarked in rebuttal that to the "dressy American," a tuxedo down to the knees appeared to be "the tony cut." The matter of accent was more serious; and on this May wrote with dry good sense: "The notices are silly; but the fact that audiences cannot understand the Co. is surely wrong—no one's English ought to be so pure as to be beyond the reach of other people's ears. I'd *make* them understand. Do you think, Pip, a little fault of dropping your last word is in any way to blame?"

The tour itself was extremely rough going. It was almost all one- and two-night stands until Christmas—even Boston only meant two nights in Symphony Hall. There was a week in Detroit and two in Chicago; then more one-nighters, and a month in New York during which the new productions both failed dismally; after that, the company set off for the Far West. Except for a week each in Los Angeles and San Francisco, it was the routine as before, with longer and tougher railroading in between. Much of this Ben knew already, except for the West Coast. But what had been bearable—even funny—when he and May were together became intolerable alone.

In December, May accepted an offer to play with Viola Allen in *Irene Wycherley*, a month's tour, a month in New York and a further tour. As usual the doctors threatened an operation, an appendectomy this time, and told her not to go. As usual, she didn't have the operation, and went. Though she liked the company, and there were no strains such as Mrs. Pat created, she too found that February and March are not the most agreeable months to spend mushing through the small towns of upstate New York, Pennsylvania and Ohio. The touring of those days has vanished for good—or bad. Despite the supposed attractions of "the vagrant gypsy life", it imposed a physical and mental strain on actors, crew and staff that sometimes proved disastrous.

The letters Ben and May wrote to each other during their travels provide a graphic illustration of what used to happen to the touring actor, even when there was no Mrs. Pat to make it worse.

The sequence begins with Ben traveling up through New England toward Canada and back through upstate New York. On the first jump there are no proper train accommodations and he thinks "everything is going to be hideous and muddly." He is told he must pay for his own sleepers. Mrs. Pat has a private car on the train, but it is several weeks before the company get a sleeping coach to themselves. From Worcester, Massachusetts, he writes: "Everything is as usual—the Co. disagreeable and unhappy, the theatre at Norwich not good and the heat in it hellish." May, meanwhile, is in New York staying at the St. Paul Hotel "in great fear of mice," seeing friends and plays (Nazimova in *A Doll's House*—"a great actress with a revolting personality"). She begins rehearsals.

The week before Christmas the Mrs. Pat company have a few days' layoff in Detroit and May manages to join Ben for two of them. But rehearsals for the new productions are studiously arranged so that nobody has any free time, or so it seems to the actors. Those who are to be in *Electra* are called upon to provide their own sandals at eighteen shillings a pair, and are in an uproar. May goes back to her final rehearsals. Ben tells her she cannot possibly go on tour burdened "with Peg and Peggage," so, according to a newspaper report: "the dictatorial Margaret Webster is left in New York in charge of a nurse." The "nurse," of course, is her adoring Aunt Gretchen.

Ben spends New Year's Eve in Kalamazoo, Michigan, May in Baltimore, where the play opens smoothly and the hotel is "a horror." Ben warns her to avoid all hotels with the word "New" in them. "It just means they were rebuilt from the original frame house and have never been touched since." Ben reaches a haven in Chicago where, as usual, are many friends. He goes to lunch with the McCormicks and reports that he thinks the American rich more "jolly" than the English: "At least they never make you feel their wealth in the way English 'maggots' would." He is appalled, however, at the amount they drink. He hears Kreisler play at an At Home at Mrs. Marshall Field's. He gives a "return of hospitality" luncheon at the Chicago Club for twelve people: cocktails (a new invention), white wine and four courses of elegant food. "It ran me into $37."

He is getting into American ways. At Wheeling, West Virginia, he takes "a comfy little room in the new part of the hotel with running water, which is extravagant, but I feel needful." At Springfield it is 23 degrees and no heat in the theatre; in their sleeper it is boiling hot but no water. In Minneapolis it is 23 degrees below zero. Mrs. Pat is being temperamental and several times decides at the last moment to be "off". Ben has constant rows with her and says "she takes all heart and interest out of the work." One of the company almost sets the theatre on fire by cleaning a pair of gloves in benzine, "having a gas light in the room and a lighted spirit stove on the same slab as her basin." They all wish she had succeeded.

May's tour, meanwhile, is still in the civilized areas. She has found a pleasant companion in a young man named Walter Hampden, who is going, she thinks, to do fine things in the theatre. Philadelphia is agreeable; the Bradys are playing there; she only pays $12 a week for her room and all meals; but she is outraged by the price of whisky, which is $1.25, five shillings in hard, English cash.

Both companies open in New York at the end of January; neither is much of a success; by the end of February they are both crazily zigzagging across the United States in opposite directions, trying to figure out where they can catch up with each other by mail, suffering for each other as well as for themselves. To May, getting up early for a morning train-call is the worst torture; to Ben, carrying his everlasting "grip".

Both have company-manager trouble. May's is "a horrid ill-mannered little man with a suspiciously red nose" whom she nicknames "Vladimir." The company blames him for all their irritations and discomforts; actors always do; it is an occupational hazard for company managers. But with May, Vladimir has a special problem; before the tour started she had flatly refused to sign the form contract provided for her. She had described it as a ludicrous document, containing countless iniquitous and tyrannical provisos set forth in four pages of fine print, and finishing up with the clause: "And the Management reserves the right to terminate this contract for any of the aforesaid reasons, or for any reason whatsoever." The final phrase, she had said, made the whole thing a waste of printing. She had started out on the tour without signing it. The ensuing discussions are, by her own account, spirited. Knowing her capacity for dialectic, my sympathies are with Vladimir. In the end there is a showdown with George Tyler himself, whom she knows and likes. "I don't trust you an inch," says she to him, "but I'd rather take your word than sign your contract." The American members of the company tell her that she is mad; that she will be black-listed and never get another job. She says she isn't dependent on one, as she will be going back to England anyway. George Tyler decides to laugh and let it go. She never has a contract at all. (Years later this episode made splendid propaganda for Actors' Equity.)

The saga of Mrs. Pat's company managers is more complex. Battles rage constantly between the actors and their manageress, to whom they are under personal contract, and between her and Tyler. Company managers come and go in quick succession. They arrive in Oshkosh and leave in Peoria. In San Francisco, just as the company is leaving, there is another crisis; a friend of Stella's recommends a "nice little man" who is hurriedly pushed onto the train with them. To their astonishment, he sits up all night in the Men's Smoking Room with his overcoat neatly folded over his arm. He did not know, he explains in the morning, how to climb into an upper berth. Instructed in this art the following night, he succeeds in pulling down the iron curtain rod and cutting his head open. Mrs. Pat screams at him a good deal in public and says it is dishonest of him to have taken the job. He bows his head meekly and makes no reply. Ben privately thinks she is right, but wishes she wouldn't keep saying so. In Seattle he disappears. It is later revealed that he has taken refuge on a slow-moving cargo boat and set sail, unpursuable, for San Francisco. It transpires that his only previous experience had been that of a lay-brother librarian in a monastery.

But it is Mrs. Pat's onstage behavior that drives Ben to frenzy. In *Hedda* one night "she calmly had the book open and read it." In *Ebbsmith*, "I don't think she stopped her silly cackle once during the entire play; but I'm getting used to it now and it doesn't disturb me." In *Electra*, during a long, duologue scene with Orestes, "she walked off, twice for a drink and once for an altercation with the limelight man." In *Magda*, she has her maid come on with a glass of water during the crucial scene with von Keller. Very occasionally Ben can't help laughing. As Paula Tanqueray she is supposed to complain bitterly of the dreadful quiet of Aubrey's country home. "Why," she complains one night in Illinois, "why did you bring me to live out here, right next to a railway station?"

He is too angry, however, to permit himself to laugh often. His normally sweet temper and his inbred theatre tradition of respect for the star break down completely. "She delights in making her company feel small and mean," he writes. And again: "The carriage is a refrigerator; only the temperature of the company is at fever-heat from the selfish stupidity of one woman who has no thought for others." He becomes inarticulate with fury; he climaxes one diatribe with the adjectives "contemptible and unwomanly".

There are compensations, of course, especially on the West Coast, where Ben had never been. Los Angeles is "peaceful and alluring; the air heavy with the scent of mimosa and jasmine and the song of birds." The journey northward up the coast is incredibly beautiful; but San Francisco is still recovering from the great earthquake. "It is rather desolate seeing all the ruins and heaps of bricks . . . The City Hall seems to have been left just as it was after the earthquake—there stands the dome with the figure on top perched on some steel girders with a little masonry clinging to them here and there . . . Of course in some places tall buildings of some 19 stories have reared their heads . . . in some the brickwork has stood to the first story . . . on Nob Hill one marble portal remains through which you get a gorgeous picture across the Bay . . . On the celebrated Van Ness Avenue, where the fire stopped, all one side the shops are just wooden buildings with only the ground floor . . ."

In Seattle he sits on the roof garden of his hotel and enjoys the view and the sun "and the scent of wall-flowers growing beside me." But all too soon they set off across the northern mountains and plains: Walla Walla, Wash.; Spokane; Butte, Mont.; Winnipeg; Fargo, N.D.—"the wind howling around us, the snow swirling about." Fargo, to crown it all, is dry and you have to cross the river into Minnesota to get a drink. Ben is too exhausted. He contents himself with milk toast. Finally, on their last jump, from Grand Forks, N.D., to St. Paul, he heaves a tremendous and still-audible sigh of relief: "Played poker on the train. Won $4.30 and slept well."

Meanwhile, May dashes, or struggles, through a series of one-nighters in the Middle West, alleviated by two weeks in Chicago, where there is the usual foregathering of other companies and friends, including Ethel Barrymore, "who," says May, "usually keeps me up till 4 in the morning . . . She says she is going to be married to a penniless Philadelphia lawyer and leave the stage and is frightfully happy." Cissie Loftus is about to arrive from California, where she is having her own brand of trouble on the vaudeville circuit. She writes to May: "A lively baby in the Gallery during my imitation of Bernhardt helped to cheer things up . . . this is a rotten hotel, completely surrounded by a trolley terminus—I don't know how it manages it, but it does. The lift is not working, the telephone operator only understands German and the dining-room closes at 8. Tonight a man in the Gallery had a *fit* during 'Bernhardt' and had to be removed, all the audience standing up to witness this feat while I went on murmuring. The 'artists' who followed me there were some trained dogs (*darlings*) and a horse. One night during my imitations there was an awful row at the back which was caused by the horse having *gone to sleep and fallen down*. All the stage hands dashed across the stage and propped him up again. But my imitations were more than the poor dear could bear."

May leaves the haven of Chicago and starts going around in circles again. She and Ben almost lose track of each other. "I feel too depressed for words and I study the map in a hopeless state, for as you do get a shade—only a shade—nearer, I go a little further away. Still, it's only three weeks now . . ." There is talk of both tours being extended. They despair. May almost succumbs to poor food—bad colds—"rotten" hotels, with conventions pre-empting all the space—early trains at six or seven a.m. She has much pain. Ben is worried to death. She plays a final flurry of one-nighters through upstate Pennsylvania and Ohio. The spring begins to appear. Her last letter of the tour is written from Charleston, West Virginia:

"I was in awful internal pain yesterday and we had to get up at 5 a.m. Last night I quite collapsed and howled—in the privacy of the most awful room I've ever been in—it was very silly—My room was so awful and the place so pretty that I had gone for a walk with Janet and Mrs. McClaren . . . we stopped to admire a gorgeous wysteria in a back garden, whereupon the lady of the house invited us to make a closer inspection, gave us some white lilacs and took us into the house—a room like *Quality Street*— lovely old furniture. Of course I was charmed and she was pleased that I knew about the things . . . And at night came a gorgeous bunch of purple and white lilac for us—wasn't it sweet? and I think I cried because Janet and Mrs. McC insisted on giving it to Miss Allen and I wanted it so, it broke my heart!"

The following week both tours ended. Ben and May collected the dictatorial Margaret from the cossetings of her aunt and gratefully sailed for home. It was to be a very long time indeed before any of them came back.

The child, however, did not lose touch with America. There were a few snapshots stored inside her head: Gretchen in a fur coat and cap, standing knee-deep in snow; May at a sewing machine in a hotel room, viewed from floor level; the squirrels in Central Park, seeming as big as tigers; a large, shedlike building vaguely resembling a railroad station. There was a long series of actual picture postcards, sent regularly by Ben and May while they were touring and reinforced later by Tom and Gretchen. These were all kept and pored over. The growing child probably learned more of what the cities of the United States looked like than many of its inhabitants. Meanwhile, of course, there was the boat, clearly remembered, and especially for the sake of a friendly steward who supplied tiny jam sandwiches and taught me my first song, "Ha, ha, ha! Hee, hee, hee! Little brown jug, don't I love thee?" There are no early London memories to compete with these.

Brave New Theatre

It was at this time, in New York in 1908, that my mother first became seriously interested in Christian Science. She had dabbled with it two years before, not because of her own many and serious physical troubles, but because of me. The infant illness in New York had left me with a weakness in the muscles of one eye which gradually became apparent as a kind of squint. During the next two years there are many notes in her diary: "Peg to doctors"; but, as in her own case, the diagnoses were conflicting and no one seemed sure of accomplishing anything. Somebody suggested she should try Christian Science.

It was then in the early stages of its growth as a church. Most people thought—they still do—that it is just a kind of faith healing. Tom called it "a dollar a prayer." But it was quite in vogue. Julie Faversham wrote to May: "I shall do more with this Christian Science. It's not easy but tremendously interesting and I believe full of good. I shall have it for my constipation."

On her second visit to the United States, May turned to it again, began to study it and to realize what it could mean as a religion. She became a devoted Scientist and remained so till her death. The healing she had sought for me never did come. The crooked eye remained to plague my childhood and my schooldays till it was put right by a very simple operation when I was nineteen years old. But for May the results of Christian Science were quite exactly miraculous. Within a year or so the worst of the suffering had disappeared. She was still subject to the shattering migraine headaches, but they came less frequently and eventually vanished. The semi-invalid who has thus far been the May Whitty of this book will not reappear. She has probably been an astonishment to all those who knew Dame May in her later years, full of health and vigor. At eighty years old she had more energy than I at half her age; she led a proverbially active and social life. I think she would like it stated that this was entirely due to the effects of Christian Science; and though I did not share her religion after I grew up, I am, as they say, "here to testify". . .

CHAPTER THIRTEEN

———— ఠఠఠ ————

Some Endings...

There were no storms to mar the voyage home. The *Teutonic* was
larger and faster than any ship Ben and May had yet sailed on; but
the captain said that was nothing. The Line (the White Star) was
already laying down bigger ships with all the modern devices;
within three or four years they would launch a real Queen of the
Seas; rumor said she was to be called the *Titanic*. Travel was
already much safer, he said, because you could communicate with
other ships, and even with the shore from certain distances, by the
new wireless telegraphy. He prophesied that in time every home
would have its own "wireless". "Whatever for?" said May.

In London the changes which had been creeping up unnoticed
were sharply discernible to the returning eye. There were, for
instance, fewer horsebuses on the streets. May regretted their
friendly leisure. She had once received an offer of marriage from
a bus driver; he had promised her that he would take her and
their prospective family for a picnic on Clapham Common every
Sunday. In the new motorbuses you could never hope to establish so warm a relationship between Waterloo Station and Charing
Cross.

Some Endings . . .

But motorcars were now quite commonplace. While May was in America, Anthony Hope had written to her:

"The great event—for Betty anyhow—is a motor-car in which she dashes about the country all day and most days—and in which we are attempting a ten days' tour just after Easter. It's a nice toy, but it *eats an awful lot*—and its appetite may become too large for the meals I can give it . . .

"I am, for me, pretty well—shaking down into the middle-age of this odd life—without—well—too many pangs over not being going to do all sorts of things which I never had any real chance of doing—The motor is good for any such follies—it blows away not only all thoughts but every vestige of intelligence. Come and try!"

Electric landaus called "the Humming Birds" had a briefly fashionable career. Ben saw Marie Tempest in hers, "looking remarkably well turned-out." Electric tramways and underground trains were well established. A telephone was installed in Bedford Street. If you didn't mind standing just inside the front door in an icy draft, facing the wall and holding up a heavy ear-trumpet till your arm ached, you could talk to your faraway friends as long as your strength lasted. The United States Army commissioned some flying machines; Blériot flew the Channel; and Shaw, always a pioneer of onstage locomotion, put an "aeroplane" into *Misalliance*. The world seemed both smaller and more vast.

There were changes, also, in the Webster-Whitty families. Old William Shakespeare, alias Micawber, Ben's father, had died a few months before they got home. None of his children could really manage to be very grieved, though Ben suffered some pangs of guilt. May's dearly loved Aunt Lally, last of the friendly figures of her childhood, died soon after. The older generation on both sides of the family were gone, and there were few children; only Peggy, and Jean—daughter of Bobby and Lizzie Brough, now a lanky child of nine, with her mother's fair hair and her Uncle Ben's sweet temper. Then and always she was extraordinarily kind to her younger, much less good-tempered cousin.

In the spring of 1910 King Edward died. Somehow he had made the small English world seem more lavish, decorative and carefree than it really was, and the lights went down a little, the

231

music changed key. The funeral, however, was magnificent; it was blazing hot and there was the usual scarlet-and-gold, uniforms to knock your eye out, flashing breastplates, monarchs galore, including the Kaiser, and the King of Greece, looking a pale shade of pea green and swaying on his horse. The Websters sat on a crowded, shadeless rooftop for hours and Peggy was sick. (It seems I didn't have much of a knack with festivities. On my fourth birthday May notes: "Peg's birthday party. She very disagreeable as usual when excited.") The coronation of George V a year later was nearly as good, but not quite so hot and not quite so many kings; more than there ever were again, however, for after this the world stopped growing them. A feature of this procession was that "Cousin Freddy" Lawson was there, son of a real lord and in a real hussar's uniform, not an actor's one; and the Faversham boys, watching with Peggy, were suitably awed by him.

The Favershams' summer home at Chiddingfold had become the anchorage of the old Bedford Street fraternity. Some of them were scattered by this time, and others less footloose and fancy-free than they had been ten years before; Suzanne Ainley was still regnant, with Constance Collier, now Tree's leading lady at His Majesty's Theatre, sharing the honors. Though the actor contingent was more staid and much more married than it had been in the old days, it was still sufficiently exotic to startle the quiet village. Motorcars would come huffing around the green in the small hours of Sunday morning, and beautiful ladies in enormous hats would arrive later, by pony trap, for lunch. Lights would burn in the library through the summer nights, when it is never wholly dark, to the sound of fierce discussion and much laughter. It was said that two handsome gentlemen in white tie and tails had once been heard, at dawn, declaiming outside the rectory an ode to the pagan gods. But Will Faversham did not favor such goings-on. He was a matinee idol in New York, but in England he played The Squire.

He had acquired the Manor House from Richard and Julie Le Gallienne, who had discovered it. Julie Faversham transformed it. "Oh God!" wrote Will to May, "come to Chiddingfold soon . . . see the extent . . . my wife dreamed I was Pierpont Morgan . . ."

Some Endings . . .

A Georgian front decorously faced the village green; a rambling assortment of oak-beamed Tudor rooms and latticed windows looked out on the garden. There was a shaved lawn, an ancient sun dial, a huge cedar tree admirably adapted to the pleasures of the climbing young. The village had, and has, the full complement of picturesque accessories: a church with a lych-gate; an ancient black-and-white inn; a village shop which sold everything, candy and cricket bats, soap, sunbonnets and paraffin, and smelled of them all; an open blacksmith's forge, which rang merrily and glowed orange-bright. It was an ideal setting for The Squire.

We children loved him because he treated us as equals; he entered into our activities with the utmost solemnity. He gave Billy and me gorgeous red-Indian costumes, with scarlet and feathers and moccasins and tomahawks; poor Philip had to be contented with a castoff cowboy suit, and was known as "the Little Papoose". (I have often wondered how he managed to grow up so unscarred.) The Squire organized wonderful picnics by motorcar to the beaches of Bognor or Selsey Bill. The ladies would climb up into the puffing, shaking machine heavily encumbered with capes and motoring veils. The men were gloomily certain that at some point they would be called upon to "get out and get under", as the song said; the children hoped fervently that they would. The machine would leap off like a kangaroo in a series of explosions, and more often than not the children's hopes were gratified. Frequently, also, the motor would have to rescue other stranded automobilonauts, and would return romantically late at night, loaded to its running boards with human barnacles.

It is during the Chiddingfold years that the isolated snapshots in my head begin to acquire continuity, like a film, and that the two-dimensional figures begin to emerge in depth. Aunt Julie was a Junoesque woman, with a loving heart of true gold and a voice, Cissie Loftus said, "like a haunted frog-pond." She was a little overwhelming for a small child. Constance Collier, with her proud, dark, Cleopatra beauty and her enormous sense of life, was a little awe-inspiring too. It was not until later that I realized her sagacity and courage, her unfailing help in time of need. Suzanne, of the flaming, red hair, was stimulating and unexpected and played soldiers wonderfully well. She and Uncle Will organized a splendid funeral for our Captain Greenjacket, and led the whole house party in procession to attend it. I wrote to my mother:

"We went to the party on Wednesday and it was lovele their were Races and a lovele tea Philip eat a pate of sangwiches . . . yesterday one of our Bravest Toy Soldiers died we aranged to have a funrel we Put him in a mach-box and Put a [here, a small drawing of the Union Jack, flying the wrong way round] on it and we made speeches I wrote them out We shal drive in London on Monday."

Eva Le Gallienne was often at the Manor House with her mother, but though she was with us, she was not of us. Having the advantage of some five years over Billy and me, she pursued her own solitary purposes with silent concentration. She climbed to the top of the cedar tree in order to read in peace. She had her own bicycle. She was a Girl Guide and wore a uniform adorned with belts, cords, clasp knives and insignia of merit, most dazzling to my eyes. It became my ambition, when I grew up, to become a Girl Guide, like Eva Le Gallienne. (I never did.)

Squire Will had initiated the Village Sports—or at least, he supplied the impetus, the organization and most of the prizes. I remember best the year when Eva and Billy were both entered for the Juvenile Fancy-Dress Race, she as a vivandière on a recalcitrant donkey with kidney trouble and he clad in a suit of shining armor and mounted on an equally handsome steed. He carried off the costume prize with ease; but the race was another matter. Eva, the light of battle in her eye, urged her ancient animal around the course by sheer will power; she even got off and pushed. She passed the winning post amid deafening cheers while Billy was still completing the first lap at a majestic walk. She won a clock. She tells me she has it still, and it still keeps excellent time.

My American education was continued by the Faversham boys and their nanny; I learned about important, un-English things, like cornflakes for breakfast and salad for lunch and comic strips in the Sunday papers. "Buster Brown" became my hero. I learned about baseball before I knew about cricket, and never, ever, referred to it as "rounders."

Some Endings . . .

In 1913 Julie Faversham's doctors told her she had tuberculosis and ordered her to Switzerland. I did not know this, of course; but I vividly remember standing beside the much-loved motorcar which was to take us Websters to the station one drizzly Monday morning. The Favershams gathered around us and we all said rather solemn goodbyes. I didn't know why I felt so miserable and bereft, since this had often happened before. But I was quite right. It was the last of the Chiddingfold summers.

Perhaps it ended, for that little group of people, the world they had known and lived in; though the accepted, epochal date was on an August morning eleven months later. The gracious living, the ordered pattern, the solid present, the secure and predictable future never came again. We children only just knew them. But I am glad I was old enough to have caught a glimpse of that lost world, and of some of those who lived, and lived well, in it. The honorary "aunts" and "uncles" of my childhood were truly, I believe, touched with brilliance and magnetism. They were not wealthy, though they were self-sufficient. They were artists in their own field and therefore self-critical, not smug. They were loving, gay, fastidious, intelligent, witty and, on the whole, charitable. They lived in a happy time when they could afford to indulge these qualities and not apologize for them. I am grateful that, child as I was, I knew a little of this time.

In the years before the First World War it cannot have seemed that the stage was changing very much, either as a profession or as an art. It had, of course, become quite respectable to be an actor. A whole phalanx of knights had followed in the wake of Irving's solitary honor: Bancroft, Wyndham, Hare, Tree, Pinero and Alexander, approved and venerable bedesmen. Fashionable acting in London and New York was at a high level; plays were common to both cities and stars still crisscrossed the Atlantic. Romantic drama and perishable farce were still the popular fare. In the provinces actor-managers like Martin Harvey and Fred Terry toured a costume repertoire of familiar plays; Benson's companies maintained the Shakespearian tradition.

Young Ben and May

Perhaps the London actor began to feel a slight twinge of uneasiness. The pattern of employment was changing. There were fewer seasonal engagements and more individual productions which succeeded or failed on their own merit, with a very large slice of luck. There were more actors, more managers and less security.

But it was not very hard for an established actor like my father to maintain his position. Comedy and drama still moved on much the same social levels and were as lavishly adorned with scenery and costumes as they had always been. Women were expected to be beautiful, rather on the opulent side, generally blond if heroines, raven-haired if villainesses or "femmes fatales." The men had to be handsome, sonorous and male; and so they were: Henry Ainley, Lewis Waller, Matheson Lang, Godfrey Tearle. Inevitably, Ben got caught up among these picture-postcard heroes. He moved in high society. He was nearly always a baron or a count or even a prince, all made of the best gilded pasteboard. He wore braided shakos or lace cravats, doeskin breeches in *The House of Temperley*, kilts and a powdered wig in *Proud Maisie*, doublet and hose in *Count Hannibal*. In this piece he had to fight a fierce duel with his actor-manager-boss, Oscar Asche, whose swordsmanship was so ferocious that it almost cost Ben an eye. May would wait up every night for him, armed with lint, bandages, lysol and sticking plaster.

In 1912 he played with Oscar Asche and Lily Brayton again as the Caliph of Baghdad in *Kismet*. May was alarmed to learn that Asche had to try and assassinate him; but this time he was adequately protected by four very large supers with spears. He was resplendent in robes of black-and-gold or cloth of silver, except for one scene when, supposedly incognito, he wore little but a becoming khaki make-up whose removal made the bathtub extremely dirty every night.

Kismet was a superbly mounted Arabian Nights fantasy. Asche had expert advice and direction on all its aspects. Ben was asked not to stand with his arms folded; this, the expert said, was the attitude of slaves. Napoleon had for years been known in the East as "the Emperor of the Slaves", because of the arms-folded

Ben and May

Ben and May at Woolacombe, 1892 (also see Plate XXIV)

The Websters

Ben, Booey, and Lizzie

Anna Sarah Johnson,
mother of Ben III
and William S. Webster,
father of Ben III

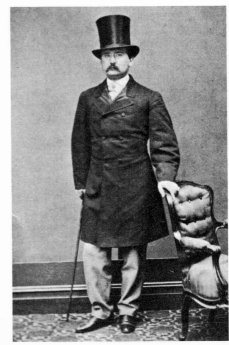

Ben Webster III

In the first production
of *Lady Windermere's Fan*
(*at far left*): "What's
the difference between
scandal and gossip?"

As Sir Lancelot,
in *King Arthur*

". . . all made of the
best gilded pasteboard . . ."
(in *The Prince Consort*)

May Whitty

In *Prince Karl*

In *The Last of Mrs. Cheney* (just right of center), St. James's Theatre, 1925; Gladys Cooper holding the parasol and Gerald du Maurier (at far right)

Ellen Terry [signature]

Bedford Street Days

Ellen Terry

Edith Craig

Marie Tempest

Ethel Barrymore

Hilda Trevelyan
and Cecilia ("Cissie")
Loftus in *Peter Pan*

May Whitty becomes a Dame Commander of the British Empire, 1917

Annual meeting of the Theatrical Ladies' Guild at the Haymarket Theatre, December 9, 1909; Peggy Webster has presented a bouquet to the Princess Helena Victoria of Schleswig-Holstein

Ben as the Caliph Abdullah in *Kismet* (surrounded by spear holders), 1911

stance depicted in his portraits. Everything in the production was real except the play—perhaps I should say the "book". There was a real pool, into which a young lady daringly attired in fleshings gingerly inserted herself; there were real oriental lamps and fabrics and rugs and jewels; and every night for nearly a year Ben brought home three real red roses—two had a function in the play and one was an understudy—which were added to a big, silver bowl in the middle of our dining-room table.

Kismet was the forerunner of Asche's fabulous *Chu Chin Chow*, which had all the same ingredients (except my father) plus a real camel. It ran for 2,238 performances. In the Nineteen-fifties *Kismet* cropped up again, plus the music for which it was so eminently suited, and Eddie Knoblock's "book" proved as durable as ever.

It cannot have seemed as if the new currents in the theatre, heralded by the little theatre societies and Barker's seasons at the Court, were making much headway. You might have thought that the Establishment was absorbing the new playwrights and perhaps disarming them. Pinero remained supreme, though a little insecure, as if he were trying on the mantle of Ibsen to see how it fitted. Max Beerbohm described the results in scathing terms: "Latest assortment of Spring problems. Scandinavian gents' own materials made up. West End style and fit guaranteed." Ibsen himself remained a special-performance dramatist. Ben once got a chance of breaking free of his two-dimensional aristocrats to play Torvald in *A Doll's House*. He did it with less pomposity and more charm than was then customary. But this kind of performance, though enjoyable, could not possibly earn anybody a living. Indeed, it was a little suspect. Years before, following his success as Hippolytus, he had written to May: "It's a bad thing to be an ancient Greek. It limits one's chances of employment."

Nevertheless, under the surface, and mostly outside of London, the new theatre was stirring, the new dramatists were showing themselves. The Abbey Theatre, subsidized by a devoted woman, Miss A. E. F. Horniman, produced Synge's *Playboy of the Western World*, and thereafter sustained itself. In 1908 Miss Horniman moved to Manchester, where she fostered new staging, new play-

wrights, new directors like Lewis Casson and new actors like Sybil
Thorndike. A "people's theatre" in Glasgow staged *The Seagull*,
the first Chekhov ever to be done in England. Within the next two
years the Stage Society put on two performances of *The Cherry
Orchard* and two of *Uncle Vanya*. Nobody else, either in England
or America, took any notice of Chekhov for another fifteen years.
But the special-performance societies were not idle. The example
of the Court Theatre seasons was not wholly forgotten.

It was, as always, a question of money. The new and unortho-
dox theatre had to be subsidized, either directly by wealthy patrons
or indirectly by theatre people who were willing to work for nothing. William Archer wrote: "If the Shaw drama had been forced
from the first to pay its way, as were the Robertson and Pinero
drama, it would long ago have died of starvation." The pattern has
not varied very much since.

When Vedrenne ran out of money at the Court Theatre it
seemed as if Granville Barker's experiments had been indefinitely
blocked. His career as a producer was frustrated, and this had
forced him to turn to playwrighting. He was learning to be a
dramatist of power. But he had one overriding ambition, and he
never lost sight of it as long as he himself remained active on the
stage: to found a British National Theatre, playing repertory. In
1910 an American manager, Charles Frohman, gave him the backing he needed. He leased the Duke of York's Theatre and prepared
to try again.

This time it was to be true repertory. There were to be several
different plays in any one week. This involved a series of miracles
in the technical departments, since the stage of the Duke of York's
is not much larger than that of the Court, and is broken up by a
series of fiendishly devised obstructions. The roster of stars included Irene Vanbrugh, Dennis Eadie and Hilda Trevelyan. They
often played no more than two or three times a week. This, of
course, increased the salary list considerably. In addition, there
were special matinee performances so that actors who were employed in regular runs could appear in particular productions. The
list of authors was a guarantee of quality: Shaw, James Barrie
(then at the height of his fame and popularity), Pinero, Meredith

and Barker himself. The opening bill was to be Galsworthy's *Justice*.

Jan. 17th 1910

Dear Miss Whitty,

Would you be insulted if I asked you to play an old woman? The fact is, the only actual old woman who can, I think, give me a comedy performance and be as fragile as I want the part to be is not obtainable, so now I must choose between real age and what I want with age assumed. Are you insulted at the suggestion?

Very sincerely yours,
H. Granville Barker.

It's rather a nice part (in my new play) though I say it as shouldn't.

The play was *The Madras House;* Amelia was a character part of a kind May had never before attempted. Barker's methods, too, were different. She was trained for difficulty; she had rehearsed on trains or walking down the street with another actor, or while the stagehands were "setting up", or not at all. She was prepared to "go on" with only the most elementary direction in the matter of positions and business. But Barker would rehearse nowhere but on the stage itself. (How on earth did the stagehands ever clear the last production and set the next?) He was a stickler for absolute quiet; the smallest whisper drove him to frenzy. Moreover, he supplied the actors with a wealth of psychological background which May found fascinating but alarming.

He didn't discuss the play at any length before the actors "got on their feet"; the instruction was given as you went along. At the first rehearsal of May's first entrance in *The Madras House* he told her: "From the moment you come in you must make the audience understand that you live in a small town in the provinces and visit a great deal with the local clergy; you make slippers for the curate and go to dreary tea-parties." She realized the value of these admonitions. But she was used to working through the lines; and the line, in this case, was "How do you do?"

Some of the company vented their disquiet in sarcasm. Sydney Valentine suggested he might carry on a pot of honey to show that he kept bees. Barrie would watch the proceedings, as was his habit, silently hunched up in an Orchestra seat, "eating his little pipe," as someone put it, his face barely visible between his hat, pulled down over his eyes, and his muffler, pulled up around his neck. He held a rather ambivalent position in the enterprise, since he was not merely "an" author, but Charles Frohman's favorite and particular author, through and because of whom the Frohman backing had been obtained.

He was not altogether in sympathy with the Barker methods. Once, when Barker had driven Dennis Eadie to the point of frenzy, he arose, walked down to the orchestra rail and removed the pipe from between his teeth. "My boy," he remarked pacifically, in his soft, Scots speech, "do ye not think, when ye walk upstage there, with y're back to the audience, ye could convey that ye had a brother in Shropshire who's awfu' fond o' reading Shelley?" The company laughed delightedly and felt much relieved and consequently more receptive to Barker's peculiarities.

Like Stanislavsky, though the connection was so very tenuous, Barker was feeling his way to a revolt against the accepted theatrical conventions, toward a new realism, not at all Russian, but indigenous and powerful. He wanted to destroy a school of acting founded on vocal histrionics, a wealth of gesture, technical facility and surface competence. He tried to get back to the inner compulsion. He had no use for actors who began the process of creation only when the audience saw them—or sometimes only when they themselves spoke to it. He disdained playwrights whose characters existed only within three canvas walls and a set of footlights.

It must have been a blow to him when the success of the season turned out to be a revival of Pinero's *Trelawny of the Wells*, charming but hardly trail-blazing. At five years old, I thought it thrilling and wonderful. I don't think I was altogether wrong; adult audiences seemed to like it too. But sterner critics have always declared that a "popular" piece was one which appealed to five-year-olds.

My mother played the desiccated Aunt Trafalgar, another

character part. The director was Dion Boucicault, whom she had met so many years before, in her first job at the St. James's. He had become a good character actor, a director in his own right, and, naturally, the preferred director of his wife, Irene Vanbrugh. He was as different from Barker as chalk from cheese, not altogether unlike Pinero in method, and another new experience for May. She found him terrifying.

Lewis Casson has told me that Barker laid stress on the value of silences in tempo and phrasing—"filled" silences, of course. His previously plotted "choreography" was not elaborate; the moves evolved from an inner necessity. He was interested in the precision of inflections, but only insofar as they concerned the exact interpretation of thought. In this he had been much influenced by William Poel and his "new" speaking of Shakespeare. But Barker, within his own terms and terminology, allowed a latitude of interpretation to the actor. "Dot" Boucicault, on the other hand, was a martinet. Marie Tempest has left this description of him:

"His chief weapon was irony and he was never charming until he had impressed you with his power. He never shouted, he waited for silence, and then he spoke in a voice which was calm and deadly. His patience was endless—he would spend an entire morning over one scene of ten minutes. He insisted on definite movements, never varying, definite inflections, and perfect timing. An actor took out a cigarette as he was standing on a definite flower in the pattern of the carpet; he took two steps, and, as his foot came down to the carpet again, he tapped his cigarette on his case. He spoke a line, took one more step, and struck a match. A few more words, a step, and the match was blown out. Then the phrase was finished. His mechanics were as fine as those of a watch, and the length of his performance seldom varied by a minute. The same method was employed for the lifting of a fan—one never toyed with it at will. One's coffee was drunk at a given second, and gloves were taken off by numbers."

At her Jubilee matinee Marie Tempest says that she remembered the scene from *The Marriage of Kitty*—movement, inflection, timing, like a childhood verse recalled.

May found the system of universal tunes particularly unnerving. She would walk along the street trying them out to herself till the passers-by turned to stare. Dutifully she went through the prescribed motions and inflections. At the dress rehearsal of *Trelawny* she saw, among the Victorian decorations, a daguerreotype of a small child brandishing a whip, its chest encircled by a sash, much like a bandoleer of cartridges. She whispered to Irene: "Portrait of Dot as a baby."

The success of *Trelawny* imperiled Barker's whole repertory ideal. Because of the limitations of the stage, the productions not in active use had to be carried off to a warehouse and brought back when next required. The expense of carrying a large company and paying them whether they played or not was very high. *Trelawny* began to be played more and more often, the less popular plays less and less. Even so, by the end of the season Frohman had lost more money than he could afford.

All of these hazards have beset repertory experiments ever since. (As I wrote the preceding paragraph, I had a piercing vision of the scenery of the beautiful "Old Met" in New York, sitting on the sidewalks of Seventh Avenue and ruining itself and the opera house.) Barker never stopped trying. His Shakespeare productions during the following years were revolutionary and fruitful. He threw out cartloads of scenery and restored large slices of text that had scarcely been spoken on the English stage since they were written. Later he collated his theories and his experience into a series of Prefaces to Shakespeare which still have an immense influence. Yet he never crystallized his director's thinking into a codified "method"; there was no Barker "school". He was one of the most powerful influences in the transformation of the British stage. But the National Theatre he envisioned did not come into being until many years after his death.

In the meantime Shaw, his great collaborator, had crashed through into the commercial world, baiting traps for the actor-managers with parts like Dick Dudgeon and Julius Caesar. Barker himself had produced his greatest popular success to date, *Fanny's First Play*—"a pot-boiler," said its author contemptuously. In 1913, at the St. James's Theatre, Barker was to do Shaw's newest script, *Androcles and the Lion*. Ben, very delightedly, came back to them to play the "handsome Captain".

Actors and audience were introduced to another innovation, startling at the time—a flat stage without footlights. The actors missed their cozy, protective glare, but the front row of the Orchestra stalls loved it. They parked their hats, their coats and even their feet on the convenient stage platform. Since the floor of the stage was more visible than usual, Barker had a special ground cloth painted. He asked the actors to protect it by rehearsing in slippers. Ben wore a pair of American sandals, bought many years before. Barker, in the midst of all his other preoccupations, recognized them instantly. "Why," he said, "*The Philanderer!*"

In these sophisticated, modern surroundings, however, Ben came closer to being murdered than he ever had in melodrama or in his ferocious duels with Oscar Asche. The actor who played Ferrovius apparently caught the Early Christian fervor of the part. He became convinced that Ben, with whom he shared a dressing room, was a reincarnate Jesus of Nazareth, destined, like Him, to a sacrificial death. Ben treated it as a joke, but he became a little apprehensive. One night Ferrovius came storming out of the stage "arena," gladiator's sword in hand, filled with godly fury and determined to perform the rite immediately. Fortunately, Ben was wearing a breastplate and was also armed. The duel, ludicrous but dangerous, was interrupted before serious damage was done. Poor Ferrovius was removed by the Imperial Guard.

My own theatregoing memories begin during this period. The first, I think, was Tree's production of *Pinkie and the Fairies*—I was not quite four. Soon afterward came his *Midsummer Night's Dream*, with real rabbits, so I've been told, but I don't remember them. There was *Charley's Aunt*, of course; Maeterlinck's *The Blue Bird* (my aunt, Lizzie Brough, was in it); *Trelawny* and *Kismet*, as well as a variety of plays of lesser note. By the time *Androcles* came along I was an experienced theatregoer of eight. Martin

Harvey was my first Hamlet, unless you count Forbes-Robertson the night before I was born. Barker's *Twelfth Night* has left a clear, pure echo in my mind, like a phrase of Mozart; Reinhardt's *The Miracle* an enormous smudge of sound and color and the smell of incense, all framed by the huge arena of Olympia. I must have been about six when I gained my first experience in professional company, as an angel, with an extremely wobbly halo, in a Pageant of the Stage organized by my mother and Edith Craig at the Albert Hall.

But the love of my theatre life was—need I say?—*Peter Pan*. I went every year to its Christmas revival, usually several times. I knew it by heart. I sang its Pirate Songs, suitably dressed in a white sailor suit with a red collar, to which I was much attached, and one of my black eye patches. Dot Boucicault was the producer, and the annual and perennial Wendy was Hilda Trevelyan. My mother would prevail upon them to let me come backstage and watch from the wings; and once Wendy actually offered to take me up in the Little House in which she and Peter ascended to the treetops in the final scene. We went down under the stage and climbed onto a platform where stood the tiny house "with darling little red walls and roof of mossy green" that I had seen so often from the front. Wendy and Peter made me stand in the very back corner while they took their places shoulder to shoulder in the doorway, completely hiding me from view. The music swelled, the platform started to move; upward and upward it went, through the trap door, onto the stage level, way up into the air. I crouched, entranced. I watched Liza fly off into space, noting, but with no disenchantment, the gleam from her flying wire as it passed through a spotlight. I heard Peter and Wendy speak their well-known final lines; all the little fairy lamps began to twinkle, the music soared to a climax and the curtain came swooshing down, with me in a haze of rapture such as I have seldom if ever experienced since.

And yet, when I came to see the play again—it may have been all of two weeks later—I did not think of the mechanics of the trap door, the cables and the flying wire, nor even of my darling Hilda Trevelyan. Wendy was Wendy; the Little House was in the treetops; Liza flew. Once I remember going with the Hope-Hawkins children in a box. Millie got very agitated about Wendy's plight among the Pirates. I told her tersely that she need not worry; the Pirates would soon go back to their dressing rooms and take their make-up off; and that if she couldn't stop crying she had better go home. Nevertheless, so long as the Pirates were onstage they were desperate villains; and all through the ship scene I would wait, practically suffocated with excitement, for the thrilling climax, every detail of which I knew by heart. It was the same with all my theatregoing. I was a rapt and ideal audience; yet I took pride in finding out how it all worked, and would crane my neck from the box to get a glimpse of the electrician on his wooden "perch" on the opposite side of the stage.

I am sorry, now, that my father never took me with him on his film-making forays. Perhaps film directors were not tolerant of small children asking questions. The industry was still in its infancy, in England, when he made his first film. It was an adaptation of *The House of Temperley*, which he had played in the stage version. This made it easier, since there were actual lines to say and you didn't have to make them up as you went along. The rhythm of waiting around seems already to have been established, varied by bursts of frenzied activity to get the shots that were needed when the sun came out. "The day has been more or less wasted," he wrote, "and tomorrow more waste of time, and on Friday, Epsom Downs at sunrise." He had to gallop about—he was an insecure horseman—and fight duels, and his breeches split and the property man charged his pistols with real shot; fortunately he had had the sense to aim past his opponent, not at him, and missed by a couple of inches.

Not long afterward he had to submit to the dangers of drowning in *Enoch Arden*. He survived, but with the loss of his wig in the sea. A few days later sharks were seen in the locality; and since this was an unprecedented happening on the Cornish coast, May felt convinced that they had devoured the wig and come, like the crocodile in pursuit of Captain Hook, "licking their lips for the rest of him." This was, I think, my mother's first experience of movie-making.

Young Ben and May

Most of the picture was shot in Polperro village, subject to many delays because of the uncertainty of the English weather. There were also some difficult double-exposure shots, which were finally solved by fastening a piece of sticking plaster over one half of the lens and then photographing the same shot with the sticking plaster covering the other half. The fishermen and cottagers did not seem to resent in the least the invasion of their village by a company of lunatics in peculiar clothes, with bright-yellow faces. Such things were a novelty in those days and tourists were unknown, so that the invasion was both exciting and profitable. The villagers were enlisted to appear as themselves, adding only the yellow grease paint, and did so with great conviction. Polperro turned out to be the star of the picture, even though the photographic limitations of the period made it seem as though rain poured across the screen without cessation.

I bitterly resented my exclusion from this frolic. But I was a little consoled when I was taken by my Aunt Lizzie, with Jean, for a holiday at Lulworth, in Dorset. For there, on the rocks, was an abandoned castle, entirely made of wood, with towers and battlements and wooden cannon, painted to look most menacing. Here, I was later told, "the buried majesty of Denmark did sometimes march"; here Forbes-Robertson had first seen, on celluloid, his father's Ghost.

May's activities as an actress, though they did not cease, came only by fits and starts. As her health improved, her energies sought other outlets. The first of these was the Theatrical Ladies' Guild. Her diary records attendance at a meeting as early as 1892. The organization had been formed to help "distressed" members of the profession—not just actors, but stagehands, wardrobe mistresses (who always seemed especially vulnerable to "distress"), anyone in need. It hated the word "charity" and abhorred red tape. It took care of children, paid doctors' bills, provided coal and blankets in winter, and did a brisk business dispensing such brittle items as spectacles and dentures. May became a member of the committee; later she was for many years its chairman. I find a note in her diary

Some Endings . . .

for 1909: "T. L. G. Annual Meeting Haymkt Peg bouquet to Schwig"; which means that I, very small in huge spectacles and a huge bonnet, presented a huge bouquet to Princess Helena Victoria of Schleswig-Holstein, the presiding Patroness. The stage was graced with the most famous ladies of the London theatre.

Other similar organizations drew May into their orbit, including the Actors' Orphanage, with its famous annual Garden Party, and the Three Arts Club, with its equally famous annual Ball. May arranged innumerable benefits, made vast quantities of "appeals", sat on one committee after another, invariably gravitating toward "the Chair", from which she dispensed order and tactful arbitration to distinguished but sometimes obstreperous colleagues.

It was inevitable that she should be drawn into the Women's Suffrage movement. In 1908 she notes, "to meeting to hear Mrs. Pankhurst." All her sympathies were already enlisted by the struggle of women to become qualified doctors, lawyers, teachers. It was intolerable that women should be legally bracketed with "children, criminals and lunatics" as being incapable of casting a vote. Even in the theatre they were not as yet recognized except as actresses. They might just, with their new Twelve Pound Look, be accepted as the manager's typist; but certainly not as stage managers, directors, let alone managers. Yet the remarkable Miss Horniman and the no less remarkable women of the Old Vic, Miss Cons and Miss Baylis, had contrived to break through these taboos and demonstrate that women could not only follow such professions, but lead them; and actresses had a long tradition of independence both as wage earners and as individuals. One day at a luncheon party there was vociferous argument about the suffrage movement, and May, with her built-in Irish passion for being "agin' the government", found herself becoming eloquent in defense of women's rights. At last, one of her friends remarked jokingly: "Why, May, I believe you're a suffragette!" May paused, slightly astonished. "Why," she said, "I believe I am."

There was, of course, violent family opposition; not from Ben, who was angelic and understanding as always, and was even prepared to argue the case for the suffragettes within the sacred precincts of the Garrick Club. The Whitty Aunts, however, aged but still dynamic, disinherited May all over again when they read that she had signed a suffrage petition; and Booey raised a furious outcry about the family "name". May therefore resolved that in all these activities, and the others which unexpectedly grew out of them, she would never besmirch the name of Webster, but would stick to the old, rebellious Irish Whitty; and it was eventually as May Whitty and not May Webster that she became a Dame of the British Empire.

As a suffragette she found support close to home, indeed within the very precincts of 31 Bedford Street. Edy Craig and Christopher St. John in the flat below were ardent suffragettes. Some of the most determined of the "militants" would take refuge with them, either before they set out on some mission or after they were released from prison. To me, as a small child, the accounts of their escapades were as fascinating as any cowboy-and-Indian saga. Yet they all seemed to me either very fat and jolly or very frail and gentle; I couldn't imagine them being "violent"; I couldn't imagine them in prison; and they never spoke of what they had been through, or at least never before me. Years later, when I read of the hunger strikes, the forcible feeding, the police brutality, the dreadful "Cat-and-Mouse" Act, I was incredulous and appalled. I remember that my mother, though she did not believe in militancy as an effective weapon, was abashed by the heroic courage of these women. Sometimes she felt she ought to go straight out and break the windows of Bedford Street Post Office. "I'm a coward," she would accuse herself furiously, "I'm nothing but a miserable coward"; and she would go to four more meetings and march in three more processions to make up for it.

Sometimes there was a lighter side. I remember walking up Regent Street with my mother and two of her friends, one a fearless little terrier of a woman who had been in prison several times, and the other a rather large girl who affected the mispronounced r's of high English gentility. We passed some thoroughly shattered plate-glass windows, at which the first woman pointed proudly. "My mother broke those," she said. The girl stared solemnly. "Vewy cweditable," she pronounced.

Some Endings . . .

May eventually joined the Actresses' Franchise League and inevitably became its chairman—or -woman. The League was neither for nor against the militants and did a certain amount of skillful fence-sitting in this respect. Its function, however, was to hold meetings, write and distribute literature, organize and participate in deputations and mass demonstrations, above all to prepare and produce various kinds of propaganda shows. Actually, the League was performing an educational function of much wider scope, though its members did not know it at the time. Women playwrights emerged to write the necessary plays and pageants, or to ghostwrite other people's speeches. Women organized performances, directed them, stage-managed them, attended to the box office, made up the accounts, handled the publicity. For the first time, they became more than just actresses; they learned everything there was to know about how to run an organization or a stage. Out of this grew such enterprises as Edy Craig's Pioneer Players, which pioneered many things women now take for granted in all the entertainment professions. The training the suffragettes gave themselves was wider, even, than that. They learned how to raise money, how to run a public meeting, how to think on their feet, how to turn hostility or apathy into laughter and enthusiasm.

In July 1914 the suffrage movement, though it had won a great deal, did not seem much closer to getting the vote. But women had got a foothold in many professions hitherto closed to them; they had sharpened their wits, tested their courage, shared comradeship and mutual trust, taught themselves discipline and obedience. They did not know that these qualities, absorbed in a different service, were to win them the vote three years later, when most of them were too busy to bother about it.

On July 13th, 1914, the Webster family left for Woolacombe, where they were joined by Norman Hapgood, then editor of *Harper's*, and his wife and daughter, friends from the Chiddingfold days. Ben and May had to be back for rehearsals in the middle of August, but they looked forward to a month of sea and, with luck, sun. Hapgood was more dubious; he thought the international situation was very alarming indeed. May scoffed at it. She was far

249

more concerned with the Ulster gunrunning and Prime Minister Asquith's latest broken promise to the suffragettes. Ben didn't see how the murder of an Austrian archduke in Sarajevo could possibly affect England, and especially not Woolacombe, between the golden sands, the heather and the sea. But the sense of war grew nearer and larger. Even we children became aware of it. It sounded exciting. I scanned the horizon eagerly, prepared at any moment to see German uhlans in bright brass helmets come charging up the beach; whereupon my father, who would somehow have changed into costume, would confront them dauntlessly, sword in hand, as he did in *The Fires of Fate*. The Hapgoods, more realistic, packed up hurriedly and left to catch the next possible boat for New York.

Every day bulletins, written in pencil on telegraph forms, would be posted in the window of the tiny post office. The whole village, residents and summer visitors, clustered around to read them; for newspapers came slowly to Woolacombe, and the telegraph wire would be first with the news. On August 2nd appeared the announcement that England had declared war on Germany. It was premature; we had anticipated the rest of the Empire by forty-eight hours. But on August 4th the King and the Government caught up with our postmaster and England was indeed at war.

As we returned to London, troops were already on guard at strategic railway junctions; we didn't know against what, but it looked efficient and reassuring. The city was full of excited crowds, waving flags and singing patriotic songs, riding on the roofs of taxicabs, massed in cheering thousands in front of Buckingham Palace. It all seemed like an exciting game. England had been bred on a history of wars and our side had always won; a battle had been lost here and there, always gloriously, but never a war. Everybody was full of romantic notions vaguely connected with the Charge of the Light Brigade and the "thin red line," and Nelson at Trafalgar. Few had any idea that it wasn't going to be at all that kind of war.

Some Endings . . .

The theatres rocked as they always do under the impact of a national crisis. New productions didn't dare open and old ones closed hurriedly. Nobody had realized the essential place that the theatre, with little cinema and no radio to share the responsibility, would have to fill during the years to come. The King and Queen announced, as a patriotic gesture, that they would not visit a theatre again until the war was over; nor did they, except for Charity Benefits in aid of some Good Cause. Their example was a big help.

I remember that my father pinned up on a screen in the dining room a large newspaper map of the Western Front marked with little flags for the opposing armies. During the first four weeks the black, yellow and red of the German emblems swept across the whole face of it, bending the Tricolors and the Union Jacks before them like a twist of ribbon. Unknown names leaped from the map into a sharp reality—Liège, Naumur, Mons, Cambrai, Arras, Soissons, the Marne—the battle of the Marne that meant Paris. Then slowly the sickening curve of the little flags straightened, not very much, but enough. Then the northern end of the line repeated the same pattern; Bruges, Zeebrugge, Ostend—the little Belgian flags bent back almost to Dunkirk. Again they wavered and slowed; a cluster of all the Allied colors grew thick around a place called Ypres. They stayed there. But it began to dawn on everyone that the war would not be over by Christmas.

The Actresses' Franchise League was the first of the suffrage societies to put its talents and training to wartime use. The Women's Emergency Fund was started by Eva and Decima Moore during the first weeks of the war to help deal with the refugee problem. Next came a fund for the thousands of members of the artistic professions thrown out of work by the general dislocation. Workrooms were opened where the untrained and otherwise unemployable, the frail and elderly, could work for pay; the others were helped to find different kinds of jobs. It was discovered that almost all the toys which had delighted British youth at Christmas time had come from Germany. A soft-toy industry leaped into being, frugal, because there was no money for raw materials, but frenzied. Elderly wardrobe mistresses, those natural distressees,

251

did astonishing things with old woolen stockings; ex-property-masters were marvelously inventive with glue and paint and scraps of wood. The Fund clambered onto its feet. Even after the early wartime crises had shaken down and normal employment was to some extent restored, the Three Arts Women's Employment Fund remained in being for over ten years.

The AFL initiated a farsighted program, much ahead of its time, for drafting women to replace men in jobs they had never held before, not only in offices and hospitals, but as factory workers, cab drivers, and, most importantly, on the land. The government which had fought the suffragettes so bitterly now made eager use of them. The famous militant Charlotte Marsh found herself drafted as chauffeur to the minister the women had most detested, Lloyd George.

It was not long before the whole rhythm of our lives in Bedford Street underwent a subtle change, due, indirectly, to "enemy action", but known to my father and me as "Mamie's committees". The dining room practically became an office. I was always surprised that we still managed to eat there, the table was so littered with pamphlets and leaflets and stacks of writing paper with boldly printed letterheads. I can still see the succession of them: THE ERA WAR DISTRESS FUND, THE WOMEN'S EMERGENCY CORPS, THE THREE ARTS WOMEN'S EMPLOYMENT FUND, THE BRITISH WOMEN'S HOSPITAL, THE NATION'S FUND FOR NURSES, THE EDITH CAVELL HOMES, and half a dozen more. The printing usually started in boldface capitals with PATRON: H.M. THE QUEEN, or some lesser royalty, and invariably, somewhere down below in smaller print, came the notation, Chairman: May Whitty.

The Actresses' Franchise League dropped its suffrage label, not without a clang and some affronted resignations, and welcomed new non-suffrage recruits, such as Lilian Braithwaite, Elizabeth Asquith and Lady Cowdray. When its earlier activities were established and organized, it rechristened itself the British Women's Hospital. The objective was to send a hospital unit to France, under the aegis of the Red Cross, but financed, maintained and completely staffed by women. The authorities had a fit. The Queen's surgeon, however, induced the Red Cross to offer an alternative. The famous old Star and Garter Hotel, which for more than a hundred years had crowned Richmond Hill with glamorous festivities, had been offered as a gift to the Queen, if the money could be raised to rebuild it, equip it and endow it in perpetuity as a home for permanently disabled soldiers and sailors. The committee agreed to do this. For good measure, they threw in an additional rest home on the south coast for the patients and a Compassionate Fund for their relatives. In eleven months they raised £150,000—or three quarters of a million dollars.

They did not neglect their original intentions about a women's hospital. When such units were finally permitted, they financed and staffed them. The Red Cross, which had viewed them with grudging suspicion, gave them more and bigger work loads. They were asked to form the Nation's Fund for Nurses, which turned into an enterprise of gargantuan ramifications and became the nucleus of the entire system of education, endowment and welfare of the nursing profession in Great Britain. Successive committees of this organization raised a quarter of a million pounds in four years. The over-all expenses, such was their proud boast, were less than four per cent of the money raised. I used to think that at least £10,000 was saved right in our dining room at Bedford Street.

All through my growing-up years I have visions of my mother sitting before her blue leather writing case until one or two o'clock in the morning, covering sheet after sheet of letterhead paper with her swift and dashing script. On one occasion Queen Mary, having been induced to attend a function that she didn't much care about, responded to my mother's greeting with a huffy: "You write very clever letters. The people you work for should be grateful." Often "Madam Chair" could be heard to mutter over her never-ending letters: "Dear So-and-so, she does work so hard . . . and then I have to work twice as hard unpicking . . ." or "I think we're going to be able to get the Prince of Wales, but who on earth can I put next to him? They'll all bore him to death . . ." or "I don't care if she *is* a Duchess, she can't make the collection speech."

Madam Chair was also envoy and office boy, writer of publicity, maker of the appeal; and more importantly, peacemaker,

umpire, conciliator, healer of wounded vanities and ruffled feelings. High Society, social workers, temperamental stars, belligerent members of the Labour Party, imperious matrons of great
hospitals at whose nod strong men trembled, all deferred, in the
end, to Madam Chair. They respected her integrity and were a
little afraid of her wit.

In the meantime she never discontinued her "agin' the government" politics. She was successively—and to some extent justifia-
bly—accused of being a pro-German, a pacifist, a Sinn Feiner and
a bolshevik. She cared not at all for any of these labels, but
continued to pursue the work in hand. It involved ironies; such as
lunching at Number 10 Downing Street with her mortal foe,
Prime Minister Asquith; and a certain amount of what she called
"hob-nobbing with royalty", a more restricted pastime then than it
is now. Although this amused her (especially when she thought of
the Whitty Aunts), I think she never took it in quite the proper
spirit—unless, which is possible, irreverence is the proper spirit.
When the Star and Garter buildings were finally finished and
equipped, and dedicated with great ceremony by the King and
Queen, she had to make the speech of presentation. Afterward the
Queen congratulated her, adding: "I'm sure everyone could hear
every word you said." "I meant them to, Ma'am," replied May
tartly. This was too much for the press, who credited her with the
reply: "I meant them, too, Ma'am." This was true enough, and
far more respectful, but not at all in character.

The kind of money which she and her colleagues managed to
raise was extraordinary within the context of war, when other
demands were so enormous and so vital. The toll of the First
World War was grim, exorbitant, unsparing. People read the
casualty lists—or suffered them—with ever-increasing horror.
They learned for the first time about submarines—the U-boats
sank over a thousand ships—and air raids, and bungling disasters
like Gallipoli and the wholesale butchery of the Somme. The
nation was very far from festive; yet the money had to be raised by
festivities. It could never have been done without the theatre. May
Whitty, Lilian Braithwaite and half a dozen others were engaged
in almost all the work which meant so much to so many. The

upshot, not unnaturally, was that Madam Chair got Damed.

The Order of the British Empire had only recently been instituted. Women had for the first time been awarded a title in their own right. Only two actresses had before received it, the veteran Geneviève Ward, and Ellen Terry. May felt strongly that she should refuse the honor. She did not think it was a time to decorate civilians for any reason at all; but if it were, many others deserved it more than she. Secondly, she didn't want to accept any honor recommended by a Lloyd George government. Thirdly, she would feel like the Dame in a pantomime and nobody would know what to call her. She was duly overpowered by her friends. I believe she always felt an obligation to live up to the title which she felt she had fortuitously earned. It seems to me that she succeeded.

But her fears about what people would call her proved amply justified. "Dame Whitty" was the most frequent and persistent. "Dame *May*," she would plead wistfully. "You wouldn't say 'Sir Irving'—or even 'Sir Falstaff.' " The correct vocative was also a puzzle, even to the Debrett-minded. It was being hazily discussed at a luncheon, when the butler (there still were some) appeared Jeeves-like at her elbow and asked in a penetrating voice: "Claret, *my lady?*" Ben got involved in the general confusion and was often ennobled too. At the first official function they attended together they were announced in stentorian tones as "Mr. Dame Webster and Mrs. Webster." But the most acute difficulties arose a few years later in New York, where, among other embarrassments, the stage door keeper of the Empire Theatre threatened to knock down an affrighted visitor who had "dared to call our Miss Whitty a dame."

PART THREE

. . . and Margaret

CHAPTER FOURTEEN

Some Beginnings

During these war years a self I begin to recognize arrives on the scene. I have, of course, the closest and sharpest identification with the Peggy of the Peter Pan house and of the toy soldier's "funrel". No place that I have ever seen or will see means to my heart what Chiddingfold and Woolacombe (those charming, chiming names!) have meant. It seems to me incredible that only six years elapsed between the return of the Webster family from the Mrs. Pat tour, when I was only three, and the outbreak of World War I. "The day was at first as a year when children played in the garden . . ."; but between three years old and nine is a great gulf fixed. A pleistocene age passes by. During the First World War there enters the cold, cause-and-effect figure of reason. I am ceasing to be a small animal to whom things, mainly pleasant things, happen. The film runs more steadily from the reel. There is a continuity which indicates "because of this . . . this."

The war, to a child, was "tremendously thrilling"—it is Hilda Wangel's phrase. The hint of danger sharpened the excitement. I was filled with nationalistic fervor; I am appalled, now, to watch this emotion, very proper in a child of ten, engulfing and imperiling the world. I was, naturally, sure that everything would come out right in the end and that the last-act curtain would be a happy one. (Happy!) I was spurred to flights of patriotic versification in which I celebrated "England's Glory" in strict meter and simple rhyme. On the flat roof at Bedford Street was a small water tank, about four feet by six, and I would clamber on top of it and stride to and fro, composing and declaiming. The fact that neither the cistern nor the roof had any guardrail never occurred to me, though it alarmed my mother considerably when she first caught sight of me, dramatically poised in space. But she let me finish the verse before luring me to safer ground.

"England's Glory" was published in a London newspaper and reissued as a glossy leaflet with the King's picture, in admiral's uniform, on the front and an appeal for The Fund on the back. I forget which of Mamie's Funds it was. During the war, as I advanced toward my teens, my poems grew more somber. I also became drawn increasingly into the orbit of Mamie's Good Causes. I appeared as things; I collected for things; I presented bouquets to H.R.H. or Her Grace the Duchess of; I peered over the tops of bazaar stalls; I sold programs, flags, everything in sight. By the time I was twelve I was a veteran of the whole business. It continued through the postwar years and to this day awakens answering tremors in me of "Oh yes, of *course* I will . . . (Oh Lord! not *again!*)"

Flag Days, I think, were the first and the worst. They were a punishment to buyers and sellers alike. The sellers were frequently actresses, or embryo ones, and I suppose it was good training in making contact with your audience. First you had to tie a string around your neck, from which hung, precariously, a cardboard tray stuck all over with little emblems impaled on pins. These were the insignia of the cause. I remember especially the wild roses of Queen Alexandra's Rose Day—harmless as to color, but the crimp came out of them; violets—the Edith Cavell Homes, I think—which empurpled everything within reach; and, later, the Flanders poppies, which were then and have remained the most durable.

Armed with these you prowled your allotted beat, shaking a metal container at the passers-by and murmuring at them exhortation, appeal or threat. The eyes of the pedestrian would immediately assume a blank expression, as for blindness, or she would dive madly across the street under the wheels of a bus, or he would stop resentfully, and, after much fumbling, produce a penny. Your collecting tin grew heavy with them, while your shilling emblems remained unsold, and if it was raining, which was usual, the dye of the flags left stains all over you which never came off again. Flag Days, during the war, reached the proportions of an epidemic.

Then there were Sunday Concerts, given regularly at one of the big music halls, like the Alhambra or the Palladium. They were strenuously opposed by the Lord's Day Observance Society and held in the teeth of the licensing laws. You might legally sing on a Sunday, but not, if you were George Robey, paint on those famous eyebrows or wear a funny hat. You might recite, but not act. If two or more stars played a sketch together they had to veil it under the pretense that they were each, severally, "reciting"—which, indeed, they sometimes were. May always had a lurking fear that she would end her Charity Concert career in jail; and I, selling my programs humbly in the upper reaches of the theatre, never quite lost the hope of seeing uniformed "bobbies" come marching down the aisles below.

Most profitable of all were the All-Star Matinees. For the organizer they must have been sheer hell, but the innocent bystander like me had a wonderful time. I was usually allowed to attend the dress rehearsal, where the most celebrated figures of the English stage would flock together, many of them never having attended any previous rehearsal, and greet each other with surprised delight. "Darling! Are *you* in this? How lovely! No, I don't really know who I'm supposed to be, but it's in the Ball Scene and I have two lines with darling Gerald. No, I haven't seen him yet—we did have one rehearsal for the Minuet—of course you weren't there—well, practically nobody was, so I expect they'll have to do it all over again—but it's getting terribly late—I must go in ten minutes . . ."

Benefits never changed much, though fortunately there are fewer of them nowadays. Here is one from the postwar years, described in a letter I wrote to my mother; the last scene from *A*

Midsummer Night's Dream was to be the gala item on a variety program. Almost all the actors were ex-members of the Benson Shakespeare companies and all had firm, but conflicting ideas of the traditional Benson business.

"Theseus firmly took charge of the proceedings. 'No, no, *no*, old boy, don't you remember? Quince turned round there and banged into Snout and he fell over Bottom's sword—it was a sure laugh.' 'Well, we never did that in my day, old man.' 'Oh, yes, yes you must have . . . now come along, Clarkie my boy, you say "Moon, take thy flight," and he's asleep so you poke him with the sword . . .' 'No, *no!* in *my* day *Quince* went to sleep and *I* said . . .' 'Well in *my* day *I* used to wake him up . . .' etc. etc.

"Later, the eighty stars who were walking on as wedding guests turned up—or about half of them did—and were duly divided into Groups and were pushed about and shouted at by Edy [Craig]. 'Where's Group Seven? Come along, now, come along—I told you your Groups—*can't* you remember? You there on the right—Group SEVEN!' and eventually Marie Lohr or Violet Vanbrugh would appear, very sheepish and self-conscious, trying to look like a Group and nervously anxious about whether or not to curtsey . . ."

Nevertheless, some notable things, vaunting not themselves, were accomplished in the cause of Charity. I remember in 1915, in aid of the King George's Pension Fund, a profoundly moving and magnificent All-Star performance of *Henry VIII*, produced by Sir Herbert Tree with as much care as if it had been going to run forever. His own Wolsey still seems to me, in retrospect, incomparable, and probably much closer to Shakespeare's intention than Irving's. Irving must have been the arrogant Prince of the Church and the broken figure of the final scene; but Tree was also, combined with these, the butcher's son from Ipswich. The cast was diamond-studded. My father had two lines; and I fell in love with Henry Ainley as Buckingham.

Tree, again, produced an even more scintillating *School for Scandal* with a full complement of brilliant performances. Among them I remember best Fred Terry, Ellen's younger brother, as Charles. There was never anyone, in my time, who could wear a square-cut coat and lace ruffles, a white wig and a rapier as could Fred Terry, with such grace and dash and virile magnificence. It was as if these were indeed the garments he put on every morning when he got out of bed; as if they were not costumes but clothes. He had a warm, infectious gaiety and a laugh which came from his blood and was not just a small, intellectual snigger. Yet he was the most elegant creature imaginable.

Occasionally these all-star revivals were expanded into a brief run with the profits devoted to the Good Cause in question. Such was the case with Forbes-Robertson's production of *The Passing of the Third Floor Back*, which moved to the Queen's Theatre and settled down there. Both my parents were playing in it, and when Forbes-Robertson left, my father took over his part. On matinee days I would always go around to the theatre on my way home from school and crouch under the window of the set, listening to the play. After the first few times I knew it by heart; I secretly nourished the dream that Lady Forbes-Robertson, who played Stasia, the little "slavey", would meet with a sudden accident and I would leap into the breach in her stead. Stasia could easily be a child of twelve, I thought—better, indeed, than an old woman just over forty—and though I was small for my age I was very grown-up, really. It might have happened. But it didn't.

I cannot claim ever to have made a genuine and official debut. I rather seem to have attained professional status in a few peculiar jumps and a series of slithers. There was a very little one early in the war, when I took part in a masque in the gardens of the Inner Temple. The chief item on this program (in aid of something-or-other, of course) was the Garden Scene from *Much Ado About Nothing*, with Ellen Terry as Beatrice. I can still see the stooping, golden figure dip and glide onto the green lawn as swiftly as a bird in flight.

In July 1917 my mother was one of a company of star actresses who were to play a benefit performance of a new piece specially written for the occasion by Louis N. Parker. It was called *The Women's Tribute*. The characters ranged through the realms of allegory from the abstract to the concrete, variously embodying Peace, Courage, The Mother, The Nurse, Britannia, New Zealand, and so on. It was very stimulating and patriotic and mostly in very blank verse. The night before the matinee, the actress who was to play Youth was taken ill. Clara Butt, who had heard me recite some poetry at a lesser fund-raising occasion, telephoned my mother to ask if she thought I could play it. May was extremely doubtful and said I was already in bed and asleep. She agreed to wake me up, however, and ask what I thought. She warned me that the part included a newly written speech of thirty lines which Mr. Parker would have to bring around himself later that night. I said of course I could do it and then went to sleep again. In the morning when I woke, the part and the new speech were lying beside my bed. I sat up and learned them.

When the time of the performance came, I was not nearly so lighthearted. The grease paint on my face felt hot and sticky and I thought I looked stupid in a kind of Greek tunic, rather too big for me, and a fat, scratchy wreath of artificial flowers. Besides, Mr. Parker had terrified me at the one, brief rehearsal, with his ebony stick and his ear trumpet and his brusque, rapid commands. My heart pounded like mad and I felt sick. Maybe I looked it, for Lilian Braithwaite, as Britannia, laid aside her shield and trident and held my hand in the wings till it was time for me to go on. I still remember how the footlights seemed to glare up at me as I advanced toward them and the auditorium beyond was like a limitless black cavern, stretching away to infinity. I didn't dry up or anything, and went and took my place among the Abstracts while the Colonies said their pieces. At last it was over and we marched off in turn while Clara Butt sang the concluding anthem. I was the last to go; and I have wondered since what we looked like standing together, me, stiff as a ramrod, very small, in pink, and she towering above me in black, fully six feet two and statuesque to match.

Everyone was very kind to me, especially Marion Terry (Peace), and the following week *The Stage* described me as "a brilliant young lady of undoubted histrionic gifts." I was elated, naturally, but not, in my heart, satisfied. I felt I had merely "got through". I suppose this was the nearest I ever got to a genuine "debut"; but it was only a Charity matinee, so I never felt that it really counted.

It was obvious by this time, even to a child like me, that the war was not all excitement. Young men we knew went off to France and never came back. A cousin of my mother's appeared in hospital blue with only one leg. Some of the American "uncles" began to turn up in mysterious uniforms. Gretchen's letters, long filled with gloom and misery, became hysterical with relief when the United States entered the war. My father kept trying to get into some branch of the army and my mother kept trying to stop him, not so much because she was afraid of his going to France as of his being sent to Ireland to serve with the terrible Black-and-Tans. Anyway, he was over fifty and nobody would have him. He felt a little ashamed of having to play heroes in war films. He was paradoxically a little comforted by nearly getting his head blown off by a too-real bomb. My mother was not. The medium, however, was even then more lucrative than the theatre, and as "Mamie's committees" did not pay the rent, he was pleased to think he could. He did a three-reeler in a week, and wrote of it: "My terms are £6 10s a day [$32.50]. Harry Ainley tells me he started at £3, went to £5, got £7 10s for Rudolph in *Zenda*, but for *Brother Officers* he got only £5 again, so I don't seem quite out of it."

The trend of the London theatres inclined, inevitably, to farce and light comedy, and in these Ben duly appeared. He managed one more Prince, at the St. James's, but Rudolph of Ruritania had been mortally wounded along with Archduke Ferdinand at Sarajevo. So had the actor-manager, though he didn't know it yet. The theatre had to "entertain", and it did so with all the vim it could summon. Musicals did gloriously and were, like *The Bing Boys*, glorious—or seemed so to all who saw them. Sentimental pieces like *Peg o' My Heart* and *Romance*, both with American stars, ran forever. The brave forward-looking repertory companies went under; with the very notable exception of the Birmingham Repertory, which had started in 1913 and, thanks to Barry Jackson, survived to do wonderful things. In 1916 the Government, for the first time, imposed an entertainment tax; in the next seven years it brought the British treasury £57,000,000.

Meanwhile there were other trials. Something called "rationing" came in, which was a great worry to my mother and to Frances, once more in command of our kitchen. There were queues— Frances called them "queebs"—outside the shops, which made Mamie late for her committees. The dignified Victorian establishment at the end of our street which supplied everybody with food and was universally known as "the Stores" acquired the stature of a club; rumors, anxieties, hopes were interchanged among its waiting clients. If you had meat coupons it by no means followed that you could get meat, or if so what meat. At one time May felt convinced that "the Stores" had bought up a camel which had been forced by ill health to resign its part in *Chu Chin Chow*. None of this ranked as the kind of food shortage that Great Britain grew to know during the Second World War—indeed everything was lavish and plentiful by comparison. But it was new, and nobody liked it.

Another unpleasant novelty appeared, and multiplied: the air raids. Very insignificant and puny they seem now, the bombs so few and small, the targets so limited, the damage so slight. Nevertheless, if the bomb did hit you it killed you; and Bedford Street was well in the line of fire. The attacking planes could not carry enough load to bomb indiscriminately, nor did they have the navigational devices to which we have grown accustomed; in the final stage they had to use their eyes. This meant that they would approach London along the line of the river and unleash their bombs in the central area just north of it, for in this vicinity lay the Houses of Parliament, Buckingham Palace, the railway terminals, most of the London theatres, and coincidentally Bedford Street.

The Zeppelin raids came first, ominous, clumsy pioneers. They struck only on dark nights, and we learned to look upon the moon as a friend. But "the Zepps" proved too vulnerable, and in the plane raids which followed the moon was an enemy, silvering the telltale ribbon of the Thames. Several theatres were hit almost immediately, and theatre business was apt to "ebb and flow by the moon." There were very primitive warning systems and street black-outs which were more exasperating than effective, except in the damage they did to the theatres.

The daylight raids came last. One Saturday morning, as my mother and Frances were sitting in the kitchen placidly discussing what form of camel we could have for Sunday lunch, May suddenly caught sight of the planes. They flew in V-shaped formation, gleaming in the sun, beautiful and swift, heading straight for 31 Bedford Street. She called to me and I yelled to Edy and Chris below and we all rushed to the nearest window and hung out of it, watching till they were vertically above us. "How lovely!" we all said. A few seconds later came the crashes and the puffs of smoke.

The daylight raids never became very frequent or very severe, but the night raids were both. Covent Garden Market was hit, Charing Cross Hospital, and other targets too close for comfort. When Ben was playing and May was not, she preferred to join him so that they could both be killed together. If I was not at school, she would take me along too. She collaborated with a friend whose husband was an early species of air-raid warden and who received telephonic warning when a raid was expected over the "Metropolitan Area". The news was supposedly top-secret, so a code was devised between them. The Metropolitan Area was "Ma". If Ma was reported as breathing freely, we would deduce that there was a high wind and no planes were expected; if Ma's temperature had not yet been taken, we would remain uncertain, waiting for the telephone to ring. But if Ma was worse and they had sent for the doctor we would put on our hats and coats and walk over to the theatre in case Ma suddenly got spasms.

Outside London it was often more severe. From Hull, in October 1916, Ben wrote: "The poorer people troop out in thousands to a little village about three miles out and sit under hedges until the raid is officially over when the trams go out and bring them back free of charge." In Nottingham, during a dress rehearsal, there was a total black-out of all electricity the moment the alarm sounded. In a strange theatre, no one could find his dressing room, let alone his clothes, and Ben finally decided to feel his way back to the hotel in what he was wearing, which was the uniform of a German general.

In 1917 Ben and May were playing together, for one of the few times in their careers. There had been a benefit revival of *Trelawny of the Wells*, successful enough to be continued for a run at the New Theatre. Ben was playing Tom Wrench, with Irene Vanbrugh, Dion Boucicault and May herself in their original parts. When the raids became an almost nightly occurrence, every other "straight" play in London either closed or switched to matinee performances; but not *Trelawny*. "I will not," said Boucicault firmly, "give the Kaiser the satisfaction of knowing that he has closed the New Theatre." During the Second World War such stories were repeated many times under conditions inconceivably worse. But there has to be a first time for everything, and this was London's first time.

In those days the County Council Fire Department insisted that every stage should be partially roofed with glass, so that the actors could be roasted by upward-roaring flames and the danger deflected from the auditorium. They could also, of course, be the more easily killed by any stray piece of shrapnel or chunk of broken glass; so when Ben was in a scene without May, she would stand in the wings. Not so the stage crew. "Why these 'ere bombs," said one of them, "is 'oppin' round us like fleas," and they very sensibly retired to the stone staircase below ground level. One night Suzanne Ainley appeared and insisted on massaging everybody's back to relax them. She gave May a bizarre-looking helmet which she said she had got from a German uhlan, and, being Suzanne, quite possibly had. May passed it on to the wardrobe mistress, who was of a nervous disposition. At the next loud bang she gave an involuntary jump which caused the helmet to fall off and clatter down three flights of stone stairs, creating near-panic among the theatre firemen, who forthwith barred everybody from their dressing rooms except May, who had a quick change and fought her way in with tooth and claw.

Sadly, I missed all this fun. The husband of May's committee companion, Lady Cowdray, was Minister for Air; and he had warned May that the raids were likely to get much worse during the autumn months. She packed me off hurriedly to a small Christian Science school in Devonshire, where I was very homesick and furious at my exile. Within a week or so, however, I managed to organize a consolation prize. The school was to give a Christmas show at the end of term; the star turn—at my suggestion—would be the Trial Scene from *The Merchant of Venice;* and somehow I was cast as Portia. I announced this in a letter, with five exclamation points to indicate my astonishment.

I was full of demands for make-up and clothes. My mother made me a replica of Ellen Terry's red barrister's robes. I wrote: "Gratiano's knickers are still rather a problem." (Gratiano is now Mrs. Boris Karloff.) I was not supposed to have anything to do with the direction, being merely a new girl. But I wrote my skeptical comments: "Nerissa has a tendency to sit with one hand on her hip and the other in her mouth which must be overcome." The show finally passed off with great aplomb to an audience which just outnumbered the cast. I also contributed a Muff Dance. The next day we all went home for the holidays.

That very night there was a raid—a real one, lasting over four hours. The sirens went exactly as soup was being placed on the dining table. Back went the soup, and we all trooped down to the first-floor offices, whose owners let us have the keys for use as a night-time air-raid shelter. Edy Craig and her friends joined us, clad for a peaceful evening in a colorful assortment of turbans, sandals, corduroy pajamas and Chinese robes. We all sat around playing parlor games and charades. Edy was splendid as an elephant. I enjoyed it all tremendously, including the Big Bangs, and was only sorry when the Boy Scouts came tootling down the street with their bugles to announce the all clear.

When the run of *Trelawny* ended, Ben stayed with the same management in a play of Pinero's called *The Freaks.* He played the skeleton man in a circus troupe which also included two dwarfs. Pinero and Boucicault each conceived a passion for the dwarf scenes. They would rush onto the stage, pushing the two little actors out of the way, and show them how to do it. Back and forth they would go, Pinero glaring down from beneath his bushy eyebrows at Dot, Dot throwing out his chest and glaring up at Pinero.

The company was entranced; but the public never knew what it had missed and didn't, rightly, think much of the play. It was replaced by A. A. Milne's *Belinda* and that, in turn, by his *Mr. Pim Passes By*, in both of which Ben had the very great pleasure of being married to Irene Vanbrugh.

She was a charming woman "of no airs but many graces," my mother used to say, adept at playing that clever, delightful lady who twists the stronger but dumber sex around her little finger. (The type has not gone out, but the technique has changed.) Her comedy was as smooth and dextrous as that of Marie Tempest, but less brittle, and she had a far greater emotional reach, even encompassing tragedy. The Milne plays were butterfly affairs with the up-to-date dialogue that dates faster than anything. A revival of *Mr. Pim* in London in 1968 caused some contemporary critics to dust off their sledge hammers—"baby, whimsical, afraid of reality (sexual as well as economic)." One of the elder critical statesmen, who saw the original, sagely advanced the view that "the modern cast often doesn't know where to look for the laughs"; nor, perhaps, how to twist an inflection or place a pause like Irene Vanbrugh. They probably think that no comedy more than ten years old, at most, can possibly have been about real people. In my youth we thought the same thing about the comedies of the Nineteen Hundreds; and the producers of 1984 had better tread carefully, should they go Barefoot in the Park.

The Milne comedies of that moment were the desired antidote to the tensions of the war's ending and of its aftermath. When *Belinda* was produced the terrible German offensive of 1918 was at its height; gradually it slackened; the Allied armies, the Americans among them, held; the Big Bertha guns could no longer shell Paris. My father wrote: "It's a horrible time, isn't it? but the play goes so well—it does one good to hear people laugh and know that for the moment they are forgetting the cares and troubles that beset us." Escapist? yes, indeed; the mixture as before and since. It is easy to condemn if you have never needed it. In the autumn the air raids slackened, the Germans were in retreat. May and Ben went on tour with escapist *Belinda*, and I was sent to a new school, made of sterner stuff than my Devonshire hideaway: Queen Anne's

Some Beginnings

School, Caversham. I had barely settled down there when the great flu epidemic of 1918 hit the nation, half the school and me. In Manchester, where the Boucicault company was playing, victory was in the air, in the streets; it was even announced from the stage of the Hippodrome next door, with cheering and full orchestra and free champagne. But Manchester, like Woolacombe, was premature; it was only a music-hall armistice.

On Monday morning, November 11th, at eleven o'clock, I and my fellow flu sufferers heard all the air-raid sirens in the town suddenly go off, with all the factory hooters and all the church bells. We climbed out of our beds and tottered to the windows, where we cheered in croaking chorus, while such of the staff as were left on their feet ran up flags on the front lawn. That evening, back in London, May and Ben fought their way to the Wimbledon Theatre through delirium and chaos. An Australian soldier literally carried May aboard an impossibly jammed train. He cried on her shoulder and told her all about his mother and the beautiful cakes she used to bake.

In the theatre, battered actors, arriving late and frantic, greeted each other shakily, old comrades of the glass-roof-air-raid days. "Overture and beginners, please!" yelled the callboy. Amid a babel of carnival noises from the street and the explosion of firecrackers almost as loud as the bombs, the curtain rose as usual, with Irene Vanbrugh in a hammock and a garden of paper hollyhocks. The war to end war had ended.

Getting educated, in the sense of "schooled," is a process which some people dislike very much. I cannot say that I went "willingly to school," except the first time, when I was five years old. I then announced to my mother that a playmate of mine went to school "in the Burlington Arcade" and that I should like to go too. She, remarkable woman, went off to the Burlington Arcade, the home of the most fashionable and expensive shops in London, and inquired of the uniformed Commissionaire whether they also harbored a school. Well, not precisely *in* the arcade, he replied, but there was

a much-respected establishment a hundred yards away in Old
Burlington Street. This was not a smart affair, but it was a sound
one; and to it I went until the air raids forced me to Devonshire
and thence, with apprehension and reluctance, to Queen Anne's
School, Caversham.

This was, and still is, a smallish version of what the English so
confusingly call a "public school," meaning what the Americans
call a "private" one. It had inherited a partial endowment from its
parent body, the Greycoat School in Westminster. This had been
founded at the end of the seventeenth century by eight tradesmen
of the Borough of Westminster, quite literally the butcher, the
baker, the candlestick maker, each of whom contributed £5. From
this foundation there is still a surplus. The balance of the school's
expenses had to be covered by fees, which were extremely moderate. At that time there were some two hundred and fifty pupils,
girls from thirteen to eighteen, mostly daughters of professional
men, doctors or teachers or members of the civil services. The
teaching, I think, looking back, was excellent.

Of course there was much emphasis on sports. This was no
good to me because of my peculiar eyesight; but I was an inveter-
ate organizer and usually ended up as the nonplaying captain of
something or other. There was also, however, an emphasis on
"work." Competition was then thought a virtue in youth, and I got
high marks which redounded to the credit of my "house" and
helped to gain it a coveted yearly trophy—a bronze replica of the
Winged Victory of Samothrace. I progressed determinedly
through various sectors of responsibility till I became "Head Girl."
I was very proud of this, and when I left I couldn't really see how
the place could get on without me. Despite this pomposity, I think
I learned some useful lessons in discipline and the proper exercise
of authority which came in handy later on.

I acquired other possessions, some of them now out of fashion:
a little Latin, for instance. This uniquely logical, structural and
liturgical language became a rocklike foundation for its many
derivatives. Considerably less Greek gave me far more pleasure,
since it opened doors for me on a world of endless magic. My
mother insisted that I learn as much French as possible; in my last

two school years it was my "special subject." For this I couldn't now be more grateful, though I wasn't then. Speaking French is an enforced education in enunciation, in the use of the tongue, teeth, lips, palate, which an actor cannot possibly obtain in the study of English. I would make it obligatory in every drama school. Though English is a richer language, the wealthiest in the world, French is the perfect precision instrument of speech.

QAS wasn't especially theatre-minded, but it fostered the usual quota of school performances. I managed to play leading parts in most of them besides reciting a good deal on white-frock occasions. I played everything from Aladdin in my first year to Abraham Lincoln in my last. As Puck at the prize-giving celebrations when I was fourteen, I went through considerable anguish. First it was about myself: "I am *rotten* and if I'm not chucked I ought to be." Then it was about my fellow actors who "just read their parts and don't act at all"; and finally the teachers in charge "who have no earthly idea of managing a play." I described furiously how one of them would tell me to do it one way and one another way and then the Headmistress would turn up and alter everything all over again and I didn't think any of them knew a thing about acting anyway. My mother replied drily that this routine was precisely what I should subsequently encounter in the professional theatre, and I had better get used to it.

I began to direct myself, finding no one else as good. In *The Prince and the Pauper* I also doubled the leading parts. A friend wrote to my mother: "The nicest part was that all the actors seemed to enjoy it so much—and Peggy is so tactful and always seems to know when to speak and when to keep silence." Would that I had managed to sustain this excellent beginning.

For a time I toyed with the idea of devoting myself to a career of classical research beneath the dreaming spires of Oxford. I passed all the necessary examinations. But Fate kept slithering me toward the professional theatre all the same, and then Edy Craig gave me a fatal gift. She was producing an All-Star Matinee in honor of Shakespeare's birthday at the little Everyman Theatre in Hampstead, one of London's first "experimental" theatres. There was to be an assortment of different scenes, the final and crowning

273

item being the appearance of Ellen Terry as Portia in the Trial Scene from *The Merchant of Venice*. Since she had officially retired many years before, it was a unique opportunity to see her. Among the preceding scenes was the meeting between Oberon and Titania from *A Midsummer Night's Dream;* Edy, with that extraordinary faith in me for which I shall always be grateful, requisitioned me for Puck; and the school authorities allowed me to come to London and do it.

I was not unduly nervous; after all, I had played the part before; I even had my own clothes. Edy, however, improved both costume and performance, the latter by some acid and sobering comment and the former by giving me a small box of the glittering, bronze-green beetles' wings which had been a part of Miss Terry's famous costume as Lady Macbeth. I was, and have been all my life, a clumsy and reluctant artisan with needle and thread; but I sewed on every shard myself, as firmly as if I meant never to part with them, and indeed I never did till an ocean came between us.

Once I was able to smuggle myself into a rehearsal of the Trial Scene, but it was not at all what I had expected. Ellen Terry was evidently disconcerted by the tiny, flat stage and the absence of footlights. Her sight was failing and she wore thick, heavy glasses. You could tell that she looked toward a voice rather than at a face and that she was nervous about getting too close to the edge of the stage. She seemed to have trouble in hearing the cues. Her own lines came hesitantly, and she continually asked for "the word." Edy, probably nervous on her mother's behalf, grew extremely irritable and shouted at her, as well as at the other actors. Everyone was embarrassed and unhappy. I crept away.

On the day of the performance my scene came early and was soon over. I judged that it had been "all right," neither scintillating nor disgraceful, and went downstairs to take my make-up off. But my mother, who was playing in another of the preliminary scenes, took me firmly by the hand and led me to Edy. She said: "I want Peggy to be able to say that she has been on the same stage with Ellen Terry. Will you let her go on at the back of the crowd in the Trial Scene?" "Of course," replied Edy without blinking an eye.

She whisked me off to the wardrobe room and snatched up what looked like a few old rags, twisted them around my head, pinned them together under the arms, flung an end over one shoulder, and there was a small but authentic-looking member of the Venetian populace. I determined to hide at the very back, where nobody would be able to see me; but at the last minute Edy, by now also transformed into a Venetian citizen, seized me by the hand. "Come on with me," she commanded and before I knew it I was standing in the very front row, the curtain was going up, and the Duke was saying: "What, is Antonio here?"

Ever since that moment I have had the most profound sympathy with Shakespearian walk-ons. At the best of times it is not an easy problem to ad-lib in Elizabethan English without sounding idiotic and feeling like a fool. On the other hand, you cannot risk a natural, contemporary remark, since this has a way of plunging into an unexpected silence with the shattering effect of a well-aimed rock. On this occasion I was doubly lost. I didn't know when the crowd was supposed to react and when it wasn't; when it was meant to make noise and when be struck dumb; I didn't even know whose side I was on; but I knew I couldn't stand there in the front row looking like a half-wit. I decided to seem intelligently neutral but rather too young to understand the issues.

I could see offstage into the wings, and in a few moments Miss Terry appeared, helped up the iron spiral staircase which led to the stage by one of Edy's assistants. She was wearing her celebrated scarlet robes and round, red cap. The hair beneath it was snow-white and she still had her glasses on. I could hear her saying "Where is it? I can't see . . . where's the entrance?" They guided her toward it. She took off her glasses and fumbled to lean her stick against the wall. Edy, beside me, was rigid with nervousness. Nerissa came on, very bright and brave. The Clerk read Bellario's letter. "You hear the learn'd Bellario, what he writes," said the Duke. He drew a deep breath. "And here, I take it, is the doctor come." In a flame of scarlet Ellen Terry swept onto the stage.

The applause smashed over her; she seemed neither to respond to it nor ostentatiously to ignore it, but moved directly to the Duke, bowed over his hand with a swift, bending movement, and stood alert, erect, awaiting his instructions. You would have sworn that this was a young woman in her twenties and that the hair beneath the cap was gold. Her first words were quiet, authoritative. She took her place at once by the advocate's stand. No time was wasted on trivialities, on pretending to be Portia pretending to be a man pretending to be nervous or "putting on an act." She cut directly to the heart of the situation and took control of it.

When Shylock stepped forward she turned and looked directly into his face, her eyes a penetrating, shining blue. Having questioned him, she turned to Antonio, very grave and gentle. "You stand within his danger, do you not?" "Ay, so he says." "Do you confess the bond?" "I do." "Then must the Jew be merciful." "On what compulsion must I? tell me that." There was a little pause and then the answer came, perfectly simple and somehow completely surprising: "The quality of mercy is not strain'd . . . It droppeth as the gentle rain from heaven upon the place beneath: it is twice bless'd . . ." The word brimmed over with healing. There was no vocalizing or trick of phrasing. The lines seemed to come of themselves, as if they had never been read or spoken before. I never once thought of how she was saying them, just of what she was saying. ". . . we do pray for mercy, and that same prayer doth teach us all to render the deeds of mercy." A small silence. There had been no "great speech." Something had been said, beautifully and totally. We thought about it for a moment. Shylock refused it, and we hated him.

The scene went on. Ellen Terry played with unfaltering assurance. She used little gesture, but when she did, her arms moved from the shoulder, generously, at full length, the fingertips alive, the beginning and not the end of thought. The mischief danced in her eyes as she teased Bassanio; but she held the tension steadily, mounting, right up to Shylock's "A sentence! Come, prepare!" He leaped forward. "Tarry a little: . . ." It rang out, not loud, but with a resonance that stopped him instantly. It would have stopped a charge of cavalry. ". . . there is something else." And then we heard what it was. At the end there was no longer any question as to what the crowd should "do"; I have no idea what we did, except that we were crying with relief and happiness. Antonio was saved.

Some Beginnings

After the crowd went off we stayed in the wings to watch the end. The gay mockery of the Ring Scene bubbled like champagne. "Well . . . peace be with you," and she danced rather than walked off the stage.

It was raining in the streets when we got outside. The stage door was besieged with people jostling and pushing each other, their faces glowing. It seemed to me that we floated to the Underground and were magically wafted home. I became aware of a fire and food; but I went to bed without really regaining consciousness and slept profoundly. My destiny was now clear to me.

The next time I saw Ellen Terry was in the Bedford Street "lift". This was not really a lift, and certainly not an "elevator". It was a large, wooden, cratelike affair which could be hauled up manually by a system of ropes. There were no gates on the upper floors. You were supposed to heave packages or trunks over the top of the banisters into the box; and the box was just large enough to take a small chair and someone sitting on it. It used to take Ellen Terry. She would be installed on the ground floor and then we all manned the ropes on the upper levels and Edy shouted down from above and we sweated (with fright—she wasn't very heavy) and pulled and hung on like grim death while the lifting-out squad extracted her outside Edy's front door and she laughed helplessly and made it much more difficult. "Benny . . . don't . . . you're tickling me . . . !" Imogen's voice floated down the years.

Later, when I was attending a drama school, Edy did a guest production of the York Nativity Play. I was a kind of prophetess who spoke the Prologue. Attired in long, flowing draperies, flung upon me with Edy's practiced and unerring hand, I had to walk down the center aisle of the auditorium and up some rather steep, makeshift steps onto the stage. Here I delivered a long speech in which came some lines describing a maiden

> *Of Nazareth in Galilee*
> *That to one Joseph wedded be,*
> *Her name is Mary.*

One day Edy brought her mother to rehearsal; she sat in the front row and listened quietly. Afterwards she asked for me; she repeated the lines from memory and then commented: "That word, 'Mary' . . . say it with love." She spoke it herself, entirely without sentimentality, but the name of the mother of Jesus glowed with light.

She came to the performance and again sat in the front row. Nervously I marched through the audience and climbed over the steps. To do this rhythmically, with dignity, easily, and without scooping up the draperies in your hand, which is cheating, is quite a trick. I managed it, however, spoke my Prologue and started down the steps again—a perfectly simple operation, which should involve no drapery trouble at all—when the golden Terry voice rang through the hall. "Very good, Peggy!" she said delightedly. "Very good!" I immediately tripped over my draperies and fell on my knees in the aisle.

During the last years of her life my father managed some of her business affairs for her, and once, when she was staying at the house of some friends in Kent, I drove him down to see her. Before he left, she asked for me and I went into the room. She was sitting in an armchair with her back to the windows, dressed in a gown of deep green-blue with a rug over her knees. Her hair, swept back from the square brow, was gleaming white. The beautiful actor's mask of her face was clear and firm, like a woodcut, the mouth wide and generous, the eyes blindingly blue. She couldn't see me; someone told her who I was and she stretched out her feeling hands to me, alive with warmth and welcome, and cried out, "Why, it's Peggy!" in the old, ringing voice. She asked me some questions, forgot the answers, asked me the same things again, began to grow tired. But the flash of laughter in her eyes was irrepressible, the bubble of mischief still lurked in her voice. Clemence Dane has best described it. She was "like Ariel in the tree."

She died soon afterwards. The funeral took place at our own little church of St. Paul's, Covent Garden. The crowds were so great that not a quarter of them could get inside. My father had to explain to the others that there was no room left except for a few of her close friends. A woman came up to him, almost in tears. "I must be there," she said, "I must! You don't know what she meant to me. I never met her but she made my whole life a different thing."

After her mother's death, Edy turned the old Kentish barn which stood in the fields beyond her house into a rough-hewn handmade playhouse, with a crooked wooden stage. Performances were given every July on the anniversary of Ellen Terry's death. Every actor was glad to play in them. Later Edy started a Barn Theatre Society and did rare and unknown plays, just as in the days of the Pioneer Players she had produced "collectors' items" from Russia and France and Japan and America that nobody had then heard of. At the Barn I remember Claudel's *The Hostage*, Yeats's *Purgatory*, the original fourteenth-century Flemish *Tale of Beatrice* from which sprang *The Miracle*, and Sheila Kaye-Smith's *Child Born at the Plough*. I was in several of them. Conditions were frequently chaotic; willing helpers fell over each other in their excitement, inefficiency and enthusiasm. Edy marshaled everybody, dragooned everybody, charged them with resolution. Suddenly, there was a beautiful, moving performance.

The Barn still stands today, with its black wooden walls and deeply sloping thatched roof, like a sturdy little ark on the edge of Romney Marsh. It is still played in and the air is still charged with vibrance; sometimes with a furious gust of wind. I have never been prone to ghosts, but the Barn is marvelously haunted.

Sybil Thorndike has said of Edy: "She was big—and simple. She hated trimmings. I trusted her utterly. I would have done anything she told me, blindfolded; her instinct was so unerringly right." Ernest Milton echoed this: "You knew, after the first searchlight gaze, that you were in safe hands." Those who worked with her were in agreement that her criticisms could be brusque and trenchant but never devious, always galvanic and often unexpected and profound.

The improvisations for which she had a real flair were partly thrust upon her, for the professional theatre in London at that time would never have accepted a woman doing the job, or jobs, she did. But in a sense I think she preferred it that way. She hated anything prefabricated, elaborate, solid, frozen. Faced with our union regulations and restrictions of the present day, she would undoubtedly have exploded in a blinding flash.

I have vivid pictures of her throughout my childhood, sitting huddled over a gas fire in an old turquoise-blue dressing gown, her white hair gleaming, her brilliant brown eyes looking right into mine. (I have always thought that "brilliant," as applied to eyes, meant blue; but Edy's were brilliant and brown, merry, meditative, penetrating.) She would discuss anything and everything, often way above my head, but striking sparks from me all the same. She could be funny or belligerent. She was wonderful with children. She was of no religion, but in her work she was religious.

I know now that I have done many things because of what I watched her do—set a light, angle a rostrum, drape a cloak, compose a picture on the stage; my eyes and hands learned these things. She made me understand what craft meant in the theatre. She knew everybody's job, from the author's to the usher's. From all she exacted workmanship, to all she accorded value. Her shows were frequently a battle, but it was always an exciting one.

She and her much more famous brother Gordon—"Teddy"—had many things in common. But he was essentially an artist of the imagination, she a craftsman in practice. She wrote nothing about herself; he never stopped. As a result, the Terry-Craig biographies concentrate on him. The references to her are scanty and misleading; some are openly hostile. She could arouse bitter antagonisms and never suffered fools with even a semblance of gladness. She loved her mother with a fierce, protective possessiveness. Ellen Terry inspired, without in the least meaning to, possessive and jealous emotions in the men and especially the women who loved her. They all wanted to be "the one" to look after her and understand her and protect her. They were united in only one thing—they hated Edy, who stood in the way.

Whatever the rights and wrongs of these faded factions, two things stand, incontrovertibly, as a memorial to Edy: one is the Shaw-Terry correspondence, which would never have been published without her. Shaw himself testifies to his own initial reluctance and Gordon Craig's continued and bitter opposition. The other is the preservation of the two beautiful cottages, and the Barn, at Small Hythe, under the protection of the National Trust, in permanent memory of Ellen Terry. For this, too, posterity is indebted to Edy.

CHAPTER FIFTEEN

———— ৪০৪ ————

A Time to Sow

The world which awaited me outside the school walls in the early Twenties was a confused, rapid-moving affair. Bright Young Things were making hectic efforts to forget the recent unpleasantness and to pretend that we could all be as gay and carefree as our parents had been ten years earlier, before the war. Women, having got the vote, didn't bother very much about it; but they had secured the entree to many professions formerly closed to them. Income tax skyrocketed and there were strikes and unemployment and everybody who voted Labour was thought to be a bolshevik. Edy and her friends in the flat below us went around defiantly in red scarves and Astrakhan caps, thereby clinching the matter. The theatre was a mirror for conflicting images. Audiences wanted something brittle which would make them forget the war. They also wanted something with a message that would help them to give a shape to the peace. The old actor-managers were a thing of the past, and the new managers were mostly theatre owners who operated a highly speculative and opportunistic business. There was a lot of unemployment among actors and working conditions were confused and deteriorating.

A Time to Sow

The school authorities did not try overtly to dissuade me from embarking on this choppy sea. They merely suggested that it would be splendid, wouldn't it, to get a scholarship to Oxford, and there was nothing like three years at this ancient university, was there? My parents agreed that all this would, indeed, be very splendid. But my mother asked gently whether I really thought I could afford to—she almost said "waste," but snatched the word back in time—*spend* three years learning things which, though of the highest value in themselves, would be of no direct help to me if I decided to be an actress. I should not emerge into the theatre until I was over twenty-one; and what did I think my contemporaries would have been doing while I luxuriated in the humanities and a punt on the Isis? "I wonder," she added speculatively, "whether you might not like to leave school at Easter and spend three months in Paris?"

I was dreadfully torn, partly from conceit, because the number of places open to women at Oxford or Cambridge in the early Twenties was still extremely limited and I was flattered by the sanguine hopes held out to me. Still . . . three months in Paris, the theatres, the Opéra, the Champs Elysées and the Louvre . . . I chose Paris.

In the United States in the late Sixties, it has become almost universal practice to acquire a college degree of some kind, very often to stay a fifth or sixth year and get a Master's; quite frequently to pursue a Ph.D. for a further couple of years, or longer. Much of what you absorb is the valuable stuff of life; much of it could quite well be acquired off campus. The theatre is a very educative medium if you want to get educated. It is also one of the very few fields left in the United States where nobody cares in the least whether you have a degree or not, but only what you've done, what you look like (which often includes how young you are), and whether you have any talent. I have visited many theatre departments in the universities of America, sympathetically, sometimes admiringly, occasionally with envy. But I have never seen reason to conclude that the decision I made in 1923 was the wrong one, or to think that I would not make the same one today.

Paris, for me, was quite an adventure. Looking back, it is hard to understand why my family so seldom went abroad. Paris is, after all, not much further away from London than Woolacombe. But in those days the Channel, actually so very small, seemed very large indeed to the insular English, and the perils of crossing it—for "perils," read "seasickness"—were deeply embedded in British folklore and much impressed upon the young.

To me it was a challenge. My French, after a few shuddering collisions with the vernacular, survived the test. In retrospect, the months I spent in Paris seem a little odd. The Left Bank was no haunt of wild Bohemians to me; I just lived there, attended lectures at the Sorbonne, bought books in the arcades of the Odéon, and never so much as saw a drunken painter or a tubercular midinette. The Grandes Couturières were far beyond my reach— or interest. I knew the Louvre by heart, and most of the other museums and churches in or near the city; but for me the Avenue de l'Opéra was simply a street leading to the opera. I never noticed the shops.

One of my honorary aunts, Eva Moore, had given me £10 as a special fund for theatregoing. Never has £10 gone further or bought greater value. At the Comédie and the Odéon I found Corneille stiff and declamatory, Racine not much better. But Molière at his own House had an inevitable rightness. Although the acting was stylized to the highest degree it seemed entirely "natural." I wrote: "How beautifully the French enunciate. No English actor talking at the pace they do could ever get half his words out clearly. Therefore they have a greater variety of pace in actual speech than we have and a much greater command of effect."

I discovered also how Lucien Guitry could sustain a silence for what seemed like ten minutes and you could follow his thought through every second of it. He would stand perfectly still in the middle of the stage and power flowed from him like a rhinoceros before it charges. The audience would be spellbound. However, it could also shout, boo, hiss, applaud, and hurl epithets when the political views expressed in a play aroused its favor or displeasure. In my stiff, English way, I found this very ill-mannered.

I was beglamoured by the great, gilt Opéra for its own sake, not deeply minding what went on there. The Russians were much in evidence, and I reveled in Stravinsky's *Les Noces* and Baliev's Chauve-Souris. I was "foudroyée," I wrote (helpfully translating, "thunderstruck"), by the Pitoëffs' production of *Six Characters in Search of an Author*, the first time it had ever been played outside Italy; and I was quite right, it was "foudroyant." I passed severe strictures on Copeau's farcical (I thought) *Twelfth Night*. Probably I was unfairly influenced by the translation, which began: "Si la musique est la nourriture de l'amour, qu'ils reprennent!" "Qu'ils reprennent!" I wrote in disgust. "Imagine!" But I loved his *Paquebot Tenacity*, a play which I was to know better.

I adored every minute of the three months, and filled them with "distance run." I also, paradoxically, put on weight. When I got home my mother was horrified. For the next five or six years I struggled desperately with the most loathsome, ruthless and abominable diets—the egg-and-tomato, the apple-and-coffee, the potato-and-milk—as well as with peculiar things like drops of iodine in spoonfuls of milk, which had to be taken relentlessly, six times a day. A gland doctor could probably have dealt with the matter without much trouble. The overweight departed for no particular reason as suddenly as it had appeared. But it lasted long enough to handicap severely my career as a fashionable flat-chested ingenue.

If there is a better age at which to see Venice than eighteen, I have not yet reached it. There must have been greater years before 1923, when it was less "discovered"; and probably more brilliant years since; but 1923 was my year and for me it was royal. One of my American "uncles," Harrison Rhodes, used to go there every summer—until, a few years later, he gave up in disgust because of the Mussolini regime. He took the whole penthouse apartment in the Grand Hotel, facing the Canal. He had his own gondola and gondolier, and an encyclopedic knowledge of the city, gained at leisure over many years. He invited the whole Webster family to stay with him for three weeks.

Knowing this, I spent part of my time in Paris furiously studying Hugo's *Italian Self-Taught* and Dante's *Inferno* with an interleaved French translation. My Italian developed along schizoid lines: "A che ora parte il treno?" varied with phrases of ancient splendor. Verdi's librettists have since lent it operatic overtones. It delighted Hal's gondolier, who called me his little quail—in a most fatherly manner—and was always ready to take me on rambling expeditions through the smellier canals.

Hal had many friends, and there were many American visitors —Lionel Barrymore, for instance, and Emily Hapgood, whom I had known at Chiddingfold and Woolacombe. She had with her a tall, bony young man with a straggling beard, like Trofimov in *The Cherry Orchard*, named Robert Edmond Jones. He said little, until suddenly a whole torrent of words would come stammering out, driven by steam-pressure enthusiasm. He seemed content to be regarded as Emily's protégé and to be described by Hal as a "very coming" young artist. In fact, he had already designed a number of productions which had jolted the New York theatre out of its preconceived Belasco-derived notions; his dramatic imagination has been one of the most illuminating of my time.

One night there was a gondola festival on the lagoon, and the distribution of personnel among the available gondolas was difficult. I found myself a probably unwanted third with two people I hardly knew, except that Sidney Howard was a playwright of fame, currently on a reporting tour of Central Europe, and his not-long-married wife was an actress, Clare Eames. I had seen her at a couple of dinner parties; she was lean, elegant, with a sharply cut profile like a silver coin. She wore fluted dresses by Fortuni. She would be by turns fastidious and remote; generously partisan; mocking, scornful, raffishly amusing; never anything by halves, never less than passionate.

I was always exceedingly shy in the presence of the nobility of my parents' world, and these two very evidently bore its patents. I felt young and ignorant and heavy and aware of my defective eye. But Clare and Sidney did not appear to see me like that. They lured me on to talk and pretty soon I began to feel that I really could do what I wanted to do, be what I set my mind to be. Amid the Chinese lanterns and the guitar music and the water lapping against the sides of the gondola, attainable mountains became

visible. Sidney and Clare, like Robert Edmond Jones, were life en-
hancers; this still seems to me the most important thing of all to be.

The record of Clare Eames's work in the theatre is not very
large; her whole professional career lasted little more than ten
years. Yet a well-known actress who was her friend said to me
recently: "I remember Clare more clearly than anything that happened yesterday." She could have had a great influence on the
theatre. She did on me. At a time when acting tended to vary from
the florid to the slipshod and "damn-natural," hers showed me
another road.

I have been told that her acting during her first onslaughts on
Broadway was harsh, extravagant, fearless to the point of being
ridiculous. She had burning convictions but no trained or tempered
instrument. But she learned fast. During the three or four years
after I met her in Venice, she played in many of the Theatre
Guild's most famous productions, including the plays Sidney
Howard wrote for her, *Ned McCobb's Daughter* and *Lucky Sam
McCarver*. She played Lady Macbeth (she would still be my
choice, among all the actresses I have ever seen, living or dead) to
James Hackett's Macbeth, which must have been a ludicrous jux-
taposition of styles. Her capacity for satire made her an incomparable Prossy to Katharine Cornell's Candida. Her Hedda Gabler,
according to Eva Le Gallienne, who probably knows more about
Hedda than any other living actress, was "still unfinished, but
potentially the greatest Hedda of our time."

The New York critics were apt to apply to her work the word
"cold." A sillier adjective it would be hard to imagine. It was
probably due to her bone structure—she looked irretrievably intellectual—and partly because she was never sentimental or mushy;
she was stripped of unnecessary flesh. But if she was cold, it was
the coldness of the metal which burns your hand.

In 1926 she came to London to play in Sidney's *The Silver
Cord*, and returned a year or so later to live and work there. By this
time she had acquired an extraordinary economy and a concentrated discipline. She "did" almost nothing; without raising her
voice she could sear an audience with irony or hatred or compas-
sion. "Do you read?" says the mother-in-law in *The Silver Cord*. "I

can," answered Clare with a raised eyebrow, quietly destroying all mothers-in-law forever.

In 1929, while she was playing in Maugham's *The Sacred Flame*, she came to see a matinee of the *Medea*, in which I was playing. That night she asked me to supper. I was at a very low point of frustration and self-doubt, and she gave me an injection of faith and courage to which I still return. She said: "You have much to give; you must give it. Never stop believing that. Never stop doing it." After a little pause she added, in a rather odd voice, as if she were surprised, "Please don't forget that I said this to you." A year later she died, quite shockingly and unnecessarily, as the result of two successive operations for an internal injury. Having taught me some of my earliest lessons about life, she taught me the first about death. I wish, even now, that she had lived. So few people ever saw her, and she was a great actress.

So back I came from Venice "with magic in my eyes," and prepared to go to work. I was going to have some further training. I didn't really consider it essential, but it filled in time while managers and agents (not many of them in those days) were failing to answer my letters or respond to my interviews with them. My father had fallen into one of those dreadfully becalmed periods which are the despair of all actors. It may have been partly because he had been associated with the kind of drama which had ceased to exist, but I do not think this was the whole reason. He was in his late fifties, but he looked much younger—and age is never the same problem to an actor as it is to an actress. He played light comedy elegantly, and directed it well too. He was good in Shaw, who was arising in full strength from his wartime unpopularity with *Heartbreak House*, *Back to Methuselah* and, presently, *Saint Joan*.

But there were new dramatists. Pinero wrote his last play in 1923—my mother was in it and found it a detestable experience. His successors were very different. There were the glorious Aldwych farces, the Edgar Wallace thrillers, the Lonsdale comedies.

A Time to Sow

There were new managements and new centers of power. C. B. Cochran was in the ascendant, Noel Coward just around the corner—all new and strange, and making shy and gentle people like my father feel horribly insecure and out of date.

Basil Dean came marching down from Liverpool, able, ambitious, farsighted, feared by his actors, disliked by many, but respected for the magnificent record of his two tiny theatres: three of Galsworthy's finest plays; Clemence Dane's *A Bill of Divorcement;* Somerset Maugham's *Rain; The Fanatics; A Grain of Mustard Seed;* the best in current serious playwrighting. He installed new German switchboards and introduced projections and new scenic devices. My mother played with him once. She found his methods dictatorial and daunting to the actor. The actors who worked with him regularly would probably disagree.

Barry Jackson brought the Birmingham Repertory Company down to London. They had conquered it already, in Drinkwater's *Abraham Lincoln*, from a shabby little theatre in a Hammersmith market, and now went on to some fabulous successes: the new Shaw plays; the opera *The Immortal Hour*, with Gwen Ffrangcon Davies; and Eden Phillpotts's homely farce *The Farmer's Wife*, with Cedric Hardwicke. Both of these ran forever. No further actors were needed.

The du Maurier school of naturalism was all the rage in the commercial theatres: rumple her hair, smack her bottom, call her "funny-face," and lo! a love scene. It was all white flannels or white ties. Du Maurier had many imitators of what my father rather bitterly called "the scratch-and-mumble school" who never for a moment realized the special quality that lurked in Gerald and was not in them. What he did was personal, extremely idiosyncratic, distilled. It was a search for truth, within his own definitions, a detestation of falsehood and fake. It was accompanied, moreover, by a flawless sense of timing and an impeccable use of the "throwaway" effect, which looks so easy and isn't. What his imitators did was often lazy and commonplace. But neither he nor his followers could stand people whom they detected "acting"; and my father didn't seem able to avoid detection. In retrospect it seems to me that the London theatre had never before—nor has it since—been so "fashionable" nor so subservient to a single standard of fashion.

Also, it rapidly became clique-ridden to a pernicious degree. Unless you lunched at the Ivy or played golf with dear old A or went to the same hairdresser as darling B, you were pretty much out of luck. One could say that the old system of the actor-managers was clique-ridden too. But in the new London theatre there were far more actors to choose from, and those who did the choosing were rarely actors—or even directors—themselves; therefore they tended to pick people for their looks, their "type," rather than for their skills. An actor was not called upon to play a repertoire, just the one part. Type-casting rose to its highest impotence.

In the provinces, the theatre was dwindling under the fierce impact of the cinema. Fewer and fewer company coaches were shunted each Sunday through Derby or Crewe junction. More and more Opera Houses, Palaces and even Theatres Royal had dark weeks or went over to films. May and Ben managed to get music-hall bookings for a couple of one-act sketches, sandwiched between comic turns and performing sea lions. Ben toured a couple of times "on the Halls" with Violet Vanbrugh, sister of Irene. He hated the work, hated leaving May, hated himself for being unable to live without acting.

In 1921 May agreed to take over the management of the Etlinger Dramatic School, whose head and founder had recently died. The school's reputation had mainly been as a training ground for singers; now it was to begin new courses in dramatic work. Here she managed to put in seven or eight hours' hard labor every day, between committee meetings. In a letter to me she wrote: "Yesterday was ridiculous. I was at the school at 10 o'clock, Comm. of King George's Pension Fund at 11:30, met Clara [Butt] at Cowdray Club at 1:30 to discuss Workrooms. Back to school 2:30, Nurses Fund 3:30, Three Arts Club 4:30, Back to school 5:00, Home 7:15, sent hasty P. C.'s to you and Daddy, on to Coliseum to see Cissie [Loftus]."

She found teaching difficult and demanding work and took the very greatest pains to discover and nourish the shyest, tiniest grains of talent. She taught by rehearsing pupils in individual parts, or groups of them in a scene. She didn't know about improvisations and sense memories. She knew and taught the interpretation of an author's meaning through the lines the character spoke —and she was a stickler for the accurate speaking of them. She wrote: "I gave the most serious, devoted work to teaching the elements of acting—tried to show my pupils what it meant—what honest, high endeavour, what devoted service it needed—tried to make them realise the qualities needed of sincerity, sensibility, truth, imagination, vision . . ."

I enrolled at the Etlinger, and there I studied the various techniques allied to acting and subsidiary to it. There were several kinds of dancing, one of which was called "ballroom" and another "Greek." This was strongly derivative from the Scottish dancer Margaret Morris, whose classes I had briefly attended as a child, along with Angela and Hermione Baddeley. It may perhaps have been breathed upon from afar by the influence of Isadora Duncan; closer contact with that tremendous artist would no doubt have shriveled it to ash. Clad, however, in short tunics, barefooted, we ran and walked and walked and ran and presently clashed cymbals and strewed flowers and interpreted various Greek emotions to a diversity of musical accompaniments tending toward Schubert. I did it all with great enthusiasm, and I think beneficial, if limited, results.

I also studied singing with an able but erratic teacher of opera who considered that her classes were the only worthy remnant of the original Etlinger School and was fiercely jealous of her prerogatives. She put a severe strain on my mother's vaunted tact. At the end-of-term shows she regularly insisted on doing bits of *Madame Butterfly*, which meant that we all had to set to and make wisteria out of crinkled crepe paper.

The studios were shared on a rental basis by Italia Conti, whose fame as a teacher of theatre children was unequaled. She had numbered among her pupils every known child prodigy, including Noel Coward and Gertrude Lawrence. It seemed that all her little girls had to be subjected to ordeal by Juliet's Potion Scene. Work in my mother's office, which was next door, would periodically be brought to a standstill by a series of childish voices shrieking "Stay, Tybalt, stay!" in ear-piercing trebles.

I took drama classes under my father, Kate Rorke and others. My mother had a horror of "voice lessons" as such, or of anything elocutionary in the narrow sense, so I never studied pear-shaped tones, but was taught to use my voice in action. Neither she nor Miss Rorke, however, had any patience with the thin, bloodless, lip-lazy speech so common among the English. Their pupils alternated between my mother's grim "The letter 'o' is *round*," and Kate Rorke's "Take care of the consonants and the vowels will take care of themselves." Between the two of them we didn't get by with anything slipshod.

Much, too much, reciting in my childhood had taught me how to handle verse without thinking about it. I rather fancied the musical quality of my voice and was often praised for it. Once someone told me, in my father's hearing, that I had "a voice like a Rembrandt." "Ah yes," he commented, "muffled and dirty." This kind of corrective my mother also took pains to supply. "You will be told, " she would say, "that you have a beautiful voice. So you have; the credit is God's, not yours. But whenever you hear your beautiful voice making a beautiful noise . . . change it." She meant, of course, to guard me against the danger of falling in love with a mellifluous flow of sound at the expense of inner truth. Nevertheless, she had taught me all my life to appreciate words and to value the patterns in which the great craftsmen of the English language have put them together. Constance Collier used to tell young aspirants to begin their acting lessons by studying the dictionary. It is wise counsel.

The Etlinger School possessed a hall of reasonable dimensions which was sometimes hired by outside groups for special performances. One day a young man named Maurice Evans came to see my mother for this purpose. He represented an amateur society, mostly office workers, who were preparing a production of *Major Barbara*. He himself had a job at Chappell's, the music publishers, and was to play Cusins in the show. He said he would like to attend the forthcoming students' performance in order to gauge the qualities of the auditorium, and gave my mother quite a stiff argument over the rental terms.

At the students' show in question I was appearing in a horrible little one-act fantasy called *Pan in Pimlico*, clad in tights and a leopard skin (it must have meant a high peak of dieting), and representing some vaguely faunlike creature. As a result of this, the Evans group asked me to play Lady Brit, the dragonlike dowager, in *Major Barbara*. I do not know who gets the credit for this piece of casting. But I think Lady Brit turned out well, and she started me on a long series of dowagers, especially Shaw's, during which I mother-in-lawed, aunted, or housekept for an assortment of "ingenues" and "juveniles" twice my age. Maurice Evans impressed us all very much. His performance was crisp, cool, humorous, with the instinctive sense of timing which is born but almost never made.

I did some more semi-professional odd-jobbery, sketches at Charity Concerts and so forth. But I wasn't designed for fashionable ingenues, perky little types with thin, babbling voices who popped onstage through French windows and asked was anybody on for a look at the tadpoles. Also, it became ineluctably clear that the further handicap of a slight cast in one eye was altogether too much. I had the first of two operations on it, and immediately afterward managed to get my first, real, genuine, professional job.

Sybil Thorndike and Lewis Casson were about to open in the original London production of *Saint Joan*. The part had been written for Sybil, but other commitments had prevented her from producing it until after the play had opened in New York. Few people in England had seen it, and it was unpublished; but a new play by Shaw about Joan of Arc was obviously an event of magnitude. Sybil and Lewis invited my parents to the dress rehearsal. "Peggy too, if she likes." Likes!

There were only a dozen of us in the dim, white-sheeted stalls. Above, in the front row of the Dress Circle, you could just catch the glimmer of a white beard, a hand, an eyebrow. Nobody spoke. The houselights went out. The curtain slid up revealing Charles Ricketts's beautifully painted medieval drop; trumpets, a haunting little oboe melody; footlights out; drop curtain up. "No eggs! no

eggs! Thousand thunders man, what do you mean by no eggs?"
shouted Robert de Baudricourt. It is probably one of the most
unexpected opening lines ever written. What follows ranks in my
memory as second in excitement only to the *Peter Pan* adventure.
By the end I was so profoundly moved that I have no recollection
of what happened. I think my father spoke to Shaw. I think we
went around to say thank you to Lewis and Sybil. I only know that
"glory shone around."

Saint Joan settled down to what was obviously going to be a
long run, and the insatiable Sybil immediately decided to do something else as well. She announced some special matinees of *The
Trojan Women;* Hecuba was already one of her most famous
achievements. Here, I thought, was a play which did need voices
and didn't need tennis rackets. I wrote and asked if I could be
considered for one of the Chorus. I received a brief note from Mr.
Casson, saying that I might read for him in his dressing room (he
was playing de Stogumber) one night during his wait. I had just
been playing Phaedra at the Etlinger in Euripides' *Hippolytus*, a
production chiefly memorable for the fact that when I said, "O
misery! O God, that such a thing should fall on me!" a pillar did
so. I decided to try one of Phaedra's speeches.

The stage door of the New Theatre was almost like home to
me, from the Boucicault-Vanbrugh days, but I shook with fright as
I entered it. La Hire, picking his way down the stone steps in
elongated, armored feet, made a noise almost as alarming as Suzanne Ainley's tin helmet had once done. Confronted with Lewis in
his robes and wig, with a tonsure the size of a dinner plate, I was
paralyzed. I was afraid of sounding too loud in that small room
where my voice bounced back at me from the walls, yet afraid that
he would think I couldn't "project," and embarrassed at pouring
out Phaedra's passion in these constricting circumstances. I wondered whether it was essential that a Trojan Woman be very
starved-looking, and whether I should tell him I would live on
apples and coffee till the end of the run. At last I finished. He made
no comment, but gave me a piercing, crusty look. "Yes. Very
well," he said gruffly, as if he were angry about it. "Useful voice.
Start rehearsing next week. Stage manager will call you. See

A Time to Sow

Bruce Winston about the clothes. Find him upstairs. Goodbye." I spluttered something and made for the door. "Oh," he added, "love to May and Ben. Guinea a performance." The final sentence didn't register till I was outside: I was not only to have the joy and tremendous honor of appearing in this production, but I was also to be paid one pound, one shilling every time I did so. It hardly seemed right.

Quite a small Chorus was used for *The Trojan Women*—nine, I think. Most of them were already appearing as ladies of the Dauphin's court in *Saint Joan*, and were slender, elegant creatures, much at home with the rest of the company, and to me very awe-inspiring. Privately, however, I conceded to only two of them a vocal equipment superior to my own. Unlike most of the Greek choruses, the women of Troy are directly involved in the play's action. Lewis therefore used us as individuals, dividing up many of the lines for successive single voices (not enough, I thought, for me). Some of the verse, however, demanded the exceedingly difficult task of unison speaking, and some was intoned or chanted.

Lewis, like Granville Barker, had been greatly influenced by William Poel, indeed had been trained by him. It was Poel who had first cleared and uncluttered the Shakespeare texts and presented them, when possible, on a non-proscenium stage. His primary emphasis had been on the speaking of the lines. At a time when everything about a Shakespearian production is regarded as more important than this, it is worth summarizing Lewis Casson's firsthand report of what Poel tried to do: Poel, he said, did not claim to know by inspiration what every tune and inflection of Shakespeare should be. What he was fighting was the Victorian method of speaking the verse, slow, ponderous and accented all over the place; whereas Poel thought it should be rapid, with as few heavy stresses as possible—about one every three lines. The meaning should be clearly represented by melody, which supplied most of the necessary accents. He rebelled also against Irving because he broke the natural rhythm of speech by trying to make it "modern."

He detested the commercial theatre and was driven to engage unknown actors for his productions because they would do what

295

they were told. He studied a play deeply and settled in his own mind the particular tunes and accents which would express what he believed were Shakespeare's intentions, and he insisted his company should follow them. The movement he dictated was very simple, but always effective; and he insisted on the play being acted with vocal continuity from one scene to another without a break. Sybil endorsed this and added "incidentally he hated accents on auxiliary words."

It was a method which Lewis himself largely followed. He would give you an idea both of the tonal quality and the emotional content that he wanted by pouring forth a stream of total gibberish, precisely scaled and cadenced and rhythmically exact. Some actors found it extremely disconcerting—a cart-before-the-horse process. So it was, until you learned to translate back from what your ears heard to the truth of thought behind it. You then got the hang of it and realized that, far from wanting you to make noise without thought, Lewis would pounce like a hawk on any noise that was not truthfully thought-filled.

He himself had an unerring sense of pressure, tempo and pitch. His breath control was stupefying and to attain the long, graded, sweeping climaxes he demanded, yours had to be too.

> *Up from Aegean caverns, pool by pool*
> *Of blue, salt sea, where feet most beautiful*
> *Of Nereid maidens weave beneath the foam*
> *Their long sea-dances, I their Lord am come,*
> *Poseidon of the Sea.*

This he spoke in a very slow, steady, climbing rhythm, and on a single breath. Try it some time, young actors. The method is not one which I have ever felt myself able to follow, as a director. Its dangers are obvious. But as an actor I shall never cease to be grateful for the superb training I had in the three Gilbert Murray–Euripides plays I did with Lewis Casson.

Sybil Thorndike's Hecuba I thought superb. Even when I was breaking my back and cracking my knee joints crouching under the shield which held the body of Astyanax (one or other of the

A Time to Sow

Casson children, all very sturdy types), the emotion transcended the extreme discomfort. It is hard to assess the real worth of the books, poetry, music, painting, dancing and acting which were the flaming beacons of one's youth; especially the actors and dancers, since you cannot re-see them. Were they really as good as all that? It doesn't matter. The debt you owe them is just as great, and the lamp stays lit even if the match has gone out. Sybil lit those lamps for me.

Little plays she could break to pieces by the very zest with which she charged into them. But just as St. Joan shone with her own faith in God, so her Hecuba was informed by her heroic vision of humanity, her sorrow for the world destroying itself. It was of truly classic stature. Sometimes it seems to me like a dreadfully wasteful and wasted business, this acting of ours, when performances like that go by forever. But the memory of them is the more precious. I am grateful that it was in that play and with those stars that, on October 3rd, 1924, I attained at last the status of a "pro".

Coming down to earth again after *The Trojan Women*, I went back to some Etlinger classes and also to some rather desultory studying of history and economics at London University. A few months passed, every month seeming to me, at nineteen, a wasted year. Suddenly I got not merely one job, but two.

John Barrymore had come to London to present, at the Haymarket Theatre, his New York production of *Hamlet*. My mother and father had barely seen him since the days when he used to call for his pocket money. Now he was the uncontested star of the American theatre, with blazing performances in *Justice*, *Peter Ibbetson*, *The Jest* and *Richard III* already behind him. By all accounts his Hamlet was greater than any of them. He brought with him the Robert Edmond Jones sets and costumes, even his American switchboards and their guardian electrician; but the cast was to be English—Fay Compton, Constance Collier, George Relph and my mother's old friend Herbert Waring. I knew that there would have to be a select quota of Court Ladies, but I did not dare to suggest that I might be one of them. Half London would obviously have the same idea; and I did not want to presume on the fact that Barrymore had once known my parents.

One day, however, he telephoned. He said that he longed to revisit the famous flat in Bedford Street and might he come to dinner. When he arrived, he greeted my father and mother with charming and affectionate courtesy, rather in the manner of a long-absent nephew who had done modestly well in Canada, and shook hands gravely with me. He then strode into the drawing room and swept its contents with an eagle eye. He greeted the sofa as an old and valued friend; also the piano and the grandfather clock. He fixed the curtains appraisingly and declared that they were "new." He uplifted the fender by remembering it and annihilated the mirror above the fireplace by declaring that it hadn't been there in his day. He was right in every case. Suddenly he wheeled on me. I became nervously aware that I wasn't part of the original furnishings either and should, perhaps, efface myself. "Constance talked to me about you," he said. "She tells me you have a good voice and can act. I guess it must be true because Constance knows all about acting. Would you like to be a Court Lady in *Hamlet?*" I made such noises as I was able, and presently we went in to dinner. In the middle of the fish course he gave me a dazzling smile. "There are some lines too," he said.

Barely had the front door shut behind him before I rushed for a copy of *Hamlet*. What lines? None of us could remember any, except for the Player Queen, which he had said was to be played by a boy. After concerted thought we decided that the lines which immediately precede Ophelia's entrance in the Mad Scene must be the ones. Traditionally they had been spoken by Horatio, but most texts ascribe them to a Gentleman, who could, conceivably, be a Gentlewoman. Anyway, I sat up and learned all twelve of them. But I wondered in my heart whether Barrymore had really meant it, or whether it had been merely an impulsive gesture to his hostess's daughter.

If it was, he stuck to it. A few days later the business manager of the production sent for me and gave me the brief letter which in those days was the whole and only form of contract anybody ever had. I treasure it still. It runs:

"This is to confirm that we have pleasure in engaging you to 'walk on' and play the part of 'The Gentlewoman' in *Hamlet* at a salary of £3 (Three pounds) a week of eight performances. In the event of more than eight performances being played in any one week you will receive for each additional performance one eighth of your weekly salary.

"If you will be good enough to confirm this, the interchange of letters will constitute a contract."

I signed it with rapture. The next day I got a message from the Cassons saying that they would like me to play the Leader of the Chorus in some matinees of *Hippolytus*. The two openings were less than a week apart. I was anguished. In fear and trembling I went to each management and explained about the other. To my delighted amazement—and I am still amazed—each one thought "it could be managed." And so it was.

The *Hippolytus* readings started first, and it was a little while before I got a call for *Hamlet*, not to the theatre but to a neighboring restaurant. The rehearsal room seemed to me extremely professional, with its broken chairs, rickety tables, unshaded lights and filthy wooden floor. Only the walk-on people were present. Barrymore's American stage manager, lean, efficient and courteous, explained the set and told us the business. In the first Court Scene everyone was to take his position on the steps while the curtain was down. It would then rise in blackness and we were to be heard whispering among ourselves in the darkness. Gradually the lights would come up, and when the stage was fully lit our whispering would subside as the King began: "Though yet of Hamlet our dear brother's death the memory be green . . ." and so forth. We rehearsed it carefully, as well as the other general scenes. I was delighted to find that we were also to be the "nuns" who carried Ophelia's body to its grave. At the costume fittings, however, it transpired that we were to be clothed in graceful white flannelette garments with white chiffon veils and wreaths of flowers. Since I had never heard of a religious order so clad, I decided a vaguely virginal approach would be more appropriate than that of any

orthodox rule. We ended by calling ourselves the Virgin Crants
(cf. Act V scene 1, l 255).

I was called to an occasional rehearsal at the theatre, where the
principals had been working for some time, on account of my lines.
To my grief, there turned out to be only four and a half of them
instead of the original twelve, and I was unable to see much of the
ensuing scene since Fay Compton, playing Ophelia, had insisted
that the bare stage be masked in with flats so that no one could
watch her. With the arrogance of youth, I thought this affected
and silly. Later I realized how extremely difficult it is to achieve
the degree of concentration, the self-obliviousness, essential to a
scene like this when you are constantly aware of the other actors,
gaping at you from a few feet away or—it is worse, almost—picking their noses and turning the pages of the newspaper.

At last the whole Court was summoned. The imposing set with
its massive central arch and wide, solid steps, had been put up on
the stage. At the stage manager's signal, we took our places,
grouped on the upstage steps. Barrymore sat below us, facing the
audience, his chin on his hand. To our left were the thrones of the
King and Queen, Polonius and the rest in attendance. The stage
manager indicated the sequence: "House lights out . . . blackout."
We started to whisper. "Curtain . . . going . . . up!" We whispered like mad. "Lights . . . coming . . . up!" Our whispering
grew frenzied. "Lights . . . now . . . up." We subsided. "King!"
"Though yet of Hamlet our dear brother's death—" "No, no, NO!"
With a piercing yell Barrymore leaped from his chair and confronted us. "It won't do at all—not at all!" We were paralyzed. He
ran his hands through his hair as if in desperation. "Don't you
understand—when the curtain goes up it's dark—BLACK!" (Sub-
dued murmurs of "Yes, Mr. Barrymore.") "They can't see you."
("No, Mr. Barrymore.") "But you're all whispering . . ." ("We
know—we did—we were . . .") "But it was the wrong *kind* of
whispering. You've got to make the audience understand right
away that this is a *very* LECHEROUS Court!" Silence. I stole a
glance at Constance. She was looking studiously aloof. We did it
again. We did it a lot of times. Finally, lechery triumphed and we

went on with the scene. Afterwards one of the Ladies went to her stage manager. "I would like to be assured," she said, "that we were not picked for this scene as types. I could not continue with the production unless I am to be considered a character actress."

The Graveyard Scene turned out to be an even greater hazard. Ophelia had to be carefully masked as she was laid to rest, being only a piece of sacking stuffed with straw. Having performed this rite the Virgin Crants withdrew to one side of the stage, close to where Hamlet and Horatio were standing. While Laertes, the Priest and the Queen spoke their lines over the grave, Barrymore would employ the breathing space by making faces, hissing asides and doing everything possible to destroy the grave demeanor of the Virgin Crants. We thought this merely rehearsal relaxation, but we were wrong. What he afterward did during performances was ten times more varied and inventive. It included a good deal of "hawking and spitting," very audible jokes and scathing imitations of the other actors, the audience, or both. We were all too young to have learned how not to laugh; and since we stood in a close group the silent shaking of one weak sister was contagious; pretty soon the entire nunnery would be quivering. With bent heads and fingernails dug into our palms we would fight desperately not to let an audible snort or gurgle give us away and pray that the scene would soon be over.

We thought the production beautiful—it was, too—especially the Play Scene, in which the Players, robed in gold, mimed the action with archaic and stylized movement. Barrymore did not unmask his full fire at rehearsals, but the glittering, lithe, demonic quality shone through like flashing steel. He made all other Hamlets seem stodgy by comparison. As things worked out, we would have been glad to settle for a little stodge, especially in the final scene.

Barrymore's behavior throughout the rehearsal period was impeccable, all dignity and charm. Things changed a bit after the opening night. To fortify himself against the strain of playing Hamlet eight times a week (which is, indeed, almost intolerable), he would drink champagne steadily all through the performance whenever he was not actually on the stage. A dresser would wait for him in the wings, glass in hand, whenever he made an exit. By the last scene he was apt to be a little excited.

The several actors who were successively bold enough to play Laertes took to wearing hockey pads under their costumes on their arms, legs and chests. It gave them a bulgy appearance, but it was safer; not, however, safe enough. Once, having thoroughly stabbed Laertes, who had already collapsed in Osric's arms, Barrymore apparently felt dissatisfied with the job. He suddenly leaped forward and slashed his dying adversary across the behind, where there was no hockey pad. He made a further practice of leaning on his foil between bouts, as if it were a shooting stick, or beating it furiously against the floor or the furniture. The blades, not being designed to resist this kind of treatment, habitually snapped in pieces during the fight, and flying pices of steel would come whistling past one's eye or ear. The Court spent most of its time ducking.

It was all worth it. Barrymore's Hamlet was a great performance in the truest sense of that much-abused adjective. He was not a "sweet prince." The description always startled me by its incongruity whenever I heard the line. But he brought to the part a kind of tragic yearning, a terrible sense of waste and despair, and moments, especially with Ophelia, of great tenderness. His final speech never failed to tear your heart with the realization of all that Hamlet might have been. Nevertheless, my most vivid memories are of the demonic Hamlet of the Play Scene, the sweep and bitterness with which he piled Pelion upon Ossa beside Ophelia's grave, the blaze of fury in "Then venom, to thy work!" Re-reading the review in the London *Times*, I was staggered by the astonishing comment: "This Hamlet appeals more to your judgement than to your nerves." I can only suppose that the writer had none.

The opening night, at all events, was spine-tingling; for me, of course, in more ways than one. The first two acts were a long agony of waiting for the third, which began with my famous lines, "She is importunate, indeed distract . . ." and so on. The same routine was to be followed, of the curtain rising in blackness followed by a slow fade-in of the lights. Constance Collier, George

A Time to Sow

Relph (as Horatio) and I took our places on the stage, I thanking Heaven for the long dress which concealed my shaking knees, and frenziedly moistening my dry lips. Constance, looking extremely regal and undisturbed, wished me luck. The work light went out, and presumably the houselights also, for the hum and buzz of the audience hushed to silence. (It is the most terrifying moment of an actor's life.) The curtain slid up almost invisibly; the stagelights duly faded on. "What would she have?" said Constance. I opened my mouth to answer—and all the lights went out again. I stood with my mouth open in the dark, aghast. I caught the ghost of a sound from Constance. "Wait," she breathed. I shut my mouth and waited. It seemed like ten minutes—it was probably five seconds —before the lights came back on. "What would she have?" asked Constance calmly, as if nothing had happened. So I told her.

Five days later, clad in the most extraordinarily unbecoming costume it is possible to imagine, I was leading the Women of Athens onto the stage of the Regent Theatre, proclaiming "There riseth a rock-born river, of Ocean's tribe men say . . ." By now I was not just a professional, I was a veteran.

CHAPTER SIXTEEN

––––––—∞∞∞––––––

Live and Learn

My next ten years in the theatre were divided between bursts of paid, commercial activity and periodic lulls. The lulls were depressing, except that during them I learned far more and worked much harder than when I was being paid. Fortunately for me, this was a period when almost any play of any merit at all could get some sort of a trial in London itself, a flourishing theatre climate which has probably never been repeated.

There were innumerable membership or "club" societies, supposedly not open to the public and therefore immune from the censorship of the Lord Chamberlain's office. They put on special performances, for a Sunday night, or two Sunday nights, or a Sunday night and a Monday matinee. In some respects they were exactly what Shaw had described to my father: "infinite worry and unbusinesslikeness and three guineas for cabs"; except that I don't remember much about the three guineas. The performances, however, were not hastily rehearsed and scrambled together—except in the matter of scenery, which was highly extemporaneous. Nor were the casts simply composed of young actors who knew nothing being directed by young directors who knew nothing in plays by authors who knew nothing, all headed blithely for that Biblical ditch. There was a predominance, I would think, of youth on-the-learn, but there was also a solid percentage of well-known theatre people who wanted a chance to act in an unusual, probably non-commercial play, or to handle a different kind of part. The performances usually took place in West End theatres, miraculously inserted within the confines of the existing set, and were attended by the first-string London critics.

Societies like this had existed since the Nineties; but from the Twenties until the Second World War they flourished. Sometimes they were dedicated to "advanced" or "daring" plays, which the Censor would not pass; sometimes to plays which might later prove "commercial"; one, the Fellowship of Players, did only Shakespeare, with actors who did not wish to spend a year at the Old Vic taking a crack at parts they'd always yearned for. Sometimes the alleged "club" was a theatre and nothing else, like the Gate Theatre underneath the arches of Charing Cross Railway Bridge. It supplied its members with coffee and wonderful oatmeal biscuits and then pushed them into the tiny auditorium, dedicated to the Expressionist dramas of Germany, France and Central Europe. The Arts Theatre Club really was a club. It developed also into a recognized testing ground where well-known theatre managements tried to allay their own fears and soothe the Lord Chamberlain's scruples. Some of the shows would run for two or three weeks, and a fair proportion transferred to the West End; a few were plays of worth and became great successes. There were also suburban theatres, such as the Q and the Embassy, which were also tryout grounds, kept alive by quenchless optimism, "still nursing the unconquerable hope."

Most of these became very important to actors. It was almost as hard to get a job in them as it was in the commercial theatre. Within the most successful groups the same clique-ridden propensities developed as were rampant in the West End. But there was also an endless variety of humbler and scruffier odd-jobbery available for those who did not mind working for nothing, or almost nothing. None of us did. The theatrical young never do. Only now the good, kind unions won't let them.

. . . and Margaret

The lull that followed my *Hamlet-Hippolytus* outburst didn't last too long. I filled it with various studies, did a special matinee or two with the Cassons, attended a summer school at Oxford (just a little wistfully), got myself a gold medal from somewhere or other for poetry reading. May—due, she always said, to lunching at the fashionable Ivy restaurant—got remembered by somebody and broke back into the charmed West End circle in Lonsdale's *The Last of Mrs. Cheyney*, with Gladys Cooper and Gerald du Maurier. She enjoyed every minute of it. But there was one scene, a duologue scene with Gerald, which absolutely could not be got right. It was crucial to the plot; Lonsdale kept rewriting it, Gerald kept saying he didn't believe it. At the final dress rehearsal he said: "Come on, May. Let's play charades. We'll make it up." They did. Also on the opening night. "Where on earth did all that come from?" demanded Gerald's bewildered understudy. "It's the only scene Gerald knows."

Later, after she had played with him in *Dear Brutus*, May wrote of him: "He was an admirable director; he interfered very little; but his one object was to get the thing true and real . . . he only stopped you when he thought you were getting unreal. He was of great service to authors because he improved their plays— made them much more human and natural. He gave everybody a sense of confidence; and he was delightful to act with." I have thought of the "truth" part since, when I have watched actors in revivals of the Lonsdale plays manipulating a series of thin, paper, fashion-plate puppets without an atom of reality between them.

In the effulgence of the St. James's, in a success, with a charming and brilliant company who were all devoted to each other, May found again the feeling of working for pleasure of which she had been deprived for so long. It was her milieu and she throve in it. For a time she tried to continue her work at the Etlinger; but the school and the committees and eight shows a week were a little too much, even for her. "I begin to feel rocky and wonky," she wrote; and finally gave it up. "I've learned from it," she said. "I've learned a lot."

Meanwhile I had resolved, with a mixture of extreme shyness and iron determination, that I was going to understudy Sybil in the

Live and Learn

tour of *Saint Joan*. I asked the Cassons to let me read a scene for them and they did. For several weeks I rushed to the door whenever I heard the postman's knock; I would not pester the Cassons by telephoning to know my fate. Finally, one day, a letter arrived for me addressed in Sybil's dashing hand. "Dear Peggy," it said, "AT LAST! You are engaged to understudy for St. Joan at £5 a week." The intervening time sped by on wings. Rehearsals came around, with Shaw himself occasionally in attendance. We opened early in September, in Manchester.

The company was largely the same as it had been in London, but most of the Court Ladies were as new to touring as I was and we generally shared "digs" in twos or threes. Our first landlady was ominously called Mrs. Cheatem, but fortunately she didn't. Theatrical lodgings were still much as they had been in my parents' day. They were still in the same places, a tram ride from the theatre on some shabby-neat back street where all the houses looked so alike that you had to be very careful to remember which was yours. They all had a minute strip of blackish grass in front, a couple of steps up to a rather ornate front door, a bay window on one side with an aspidistra in it. Yours was the one with purple glass in the transom.

In the bedrooms, iron bedsteads and lumpy mattresses were still universal and heating still unknown. Hot water was rare and usually dependent on a ferocious gas "geyser" above the bath, whose unpredictable behavior made you wonder whether it wouldn't be safer to stay dirty. Toilet facilities varied. Once, in Huddersfield, I shared an outside one with the rest of the block; you stood in line, chatting with the neighbors. It was very friendly. The normal, indoor, ones were apt to be hedged with prohibitions and bitterly cold. In one, I remember, a large notice precluded the deposit of tea leaves, and ended, "also the W.C. is not to be used for slops and oblige G. S. Sheppard."

The sitting rooms were just as they had always been described to me: filled to bursting point with a vast, horsehair sofa (which pricked you), an upholstered armchair with broken springs and a huge table covered with a frieze cloth of dark green edged with bobbled fringe. Around the walls crowded an array of furniture.

Glass-fronted cupboards sheltered hideously curled and convoluted treasures of Victorian china in strawberry pink or spinach green; behind them a few books lurked guiltily. Bamboo whatnots, several tiers high, were loaded with souvenir cream jugs from seaside resorts, beadwork pincushions and dusty confections in raffia; and everywhere, on every inch of vacant space, The Aspidistrae still reared their venerable heads. Disgruntled actors still signed the visitors' book with the jokes of fifty years before.

Landladies ran to the same pattern. Some were vinegary and apt to sneak twopences onto the shopping bill. We had one in Glasgow who refused to buy us a chicken on the grounds that it was "far too good for the likes of us." Some were warm and affable and you called them "Ma" and they took you to their ample bosoms every time you came back to their city and never stopped talking for the rest of the week. We experienced the same reactions as the Websters and little May Whitty on the Hare-and-Kendal tour: hated Manchester, adored Edinburgh, Liverpool dubious (I had relatives there—a mixed blessing), Glasgow saved by the glorious possible excursions.

The company was pleasant and united in respect for its director and star. The Court Ladies also appeared as Monks in the Trial Scene. Seated in the back row, out of the light, we sought to disguise ourselves by sinking down into our cowls like tortoises and, for some reason, making up like unshaven thugs. I took my understudying very seriously, though I knew perfectly well that no understudy in history had ever gone on for Sybil. Once, in *Hippolytus*, she almost broke her back, but went on playing just the same. This time she and Lewis missed a ferryboat driving back to Edinburgh. I think she swam the Firth of Forth, but she got to the theatre ten minutes before curtain time. But I watched and learned and loved St. Joan with passion. The play had not been seen outside London, and it went magnificently. From Birmingham I quoted the critic: " 'The greatest play of our greatest playwright with our greatest actress in her greatest part.' So that's all right." This admiration, however, was not quite universal. In the same city I overheard two people in a restaurant discussing *Hamlet* and *Saint Joan*. After a pause, one of them summed up reflectively:

Live and Learn

"*Hamlet*, yes; but *Saint Joan* is bad form all the way through."

Toward the end of the tour plans were congealing for the production of *Henry VIII* which was to open in London at Christmas. Like the rest of the company, I went through agonies of uncertainty as to whether I should be asked to be in it; conceivably, by some miracle, as Anne Boleyn? Common-sense told me no, and I flung away ambition. But as Anne's understudy? A small, cold voice implanted doubt. As anybody's understudy? As a walk-on? Should I settle for this demotion, were it offered me? Much anguish of soul. At last, very gently, this is what they did offer me, and I accepted. It turned out to include the understudy of the small part of Patience, which was an equally small salve to my pride. I need hardly say that this understudy I did play, several times.

We laid aside with regret our lovely Chinon robes and even the scratchy old monks' wear, and prepared to don Charles Ricketts's new creations for the lavish production of *Henry*. Some of us were again to be Court Ladies, sumptuously attired. Ricketts had made all the jewelry himself and parted with each piece with the utmost reluctance. He would hold it up hesitantly to the chest of the lady who was to wear it, bringing out at last, with a slight stammer, the instruction "You wear it just . . . er . . . b-between." I, however, was to be a plebeian "crowd" and also one of Queen Katharine's homelier entourage. I saw the sketch—dark-brown cloth, very full, trimmed with black; starched muslin collar and cap; a notation in Ricketts's handwriting: "Like an old French wet-nurse." I was twenty and it depressed me.

It was a large company and there were many newcomers. Among them was a young man, more alive-looking than actually handsome, with thick black hair, very curly, bright eyes and heavy eyebrows. Laurence Olivier had a few lines in the Baptism Scene and was understudying too. They said he had been wonderful as Katharine, the Shrew, in a church-school performance. Ellen Terry herself had praised him highly. He was good fun in the company. We went to the Chelsea Arts Ball together and he came to my twenty-first birthday party. There he met Jill Esmond, Eva Moore's daughter, whom he later married.

This birthday was distiguished for me by the present my

parents gave me. It was a beautifully printed limited-edition copy of *Saint Joan*, with color plates of the original Ricketts designs. Many of the actors signed the sketches of the characters they had played, and, greatly daring, I asked Shaw for his. The title page already bore the inscription "From Mamie and Daddy," with the date. Under this Shaw wrote:

> Mamie and Daddy are only the authors of your being; but I—ha ha!—am the author of your book. So I put your name in it, lest posterity should make any mistake, and also my own: thus—
>
> G. Bernard Shaw.

Twenty-one, I decided, was getting a bit old. Time was running by me. Much as I loved the Cassons, I felt the lack of some real, hard work. After many unanswered letters to stock and touring managers, I achieved an interview with Mr. Charles Macdona, who held the touring rights to almost all of Shaw's plays and ran a semi-permanent company which played them in repertory on the road. He hired me; more, I suspected, because of Lady Brit than St. Joan; and sure enough, I started with dowagers. The first of them was Mrs. Pierce, the housekeeper in *Pygmalion*. This I played in an emergency before I officially joined the company at all, learning it overnight and rehearsing it once, just before the curtain rose.

We played real repertory; that is, we alternated the different plays on different nights of the week, playing a varying number of them according to the length of our stay in the town. When I first joined the company they were doing about half a dozen plays, but we rapidly and steadily added to them. By the time the tour finished, nearly nine months later, we were doing eighteen, including two or three one-acters, and I had played thirteen parts (some of them leads) and understudied twenty others, not to mention a couple of leading ones for which I had rushed on in an emergency, though they had nothing to do with me.

In a single week's stand we would usually play *Man and*

Live and Learn

Superman, Pygmalion, The Doctor's Dilemma, You Never Can Tell and perhaps *Fanny's First Play* or (rather oddly) *Mrs. Warren's Profession.* On a two-week stand the repertoire would be enlarged to include *Arms and the Man, Candida* (later we tacked on *How He Lied to Her Husband* as a satiric afterpiece) and either *Getting Married* or *John Bull's Other Island.* Later, during longer stays in Edinburgh and Glasgow, we added *Major Barbara, The Devil's Disciple, The Philanderer, Widowers' Houses* with *The Man of Destiny* and finally, for good measure, we threw in *The Shewing-up of Blanco Posnet* and *The Dark Lady of the Sonnets.* This order of preference, though it was to some extent adjusted to the personnel of the company, must have represented fairly precisely the box-office value of the plays; for Mr. Macdona was not a man to let anything come between him and the box office.

During our first week in Brighton I watched the shows and was a little dismayed by the standard of performance, especially "on the distaff side." I went into *Man and Superman,* and wrote: "I was magnificent as The Maid, particularly in my long speech, 'The cab is at the door, Ma'am.' " I played a small part in *The Doctor's Dilemma* and was gratified by a round of applause on my exit; but I remarked conscientiously, "I'm not sure whether it is right at this point in the play." The understudy situation was completely vague, so to be on the safe side I learned all the women's parts in *Man and Superman, Pygmalion* and *Arms and the Man* within the first week.

Then came more dowagers. A slight upset among the personnel delivered into my hands a couple of old hags, including Emmy in *The Doctor's Dilemma.* From Sheffield I wrote:

"I certainly made myself look 'an ugly old devil,' by dint of nose-paste and other delights, but beyond that, the less said the better. The local critic thinks I 'made a capital show,' but Stanislavsky and I know better. My performance was NOT conspicuous by its artistic truth, being, in fact, a desperate bluff that would have taken in nobody but a dramatic critic."

A few weeks after the tour began I inherited a couple of excellent parts from Mr. Macdona's daughter, who had decided to abandon her efforts to play them; and I began to be gratifyingly cast in the plays which were being added to the repertoire. If there were another part younger or longer than mine, I generally learned that too, "in case." From Manchester I wrote:

"*John Bull* went quite well last night. I *wasn't* very good—I've rehearsed much better. But I was very scared, and also it's extremely disconcerting to have to negotiate all sorts of banks and hills and slippery boards covered with green baize cloth which you've never even seen before. I didn't know where I came on or off or what was safe to tread on and what wasn't—altogether I cursed Rosscullen Hill!"

Shades of my father's experience as Larry in the same play so many years before.

"But you see what the darling 'Manchester Guardian' says, and I'm rather pleased . . . I think I can improve 100% on last night's performance . . . Of course the thing as a whole—particularly the long political scene in Act III—suffers from under-rehearsal, even though we've had a week's really hard work on it."

The last sentence is unintentionally revealing.

As always under the repertory system, we improved as we grew into the plays, though the productions remained as haphazard as ever. In Newcastle, for instance, we picked up female brigands for the Don Juan in Hell Scene. "Quite a musical-comedy touch," I wrote disgustedly. "Jack Tanner and ensemble!" But as the work became harder for me, and also more challenging, I ceased to mind so much about other people's shortcomings and concentrated on my own. As Louka "I still can't get the walk I want"; Violet in *Man and Superman* is still "too heavy"; Blanche in *Widowers' Houses* "frightfully difficult—I can't see myself in it at all"; and Julia in *The Philanderer* "simply dreadful." I must do myself the justice to add that my father, whose touring path crossed mine once or twice, did not echo these sweeping appraisals, but gave me some valuable help.

The clothing problem is another recurrent theme in my letters. All actors who have played in stock companies know what this involves. Most of the plays were done in "modern" dress, which the management was supposed to supply. Technically speaking, they usually did so. But even I, who had no overwhelming flair for current fashions, went on strike when I saw the resources of the wardrobe. I wrote:

"I think my own cloak will do for 'Mrs. Bompas.' Mac's things are the most awful junk. How he could imagine such terrible eye-sores could be worn on any stage, I don't know. The evening dress looks like an Eastern Princess at the Chelsea Arts Ball, bought for sixteen-and-elevenpence in a suburban sale at Tooting."

On the hat question—and it seemed as if every character I ever played wore hats galore—I gave up and bought my own, without much hope that I would ever get paid for them, or be given the raise in salary I had been promised. I never was.

Once or twice my artistic conscience pricked me so badly that I plucked up the courage to ask "Mac" whether some tiny improvement might not be made in the standard of physical production. He had one invariable reply: "What does it matter? The plays are strong." Dynamite never induced him to give anybody a raise, even when they had worked for him for years, and he was always mournfully baffled by the "ingratitude" of anyone who left the company to take a better job at better pay. Nevertheless, this constantly happened, and we were forever rehearsing new actors in old plays as well as old actors in new ones.

With all the hard work, we managed to get in some hard exercise. My letters record a sixteen-mile walk over the Yorkshire moors and a sixty-mile bicycle ride from Edinburgh. In the midst of the industrial North, at Huddersfield, we were caught by the General Strike. My mother and I interchanged passionate letters praising the dignity and calm of the strikers and blaming the Government (Winston Churchill prominent among its Ministers) for precipitating it. "I can't go about much," wrote my mother, "because I cannot avail myself of volunteer services since I do not and cannot black-leg."

Our little company was in a tricky spot. Every big industry had been brought completely to a standstill, as were all the means of transportation. The banks were closed, so that no money was available. We didn't know whether we would be able to go on playing. There might be no electricity and we couldn't act in the dark. Anyway, we didn't think anyone would come to the theatre.

But we went ahead as scheduled. The local "quality" stayed nervously at home; but the striking mill hands thronged to the theatre. We gave, as was our custom, one "entirety" performance of *Man and Superman*, complete with the Hell Scene and lasting over four hours. The theatre was jammed to the rafters with the best audience we had ever played to. Apart from a few minor scuffles over black-leg attempts to run the trams, there was no disturbance in the town at all. By the time we were due to leave for the next date, the strike was over. It had been a miserable failure, and the British public beat itself on the back for its sportsmanship and restraint. The power of the unions was broken forever, exulted the Government. Well . . .

We ended our tour with a few weeks at a suburban theatre in London. I had hoped that every agent and manager would flock to see me play, and wrote letters urging them to do so. About two did. It was a disappointing conclusion; but it had been an invaluable experience. The speaking of Shaw's prose is an education in itself. It is really difficult for an actor with any ear for language to misplace a word, or even a comma; the adjectives are so unerringly chosen, the rhythm so exact and cohesive that any inaccuracy jolts a whole speech, like a missing cog in a precision machine.

To make flesh and blood out of his women is more of a task. It has been charged that some of them are mere "mouthpieces"; and it is certainly arguable that some have more muscle than heart. This is not generally true of the character parts. Lady Brit, for instance, is vigorous and whole, stated with satire but solid as a rock. But it is not surprising that I found Julia and Blanche hard to play; they are fiendishly unreal. Nevertheless, it is essential to find the heart and the blood in them; it is the kind of complementary task which the actor must perform out of his own imagination and humanity. Few of the women are readily sympathetic; but they are never dull. Neither are the plays. I have played them since in some strange places: *Candida* in a leper colony, *Arms and the Man* in a prison, *Mrs. Warren* to nuns; but the audience contact never misses.

I learned a great deal from the leading actor and director of the Macdona Players, Esmé Percy. He taught me more about satiric farce, as in *How He Lied to Her Husband*, than I have ever acquired before or since. He knew that the basis of caricature is truth, delicately incised with exaggeration so that it becomes funny but not false. He had been trained at the Paris Conservatoire and had the French virtuosity and their swift and sparkling precision of speaking. He could twist and juggle Shaw's enormously long speeches with brilliant accuracy and speed; his enunciation was like crystal, his thought as clear. Without these weapons you cannot be a good Shavian actor.

Above all, he taught me that Shaw requires a faculty for observation and comment, a satiric quality of mind. You cannot, as in Chekhov, immerse yourself totally. Also, with Percy, I could not imitate; his style was too personal and special. I began to learn the art of translating alien mannerisms into my own truth, and to ride the horse, not be the horse. I think we all fell short of the plays, but they were wonderful training. Sometimes I think it is essential to begin by acting good plays badly in order to learn how to act bad plays well.

From the Macdona Players I returned happily to the Cassons to play the Gentlewoman in *Macbeth*. It is a play with a traditional history of disaster, certainly reinforced by the events of our opening night. This took place, after long and tiring dress rehearsals, on Christmas Eve. Some of the stagehands evidently thought that the time for festive celebration had arrived. The scenery, again by Charles Ricketts, was heavy and complex, involving much hauling and pushing. The waits between scenes were agonizing. At one point Lewis, playing Banquo, dashed up to the Fly Gallery and seized the ropes himself. Everybody was nervous, neither Sybil nor Henry Ainley anywhere near their best, and the audience was preoccupied with the kids and the Christmas tree. The reviews were an ambivalent Christmas present. But, to my astonishment, there were several flattering references to the tiny part of the Gentlewoman. It was the first time I had seen my name in the big London papers. This also led to my changing it.

Hitherto I had played as "Peggy Webster." But a few weeks later I received a letter from St. John Ervine, then the critic of the *Observer*, whom I had met once or twice. He wrote:

"This is a matter which I meant to write you about before. I want you to consider it very seriously. Please don't call yourself PEGGY Webster on playbills. Margaret Webster, please, there. This really is important, and you can make the change now, but if you leave it for a year or two you won't be able to change it: you'll be too well known by it. The choice of a name for an actor or actress is extremely important and it must be one which, while easy to say and remember, is also distinctive. It must not suggest diminutiveness or flippancy or a lighter atmosphere than the one in which you are going to shine . . . I'm not trying to be funny or clever about this. I thought your Gentlewoman in *Macbeth* was a fine one. You have got character and personality and brains—and I do not want you to handicap yourself by using a name—a very nice name—which is not quite suitable to the sort of career in the theatre that you are now beginning."

The worth of St. John Ervine's contention has since been comprehensibly disproved by the career of Dame Peggy Ashcroft. All the same, I could hardly disregard so impressive a suggestion, coming from so distinguished a man. The playbills knew "Peggy" Webster no more.

I tried out my new name in what the English call "rep" and the Americans, more accurately, "stock"—weekly stock. The Oxford Players was a company of some status managed and directed by a much-respected man of the theatre, J. B. Fagan. It had already fostered several young actors of notable promise, among them John Gielgud. The selection of plays to be done during the university's Easter term was varied and interesting. The first was to be Chekhov's *Uncle Vanya*, and for the privilege of playing Sonya for one week I would cheerfully have agreed to carry a spear for six months.

Chekhov's plays had only just begun to be known in the British theatre. We had read them—the Constance Garnett translations were now published—but never seen them. In 1925 J. B. Fagan, with an augmented Oxford Players company, had produced *The Cherry Orchard* at the Lyric, Hammersmith. It had a touching laughter-and-tears quality, though it was probably more Irish than Russian. Immediately afterwards, Theodore Komisarjevsky did a whole series of the plays at a small theatre just outside London, where everything was done on half a shoestring. His productions were a revelation—tender, compassionate, aware. The lighting, even, was modulated with a fine eye for the dramatic value of shadow, really deep shadow, varied only by a single pool or shaft of light. This was new to us in those days, and is far too rarely used even now. "Komis" worked with minimal resources. Nowadays we have so many hundreds of "instruments" that it becomes impossible to turn enough of them off. The sound, too, was beautifully orchestrated, the symphony of sound in the third act of *The Three Sisters* or the peerless sequence of sounds and silences which closes *The Cherry Orchard*. The silences, especially, were a revelation to us, and almost unbearably moving.

Komis demonstrated also that the plays were gay, constantly erupting into firework "happenings," not just grey all over. Few of his actors were as yet "West End," though many of them were headed that way; they included Charles Laughton, Jean Forbes-Robertson, John Gielgud, Martita Hunt. They played as a team, achieving selflessness and unity. They never broke through the interwoven patterns or tore the shot-silk texture of the whole. We, the young, were overwhelmed. I remember driving back into London after *The Three Sisters* on the top of a bus-with-wings. I cried all the way, as far as the Albert Memorial. It is glorious to see Chekhov, well done, for the first time; most glorious if one has just turned twenty. But I think these productions of Komisarjevsky's would have stood the test of any age or sophistication; they were the finest things he ever did. I have seen—and done—much Chekhov since, but little that excelled his.

I cannot pretend that the Oxford Players' *Uncle Vanya* lived up to these standards. Mr. Fagan, busy on other matters in London, gave it only his perfunctory attention. The company was talented. It included two young men who have since made names for themselves, Alan Webb and Glen Byam Shaw; but it lacked direction, had not yet begun to find itself as an entity and was woefully under-rehearsed. There was an overwhelming tendency toward gloom; we had not yet learned where the humor lay, nor how to combine it with the humanity. We were all abysmally sorry for ourselves, which is a fatal sin in the theatre, and especially with young audiences. The undergraduates tended, then as now, to be skeptical and ruthless, with an eagle eye for the exaggerated or overdrawn. It was still the fashion to caricature all Russian plays on "oh the pain of it" lines, and some of the Oxford student body evidently came to have this kind of fun.

The Oxford Playhouse didn't help us much. It was a converted drill hall, which had once housed a collection of stuffed animals. The audience, not stuffed, sat on squeaky wooden chairs which were audible critics. The dressing rooms were in a separate building, across a yard. You reached the stage up a flight of steps which led straight into the back "wall" of the set and right through it if, as once happened to me, you missed your entrance and were in a hurry. Also it was bitterly cold.

Uncle Vanya, I wrote, was "dull, dull, dull. We all are—it's the fault of the production, known as 'atmosphere.' I can't see why it should all be played at quite so funereal a pace . . . My first act dress is pretty bad—apparently it is always worn by people who have to describe themselves as 'plain.'" After the opening I said: "I was very fed up with myself. It's so delicate. You either just get it or just miss it—'the little less and what worlds away.' I didn't play that last speech for its full value—chiefly because I was over-anxious I think." (I'm sure.) But it was a wonderful contrast to my horseback-riding with the Macdona Players. This was total immersion.

We wrestled with Barrie, with Strindberg, with Shaw (*The Philanderer* again), with the pleased-with-itself undergraduate audience, with our absurd stage, with the cold, with fatigue, with no time, with the usual conditions of stock. In the middle of the season we had a week's change-over with our opposite number, the Festival Company from Cambridge. At the railway junction at Bletchley each company had to change into the other one's train, which then went into reverse and chugged back to its home base. As we dashed along the platform, I almost collided with one of the Cambridge actors; it was Maurice Evans. "Hulloh!" he gasped. "How's your theatre?" "Terrible!" I gasped back. "How's yours?" "Extraordinary!" he answered, and we both dashed on.

Live and Learn

He was right. The theatre apparently had religious antecedents connected with the Salvation Army and over the stage door hung a lantern with the inscription "Jesus Only." Inside, its present owner had transformed it enthusiastically into the most up-to-date of theatre toys. There was a semicircular plaster cyclorama with a sunken trough for lights, an arrangement of curved steps leading from the stage to the Orchestra floor, and various antiseptic arches and pillars. This was all very fine for *Oedipus Rex*, with which the theatre had just opened; but it was a strange home for *Uncle Vanya*. Our makeshift scenery looked ridiculous, propped up inside this operating theatre and bathed in merciless light from far too many German arc lamps. We were all acutely conscious of the age-old Oxford-Cambridge rivalry, and we played abominably. Next morning, the undergraduate critics duly carved us up and served us on toast for the university's breakfast. The theatre building had a distinguished, but brief, career. It may be responsible for my ingrained mistrust of up-to-the-minute theatre buildings.

Back in Oxford we did a new play, a first play, by an ex-student of the university called Emlyn Williams, who had recently gone down. The pre-authors, or Ur-authors, of the play were Maeterlinck and Chekhov, with a dash of Strindberg, and perhaps a godmotherly pat from Barrie's *Mary Rose*. Emlyn cannot have been pleased with our rendering of *Full Moon*. We were, inevitably, under-rehearsed and the early Williams prose was incredibly difficult to learn. It was full of speeches which repeated the same content with fractional differences of phrasing and involutions of imagery. It was all very poetic. We all tried to be very poetic too, including the prompter. I hope Emlyn has since forgiven us as freely as we have forgiven him.

After a final week of Strindberg, we took off the wet towels, laid aside the black coffee and tottered back to London.

There came another lull. It was mitigated by a visit from my dear Aunt Gretchen and "Uncle Tom" Wise; also by the acquisition of something I had lusted for—the first Webster car. We parked it in the Bedford Street churchyard and I loved it like a child. I was never at a loss for an excuse to drive someone somewhere. I took the Wises to Stratford-on-Avon, where Tom, who had been a famous Falstaff, stood under the well-known statue, looking far more like Falstaff than it did. When he died, less than a year later, he asked that his ashes should be scattered there. After apparently impenetrable difficulties and prohibitions, this was accomplished. Oh feet of the tourists, "tread lightly because you tread on his dreams."

The lull went on. It lasted almost a year, and I thought that my career was finished. I did a show or two with amateurs and fought my way into a scattering of lesser Sunday-nights and tryouts. I even managed to play a couple of ingenues in the requisite tennis clothes, who called their fathers "old bean." I pestered the managements of Stratford and the Old Vic. I came to know by heart all the formulae of refusal and polite regret.

It is usually thought to be a great help and a wonderful short cut to be the child of famous parents. Few of the children would agree. Certainly a number of doors were opened for me that might have stayed closed without suitable introductions. But more often than not they were opened only for a polite interchange of meaningless remarks, ended by a dismissive "Give my love to your father and mother," after which the door shut firmly.

It is not easy to escape from the penumbra of well-known parents and establish an individuality of your own, unless you do it by flat rebellion and in some quite different field. Neither circumstance applied to me. I didn't want "pull," but my parents, however discreetly, wanted to pull for me. The employer, I found out, is less likely to take a chance with you than he would be with an unknown. He feels a certain apprehension. Supposing you aren't any good and he fires you. He is likely to run into your mother in tigerish mood at a cocktail party the following week. He senses a possible embarrassment; he decides to stay clear of the whole thing—just to write a polite note and say that the part is cast. Later, I had to look at the problem from the opposite side of the managerial fence, and I was ashamed to detect the same tendencies in myself.

Live and Learn

My mother, who loved people and parties and was immensely good at both, thought I should be "seen." When invited to a fashionable theatre gathering she would ask, could I come too? This appalled me. She would take me to lunch at the Ivy, even though she thought it terribly expensive, in order that I might catch somebody's eye. I promptly became invisible. She used the same technique with my father. He was a charming host in his own home and always urbane, decorative and useful in other peoples'; but he was shy too, except with friends he really knew. My mother was so eager and so full of confidence in us both and enjoyed the parties so much and was so gay and amusing that we both felt monstrously ungrateful to her. All the same, we would climb into our "party clothes" with the utmost reluctance, trying hard to hide our gloom as we waited in the rain for a taxi.

In the summer of 1928 I broke my current period of lull by getting an engagement, achieved without "pull," since it was quite unfashionable. It was to join the Ben Greet Shakespeare Company on what was laughingly known as a "pastoral tour." The lull turned into a frenzy. I opened one afternoon as Viola in *Twelfth Night* and as Portia on the same evening.

"B.G." was still recognizably the same enthusiast for whom my mother had played Celia in the garden of "The Holly Trees, Leyton" forty years earlier. He had beaten a rural path all over the British Isles and barnstormed from coast to coast of the United States. He had pioneered Shakespeare at the Old Vic and kept it going right through the First World War; he had run some of the earliest summer festivals at Stratford. Many young actors, and many young audiences, owed their first Shakespeare to him. By the time I knew him he was an old man of benevolent appearance, sturdy as an oak, with a shock of very white hair, eyes of the bluest blue and a cantankerous disposition. He still played such parts as Shylock, Malvolio, Prospero, Touchstone; but it cannot be claimed that his services to Shakespeare, which were very great, lay in his talents as an actor.

He viewed his company with a fatherly eye, as if we were so many puppies whose scramblings and yelpings he had watched a thousand times before in other young creatures not yet Shake-

321

speare-broken. He had done the plays so often, in so many extraordinary ways and places, that I don't think he took any of it very
seriously any more. In the face of some particularly fearful or
ludicrous happening, his eyes would twinkle with enjoyment. Anything short of total disaster simply passed him by. He had become
so accustomed to making his actors fend for themselves that he
knew we would, between us, get the shows on somehow.

Since half the actors in the English theatre were B.G. gradu-
ates, he didn't really mind which of them drifted in or out of the
company. If poor old So-and-so was ill, dear old Somebody-else
could always be counted on; he had been "a lovely Orlando"
twenty-five years before and could easily "get up" in the part. It
was recorded, and I am sure with truth, that he had once scrambled together a bunch of his old "boys and girls" in a hurry for a
special performance of *Twelfth Night* and got them all on the train
before anyone noticed that there were two Sir Andrews and no
Orsino.

When I joined the company I was appalled by the chaotic
welter of muddle and optimism from which our first shows
emerged. But as we all grew to know each other a little better, we
managed to impose some order on chaos, and I enjoyed every
minute of the absurd six weeks which followed. The general idea
of the tour was that we should play out of doors, adapting ourselves to whatever local conditions existed. This kept the staging
flexible, to say the least. We often arrived too late to make a proper
survey of the playing area or the logistics of getting to and from it
without being seen. Sometimes we got completely lost en route; at
others we would be forced to sneak up to the "stage" by crawling
on all fours behind a rose bed. Once, wearing Elizabethan farthingales, we had to climb the ancient walls of the City of Canterbury
by means of a ladder before descending gracefully into the Dean's
garden; and once Lady Macbeth had to sleepwalk down a fire
escape, opening iron gates on every landing.

B.G. was never very specific about what went on where, with
two firm exceptions: in *The Merchant of Venice*, Venice and
Belmont had to be geographically separated. It was usual for
Nerissa and me to have our first scene interrupted by B.G.'s pierc-

ing growl from behind a hedge, proclaiming:"Ye're in Venice, y'fool, y'ought to be in Belmont." Once Venice was on a driveway, and the Trial Scene was enlivened by a postman on a bicycle, riding phlegmatically up to the front door just as I was saying: "Tarry a little: there is something else." The second of B.G.'s obsessions was that in *The Tempest*, some bush, mound, arbor or "folly" should be designated as Prospero's Cave, even if no one could get inside it.

It was these al fresco shenanigans which caused the tour to be designated as "pastoral"; but the vagaries of the English summer made it an entirely relative term. For instance, B.G. had planned an exquisite interlude on the shaved lawns of Lady Warwick's house in Essex. Instead, we were driven by the weather to the village hall, where we performed *The Merry Wives of Windsor* by gaslight in front of a drop vividly depicting the Bay of Naples. The play was the last to be added to the repertoire. B.G. had not played Falstaff for many years and he had totally forgotten it, if, indeed, he had ever known it. I approached the whole thing disapprovingly. "A shockingly cut version," I wrote, "with the naughtiest 'business' imaginable, including the insertion by Falstaff of the classic line 'Come and dress me, girls.' " However, I had carefully made myself a beautiful headdress for Mrs. Ford. It was copied from Mrs. Kendal's in the Tree production. All my headgear and "accessories" were homemade—they had to be—and this was especially elegant. But when B.G. saw it, he vetoed it immediately. We were to wear "pointed hats"—i.e., hennins. In vain I pointed out first that there weren't any in the wardrobe, and second, that they were a hundred years wrong in date. Nothing would do but pointed hats. He had some business in the Letter Scene whereby the two Wives "wag their heads from side to side and the points of your hats touch and it gets a lovely laugh."

Mrs. Page had also provided her own headdress and was far from pleased. We wished B.G. would go home and learn his lines, of which he didn't yet know one, and forget about our hats. Nor was the small village of Dunmow, where we had the night off, very prolific in materials from which "pointed hats" could be contrived. We bought what we could find. B.G. didn't want to rehearse; he said benevolently that he would see us tomorrow in our pointed hats and went off to the movies, accompanied by other actors, laughing heartily. Grimly we settled down in a bedroom under the eaves of the old inn with needle and thread and buckram and far-too-heavy veiling; also a copy of the play. As dusk deepened into darkness, we lit all the candles we could find and plodded on. One of us would stab furiously at a pointed hat while the other recited all Falstaff's lines aloud, till we both knew them by heart. The next day we wore the hats, said almost all of B.G.'s lines and were the Merriest Wives imaginable.

Some performances were quite good, I think, especially *Love's Labour's Lost*, which we did well; it didn't ask too much of any of us, including B.G., was unhackneyed, and admirably adapted to pastoral purposes. *Twelfth Night* and *As You Like It* weren't bad. *The Tempest* was a hazard, partly owing to last-minute "nymphs and reapers" locally recruited, and partly because B.G.'s really dreadful Prospero was matched by an equally dreadful Ariel. It provided the low point of the tour, at Blandford, in Dorset, where we played it on a small football field. The Town Crier, complete with bell and tricorn hat, had been busily making his rounds, announcing the appearance of the Ben Greet Players in *The Tempter;* and despite a cool wind and light drizzle, the "grandstand" was packed. It wasn't so very Grand. During the performance, the wind freshened to a near gale, with furious gusts of rain. We were dressing in a small Players' pavilion at the far end of the field, and to reach the "stage" had to make a two-hundred-yard entrance through long, wet, uncut grass. It was also quite impossible to hear a cue.

The three Goddesses, including me as Ceres, waited shivering in the doorway, barefooted and bareheaded, straining to discern when we should embark. The first, Iris, went forth bravely, and presently I set off in pursuit, clutching my flapping draperies with one hand and a bunch of autumn leaves with the other; the latter became rapidly sodden and tattooed my arm with russet and yellow. I arrived approximately on time, shouted my lines into the wind, and turned to salute Great Juno with the line "Great Juno comes! I know her by her gait." I saw that she was still about a hundred yards away, plodding through the rain with a resigned, if majestic, expression. "Great Juno COMES!" I yelled again, making large gestures of hurry-up. Her gait was transformed to a sharp trot and she arrived totally breathless.

The music was appreciably ahead of us by this time, not having waited for Great Juno, and being supplied by a nervous local pianist with no one to hold down the sheets on the piano rack. We hurried on to our song of blessing, turning benignly toward Ferdinand and Miranda, who were huddled miserably together on a damp log. A violent gust of wind filled our mouths with rain and blew the music away. At this moment we had our first real chance to take a look at Prospero's Cave in the middle distance. It was a small, black hut, marked in huge white letters: GENTS. With one accord we turned around and staggered helplessly away.

Our final journey back to London notably ended a notable tour. I had borrowed the family car, and was to drive four of the company home after the late-afternoon performance in Bath, a distance of a hundred and some miles. Unfortunately the clutch, always a temperamental character, had one of its fits and I could neither shift nor engage gears unless the car was in motion. I got a downhill push to start me off and knew that I couldn't stop till London. Crossroads meant nothing, I just sounded my horn and kept going. Towns and villages flashed by in the darkness—in those days there were very few traffic lights and these, if red, I disregarded. Even the London suburbs, fairly empty by one a.m., didn't stop me. But at Hyde Park Corner a traffic cop did.

I couldn't start again, even though I burrowed in the engine and threatened it with a hammer. I gave up, and we took a variety of taxis home. I still had on my make-up, considerably overlaid with dirt, dust and car oil. My clothes were the worse for much wear and my hair disheveled by many wigs. I wanted only a bath and bed. But as I rang the front door bell, I heard ominous sounds of revelry from inside. The door was flung open by Sir Gerald du Maurier, immaculate in white tie and tails. My mother was giving a party.

Through the following year I went on playing a number of scattered shows for B.G., mostly indoors and generally to school audiences, who are, in themselves, an education of much ferocity. Sometimes I played parts I hadn't done before. He never let you know that he needed you, or for what play, or where, until two days beforehand and would be greatly disgruntled if you were otherwise engaged. The company was always different—one lot I bitterly described as "a dreadful bunch of shoddy elocutionists"— and there was seldom time to rehearse. A sort of running tradition that we all had in common, and the fast improvisation to which our pastoral training had accustomed us, kept the shows together somehow, though not without argument. Some of us started a mutiny of purists and began to restore the cuts.

Despite all the horrors and absurdities of the Ben Greet performances, pastoral and otherwise, it was basically a very healthy experience, chiefly because B.G. had Shakespeare in his bones. Shakespeare, to him, was bread, breathing and a cup of tea. He had no time for fancy theories, farfetched analogies, scholarly discussions or gimmickry. Shakespeare had written the plays and he played them; it was as simple as that. He was unaffected by "revolutions" in stage production or design because of the peculiar conditions of his own.

William Poel had aimed at stripping Shakespeare: no scenery, no pageantry, no archaeology of costume and no cuts. Barker had followed the same path. B.G. (except, Heaven help us, in the matter of cuts) had reached oddly similar ends for wholly dissimilar reasons. He had stripped his stages because he couldn't afford to do otherwise, and the variable topography made it essential. He dressed many of the plays Elizabethan because it was simpler and the costumes would fit several different shows. He didn't fuss about design, but took what God or the local authorities provided. Shakespeare had always described exactly what the place was supposed to be, and he trusted the audience to take the author's word for it. He played himself, and directed his actors, in a sort of Elizabethan manner of his own, broadly, lustily, often crudely, but at least without affectations. His actors were expected to do one thing and one thing only—to reach their listeners, to make contact and to hold it. Sometimes they did it by fair means and sometimes by foul, but they did it; and they did it with and through the lines alone. Nobody was supposed to intervene between the author and the audience with fancy twistings and distortion. For, like Macdona, his credo was: "The plays are strong."

It would have been dangerous to stay with him too long. Actors took to the old stagey short cuts, the vocalizing, the mechanical repetition of reach-me-down business. But for learning the basic rules and the basic values, for strengthening the muscles with sheer slam-bang honest exercise it was tremendous.

CHAPTER SEVENTEEN

─────────── ᘐᘐᘐ ───────────

Journey to
Piccadilly Circus

Our "juvenile lead" on the B.G. tour was a handsome and gifted young man named John Wyse. He had imagination, energy and initiative. He wasn't going to wait for the theatre to come to him, he was going to make his own theatre. Later on he succeeded in doing so; but at this time he was apt to fall out of love with a scheme as rapidly and totally as he fell in. My frequent partnerships with him usually meant that I did the dirty work while the plan lasted and picked up the pieces after it had exploded. John's feet were firmly planted in the air.

There was no theatre in London for poetic drama; we would therefore found one. We would play everything from Sophocles to Masefield, from Milton to Claudel, before a faithful and admiring membership audience. Where the money or the membership was to come from were questions we brushed aside. We combed South London for suitable premises and found a wonderful old warehouse, not far from the Old Vic, which could have been bought outright for a matter of £500, including the rats. John rightly proclaimed that this was a marvelous bargain. But it became unavoidably apparent that we did not have £500 or even £5, so he switched his attention, temporarily, to an antique shop. Meanwhile, however, he had managed to enlist the interest of two remarkable people; one was a young dancer, a choreographer for the Old Vic's ballet company, Ninette de Valois; the other was the current leading lady in its drama company, Esmé Church, whom I came to know and value as a fine artist and much-underrated director.

In between running around after B.G. and John Wyse, I played a brief part in the brief run of a charming little double bill at the Court Theatre, *The Lady from Alfaqueque* and *Fortunato*, by the brothers Quintero. "Sugar and spice and all things nice" and a cowardly evasion of absolutely everything, would, I am sure, be the verdict on it now. And indeed it proved a little too delicate and sentimental for the public even then. John Gielgud was in it; it was my first experience of working with him, and also my only experience of Granville Barker's direction. I had been brought up on the Barker mystique and had been lastingly impressed by his first volume of Shakespeare Prefaces, which had recently been published. My expectations were keen; so was my disappointment. Mostly, I think, this was because he did not really direct the plays from the ground up, but only paid rather lofty visits to occasional rehearsals in his capacity as author of the translations.

When he did come, everything stopped. Time stood still. A pulverizing sense of awe descended on the theatre. There would be long, long, long waits while he went into a private huddle with the director. After this he would deliver to the company a pontifical— and fascinating—lecture on the history of the drama, on psychology, on Spanish literature, habits and domestic architecture. After this he would disappear completely for a week. When he came again—the company by this time was brimful of Spanish lore— nothing Spanish would be mentioned at all. But he would take one tiny section of the play and go over it again and again and again, leaving other major sequences completely untouched.

He troubled me because I was so anxious to think he was wonderful and couldn't. I remember his telling me that one of my entrances—its only purpose was to build up Gielgud's—was quite "right" and needed no more "force," but that it should have "treble the amount of intention." He would then solemnly repeat the story of the play, the antecedent lives of the characters and all the minutiae of the relevant circumstances. Now it seemed to me that I was absolutely bursting with "intention," living my whole past life from the cradle up. I played a big imaginary scene in the wings before I ever got near the stage. I really didn't know what more I could possibly "intend." Evidently I was not conveying this intention; but if not, why not? I never found out. But I have thought, then and since, that it should have been part of the director's business to tell me.

I wrote to my mother:

"He has succeeded in breaking up all the old stuff but not in supplying a new version except in the patches he's taken in detail. Everyone is playing their parts as about six different people—all very convinced that what Barker says must be good and right, but thoroughly upset as to quite what they're meant to be doing, and all holding their heads and calling on the Almighty. To me there is an awfully disjointed feeling as if none of the characters have quite come alive. This is fatal . . . as the play depends entirely on its tenderness and humanity."

It taught me the valuable lesson that it is no good being a fine director in bits or too late. Never, I thought, be a last-minute Johnny.

My next director was neither remote nor abstruse nor pontifical, but animated, elliptical, vivid, democratic (everybody had one name—"ducks") and bawdy. This was Auriol Lee, now best remembered for her direction of all the early John van Druten plays. The production was an eighteenth-century comedy, *The Clandestine Marriage;* it was to be done at the Arts Theatre Club for half a dozen performances.

Gretchen was to be in it too. After Uncle Tom's death she had come back to England, and while my mother and father were away on a tour of South Africa, was living with me and the faithful Frances at Bedford Street. Auriol, who had known her for years, offered her a part which was ideally suited to her much-neglected theatre talent. I think she was very happy to feel a part of something again. "A god-send," she called it, but added cau-

Journey to Piccadilly Circus

tiously, "though I can't really think God has arranged all this in aid of his fattest and humblest sparrow." I adored her and she spoiled me—though she had a satiric eye and could be mordant on occasion. It was said that when she played with Jack Barrymore in *Richard III* she was the only person who could control him and to whom he was unfailingly kind and courteous.

This was my first attempt to play eighteenth-century comedy, that most difficult of all acting techniques. But my doubts and fears were soon dispelled by the prevailing jollity with which Auriol surrounded her work. Someone had made a "version" of the play which, as was still usual in those days, had been typed up in separate "sides" or "parts" for the actors. At the first reading many of the cast were absent—they often were when it was an unpaid production. I wrote an account of it to my parents:

Auriol:	Come on! Fanny: "Nay, then, my dear . . ." (*Pause*) "Nay, then my dear . . ." Fanny—Miss Mars, please. Got that?
Miss Mars:	I've got "Mr. Lovewell, by your leave . . ."
Auriol:	No, no. Just leave Mr. Lovewell alone. It's "Nay, then my dear . . ."
Miss Mars:	(*looks through "sides"*) No, I haven't got that at all.
Auriol:	(*to Stage manager*) Make a note, ducks, Act I scene 2 missing in Fanny's part.
Miss Mars:	Oh, here it is—in the middle of Act IV—"Nay, then, my dear, you must not be angered . . ." Is that it?
Auriol:	That's it. You're bound up wrong, ducks, unpick yourself. (*Long wait while Miss Mars does so.*) Now, then. (*Miss Mars says line. Another pause.*) Miss Sterling: "Come, sister Fanny . . ." Betty, please!
Betty:	I haven't got that. I've got "Oh, lud, Sir John . . ."
Auriol:	Perhaps you're bound up wrong too.
Betty:	(*after much turning of pages*) No, it's not in my part at all.

331

. . . and Margaret

Auriol: Perhaps it's in one of the other parts. Look and see, ducks. (*Much searching. Missing sheet presently discovered in one of the absentee's parts, whence it is disembowelled and presented to Betty who unpicks herself and inserts it.*)

We all laughed a lot and remarkably little got done. I determined that if it were ever up to me I would have full texts for all the actors. Not long afterwards this did become universal practice.

Auriol's apparently slapdash methods concealed an acute professional eye and keen judgment. Her own natural vigor was defeated in this production by three things: the assorted modern styles and thin methods of the actors—only Gretchen really knew how to tackle this stuff with the right mixture of artifice and juice; the wishy-washy gentility of the sets; and a running accompaniment of exasperating tinkle-tinkle from the orchestra pit. This was supplied by an erudite elderly spinster named Chaplin, much respected as an authority on period music, and a ladylike group of her relatives performing on the spinet, harp and other wiry instruments. At the dress rehearsal we all went nearly mad with Miss Chaplin losing the cues, Auriol altering them, the actors missing them, and much argument with the stage management as to who should have given whom a signal light. It was my first experience of this particular method of wasting time and fraying nerves. It was not the last.

Gretchen and I emerged from this bout with the eighteenth century only to plunge into another, with John Wyse. We were to hire a hall and give two performances of Vanbrugh's *The Confederacy*. Gretchen was to play an elderly female dragon and I the Miss Fix-it of the plot, an irrepressibly talkative character named Flippanta. John was determined to be completely practical. He calculated the expenses of the show at £50, and the hall held one hundred and twenty; so in two performances we were bound to "get out." In the end, naturally, the expenses trebled his estimates and the receipts halved them and I threw in my small savings from the B.G. tour. This pattern, here established in miniature, has often been repeated in my life. I look back with amazement at the recurrence of so much naïve optimism.

We believed everybody. A costume-rental firm promised us the whole set of costumes for £7 10s. and the wigs for 7s 6d. apiece. It wasn't till later that we found the costumes were impossibly Early Upholstery and the wigs strictly Gilbert and Sullivan Amateur. John then insisted that the women's costumes should be made, which they were, by a rather ecstatic female designer and many volunteer needlewomen. But the materials were sleazy because they were (of necessity) too cheap. They had none of the "body" which should make a costume of this period practically walk by itself. They looked "flimsy and miserable" and arty with it.

We begged, borrowed and stole the drapes, the props, the furniture. I slaved at sending out circulars, inviting managers and agents, preparing press releases and conducting the business of the box office—if any. At the dress rehearsal the carpenter didn't turn up and we had to lay the rostrums ourselves. The hall electrician had few lights and didn't know what to do with them. I made a mental note: "Learn about lights." The cast was always having to be changed because of other jobs, and one of them got mumps but played all the same. As might have been expected, this had consequences.

At the performances few managers came. Some of the press did, and we rather wished they hadn't. Lilian Baylis of the Old Vic placed the last straw on my back by exclaiming: "Hulloh, dear—long part, dear—lot to do—where's dear Nell Carter?—such a good actress—hasn't got enough." Had I known Miss Baylis better I should have dismissed this remark as part of her highly idiosyncratic style. As it was, I managed to laugh it off; but it was an effort. She couldn't, I considered, have thought as badly of my performance as I did. "Terrible" would have been my adjective. "It's no good," I wrote, "I KNOW. It was by a long way the most difficult comedy part I've ever played and I fear definitely beyond me. I was, as a line in the play puts it, 'insupportably brisk.'" Gretchen thought I was good; Edy Craig said so; even ferocious

333

Aunt Booey sent me £10 for the expenses, and I knew very well she wouldn't have done that unless *she* had thought I was good. But I had determined otherwise.

Nothing comforted me, not even another job. I had been engaged to play a small part in a revival of Barrie's *Quality Street* at the Haymarket; indeed, I had already started rehearsing. In the Oxford Playhouse days I had loved Miss Phoebe very much, and I worked hard not to repine at playing little Miss Fanny and to make her as good as possible. I went to museums to look at prints and drawings and find out how the clothes should be worn, the drape of a shawl, the correct tilt of a bonnet.

I appreciated the order and dignity of the Haymarket after all the hurly-burly of B.G. The rehearsals were conducted with calm and courtesy and the actors treated more like guests than employees. During the first week we already had most of the props and furniture. Charles La Trobe, who had been at the theatre for many years, presided over the stage. If a scene were not completely set up as soon as we came to it he would look a little pained and say gently to the master carpenter, "Well, old man, well . . . come along, now . . ." and everything promptly appeared like magic. The theatre housekeeper dispensed tea in the Green Room seated behind an elegant Chippendale table and wielding a silver teapot. "Be careful not to spill any," she would say, "not on that dress—it's gordious." Sir James Barrie sat in the Orchestra stalls with his hat pulled down to his nose and his muffler pulled up to his ears and his pipe just visible between them. He sometimes emitted a grunt. It was all very stately and soothing.

But it failed to soothe me. I hadn't even asked for the understudy of Phoebe, being morosely convinced that they wouldn't give it to me, but had accepted that of Patty. Bouncing maids, I said to myself, are evidently my destiny. The part was played by Hilda Trevelyan, the adored Wendy of long ago, who had done it in the original production twenty-five years before. Obviously I couldn't be a bit like her; yet the business of the scenes had become molded around her so that I couldn't escape from her personality and didn't know whether I ought to try. This is a difficult problem for many understudies, and no one pays enough attention to it.

Journey to Piccadilly Circus

It was a bitterly cold winter. We all went around with numbed fingers and dripping noses, shoulders hunched against the icy wind. Gretchen and I huddled over a gas fire in one small room at Bedford Street and shut up the rest. I got mumps. I insisted it was "glands," though I knew perfectly well it wasn't, and went on playing, looking swollen and revolting in my Kate Greenaway clothes, and praying no one else would get it. They didn't. But a bout of flu swept right through the company and all the important parts were played by their understudies, except, of course, Patty.

The revival didn't last very long. I started around the agents' offices again. I tried other forms of activity. In fear and trembling I gave a lecture—my first—to the Women's Institute in a small Hampshire village. An old lady, a farmer's wife, came up to me afterwards and asked, "Was that true, all you said about this Shakespeare?" I said faltering that indeed I believed so. "Really true?" she said, still unconvinced. I nodded. "Well, if that isn't the strangest thing! I always thought Shakespeare was another name for God."

I gave lessons in French and arithmetic to the Casson daughters, Mary and Ann, an extraordinary notion of Lewis's which resulted in my learning far more than I taught. Lewis also asked me to do a couple of weeks of the *Medea*, as Leader of the Chorus. Sybil was tossing it off as a double bill with *Jane Clegg*, while rehearsing a new play, a proceeding which would have killed anybody else. I became gloomier and more tragic than ever, in consonance with the tragic Greeks.

It was from this black gulf that I was rescued by Clare Eames. She turned my eyes outward. I stopped being what Shaw calls "a selfish little clod of ailments and grievances." She encouraged me to hope that I had something to give and not just something to get. A little Life Force flowed back into me. And suddenly I had an offer from Lilian Baylis and Harcourt Williams to go to the Old Vic. I was to play a fistful of widely assorted parts—Lady Capulet, Audrey, the Duchess of York, and, by far the most important of them, Toinette in *The Imaginary Invalid*. It was this part, own twin to Flippanta, that Williams had found most difficult to cast; and it was my performance in *The Confederacy* which had got me the job. I decided I had wasted a lot of perfectly good despair on myself and would, in future, try to save it for worthier objects.

The season of 1929–30 at the Old Vic was one of transition. Hitherto the Shakespeare productions had visibly evolved from the traditions established by B.G. during the First World War, when he and Lilian Baylis began to introduce Shakespeare to "the Home of Opera in English." It is astonishing that anything, even Shakespeare, survived the manpower shortage, let alone the clash and thunder of those two eccentric Titans. The wardrobe and scenery was then Early Makeshift, massive crumbs dropped from the tables of *Faust* and *Aida*, or loans from other managements which Lilian somehow forgot to give back again. The salaries were strictly shoestring; Sybil Thorndike got £1 10s. a week for playing all the female leads and usually doubling a lot of the male bit parts. Opera was still the paramount responsibility of the Vic and its prime source of income.

But the balance gradually shifted. By the mid-Twenties Shakespeare had drawn level, by 1929 he was in the ascendant. The productions and directing remained strictly traditional. The companies were largely drawn from the recognized pool of Shakespearian actors trained under Benson or B.G. There were some fine performances and some remarkable individual actors, such as Edith Evans, still new to stardom. The conventional cuts in the texts remained, however, and much of the business (some of it very good) had been handed down from generation to generation. Production and design began to be recognized by Miss Baylis as necessary evils which must be paid for. She was induced to spend as much as £15 on the sets and costumes for a new production. But all in all, the winds of change blew gently down the Waterloo Road.

Nevertheless, the status of the Vic had become very different. After ten years of begging, wheedling, scolding, scraping, bullying and above all, praying, Lilian had got it rebuilt and sufficiently endowed. Gifts from Sir George Dance and from the Carnegie

Foundation, plus the remission of entertainment tax by the British treasury, had all helped. But to God was the glory. There are countless stories of Lilian Baylis, that dumpy, homely, rather comic aging woman with the peculiar cockney-colonial accent, and of her total devotion to the Vic. It was said that when Queen Mary came to open the new building Lilian pointed out the two framed portraits in the lobby, one of Miss Emma Cons, who had founded the theatre, and one of King George V. "That's your dear husband," said Miss Baylis to Her Majesty, "and that's Aunt Emma. She's larger, but then she did more for the Vic."

Many of the stories about her are probably apocryphal, but everyone believed them immediately because it was impossible to exaggerate Lilian. However absurd the anecdote might be, it always cut to the heart of the matter. There was, for instance, Ernest Milton's account of having told her that he had acquired a new flat and that the telephone would be installed shortly, after which he would talk to her. "Very nice, dear," she replied. "Come to me in your joys and come to me in your sorrows, but not in between because I've no time for chitchat." This splendid aphorism should be engraved on every telephone in the world. Hundreds of people went into the stuffy, cat-smelling little office where she sat entrenched behind a huge rolltop desk, having been exasperated beyond speech by her meanness and obstinacy. They came to complain, to protest, to demand, even to resign; also, if they were newcomers, to mock. Flung onto their knees beside the desk, balanced between a saucer of cat's meat and a bubbling kettle on a gas ring, they found themselves remaining to pray.

Next to God, Lilian's Second Commandment was "her" audience. She didn't know or care very much about the art of acting; it was said she didn't know much about Shakespeare. She simply put the actors into the plays and watched their impact on the audience. She could read the resulting graph to a hair. It was, truly, a very special audience; you meet it quite often at the ballet or in an opera house (provided it isn't too smart), but rarely at a play—an audience of experts. At the beginning the Vic audience was largely local. It paid very low prices—only sixpence in the Gallery. It came to enjoy itself and did so vociferously. It could criticize

337

vocally too, and laugh with a mighty derision. If you "dried up" it could have prompted you, which is exceedingly unnerving for an actor. You knew you were on trial by comparison with a dozen others who had played that particular part before you.

Lilian watched like a hawk to see how her audience was liking what it saw. Her judgments, within this frame of reference, were devastating, but they were shrewd. I was with her once when a new member of the company, a West-End-ish sort of actor, was playing Enobarbus. During the drunken scene on Pompey's Galley he sprawled clumsily on the floor, revealing an unmistakably modern pair of white underpants, and thereby getting a laugh. Lilian clucked. "No good in Shakespeare, is he, dear? Don't think we can keep him," she said decisively. It seems like a wholly insufficient reason, but he wasn't and she didn't.

She was present—in a way—at almost every show. She would sit at the back of her box in the auditorium, with a red curtain drawn across the front of it, writing letters, addressing circulars, doing accounts. If anything in the least unusual changed or interrupted the rhythm of sound from the stage, her head would come poking through the curtains in a flash to see what was up. If she sensed a crisis, she would be backstage almost before it happened, with a speed astonishing in one of her bulk.

Maurice Evans has related that one night when he was playing Iago a cat decided to take part in the Jealousy Scene. Two seconds later Lilian's voice was heard from the wings. "Pussy, Pussy, pretty Pussy," said she in wheedling tones, and made alluring, smacking noises with her lips. When this failed she tried poking at the cat with a broom. When that, too, proved useless, she reached firmly onto the stage, perfectly visible to the audience, seized the animal by the tail and yanked it off. It was typical Baylis technique, as applied to all problems.

By the season of 1929–30 the character of the whole enterprise was changing. The Vic was being taken up. Box-office prices had risen, first-string critics attended opening nights, successful young actors wanted to go there, audiences from across the river came in increasing numbers. They started by being snooty, but they soon caught the prevailing spirit. It was still a people's theatre; there was still a unique flavor of intimacy, loyalty, mutual friendship and proprietary pride. The hard core of the audience didn't read the critics and didn't care about an actor's previous successes. It still liked to make its own stars, and when it made them, they stayed made.

The texture of the company, that year, was different, however. There were fewer identifiably Shakespearian actors, though almost everybody had had some sort of classical training and one or two, like Donald Wolfit, had done a good deal. Harcourt Williams had put together a fresh, young team with some surprising departures from the traditional casting molds. Martita Hunt, known only for her modern work, was to be the leading lady. The leading man was a successful young actor with a rather immature Romeo already to his credit, John Gielgud. That season at the Vic turned him into a star of the first magnitude, the finest young classic actor who had yet emerged in his generation.

Lilian paid him £20 a week. It was enormous, by Vic standards, and she resented it bitterly—until she saw what he meant to her theatre. Even then she thought it too much. But at this figure the star salary was firmly fixed for many seasons to come. The names got larger, but not the pay envelope. A couple of seasons later it was announced that Charles Laughton was to join the company. He was already a highly paid star of stage and screen. But Lilian was not impressed. She told me about their interviews. "Funny boy," she said, "keeps on saying God this and God that . . . didn't care for it. Told him, 'Well, dear boy, we don't care how much money you make in films—are you good in Shakespeare?' Said he'd slept with a copy of *Hamlet* under his pillow since he was seven. I said, 'That's not the point, dear boy. Can you say his lovely words?' " Which, of course, was and still is the point.

In one respect our season marked the end of the old regime. It was the last of the Old Vic as the only home of both Shakespeare and opera together. A fund had been raised to acquire Phelps's famous old theatre of Sadler's Wells. It was being rebuilt and was to open the following season. The two companies were then supposed to alternate at the two theatres. Later this proved completely impracticable and, as everyone now knows, opera remained at "the Wells" and Shakespeare took over the Vic. The ballet, too, remained at Islington, till it became Royal and adorned Covent Garden.

In my day at the Vic we played turn and turn about in any given week: Monday, Wednesday, Friday and alternate Saturday matinees for us, Thursday and Saturday for the opera, Tuesday for dress rehearsals or occasional special performances. We did nine different productions and kept each of them running for three weeks, while the opera played real "repertory." Sometimes we did, too. In a program for the last three weeks of the season, I see that we played *A Midsummer Night's Dream*, *Hamlet* in both the entirety and the cut version, and *Macbeth*. The opera did *Otello*, *The Force of Destiny*, *Madam Butterfly* and *Aida*. The dancers were just beginning to be welded into a company by Ninette de Valois and, for the first time, were allotted an occasional Tuesday night for a ballet performance. The building, which was quite small, nearly burst with all this activity. How the permanent staff, technical or executive, ever managed it at all I cannot guess. Being then as egocentric and ignorant of these matters as actors usually are, I never thought of asking. Pride, devotion to "the Lady" and a kind of cynical bravado were, I think, their motive forces. "You think it's impossible, do you? Ha! ha! you should have seen last year's dress rehearsal of *Aida!*"

Of course there wasn't enough of anything to go around—space, time, physical resources, above all, money. Harcourt Williams managed to get the average sum spent on sets and costumes for a new production raised to £20. Even so, they were still much affected by the demands of the opera. There was bitter rivalry as to whether a new set of steps or rostrums should be painted red brick for *Rigoletto* or grey stone for *Macbeth* or could be made to do for both in an indeterminate shade of brown. Scenery was built and painted in the theatre, quite a lot of it by actors doubling in paint, or by apprentices who were supposed to be learning to act by doing the dirty work which had little or nothing to do with acting. The prop department was staffed by semi-amateurs, and remained so for many years.

The new costumes, those we were lucky enough to get, were also designed and made in the theatre; but the cloaks, wigs and other adjuncts retained a visibly operatic flavor, and there was much competition as to who was to sing or speak in them. Orlando, the wardrobe master, became my very good friend. He had a bald head, rosy cheeks, a wonderfully thick Lancashire accent, and stood behind his clothes counter in a white apron, looking, as John Gielgud said, "like a magnificent grocer." He was an old-timer and a "character." He viewed with twinkling shrewdness the collisions between fresh newcomers with fancy ideas and the rocklike Miss Baylis. He judged actors and singers solely by their ability to wear costume. "That Miss Thingummy!" he once said despairingly of the current Viola, "with 'er bum and 'er bust . . . !"

He liked me, thanks to my B.G.-trained athleticism, and I did especially well on cloaks. I deferred, of course, to the priority of Martita Hunt; but she had not then had much experience of period costume and regarded a heavy cloak rather as if it might bite her. I had not dragged such garments over the walls of Canterbury for nothing, and I would conspire with Orlando to obtain the most impressive at his disposal, even if I had to share it with Brunhilde. He once gave me an entire, uncut bolt of cloth and calmly told me to pin myself into it. "Doan't y' go cutting it naow," he said, "we'll 'ave to use it fer the opera." Thus challenged, I did as he said.

The use of the stage for rehearsals was, of course, hotly contested. We spent a good deal of our time in the rehearsal room, a big, bare place under the roof, which seemed to become terribly cluttered with actors and students and everybody's hats and coats and books and cups of coffee and Harcourt Williams's tins of "Bemax," a patent food on which he seemed to live. We felt constricted and self-conscious at first. Williams was nervous—he was much more experienced as an actor than as a director, and as always happens, this communicated a sense of insecurity to the company.

But he grew in confidence and we in comradeship; so much so that Lilian thought fit to issue a warning: "I like my young people to mate," she said, "but not in the wings."

"Billy" Williams was a gentle and loving spirit, with sparse hair which always seemed about to fly off his head. He was enthusiastic, diffident, full of ideas, much influenced by his two leading actors, which did not make for good morale in the company. He had worked with William Poel, but derived his sense of verse-speaking from Ellen Terry and from Margaret Charrington, who had coached John Barrymore for Hamlet; he wanted a truth with music in it. His immediate mentor and guide was Granville Barker, whose second set of Shakespeare Prefaces was about to be published. Billy read them in proof and handed them on to us. They were invaluable; they still are. The texts we used had few of the traditional cuts; they were based, as Barker advocated, on a direct study of the First Folio versions. Billy's major innovation was to introduce playwrights other than Shakespeare through the sacred portals of the Vic: Molière and Bernard Shaw (*Androcles and the Lion* and *The Dark Lady of the Sonnets*) were to give the Bard some competition. The scenery and costumes might still have inherited trademarks; but at least he determined that the acting should wear a new look. There remained, however, Lilian's basic question: Can you say his lovely words?

Billy found that his fresh young actors "had no vowel sense . . . the words are clipped out of all recognition, and, what is worse, have no carrying power." In *Romeo and Juliet*, the first production, he strove to get a feeling of Italian vitality and speed. The result was gabble and rush. After *The Merchant of Venice*, which came next, Granville Barker wrote to him that the company's great need was still a common method of speaking verse, "to let the verse seem to be carrying them along, not they to be carrying it, and not, some of them, to be so damned explanatory."

It is an irony, repeated like clockwork, that every generation thinks its predecessors have been vocal and artificial. No sooner had Gielgud established a viable alternative to the declamatory methods still in vogue than his contemporary Laurence Olivier arose to do battle with him for being too lyric and poetic. Their successors don't yet seem to know which of them to rebel against. The lesson that music does not preclude truth, but expresses it, comes late and hard.

We got better, naturally, as we went on. Shakespeare and the audience between them honed us to a fine cutting edge. Billy grew in authority and definition. But the glory of the season was the emergence of Gielgud: first, predictably, in *Richard II*, then, much more surprisingly, as a gaunt and hunted Macbeth, and finally as Hamlet. I have seen many Hamlets since, including two of Gielgud's, and directed others, but I have never been as moved as I was by this one. It sprang fresh and whole from his imagination and his natural gifts. It was not too much overlaid by taking thought or by awareness of comparisons. It was spontaneous, glowing, and above all, young. He *was* "the expectancy and rose of the fair state"; he *was* "like sweet bells, jangled, out of tune and harsh." It was a "first, fine, careless rapture" of accomplishment such as is granted only to the very few, and that not more than once in a lifetime.

It was also, I believe, Williams's most satisfying production. When I came to direct the play myself in New York in 1938, I realized what a debt I owed him. We were each of us enormously helped by using the uncut text, which both rests Hamlet and illuminates the lesser characters. At the Vic, Martita Hunt and Donald Wolfit, both of them excellent as the King and Queen, were the chief beneficiaries. I too got a hunk more than usual, as the Player Queen, and was duly grateful. It was Billy's aim to stress the human values of the play. He said himself: "I put the characters into Elizabethan costume because I felt the spirit of the play . . . was expressed by the author in the immediate values of his time . . . When Hamlet was first produced it was as modern and provocative as a play by Bernard Shaw." The Elizabethan production, like John's performance, was as different from Barrymore's as chalk from cheese. The latter had a grandeur, a stripped and primitive quality. The virtues of the Vic's lay in a freshness of detail and a common humanity.

Between *Romeo* and *Hamlet* we were variously successful. The Vic-ites took with enthusiasm to both Shaw and Molière. I found I had learned by past errors and was able to play Toinette much more lightly and crisply than I had played her predecessor. I was, naturally, less strained and more relaxed. There was a revolutionary *Midsummer Night's Dream*, with some rather folksy, country-dancing music instead of dear old Mendelssohn. The scenery was stylized, with lots of steps and rostrums, and the costumes were "after Inigo Jones"—for the women, huge farthingales on rigid, wooden frames and high, wired collars. Martita and I found that to lie on the former clad in the latter for some fifteen minutes, supposedly "asleep," was an excruciating torture. Lilian must have hated the whole thing—for different reasons—but she loyally backed up her director and there were few complaints. Fortunately the Clowns were played with real comic invention. The Pyramus-and-Thisbe interlude was actually fun to watch. If only audiences could know what actors suffer when, night after night, they have to pretend to be audiences!

My greatest success was as Audrey in *As You Like It*. I romped around in nose putty and a flaxen wig and some padding and was chagrined to find that everybody thought it a wonderful piece of casting. *Macbeth* is chiefly notable in my memory as the only production of that play with which I have ever been associated to escape the trail of doom and disaster which is supposed to follow it. In my experience, it almost always does. Since the play is concerned with the power of evil, this is by no means surprising.

The season drew to an end. I was offered a return engagement for the next one, but I didn't think the parts were good enough. I nerved myself to refuse; so when the last night came it was tinged with sadness. It wasn't a completely "last" night, since *Hamlet* was to be moved to the Queen's Theatre for a three-week run, the first invasion of the West End from the Waterloo Road. But this was the last of the Vic, and by tradition it was a shouting, tumultuous affair, a jamboree for the faithful audience. They showered all of us, not just the stars, with bouquets and gifts of all kinds. Trestle tables stretching the whole width of the stage were piled high with little parcels wrapped in tissue paper, with cards saying "To my favourite Guildenstern" or "Shall never forget your Third Witch."

344

Even the stage managers, those generally unsung heroes, were not forgotten.

Innumerable speeches were made and finally "the Lady" took stage center, a dumpy figure in the robes of her Oxford doctorate, which she wore on festal occasions, with her spectacles and her crooked smile, making clumsy, inept remarks about each of us and bullying the audience to keep the house full next year. She announced the names of the new company, including several actors, Ralph Richardson among them, well known in the West End but not on the South Bank. Her face wore a dubious expression. "Don't know 'em myself," she said tartly. "Billy says they're all right. They'll have to show us, won't they?" The audience agreed. We all felt rather sad and sentimental. "Never mind, dear," she said to me afterwards. "You'll be back."

Hamlet with Gielgud settled down at the Queen's Theatre, next door to *Hamlet* at the Globe with Moissi. I started rehearsals at the Arts Theatre Club for Vildrac's *S. S. Tenacity*, directed by Clare Eames. She had not yet fully mastered the art of imparting to others what she could do herself; but she was enormously stimulating and perceptive and brimming over with plans for the future. Gretchen had taken a cottage at Maidenhead, near the river. I commuted from London every night, walking across the Thicket under the silver June sky, smelling the sweet-scented hedges and the delicate wild roses. It was a happy time. I didn't even mind that I was soon to be unemployed—"and for turning-away, let summer bear it out!" It was here at Gretchen's cottage, the following November, that I learned of Clare's death, when I got back one night from a Schools' Theatre performance of *Macbeth*.

The Schools' Theatre was an organization formed by John Wyse, Esme Church and myself to give what are now known as "concert readings" of Shakespeare and other plays at schools and colleges. We had started off rather grandly with a full-scale production of *The Tempest* in the Speech Room at Harrow on the openest-possible stage. I should think it was about a hundred feet wide by eight or ten deep. Later we did one of *Macbeth*, which turned out sheer hell and was more full of serio-comic disasters than I care to remember. Meanwhile, however, we had got ideas. Esmé Church evolved a production scheme designed for about eight actors in which the plays were partly read and partly acted out. John Wyse flitted on to something else and we acquired a colleague with a genius for costume who made us a set of Elizabethan clothes. The shows were pleasant to the eye and blended together by Esmé with remarkable imagination and skill. The promotion side of it, however, was a vast and dreary job. I sank under the weight of gigantic school directories, mountains of circulars and piles of yellow envelopes. I loathe yellow paper to this day. The performances were excellent, and succeeded admirably in their purpose. So far as I know, they were the first example of a breed that has become very popular since. But the practical and promotional problems were too much for us and ended by exhausting our energies and our cash.

Meanwhile, my mother played in some short-lived plays, my father in a long run, Ivor Novello's *Symphony in Two Flats*. Ben had appeared with him before in Molnar's *Liliom*, an unaccountable failure in London; and my cousin, Jean Brough, was a constant member of his companies. Like everyone else, she adored him. As a writer he was midway to the creation of those dazzling musicals which later crowned his career. It was an inevitable progression; his plays all pointed that way. In my lofty, Chekhov-worshipping manner I wrote to my mother of this piece: "Ivor has a wonderful eye for what they *wear*, what they *look* like, what they *say*, what they *do*—though he exaggerates and makes fun of it—but not what they *are*—complex and half revealed and full of shadows. They're all bright and new and two-dimensional and charade-ish. 'You play the fat old mother who drinks and you play the henpecked father and you play the good girl and you the bad and all of *you* the comic neighbours and I'll be the bold, bad attractive foreigner and we'll all have such *fun!*" And everybody did, including the audiences, and my father was happy and we were happy for him.

Ivor was the inheritor of the popular costume-melodrama traditions of the past, though he hadn't yet got into those beautiful Ruritanian uniforms and burnished boots. And my next engagement was in a play which both shares and satirizes the genre. It was Shaw's *The Devil's Disciple*. Sir John Martin Harvey had announced a new production of it and it was assumed that the part of Judith would be played by his wife, who had been his invariable leading lady ever since anyone could remember. But the passage of time, more cruel to women than to men, had caused both critics and public to groan audibly when she reappeared, year after year, as the dewy young heroines of the Harvey repertoire. She and Sir John had privately resolved to let another actress open as Judith and receive the impact of the press before retiring gracefully in favor of Lady Harvey. This, as can well be imagined, involved them in a casting problem, since no established actress was likely to accept such peculiar conditions.

I had written suggesting that my previous experience in the play might make me a useful understudy, and presently I was summoned to meet them at their home. They received me alone. After the initial introductions, they asked me to stand up; they then circled around me in silent appraisal. I became acutely embarrassed, the more so since they were both unusually small and I found myself looking slightly down on them. Suddenly Lady Harvey said, "Can you nestle?" Light dawned. I buckled at the knees, folded slightly at the hips, put my arms around Sir John and gazed fondly *up* into his eyes. I got the job.

He was quite a martinet in the theatre and a little on the regal side. His direction was the result of vast experience in a rather limited type of material and was inclined to be rigid. He imposed on his actors precise gestures and exact inflections—not like Lewis Casson's cadenzas of sound, but rigorous and, I thought, mechanical. It is a practice I have detested and shunned ever since. I was conscious, also, of Lady Harvey's brooding eye. But she was kindness itself to me. She supervised personally, and with great knowledge, all the details of my costumes, and out of her "long-experienced time" helped me with a most difficult part. Nature had hampered her with a thick, ugly body and art had not helped with

347

the application of too much henna and rouge. She really did look, as a detractor once put it, "like a Buff Orpington hen which someone had left half-plucked."

Yet she moved most beautifully. She showed me how to faint in a single, flowing line which I couldn't reproduce nearly as well, for all the suppleness of youth. Once, at the end of a costume fitting, she looked at me for a moment and then said: "My dear, if I could be born again, and could choose to be given one quality at the expense of all the rest, do you know what I should ask for?" "No, Lady Harvey . . ." "Charm, my dear, charm."

Harvey's performance as Dick Dudgeon echoed something of his old, perennial vehicle, *The Only Way*. The analogy of the execution scene provoked witticisms about "the old Cartonians." He was a trifle noble. Yet he did a remarkable thing in that scene —he really did come on like a man about to be hanged. The dew of death was on his forehead. He was not easy to play with because he had such a very disconcerting, directorial eye. You kept thinking, "Did I do that right? was that what he wanted?" He would come striding on in the first act, where the family is settled for the reading of the will, sweep the whole circle with an eagle glance to see that we were all in the prescribed attitudes and remark quite audibly, "That's right!" before going on with the scene.

On the few occasions since that time when I have acted in plays that I had directed myself, I have tried very hard to suppress that directorial glint. It isn't always easy. I remember asking a friend to come and watch a performance of *Othello* for me after it had been running some time, since I was playing in it and couldn't judge it from the front. We discussed various points, and at last I said nervously, "What about me?" "Well," she answered reflectively, "do you mean to play Emilia as an efficiency expert?"

The Devil's Disciple was my first experience of a leading part in the West End. Lady Harvey finally decided that the run would not be long enough to make a change worthwhile, and I was presently moved down from the small dressing room three flights up which I had meekly shared with two other people, to the star dressing room which had been kept for her. It was quite a transition. I had had a good personal press and quite a lot of praise. Even the author had said that he thought it a splendid performance, not in the least like the character. But I might have been pardoned for supposing that it would lead me onward and upward. It did no such thing.

My memory has always been that the following eighteen months were a period of general inactivity and total frustration, broken only by a small part in a complete flop with Emlyn Williams and a two-month tour in a thriller *by* Emlyn Williams. But piecing the records together, I discover that during this time I played in no less than twenty-two plays, not counting a considerable number of Schools' Theatre shows and some odds and ends too odd or too soon ended to leave anything but a faded snapshot of recollection. I thought then that it was a setback, a dead end, eighteen wasted months. I see now that Fate had bestowed on me a whole treasury of experience and opportunity for growth. I was being done-good-to by force, far more effectively than anything a West End success could have done for me.

A few of the productions in which I played were stock revivals for small companies around London. Three or four more were done on a sub-subway circuit, consisting of a night apiece at six of the worst theatres in six of the most inaccessible suburbs surrounding Greater London. Yet another was in Italian for a strange organization grandiloquently entitled the Anglo-Italian Theatre. In this language, of which I really knew very little, I had the incredible temerity to attempt a part which had once been played by Eleonora Duse. I even learned how to suffer a "souffleur," muttering and burbling away at my feet like a species of manic kettle. I even ad-libbed in Italian when somebody missed an entrance. But most of these activities were in new plays done by Sunday-night membership societies or tried out at the Arts Theatre. I think it was during this year that I put an ad in an actors' trade paper with my name and the caption: "Has played every Sunday for the past six months. Has no religious scruples about playing on week-days."

This diversity of modern work was exactly what I needed to fill the gaps in my training. The stock company shows usually meant no more than a week's rehearsal, but they were not carelessly done and the casts were talented. A program of *Dear Brutus*, for instance, begins with the unknown names of three Margarets in a row, Webster, Rawlings and Rutherford. The Sunday shows were rehearsed for three weeks and I worked with good directors and good actors. Most of the plays had some worth or quality—one of them rather more than that.

It was a first play called *Musical Chairs*, by Ronald Mackenzie, which had been sent to John Gielgud, who, in turn, had taken it to Bronson Albery, owner and manager of several London theatres. It was considered a doubtful commercial proposition, but John believed in it and wanted to play it. As he was then tied up in a long run, they decided to put it on for a couple of shows at the Arts. The director was Komisarjevsky. The cast was Gielgud, Frank Vosper, Carol Goodner, Roger Livesey, Jessica Tandy, Finlay Currie and myself, all of us "rising" young actors, only the first two yet "risen."

It was one of those productions where everything drops sweetly into place. Perhaps it is the highest praise of Komis's direction that I cannot remember, analytically, exactly what he "did." I only know that I felt happy, assured, on center. The play was very much in the Chekhovian manner and he understood it completely. He guided us, but he never pushed; he allowed the subtle relationships between the characters to develop gradually, with a hint here and a comment there, until we had absorbed the play into our blood, into our skins. It grew together organically. We all trusted him and each other and the script. There was a good deal of progress by "feeling it out," but not by chopping and changing, which is a very different thing.

The press was amiable, though not ecstatic, the audience reaction all we could have wished. Four months later, when John was free, it was put on at the Criterion Theatre with substantially the same cast. After a perfectly ghastly dress rehearsal at which every conceivable thing went wrong and everyone threw temperaments and tore their hair, except Komis who hadn't any, the opening night was as smooth as oil and went like a charm. It was one of those theatre miracles which are mystically supposed to happen, and very, very occasionally really do. John gave a big supper party at the Savoy and we were all very happy.

Next morning, critical hats were well and truly thrown in the air; the papers were dense with complimentary superlatives. Cast, individually and collectively, director, play, playwright, all of us were superb. We knew we'd be at the Criterion for many months to come. But there was a tragic epilogue: Ronald Mackenzie was killed in a car crash a week after he had finished his second script.

Looking back over those eight or nine hard, full years of my apprenticeship, I realize that the training I received from them is no longer obtainable anywhere, and I doubt that it ever will be. It is, in that sense, "historic." In the United States, union regulations would blot out most of those activities totally. In England they have ceased to exist, many of them, or have been greatly reduced in number. Rising costs, the competition of television, changed habits in theatre-going, different demands and needs both from actors and audiences—all these are responsible, the first villain being the worst.

It is also true that actors no longer dare to tie themselves up for three weeks to rehearse a Sunday show for fear of missing an odd day or two's television. Also, budding authors tend to write scripts for submission to television rather than plays for the few remaining experimental groups.

Of course other, different, training grounds are now available to actors: more and much better "approved" drama schools in England; far more, and again much better, college or university departments of drama in the United States. Schools, however, are one thing; active, professional experience of playing to the public is quite another. There are new stock and repertory companies in both countries, generally better housed, better cushioned, and playing, very often, exciting repertoires. There is also a flood of supporting money available, especially in the United States, which we never dreamed could be possible. But there is still nothing to compare with the variety and extent of the pay-as-you-go training resources available to young actors in England in the Twenties and Thirties. The innumerable Sunday nights, the special mati-

nees, the little do-it-yourself shows, Ben Greet, the Macdona Players, even the Old Vic in its 1930 format, all such workshops in
which I and my·generation forged the tools of our trade have
ceased to exist.

I am not idealizing the work done. Much of it was apprentice
work in every sense. But it certainly produced actors: all the
now-famous names of the British theatre: Olivier, Gielgud, Ashcroft and the other Knights and Dames, and many of the character
actors and actresses who are of lesser fame but not of lesser value
inside a theatre. It also trained the authors of the day and brought
to light a number of fine plays, a few of which, like *Journey's End*,
may even survive to tell future generations what we were like.

At all events, when I settled down in Piccadilly Circus, playing
a good part in a good play which was a hit, I felt that I had reached
the end of Act I. The rest of the play might turn out to be dreadful,
but the first part had been exciting and rewarding, and I was grateful. I still am.

CHAPTER EIGHTEEN

———— ୨୨୨ ————

Journey to New York

"Everyone asks me if I don't see great changes—and I don't. There are all these amazing towers, but on the level it's much the same." Thus my mother from New York in 1932. She was playing in John Van Druten's *There's Always Juliet* with Edna Best and Herbert Marshall. Park Avenue and Grand Central were new to her and "very imposing"; Broadway, the Great White Way of former years, had become "very shoddy, shabby and sordid." Beekman Place was now the height of fashion; Gretchen had once been the butt of many jokes for buying (and alas, selling far too soon) a house in such a "slum." Gretchen herself was dead, and the town seemed strange mostly because she was no longer in it.

The theatre district had moved several blocks uptown and there were nearly four times as many theatres as there had been when May had last played in one of them in 1908. The whole focus of the American stage had changed entirely. There was still a reasonable amount of touring activity, but New York reigned supreme. The greatest peak of Manhattan's magnitude was just past, because the United States had already entered on the Depression years; but it was, and remained, the arbiter of the American theatre's professional destiny.

This, however, was not especially apparent to a visiting actor. The city was full, noisy, lively. May found crossing the roads a hazard after the more dignified progress of the London traffic. "Cars come at such a pace," she wrote, "that you can't believe they'll pull up in time. Their brakes must be marvellous." Once, in the middle of Times Square, the light changed while she was in transit and she took refuge with a policeman. "I feel safe with you," she confided. "Safe?" he said. "Why, you're as safe as if you were in God's pocket." He must have recognized the Irish in her.

Her letters reveal her astounding vitality and vivid interest in things and people. She describes their houses, their plays, their meals and conversation. She is always "arriving home at 4 a.m.," or going to lunch with A, matinee with B to see C and D, cocktails with E and so to the theatre. There were many English friends in New York, and many American friendships were happily renewed. Cecilia Loftus had an adjacent room in the same hotel, and they disturbed the other guests by persistent trans-airshaft conversation. She saw the Lunts in *Reunion in Vienna*, Katharine Cornell in *The Barretts of Wimpole Street* and Constance Collier in *Hay Fever*. She frequented "21" and went to the top of the Empire State Building.

She addressed Women's Club luncheons, a form of activity which was new to her and which she viewed with some astonishment. She wrote: "One woman terrified me—came up and shook my weak, limp hand and barked out: 'Mrs. Whitestone of Minerva.' I hadn't an idea of the answer." At another party "a man trapped me on a sofa and raped me with talk—talk—talk—a poor form of that over-rated pastime." Because there was so little time left for letter-writing, and she had only one real wait during the play, she had a little table and lamp set up at the side of the stage so that she could continue with her voluminous correspondence between entrances.

This was the Prohibition era, and at first she wrote: "Oh, the farce of this absurd and pernicious Prohibition!" But very soon she became an experienced and skillful lawbreaker. She complained over the phone to the "vegetable man" that "those Brussels sprouts you sent me reeked of gasoline," and she learned to make the best bathtub gin in the Times Square area. *There's Always Juliet* closed unexpectedly in the midst of its success because Herbert Marshall was summoned to Hollywood; and her most urgent problem, before sailing for home, was how to dispose of her superfluous stock of Brussels sprouts.

After she came back to London, managers began to realize for the first time in many years that the Dame was an actress by vocation and a Chairman of Committees by avocation only. She played with Gerald du Maurier and Gertrude Lawrence in John Van Druten's *Behold We Live*—the first time that a Dame had played a Dame. She played in *The Lake* under a new young director, Tyrone Guthrie, who, she said, "helped me very much." The result was, in the words of Martita Hunt, "a brilliant, subtle commentary on a terrible type of woman, so much more than photographic and true—true—true." She also appeared in one play which lasted one night and one which lasted two. "I prefer," she said, "to draw a veil."

Meanwhile, happily ensconced at the Criterion Theatre, I continued to utilize Sunday nights and other varied opportunities. I had always kept up my association with the Old Vic. Lilian Baylis regarded me as one of her standbys. I played several times for one of her pet "causes," which was a leper colony in Essex. I was roped in to help with New Year's parties for the children of the slum areas adjacent to the Vic. She would exhort me to count the buns and make sure they only got one each. (*"Such* a clever girl, *such* a clever mother," I heard her mutter to a visiting patroness.) I had agreed to go back for the season of 1932–33, but she released me when it became obvious that *Musical Chairs* would run well into that period. She stipulated, however, that I be allowed three weeks' leave of absence to play Lady Macbeth. Bronson Albery agreed; I can't think why. People, throughout my life, have been very generous to me.

I wasn't really ready for Lady Macbeth in terms of inner experience, though I had acquired the necessary technical equipment. Edy lent me the first of the Ellen Terry prompt copies and I studied it avidly. I didn't believe I could approach the character as she had done; but I was fascinated by the illumination she cast even through the most down-to-earth comment. "Get sleeves out of the way," for instance, when she holds out her bloodstained hand to Macbeth's after the murder; the exact note for downward inflection and gesture and an enormously enlarged full stop after the controversial line "We fail". " 'My hands are of your colour'— creeps on." The breath marks—extremely revealing to an actor. After "Hold, hold!" when she and Macbeth first meet, the interesting note: "I must try to do this—two years ago I could not even have *tried*." And a wistful comment at one point: "It is wretched to be discovered"—that is, "onstage at Rise."

My own wretchedness onstage was partly because there was absolutely nothing on the stage—at least in the Murder sequence and the Sleepwalking Scene—but a semicircular piece of burlap surrounding it; not a step, not a stool, not a block to put the candle on. But on the opening night I realized that the shortcomings were mine alone. When I came off after the Sleepwalking Scene, I walked down the long, narrow corridor behind the stage with a bleak heart. Lilian was coming from the other end. We met in the middle and stood still. At last, in a voice rough with commiseration, she said, "Yes, dear. Just like giving birth, isn't it?" I was grateful; though I didn't quite see how either of us should know.

She was very kind to me during this run, and perhaps I deserved her sympathy; for I suppose I am the only Lady Macbeth who has ever had four husbands in three weeks. Malcolm Keen was the first. At the end of a week he strained a muscle in his back during the fight and couldn't go on. I rehearsed with his understudy, Alastair Sim. He at once developed a quinsy throat and couldn't go on either. Posterity was robbed of what might have been a unique interpretation. A boy in the company, Marius Goring, who had once played the part at school, threw himself magnificently into the breach. But Lilian felt that a Lady M of twenty-seven was quite young enough, without a Macbeth six or seven years younger still. She engaged John Laurie, an old stalwart of the Vic, to play it for the rest of the run. It was all very instructive.

After this I only occasionally went to the Vic again. In 1934 my mother was playing in a revival of Barker's *The Voysey Inheritance* put on for the benefit of the Sadler's Wells Endowment Fund. I find an entry in her diary: "Dragged Maurice and Lilian together." This effort was called forth by the moans of Miss Baylis, who complained, "Can't find a leading man for next year, dear, simply can't—don't know where they've all gone to!" My mother replied: "There's one in this theatre—Maurice Evans." But Maurice, when approached, was reluctant, said that he'd never played Shakespeare, wasn't sure whether he could. My mother went on dragging and Maurice was persuaded to try. It worked.

At one of the Birthday Festivals I played the Wooing Scene from *The Taming of the Shrew* with him. It was the last time I ever saw Lilian. She died in 1937—during the dress rehearsal of Larry Olivier's Macbeth. During the Second World War the theatre was partially destroyed and the company went into a long exile, but acquired much glory. In 1952 it came back home to the Waterloo Road. The Old Vic is now only the name of a building which temporarily houses the National Theatre company. But Lilian Baylis's old rolltop desk still stands in the star's dressing room, and I should suppose that her imperious mumble still sounds audibly from time to time in the august ear of Sir Laurence.

In 1897 my father, on tour with Irving, writes that he is "going to complain to the A.A."—Actors' Association—about the conditions of the Cardiff theatre. In 1904 there is a letter in which he says he has been to a "long and tiring [committee] meeting of the A.A." dealing with its financial problems. In 1912 *The Stage* reports a meeting chaired by Sir Herbert Tree, at which Ben opposed the Sunday opening of theatres on the grounds that actors were already being asked to play regular matinees for no extra pay and probably wouldn't receive any for Sundays. Through the post–First World War years the references grow thicker. The initials "S.G." begin to appear in my mother's diary. In December 1929 comes "Actors' Meeting, Duke of York's." In March 1930, "See Wall and Gilmer re Equity"; and two weeks later, "Equity.

Here." This last is a sinister notation. For the next five years it occurs with the regularity of a minute gun and sometimes becomes a positive salvo.

The first real banding together of English actors, known as the Actors' Association, took place before the turn of the century. It was not a trade union but a sort of club and protective society formed "to remove all or some of the abuses detrimental to the welfare of actors and actresses and to the theatre calling." It was, of course, a voluntary organization. The leaflets embodying its aims and objectives were dignified and high-minded. One section was headed "Obligations to your Manager"; it laid down rules of good behavior and discipline. A further list of "Obligations to your Public" began: "Your obligation to the public should be one of your first and greatest thoughts. It is through the public that you earn your livelihood and the public deserves your best efforts at all times."

After years of effort and mild achievement the Association realized that it was going to have to do some fighting, and needed the protection of the trade-union laws. It re-formed as a union in 1919, under the leadership of Sydney Valentine. It had to face an exceedingly difficult task. The stage was no longer the known and controlled profession that it had been. "Bricks-and-mortar" men now owned the theatres and leased them to middlemen who, in turn, let them to producing managers who appeared from nowhere and vanished as quickly. In the provinces, and even in London, bogus managers sprang up, failed to pay their actors, left them stranded in remote corners of Great Britain, and then escaped, untraceable and unpunishable. At last the A.A., in negotiation with the reputable London managers, secured the Valentine Standard Contract, to which most of them adhered. There was even the beginnings of a provincial contract. But the London actors, having got what they wanted, began to lose interest; the rank and file of the profession was apathetic; the fighting remnant grew increasingly extremist and bitter. The London contract began to be openly breached, the touring agreements completely disregarded. Sydney Valentine died of overwork, strain and disappointment. Because there was no such thing as a "union shop" under which all actors could be compelled to join the A.A., and no effective association of managers with whom to deal, nobody could control anybody.

In 1924 an ingenious group from among the managers seized upon the situation to form a rival organization called the Stage Guild. It was not a union, Heaven forbid. On the contrary. It was a kind of get-together friendship club. Each element in the theatre, actors, and managers had a separate section, but all were neatly tied up in a parcel so that nobody could take action against anybody else. For some obscure reason the vice president was H.R.H. Prince Paul of Greece, and among the board members was Dr. Marie Stopes, the expert on birth control. A Royal Charter was envisaged. "The lion is to lie down with the lamb," wrote my mother, "and all is supposed to be well." Conditions in the theatre became rapidly more chaotic than ever. Blandishments were held out to my father and other stalwart A.A. members, but they stubbornly held out. He wrote: "The Stage Guild has been the ruin of all the A.A. built up. It has been proved to the hilt that they are powerless to uphold the Standard Contract . . . and obviously hopelessly unfit to deal with any difficulties that may arise." There was some talk of fusion with the scattered remnants of the A.A., on which Ben commented: "I can't see how we are going to fuse except as electric wires do, with a sputter of fire and then darkness."

In 1930 there was a particularly glaring instance of a company being stranded on tour without notice and with all salaries unpaid. It was called, appropriately, *Open Your Eyes*. The Stage Guild opened one, but helplessly shut it again. It became vitally necessary to form a new actors' union. Bearing in mind the record and example of the American actors' counterpart, it was decided to adopt the name of British Actors' Equity. Advice on labor laws and organization was supplied by Alfred M. Wall, an official of the London Trades Council, a man of moderation, wisdom and skill. The embryo began to take shape. Many of the discussions took place in Bedford Street. So did the first committee meetings. The dining room became more difficult to eat in even than it had been during May's wartime campaigns; it was generally occupied by anything from four to forty actors. Among them were the members of the first elected committee, which included, besides all three Websters, Sybil and Lewis Casson, Raymond Massey, Godfrey Tearle, who became Equity's first president, and Felix Aylmer, who, as I write, is still its present one. The first council brought in representative leaders of the profession and a solid contingent of chorus members. The Bedford Street dining room bulged at the seams. When Equity finally acquired premises of its own, it took along the big mahogany table around which its founding committees sat. Suitably inscribed, this table still adorns its Council Room.

The fact that Equity was registered as a trade union made it anathema to the elder statesmen of the Stage Guild. We were "sold to labour"; we would be "dragged at the chariot-wheels of Moscow"; actors would be called upon to strike at the behest of "the boilermakers of Barrow." The boilermakers became a great slogan. They also boomeranged and became a great joke. The Stage Guild was quite evidently fighting a hopeless rear-guard action, much like the "Fidos" who held out against American Equity. But it was not until 1933 that its remnants finally agreed to incorporate with the new union. One of them observed wistfully that it was, by this time, much like the incorporation of Jonah with the whale. Equity magnanimously allowed for "conscientious objectors" in cases of dangerously high blood pressure.

Throughout these years there was an immense amount to be done. The fledgling union had to recruit its own membership and consolidate the profession behind it. Actors did not consolidate easily. It had to thrash out regulations to deal with existing abuses, embody them in contracts, negotiate the contracts and, which turned out to be the crux of the matter, devise the machinery to enforce their universal observance. It was evident from the start, though many actors refused to recognize it, that this would have to be the "Equity shop." Only if every actor were an Equity member could the contracts be made to stick.

Committee meetings were practically continuous. Many of the members concerned were quite strange to this kind of thing. "Parliamentary procedure" meant nothing to them. They regarded Alfred Wall, by now the union's general secretary, with amazement and awe. He, in return, was bemused and fascinated by them. Edith Evans especially entranced him. Her sprightly and inquiring mind somehow led her to make the most eminently sensible suggestions after a welter of apparent irrelevance. My mother, appearing as "Dame Chair," steered the proceedings with a mixture of asperity and tact. Once, I remember, she read a routine announcement regarding an application for an Honourable Withdrawal card. Ernest Milton was enthralled by the phrase. "An Honourable Withdrawal card!" he remarked. "How Japanese!"

The Equity years taught me much, just as the suffrage movement had taught my mother: to think on my feet, to speak and write, to conduct committee business with order and dispatch. For three years I was chairman of the editorial board which produced British Equity's first magazines. They made their debut in the form of a small leaflet called the "Equity Broadsheet"; then we expanded to something far more impressive; Ernest Milton called it the "Equity Bedspread." Having spent a good deal of the Association's money, we contracted again; but we were never the "Equity Featherbed." For the battle was on. "Clause M" was nailed to the mast. It stated that "The Artist shall be required to work only with members of the British Actors' Equity Association." The managers wouldn't have it, and for two years we had to maintain it by voluntary efforts of our membership.

In January 1933 we declared that the Equity shop was to be made effective. The trouble began at once. George Robey, a great "comic," adored by the public, was about to appear in a show called *Jolly Roger;* and he refused to become a member. He talked about "agitators" and "red soup" and "taking orders from Moscow." Should the other actors be allowed to play with him? or should we pull them out and stop the show? Persuasion was tried, and failed; the first night approached; our first real crisis was upon us.

For days on end the pale and weary "agitators" of the Equity Council met in almost constant session. There were too many of us for the Bedford Street dining room, and we hired a room at the Irish Club. We sat on either side of a long, narrow table; my mother, in "the Chair," at its head. From the walls the whiskered

and bearded visages of nineteenth-century Irish patriots stared
grimly down at us in lithograph. Feeling was tense. At the climac-
tic meeting tempers became very strained indeed. A deadlock was
reached; to strike or not to strike? At this point my mother wrote
something on a piece of paper, folded it, addressed it to me and
handed it to the Councilor next to her. It traveled from hand to
hand, right down the length of the table, watched furtively by
every eye. The debate faltered. I opened the ominous missive.
Sensing the charged atmosphere, heavy with suspicion, I asked
permission to read it aloud. It said: "Look on the wall behind you
at the picture of Cedric Hardwicke as Moulton-Barrett, erro-
neously labelled Joseph Biggar." In the resultant relaxation we
passed a unanimous vote.

We called a meeting of the whole membership at Drury Lane.
It is vivid to my eyes even now: the vast, empty stage, stretching
back into darkness; a semicircle of chairs, half-shadowed, for the
Council, reaching the whole width of the proscenium opening; a
table for the speakers under the hooded work lights, as brilliantly
lit as a billiard table; the famous auditorium, only dimly visible,
crammed with the whole of the British theatrical profession. "One
of the most memorable and dramatic performances in the history
of the Lane," someone wrote, and rightly. There was no rabble-
rousing, no dramatic outbursts, but a great feeling of comradeship,
unity and determination; the first time it had ever been manifested
in such strength. We would strike rather than give way; and it
looked as if we should have to . . .

We didn't, however; the *Jolly Roger* flag was struck instead.
It wasn't, by any means, the end of our troubles, though it was a
major battle; only once again did we come as close to the necessity
for a strike. Among the smaller skirmishes was my own over the
Brontë play, when I first met Old Ben. It was successful in that the
manager concerned was forced to engage a wholly Equity cast,
unsuccessful from my point of view, in that he wouldn't include me
in it. But then I had never supposed he would. It was a price we
were prepared to pay.

There were other agitations, one of which has proved perennial. It concerns the relationship between American and British

Equity in the matter of "alien" actors. From the beginning, AEA
had been extremely helpful to its fledgling British relative. But in
1932, while my mother was in New York, the first storm blew up.
British Equity was supposed to have refused a permit to an American actor and there was much righteous American indignation. In
fact, BEA was quite innocent of any such action and reciprocated
the anger. May visited AEA in person, loaded with olive branches
and accompanied by flights of doves. She collected the signatures
of twenty British stars in Hollywood and New York on a cable to
the Ministry of Labour in London, urging "the importance of a
free interchange of artists in the legitimate theatre." The storm
subsided.

It blew up again in 1934 over the American Dickstein Bill,
then before Congress, to restrict the admission of alien actors.
AEA's president, Frank Gillmore, voiced the view that "we have
no quarrel with the foreign star; but in times like these it stirs us
deeply to see alien actors from the lower classifications being cast
for parts we could play just as well ourselves." British Equity was
prim and soothing and urged "the desire of the public for the free
flow of the finest art." The waves subsided once more. In 1936 they
blew up again. Again each Equity reiterated its pious faith in the
freedom of art, together with its iron determination to protect its
membership. I find in the "Equity Bedspread" an article over my
own signature entitled: "The Theatre is International." Later, on
the other side of the ocean, I became a Council member of American Equity, and during my ten years of office I suppose I fought
this weary battle at least three times more. Now, as an onlooker, it
seems to me that the London stage suffers from exasperatingly
inadequate performances of American parts and plays by Canadian and British actors with ludicrous accents, while New York is
rich in good English performances. Clear gain, of course, for New
York. The dilemma, precisely stated by Frank Gillmore, is a real
one and there is no point in pretending it isn't. But the ultimate
values, and the ultimate good sense, still lie, or so I believe, where I
thought they did.

Toward the end of 1934 British Equity felt strong enough to
impose its one-hundred-per-cent-Equity policy in all contracts,

whether the managers liked it or not. Most of them accepted it as inevitable; but there was some rear-guard action, not only from them but from our own members. The elderly Victorian lady who owned the Duke of York's Theatre proclaimed her readiness to "roll up her sleeves if there is any fighting to be done." Some aloof patricians in our own ranks were lofty about "co-ercion"— and Moscow cropped up again.

Unexpected help was provided by Dame Marie Tempest, who could not by the wildest stretch of the imagination be pictured as a communist agent; nor had she ever seemed much interested in these questions. Suddenly she commanded all the elite of the London stage to a luncheon at the Savoy Hotel. They came, one and all, much flattered. They consumed impeccable food and drink. She then arose, exquisite and imperious, and issued her instructions. A Roll of Honour had been prepared and was laid out on a table beside the exit door. It pledged those whose names appeared on it to sign only one-hundred-per-cent-Equity contracts, containing the famous Clause M. She had much enjoyed their company at luncheon, and after signing the Roll of Honour, they might go. They laughed, applauded and signed.

We had one more battle to fight. At an all-night meeting of the Executive at Bedford Street, with reporters encamped on the stairs, January 1st, 1935, was decided upon as the official, effective date for dear old Clause M. The dissident managers immediately picked a showdown case to issue contracts without it. They chose cannily, for the production was Ivor Novello's *Glamorous Night* and the management was that of Drury Lane. Everybody loved "darling Ivor", no one wanted to wreck his show. There was another wholesale meeting, this time at the St. James's since we could hardly use the theatre we were about to strike against. As it turned out, we didn't have to.

Wise counsel on either side suggested that the dispute be taken to the Ministry of Labour for mediation. Less than a month later the London Theatre Council came into being. It comprised ten managers and ten actors under the independent chairmanship of Lord Esher. I was one of the actor delegates. The first thing we did was to evolve jointly a formula for putting the Equity shop

Miss Margaret Webster in fancy dress, 1909

Peggy as Puck
in a school production,
age fourteen

Margaret Webster in *Medea*,
Wyndham's Theatre, 1929

May Whitty, Peggy Webster, and
Ben Webster in a charity pageant;
Peggy was twelve

Margaret

As Rosaline

In *The Devil's Disciple*, 1930

Opposite page: As Lady Macbeth at the Old Vic, 1932

Richard II directed by Margaret Webster, with Maurice Evans as Richard, New York, 1937

Dame May Whitty in the
movie version of *Night Must Fall*

Margaret Webster, director

Ben and May in 1942,
their Golden Wedding Anniversary
(also see Plate XI)

into effect and enforcing the Equity contracts. The managers undertook to police their own side, we ours. The campaign was over; but the London Theatre Council went on, a meeting ground for both sides to examine disputes and try to settle them before they became open warfare. Neither side was legally bound by the Council's decisions, but in effect both accepted them. It established a remarkable precedent in labor relations in England. The Ministry of Labour's representative said of it:

"The agreement between the London Theatre managers and British Equity probably represents the highest point reached in voluntary self-government . . . The agreement was remarkable in that both sides accepted the need for complete organisation and, that being taken for granted and no longer a matter of controversy, attention was given to the method by which they could join hands for the good of the profession and those engaged in it . . . Both sides mutually agreed that unfair conditions should neither be imposed nor accepted and a joint system was adopted for confining employment to those who were prepared to accept this obligation. It is highly desirable that mutual consideration and agreement should be substituted generally for opportunist stealing of advantages and periodic trials of strength."

Not the least notable point about all this was that for the first time the managers were both able and willing to police their own ranks. The "bogus manager" ceased to exist. It was a good fight and a constructive ending. The nature of it, the individual responsibility and sacrifice it demanded, the philosophy which prompted its leaders, the unthought-of disciplines it imposed for the first time, all these are now practically unimaginable. They are either wholly taken for granted or largely superseded.

My mother once wrote: "To me the theatre still remains a temple to which we artists are privileged and under service; we must not look on it merely as a means of making a livelihood." Sybil Thorndike said: "Let us give our souls to the work; let us be witnesses, not profiteers." I think it may fairly be said that they, and we all, were united in a sense of responsibility, an obligation to "see the actors well bestowed." We saw the union as an instrument of service and felt that when its struggle for recognition

ended, its work had only just begun. In 1937 my mother wrote:
"So we have succeeded. Now we have to see that we carry our
success wisely. Success means power—that is a great responsibility. Who was the wise man who said 'success means you either
grow or you swell'?"

In 1952 Dame Sybil Thorndike reached her seventieth birthday, having served on the Council of British Equity for twenty-one
years. She was asked for her views on the changes she had seen.
She wrote:

"I can recall the changes, certainly, but as to my having, as a
result, any words of wisdom to contribute to the solution of theatre
problems, I can only say that I am more perplexed than ever I was.
I am more muddled in my mind about what people want of the
theatre, what actors think they are giving to the community, or
getting out of it, and what we are all making for . . . In London I
have seen my profession change from that of 'Rogues and vagabonds' and rebels, to obedient trade-unionists with the ideal of
dignity and security. Now anyone can come into the theatre without any danger . . . As things seem to be moving, I imagine that
we may soon become a solid, safe profession, drawing regular
salaries from theatre, film, B.B.C. and television . . . Is this all
that we ask of the theatre? That's what I'm still wondering . . ."

While *Musical Chairs* was still running, John Gielgud arranged a
Sunday night tryout of a new play about Richard II called *Richard
of Bordeaux*. It was by a new dramatist, "Gordon Daviot," in
reality a Scotswoman of the clan Mackintosh, now known to thousands of readers for the brilliant thrillers she wrote under the pen
name of Josephine Tey. The play was received with enthusiasm,
and as soon as John was free it opened at the New Theatre for
what turned out to be a fifteen-month run. My father played John
of Gaunt; Gwen Ffrangcon Davies, the Queen. I had only a "cough
and a spit," and during these long months I began to turn my hand
to other things.

A play of Emlyn Williams, *Spring 1600*, and another of Gordon

Daviot's called *Queen of Scots* followed. John directed both but played in neither; both were distinguished, neither a success. In both I began to discover from John's unending stream of new notions and suggestions and changes and improvements that there may be such a thing as having too many good ideas. The cast of *Queen of Scots* was, I think, the most brilliant with which I have ever been associated. It was headed by Gwen Ffrangcon Davies and Laurence Olivier, and there was a whole phalanx of those fine character actors in whom the English theatre has always been so enviably rich. Moreover, it was the gayest, friendliest and most harmonious company I have ever been in. There is no such thing as having too many good actors.

After that, more Sunday night plays, the Gate Theatre, the Arts Club; a rewarding, if not wholly successful, tussle with Hilda Wangel, Donald Wolfit as Solness; some scrappy London shows that didn't run; some fun, some heartbreaks. But it was the interminable fifteen-month run of *Richard of Bordeaux* that really "drove me to drink", or, more precisely, to directing. The seeds of this vice had been planted some years before, with the production of *The Merchant of Venice* on a very modest scale at a girls' school. The Shylock would not have threatened Irving's pre-eminence, but I got my first lesson in mechanics and locomotion. Then I had done various modern plays with amateur groups, learning to mistrust "French's Acting Edition" as being a little less than omniscient. I undertook the judging of various Regional and National Festivals organized by the British Drama League. All the best amateur dramatic societies in the United Kingdom competed in them, and the awards were keenly contested.

The task of dissecting and grading the component parts of a performance was admirable training. You had to observe the "what" of completely disparate play material, analyze the "how" of performance and come out with the "why" in terms comprehensible and supposedly constructive. Like a newspaper critic, you had to turn personal reaction instantaneously into reasoned and precise comment. Unlike a dramatic critic, you could not disguise personal prejudice in witty print. You were not supposed to demolish. You were there to promote future growth. I found it a heavy responsibility; but it forced me to clarify my own thinking and sit in judgment on my own knowledge and standards.

During the run of *Queen of Scots* I was engaged on a directorial task of some size, though still in the amateur field. The Women's Institutes throughout the county of Kent joined together to do Shakespeare's *Henry VIII* as a pageant production in an outdoor setting. The principal parts were played by the same actors throughout, but each of the different crowd scenes was allocated to a separate village or locality. The Baptism Scene at the end was to bring together the entire cast of more than eight hundred people.

For two or three months, during the spring and early summer, I would drive twice a week to different parts of Kent and rehearse different pieces of the play, returning to London in time for my own performance at night. I would date the progress of the play by the flowering of the cherry blossom, the pear trees and the pink-and-white apple blossom, the lovely unfolding of young summer in the Kentish valleys. We did not rehearse more than four or five times on the actual site of the performance, and each half of the play, with its full complement of womanpower, had only one dress rehearsal, necessarily brief. Complicated music cues had to be timed with entrances involving a couple of hundred people over distances from a hundred yards to a quarter of a mile. Costumes which I knew only from the sketches had to be put together in mass groupings. Vocal qualities of pitch and balance had to be adapted to new requirements. I offered up silent prayers of gratitude to Ben Greet and his training. It all came out more or less as was meant, and with considerable effect. Many years later, at the Metropolitan Opera House, I was confronted with two hundred and fifty people onstage at once and no time flat in which to rehearse them. Then I offered up my grateful prayers to the eight hundred women of the county of Kent who had been the guinea pigs of my first effort in mass direction.

In 1935 and '36 I directed nine different plays at tryout theatres or for Sunday societies. All of them included well-known, experienced actors, so I was spared the dangers inherent in the blind leading the blind. They were all new plays except one, which was a revival of Ibsen's *Lady from the Sea*, with Flora Robson as Ellida. Once again, I found Ibsen an absorbing challenge. Fortunately the Archer copyright on this particular play had run out. I was therefore able to use a fresh translation and strip away the Victorian whalebone which Archer's prose clamps around Ibsen's thought. The comedy in the play emerged also, as it always does if you give it a chance.

A South African play at the tiny Gate Theatre taught me the elements of lighting. We had to supply everything, from lamplight in the parlor to sunrise over the veldt. The stage manager and I spent all one night lighting it with our own four hands, a dozen or so small spots, some tin reflectors and a deal of ingenuity. By five thirty a.m. I was filled with enormous satisfaction. We went to Lyons' Corner House and ate bacon and eggs, and I maneuvered my car home through the crush hour of Covent Garden Market feeling godlike. I had yet to learn that when you have electronic switchboards and several hundred different instruments it gets much more difficult and not nearly so much fun.

Bit by bit I accumulated the experience which later enabled me to deal with more complex productions on a large scale. Naturally not all of this, not even the most important part, came from actually doing shows; especially since I had no ambition to direct and was not consciously training myself as a director. But as an actor I had learned to look and listen and watch all sorts of people and places and things, everywhere from the Munich Pinacothek to the London zoo. I learned from the people leaning over the roulette table at Juan-les-Pins—a brief and timid initiation, for I am not a natural gambler. I learned from the audiences at Wormwood Scrubbs Prison, where we would give Sunday performances of a very scratch nature. Here, for example, I learned that Othello is not necessarily a hero nor the play a tragedy. Sometimes it is a comedy and the hero is Iago and the actors must take what comes.

I went to Germany, already much too Nazi for comfort, to Italy (too Fascist) and to the Moscow Theatre Festival. This was in 1935, during the brief period of comparative cordiality between the USSR and the West. The British Drama League sponsored a delegation to the Festival, led by Lewis Casson. They were mostly amateur enthusiasts, with a leavening of professional actors and designers. There was one particularly rugged Scottish individualist who spent most of her time in Russia remarking: "Och! the puir wee things!" We absorbed delightedly the incomparable beauty of Leningrad; the pictures in the Hermitage and the Museum of Western Art; the onion-domes of Moscow. We made ourselves very unpopular by refusing to visit the Underground, from which we felt we had little to learn. From the Festival, however, there was much.

The original plays were either negligible or actively irritating. One of them was done in the round, or the oblong, by Okhlopkov, pioneering a geography that has since become very widely used. It was very Soviet-heroic and noisy and acrobatic, and we felt a little embarrassed by the close proximity of these dashing People's Heroes prancing on our feet. "Och, the stupid things!" said the Scots lady. We were a little stupid too, I think, for there was much in Okhlopkov's balletic style that is of value in our theatre today.

The greater part of the Festival program consisted of classic plays, since they were comprehensible to the visiting delegations. There was an extremely controversial *King Lear* done in Yiddish by the great Jewish actor Mikhoels; and Fletcher's *Spanish Curate*, own cousin to productions I have seen in the West by Komisarjevsky and by Michael Chekhov. The physical productions were always lavish and ran a gamut of style in design, remarkable for boldness and freedom. The acting varied; sometimes it was fluent and full of color, sometimes flat and insipid. We agreed that, all in all, the best came directly from the past—from the overt Stanislavsky influence; and especially in Nemirovich-Danchenko's production of Shostakovitch's *Katerina Ismailova* (or *Lady Macbeth of Minsk*), the most magnificent translation of music into drama that I have ever seen.

Next only to this was the accomplishment in the field of children's theatre; the best acting, the best design, the best use of all theatrical and circus resources to entertain the young—and to instruct them too. Till Eulenspiegel became a Soviet forerunner; but never mind, he still, miraculously, split the apple. There was also a play, in 1935, about splitting the atom, another kind of magic. The Soviets had realized from the start the immense potential of living theatre as propaganda, and as training for the minds and hearts of the next-generation citizens: no shoestringing around school auditoriums by truncated groups of students or "community" actors, but the finest resources they could command. We envied our Russian colleagues, too, their jam-packed theatres and voracious audiences, and reflected wistfully that the Soviets inherited a passionately theatre-minded society, such as had never existed in England. But we noted the positively shouting absence of Meierhold, the most famous Russian director of his day, for whom a fine new theatre was actually being built. Whenever we inquired about him the silence became deafening. He never played in his new theatre; it was renamed.

We came home full of food for thought. There was a ship's concert—it was a Soviet boat and we thought we ought to try and demonstrate that we could act too. Lewis and I volunteered the murder scenes from *Macbeth* on top of a table during a thunderstorm in the middle of the North Sea. I doubt that we convinced anybody.

The following summer I translated and adapted a play of Molnar's. I also played in it—one of those sympathetic friends who stand (or sit) slightly downstage of the leading lady and say at intervals: "No! Really? What happened then?" or "What you must have suffered!" or, quite simply "Oh!" I was good at this. I had had a lot of practice. The play was a total flop.

I then tossed off the direction of a couple of try-outs and was summoned from an abortive holiday to join the cast of *Parnell* which was already in rehearsal. This time I was an extremely sour and unsympathetic cousin and had little to do but give Kitty O'Shea "the back o' me hand". I enjoyed the change very much. Meanwhile, my father and mother were playing in New York. The story behind this is highly instructive for every actor who has not yet flung away ambition.

Journey to New York

In the spring of 1935 Gielgud was projecting the production of a three-character play by Rodney Ackland called *The Old Ladies*. Edith Evans and Jean Cadell were to play two of the parts, and John suggested my mother for the third. She fell in love with the play and the part and set her heart on playing it. But differences of opinion arose between author, manager, director. Someone evidently thought May Whitty was "not sweet enough" or "not fragile enough" or not something enough. At all events, they engaged somebody else. I had seldom seen my mother so deeply upset and disappointed. She was engulfed in gloom and despair.

At this point, Emlyn Williams sent her the script of his new play. She read it. "Well," she said, "it's just a thriller and it won't run and the part's an old beast in a wheelchair, but I suppose I'd better do it since they won't let me play anything but old beasts anyhow." In this glum mood, she accepted. In April *The Old Ladies* opened and ran three weeks. On May 31st, at the Duchess Theatre, came the opening of *Night Must Fall*. It ran a year in London and led my mother to New York and thence to Hollywood. It undoubtedly changed the pattern of her life more profoundly than any other professional event that ever happened to her. She was then seventy years old.

After a short provincial tour, the *Night Must Fall* company sailed for New York, where the play had a rather mediocre press and was not a great success. There were accolades, however, for my mother's performance, and Hollywood began to take notice. The movie rights had already been bought by MGM as a vehicle for Robert Montgomery and Rosalind Russell. They decided they would like May Whitty for her own part. Tests were made. Agents sprang up. Contracts impended. Meanwhile, a closing notice had been posted for the New York run, and my mother, with a rooted mistrust of all things pertaining to Hollywood, had booked a sailing home.

During her visit, she had been seeing something of Maurice Evans. He had already played with Katharine Cornell in *Romeo and Juliet* and in *Saint Joan*, and had just scored a tremendous personal success as Napoleon in *St. Helena*. Out of the blue, there appeared in his life Joseph Verner Reed; a man of multiple activities, whose most notable trait is a readiness to back his enthusiasms and put them into effect. He admired Maurice as an actor, believed in his ambitions, and one evening left for him at the theatre an envelope with a check for $35,000. In 1936 this was a theatre fortune.

Maurice instantly began to make plans. He wanted to do a series of classic revivals, not just one play. He said to my mother: "We'll do some Shakespeare and get old Peg out here too." This too she took with a spoonful of salt. But discussions progressed, letters crisscrossed the Atlantic, and there was much debate. *Richard II*, *The Beaux' Stratagem* and *Major Barbara* emerged as possible plays. The west wind began to blow for me. Another play which I had adapted was bought for American production, though I doubted, rightly, whether it would ever get produced. Meanwhile, the small Webster affairs were conducted against a background of some turbulence. First, the United States underwent the convulsions of a presidential election. The tumult and the shouting bewildered my father, who innocently stood and listened to the sound trucks electioneering in Times Square, in the hope of really learning something of the issues. He emerged battered and baffled. My mother responded gladly to all the excitement, was fanatically pro-Roosevelt, and had great trouble in remembering she was British and mustn't talk. No sooner had the election turmoil begun to subside in New York than a hurricane swept over London.

Very little had appeared in the English papers up to this time about King Edward and "the Wally Simpson situation." Its gravity had been almost wholly concealed from the British man-in-the-street by a tacit agreement among the press. Not so in America, where, my father wrote, "our Royal Master's doings are a fruitful and flaming topic of conversation." So that when, one fine November morning, the news of the King's projected marriage finally broke in the British papers, the great, black headlines exploded like bombs. The whole country was rocked. No business got done. The streets were full of people discussing and arguing. Perfect strangers on buses almost came to blows. Shops turned into debating societies and customers flounced out of them, quite forgetting to buy what they had come for. When I arrived at the theatre I found actors and stagehands engaged in feverish discussion, utterly disregarding the callboy's frantic "Fifteen minutes, *please!*" At this moment the stage door man came up to me. "Transatlantic telephone for you, miss," he said. "Personal call. Mr. Maurice Evans from New York."

Maurice was organized for brevity. He said first that the Royal crisis had precipitated everything. The abdication theme was on everybody's lips. We would open with *Richard II;* history had taken over the advance publicity; all was arranged. He had engaged David Ffolkes to design the sets and costumes, and wanted me to direct and to play the Duchess of York. He ticked off rapid questions: 1) Would I do it? I said yes. 2) Could I give a two-week notice and leave the cast of *Parnell*—earlier, if possible? I said yes. 3) Would I accept such-and-such terms? I said yes. 4) Would I confer with David Ffolkes according to the tenor of notes and plans already in the mail to us? I said yes. 5) Would I sail on the *Berengaria* on December 21st? I said yes. "Good," said Maurice. "We've got thirty seconds left. How's the King?"

The settlement of my mother's affairs with MGM was not so clean-cut, since discussions had to be conducted through the usual chain of middlemen on opposite sides of the American continent. She was determined to sail for England as arranged, contract or no contract. Agents pursued her to a midnight party the night before she sailed, and still the argle-bargle was not concluded. On board the *Queen Mary* it still went on, with the representative of MGM dashing up and down the gangplank to the telephone booth on the pier. Five minutes before the ship's moorings were cast off, the quintuple May Whittys and all the multiple initialings were finally affixed to the ten-page documents and the emissary of MGM, together with her own agent, snatched up their hats and coats and ran for the already loosened gangplank. Little, puffing tugs nosed the *Queen Mary* into the river. My mother fell on her bed and went to sleep.

In England, my parents and I barely saw each other. I opened up the flat in Bedford Street and met the arriving boat train at Waterloo. After ten days of hurly-burly, I closed my own flat in Hampstead and they waved off the departing boat train from Waterloo. I spent Christmas at sea; very rough it was, too. A concert was given by Myra Hess, Buck-and-Bubbles, the soft-shoe team, and me. We outnumbered the audience. Tugs escorted the *Berengaria* up the Hudson River and nosed her into her berth, me hanging over the rail. There, far below, I could see Maurice standing on the dock; and couldn't see, just out of sight, many magic things awaiting me. I walked down the gangway—and into that same shedlike building that I had dimly remembered for twenty-eight years. It wasn't a railway station; it was the pier of the Cunard Line. It looked just as I had always thought it did, only of course a little different.

EPILOGUE AND PROLOGUE

———————— ဝဝ ————————

My first impressions of New York were kaleidoscopic and dominated by a sense of rush. This was not surprising, for we had very
little time. *Richard II* was to open "cold" five weeks later.

Maurice decided that I should "see a bit of New York," since I
wasn't going to have much chance. We hurtled up the newly built
West Side Highway and through Central Park, a lake of darkness
—stark, winter trees between the piled towers. In a small hotel on
the canyon of West Fifty-eighth Street, half a block from the place
where I was born, I flung my suitcases onto a studio bed and went
off to Maurice's apartment for dinner.

There David Ffolkes awaited me with sketches and ground
plans, and Maurice brought out sheet after sheet of cast lists, time
schedules and tabled estimates of costs. Outside, the huge towers
of Radio City climbed up into the sky, columns of blackness
patterned with rectangles of orange, yellow and blue-white. They
hypnotized me. At last I begged Maurice to close the curtains and
nailed my attention to the figures (which seemed to me enormous), the blueprints and the string of unfamiliar names, to which
I frenziedly tried to affix functions and personalities.

. . . and Margaret

Next morning came my introduction to Broadway, attended by a sense of shock. I had heard so much about the Great White Way; it had glittered in my imagination like a necklace of diamonds. I was quite unprepared for the drab and dirty clutter of its daylight wear, the noise, the jostling crowds, the shooting galleries and peanut stands, the cinema marquees, the enormous hoardings covered with glaring ads. This was another New York. I progressed, in some dismay, to the St. James's Theatre (I had to remember to call it "the Saint James"), where *Richard II*, Inc., had their offices and where we were to play.

I met the "Inc." part. One was young, gentle, smiling; one an intimidating Russian businessman who knew nothing of Shakespeare and cared less; one a professionally Irish trouper, hat tilted back on his head, feet on the desk, who beamed upon me and instantly called me "Peg". The fourth I did not meet until several weeks later: the man whose faith had made the whole thing possible, the enthusiastic, generous, elusive, imponderable Joseph Verner Reed. Their ideas about absolutely everything were, as I later discovered, invariably and totally in conflict. Maurice was the axle of this Ferris wheel. I eventually christened them the Incorporated Incompatibles.

Casting began. Neither Maurice nor I was familiar with standard Broadway procedure. It ran something like this: The producers' secretaries would send out a raft of audition cards, more or less at random and usually summoning twenty-five people to be at the theatre at the same time. Other actors would hear about this and come too. The producers, director, star, several hangers-on and the theatre cleaners armed with vacuuming implements would assemble in the dark auditorium. A naked two-thousand-watt work light on the stage effectively blinded everybody. The actors, one by one, reached the stage manager, who would give them a book and thrust them onto the stage, sometimes, but not often, announcing their names. He would then read their cues in a meaningless mumble: "Old John of Gaunt . . . uh . . . hast thou . . . blah-blah—long speech—coming down to . . . Duke of Norfolk, Thomas Mowbray?" "I have, my liege," the bewildered actor would faintly reply. A few lines later somebody in front would say: "Thank you—that will do," and the actor would stumble off again.

After a couple of hours of this everybody would be stupefied and decide to go out for lunch. The director would say he liked the boy in the red tie for Mowbray; but no one else had seen him as they'd all been out making telephone calls. The producer thought the tall blond had talent, but not for this. Another producer was absorbed in trying to remember the name of that wonderful actor who was so good in that play that didn't run a couple of seasons ago. Martinis would be consumed, the queue of actors would lengthen to impossible proportions, most of the producers would leave and it would start all over again.

Maurice and I didn't know about this, and our producers gave us a free hand. We saw each actor alone—a hundred and twenty in the first two days. We made polite inquiries about their previous experience, with apologies for not knowing it, and, if we thought them possible, gave them a book, explained about the part, and asked them to come and read later. These procedures struck New York with astonishment and tired us very much indeed. I felt as if my skull were being pulled off my head, in the effort to make room inside for all the unfamiliar names, faces and voices.

We didn't want a British-English cast, which would have been silly in New York, but we had to try for a certain standard of good, international speech to maintain a balance between the company and its star; and, desirably, some distinction of style and manner. We found these things hard to come by among young actors who had no experience of speaking Shakespeare and had seldom even seen him played. We had particular trouble, for instance, with the King's three favorites, Bushy, Bagot and Green. I wanted three distinct and individual characters, not anonymous triplets, the kind of elegant young men Richard would have liked to have around. We must have heard at least seventy-five young stalwarts announce with honest zeal that "the Dook hath broke his staff, ruh-signed his stooardship." "Duke—steward," Maurice would murmer politely, while I felt pedantic and baffled.

One actor whom I hadn't met, a distinguished "character" man, refused to consider the part of John of Gaunt because he would not, he said, be subjected to the whims of a woman. Another, whom we asked to read Northumberland, insisted there was no such part. He had been in the play with Edwin Booth, and he knew. He brought us the Booth version, and there wasn't.

Our last hurdle was the Duchess of York. Maurice wanted me to play it, as I had done with Gielgud at the Old Vic. I had quite liked my own performance and would have been delighted. But I decided, after much cogitation, that the York scenes had never been in Shakespeare's original script and oughtn't to be there now, except, perhaps, for the Duke's famous speech describing Richard's entry into London. I cut the rest of the scenes, and myself.

Finally we got a cast, and a good one. We had evolved a production scheme which used a permanent basic set of pillars and arches; certain scenes were played downstage, in front of a traveler curtain, while the necessary changes were made in the aspects of the main set. The playing areas were flexible and good for the crowd scenes. It was a swift and serviceable method, very simple in comparison with the heavier scenery then in general use. The theatre as a whole has made enormous strides since 1937 in its reliance on spatial areas or levels, lights, a prop or two and the imagination of the audience. Our scenery would look cumbersome now. Nevertheless, *Richard II* is a play which benefits from the flash and color of its background, the banners and heraldic devices of medieval chivalry, the aura which invests "this royal throne of kings, this scepter'd isle." David Ffolkes had done all this very finely.

He had also designed all Maurice's costumes, rich in color and beautiful in line. But most of the smaller parts were clad from the New York production of *Richard of Bordeaux*, which had opened and closed again with dreadful rapidity only a few months earlier. They were the same clothes by Motley, varied somewhat by Ffolkes, with which I had lived for fifteen months. It never ceased to disconcert me, when the curtain went up, to see Maurice on his throne flanked by three carbon copies of John Gielgud, or to watch the Queen making an entrance attended by two little Gwen Ffrangcon Davies-es, one in blue and one in pink.

In the midst of these frantic preoccupations I found myself, one morning, back on the Cunard pier again, gazing up at the *Aquitania*. My father and mother had arrived from England. They spent three hectic days in New York, and then I took them to the smoke-filled caverns of Grand Central Station and put them on a monster train bound, via Chicago, for Los Angeles. I thought my father looked a little lost and wistful, but my mother displayed her usual zest and courage, setting forth at the age of seventy-three to beard the MGM lion and conquer Hollywood.

Rehearsals began. Everything settled down to that blissful concentration, that total commitment which characterizes all serious theatre work. The outer world dimmed. Newspapers went unread, letters unanswered; I ate as close to the theatre as possible (Sardi's, in this case), and went home only to do my homework. It goes without saying that I was frightened. I had every reason to be. Even now I never come to a first rehearsal without feeling a panic-stricken impulse to rush to the nearest airport and take a plane to the South Pole. But I knew that a director cannot afford the luxury of fear. The vibrations of insecurity are infectious. They can be just as destructive as the opposite vice of arrogance. I tried hard to appear authoritative and perfectly calm and to acquire, as fast as possible, an understanding of my actors. To know his actors is the first thing a director needs to learn; and here was I, confronted with thirty large-size Americans, all total strangers to me. One day in Sardi's I overheard a remark from a neighboring table: "One woman and all those men—she must be fierce."

I didn't feel so, and there was no need to be; they were gentle as lambs. I soon discovered certain fundamental differences between American and English actors, especially when confronting Shakespeare. The Americans worked harder, were more concentrated and more direct. They were also more self-conscious. The English actor would toss a Shakespearian part lightly over his left shoulder, as something all in the day's work; but the American treated it as something very special and rather awesome. He was apt to approach the verse cautiously, and plow his way through it as if it were a wet, muddy field and he had heavy boots on. But the Americans were quick to treat the characters as people, not as mouthpieces, as soon as you had performed the necessary introductions. They had less gloss than their English counterparts, but more reality and more guts.

I had loved the play since my schooldays, and thought I knew it well. But, as always, it revealed itself in a hundred new ways as the words became people and the design grew alive and moved. We were all, I think, remarkably relaxed; I, probably, out of sheer ignorance of the pitfalls surrounding me, and most of us because we had so little to lose. We had no comparisons to fear, because *Richard II* had not been played in New York within living memory —it was, in effect, a new play by Shakespeare. A succès d'estime with a bonus for good intentions was the summit of our hopes.

I was luckier than I knew in my producers. At rehearsals they left me alone. They did not hiss in my ear at the very first reading: "He isn't going to say it like *that*, is he?" At the dress rehearsals, when the switchboard failed utterly, they didn't rush down the aisle protesting that really it did seem just a *little* too dark. They didn't ask me to put Act III scene 2 into the middle of Act II scene 4. It was a forbearance more unusual than I then realized. Meanwhile Maurice, who had most at stake, remained cool, affable and unassuming, and kept his eye on the budget like a hawk. Around his flexible and brilliantly spoken Richard a pattern began to take shape. A sense of inner happiness gradually crept over me, not of accomplishment, but as if I were listening to the smooth, sweet hum of a well-tuned machine, music to my ears.

At the dress rehearsals, naturally, all this disappeared. Our set not only looked massive, it was. Flint Castle was harder to move than an army tank; the "Little Arches drop" seemed to have been built of stone. I had been astonished to learn that the entire lighting equipment had to be hauled into the theatre and hung, instead of being part of a permanent installation, as in England. When it arrived, I fell in love with its resources, but it was complex beyond my English dreams. Also I had to learn a new technical vocabulary: "foots" for "floats", "X-rays" for "battens", "projectors" for "pageant lamps", as well as glorious new things like "lekos", and gelatines of rainbow hue with sugar names like "surprise lavender". Once, from the darkness of the auditorium, I wailed that I had lost my torch. Ten minutes were wasted before it was discovered that I meant my flashlight.

When the actors appeared in their costumes, a new set of problems emerged. Few of the men (with the blazing exception of Ian Keith as Bolingbroke) had the smallest idea about what to do with a cloak. They just hung it around their necks like an oversize muffler. The Queen was terrified of her trains and behaved so timidly toward them that they immediately wreathed themselves around her hesitant feet and tripped her up. I seized a large bunch of safety pins, invoked the memory of Edy Craig, and attacked the cloak brigade. I gave a practical course on the taming of trains. Urged on by David, I told the male cast about what to wear underneath tights—also what not to wear, such as long, woolen combinations.

At these dress rehearsals my own education in crew costs began. In England, if there was a lamp standard to be moved in a given scene shift, whoever was standing closest to it picked it up and moved it. If it was simple for an actor to walk on during the change carrying his own stool and be sitting on it when the lights came up, he did so. But not, I discovered, in New York. Nobody but an electrician might move the lamp standard, even though three members of the carpenter's crew were standing idle at the time. This meant an extra electrician or no lamp standard. Under Maurice's vigilant eye, and with a terrifying sense of being responsible for spending money which might be more vitally needed, I would meekly agree to the elimination of the lamp standard, along with the shaft of sunlight, moonlight, firelight or whatever else it was designed to create.

Similarly, I brought on Pages visibly to move stools; or caused the actors to perch on ledges on the scenery, or not to sit down at all—which could subtly alter the emphasis of a whole scene. These obstacles, at first, challenged and intrigued me. Sometimes I swatted at them irritably, as one would at a mosquito. It was only later, and by degrees, that I realized the formidable nature of this swarm of poisonous insects; that from their bite the victims often die.

However, along this craggy path I became fast friends with

our production crew, carpenters, electricians, property men. This has rarely failed to happen to me since. My sense of comradeship and gratitude to "our boys" in *Richard II*, and to very many of their successors, will stay with me long after the chronic state of exasperation with their union regulations has burned itself away in weary despair.

Our dress rehearsals were reasonably smooth and well integrated. At the previews the rhythm almost, but not quite, returned. It was always being checked by technical imperfections, and then the tempo faltered and the strength of the performance was weakened. After the second public preview, I took my courage in both hands and demanded the "scene and light run-through"— every technical cue in unbroken sequence—which we had never yet had time for. It meant paying everyone in the theatre overtime. The producers turned pale, especially Maurice; but God bless them, they gave it to me. In the small hours of the morning I went home to bed. I had done everything I knew how to do; now I could only pray.

During rehearsals I had moved from my cozy little dog kennel on Fifty-eighth Street to share an apartment at Number One Fifth Avenue with Peggy Ashcroft, then playing in *High Tor*. It was high up on the twenty-sixth floor; the windows of the living room looked north over Manhattan, and my tiny bedroom, about the size of a ship's cabin, seemed perched in the sky, with nothing between me and the Hudson River. The big ships hooted as they came into harbor, or headed down toward the sea, and I learned to identify them by their voices. At sunset you could see the whole vista of the city washed with rose-gold, and then the pattern of lighted windows began to star the dusk. On the evening of February 5th, 1937, I said goodbye to this fairyland and called for a taxi to take me to my execution.

There is nothing I have experienced to compare with the agony of a director on the opening night of a big and complex production. You anticipate in imagination every possible flaw, every hypothetical disaster. As soon as you have sweated past one of them in safety, you start oozing blood in preparation for the next. To begin with, you never know until you have seen him what sort of an "opening-nighter" an actor will turn out to be. Some overplay, some underplay; some shrivel with nerves, some become strident with challenge; you can count on only one thing: that almost everyone will give a performance you have never seen before. Fortunately for us all, Maurice, on this and every opening I ever saw him play, was better than he had ever been before. Invariably he rose to the occasion with reserves one had not known he possessed. This time he didn't know it himself. He was in agony with an abscessed tooth and was practically oblivious to the play's reception until after the following Sunday, when he had had the tooth out.

The director's agony begins with the audience. It comes late; the curtain is delayed, excruciatingly; you want to go out into the lobby and lash them in. The actors are nervous at first and hard to hear; more latecomers and ushers with flashlights. You could kill them all. You nurse the actors through every speech, thrust every point home by muscular force, grin like a skull just ahead of every laugh. The members of the audience are thick-witted idiots with influenza. Every cough is a criticism. The pace is intolerably slow, snail-like; what on earth do they think they're doing?

The scene changes are torture—or used to be, when we had changeable scenery. You would watch the hairline of light between the traveler curtain and the floor, praying that it would go out, indicating that the change had been completed before the line or music cue. Open, or "thrust", stages have at least delivered us from this particular anguish; not, however, from the light-cue ordeal: the missing set of number 41 in the X-rays, the essential pin spot that isn't there, the dim that goes much too fast . . . "Oh, dear God, make them take it slower . . . make them bring back the blues . . . all right, just make them let it *alone* and not do anything *idiotic* and let no one notice but me." You resist a wild impulse to charge backstage through the pass door. You are completely helpless.

In the intermission you go around and tell everybody that it's going beautifully and they're playing like angels. You extend an ice-cold and trembling hand to the stage manager, who takes it in a palsied and sweating one. You remind yourself that he is not deaf, dumb and blind and is perfectly capable of dealing with any disaster long before you could. You surreptitiously check the props for the second act and go back for another dose of torture. It all comes to an end somehow; the last curtain comes down with a smooth, sliding finality, like a blessing; or it used to, when we had one.

They told me the opening night of *Richard* was "a smash". I had no barometer for New York audiences. Certainly, it had gone well, astonishingly, even. At the end of Maurice's "death of kings" speech there had been an outburst of applause that stopped the play for almost a minute. I had never heard such a thing in a theatre before. Also there had been long, wonderful rapt silences . . . At the end there was a tremendous noise, and I realized I hadn't arranged for more than four calls and they went on and on and Maurice made a modest little speech. A tide of mink coats and white shirt-fronts swept over us all, and everybody kissed each other and superlatives hurtled through the air and it was all very dizzying. I kept wondering whether the *play* had really got over and whether all this was really happening.

I went to Sardi's for a drink with the stage manager and his wife. I had never heard of the masochistic American habit of listening for midnight radio comments, far less of sitting up for reports of the morning notices, gleaned from gremlins in the press room. Pretty soon, I got up and went home. Peggy Ashcroft was out at a party. I stood by the windows and looked at the darkened city, only sparsely jeweled now. "We all know, don't we," I thought to myself, "about those triumphant opening nights and those appalling mornings after." I had quite forgotten to order the papers except for my usual *Times*. I fell into bed.

When I awoke next morning my little room was filled with white, winter light. I got up to make breakfast. The edge of the *Times* was showing underneath the door. I looked at it cagily and went on into the kitchen. I came back with the coffee and eyed the *Times* once more. I opened the door, picked it up quickly and carried it to my room. With the second cup of coffee I turned to the drama page: Brooks Atkinson's by-line. I read the column. Shakespeare was superb. Maurice was superb. Even I, personally, was pretty superb. Above all ". . . it dismissed us from the theatre with a feeling of high excitement and a conviction that there is nothing in the world so illustrious as drama and acting." I burst into tears. At last I went to the telephone and croaked down for the other papers. I read them. Then I reached for the phone again and dictated a telegram to my mother in Hollywood. "It looks like a hit," I said.

I was quite truthfully amazed at the furor which followed. In England it was then quite rare for the press even to mention the fact that there had been a director ("producer") at all. I was entirely taken aback by the compliments paid me. Of course there were one or two sour notes, which I welcomed as valuable correctives, and various wild statements. A slight flurry of Anglo-American ill-will was caused by the critic of the *Herald-Tribune*, who proclaimed that Maurice Evans was worth two John Gielguds. He afterwards emended it to six. This earned us a rather mean little paragraph in the London *Times*, and the intervention of James Agate. This vastly overrated pundit of the British stage announced pontifically that the Richard of both Evans and Gielgud was "six times less good than that of Benson. Evans is all hocus and Gielgud is all pocus"; whatever that may have been supposed to mean. The embarrassed protagonists were happy to let it go.

But these were motes of dust in the general wind of triumph. I had been brought up on the reticence of London managers who, if they had a success, simply printed a fresh batch of tickets and said no more about it. I was dazed by the newspaper advertisements, the banner headlines, the personal interviews, the luncheons, the dinners, the wholesale allocation of laurel crowns. "A play by William Shakespeare is the outstanding drama of Broadway," said the *Telegram*. (Yes, I said to myself, let us by no means forget the author.) The advance booking grew by leaps and bounds. Long lines formed in front of the box office. Most of all, I was impressed by the audiences. The enthusiasm remained just as great as it had been at the opening. At every performance I would watch the still, intent faces, listening spellbound as Shakespeare's magic became potent and alive. For if I was incredulous, I was not ungrateful. The wholehearted warmth of the welcome we had received, the

generous delight of our own colleagues in the theatre, the un-
stinted enthusiasm of the public filled me with a deep sense of
gratitude and obligation. This, I thought, I must study to repay.

The repertory idea had to be abandoned, though for the most
agreeable of reasons—the success of *Richard II*. It would run till
the hot weather, be revived in the fall, and then go on a long tour. I
should come back to redirect it; but in the meanwhile I had nothing
to live on in New York. When I made my contract I had not realized
that American directors all got weekly royalties; and I had cut myself out of the acting job. I booked a sailing home.

One night Maurice and I were at a grand party, sitting close to
Mrs. Patrick Campbell. She said wasn't it wonderful for me and
wasn't I making lots and lots of money. I said yes, and no. Hadn't I
got a percentage? Well, no. She proceeded to proclaim this fact to
the world in her most Campbellian tones. "You poor child, you
ought to have a percentage. Listen! this poor child hasn't got a
percentage!" To Maurice: "*Why* hasn't she got a percentage?
Have *you* got a percentage? But the poor child *must* have a
percentage. *Why* haven't you given her one?" Maurice laughed
amiably and said: "Because I'm too mean!" I stopped blushing and
was delighted.

Before I said goodbye to this golden New York interlude, as I
still thought it, projects of all kinds sprang up around me like
mushrooms. I was a novelty, and so everyone seemed to imagine I
could direct anything. I thought this charming of them, but not
very well judged. However, I made the mistake of supposing that
their plans were really serious, instead of just an emotional release
on the part of the planners. I got involved in a welter of hopes,
fears, promises, determinations, hazards and cross-purposes.
Among the more active ingredients of the cauldron was a "whacky"
comedy which I should have directed very badly. This piece was to
be done in New York—in London—this season—next season—at
once—not at all. This producer was interested; so was that actress;
but not this producer in that actress. Another producer became involved with the same actress—also another actress with the same
producer. The authors sobbed on my shoulder—backers and agents
came and went—everybody planned, fussed, accused, explained, got

hot tempers and cold feet, and nothing ever came of anything. Bedlam, I thought; just my luck to get involved with something as unique as this. It wasn't unique at all, as I later discovered; it was just Broadway behavior.

The date of my sailing drew near. I tried simultanously to buy some clothes, go to the top of the Empire State Building, visit the Metropolitan Museum, see some other shows, repay some of the hospitality which had been showered on me, and provide for every contingency which might arise in the life of *Richard II* after I left. In those happy days the big transatlantic ships would sail at midnight or thereabouts, so much more gaily than the drab, sober morning departures of today. There was a party in my cabin, already overcrowded with luggage and flowers and champagne and telegrams—and two more scripts, I noted sourly. The last bugle sounded, the guests departed, the ship moved down the river. I waved a grateful goodbye to where Number One Fifth Avenue probably wasn't, gave the two scripts a disillusioned look, and made room for myself in bed. So that was New York, I thought. Goodbye and thank you! (But it was not goodbye.)

During the voyage I did a few addition sums. I had had, by good fortune and God's grace, the experience of success. It had come to me fairly late, as theatre careers go, and it was an oddly oblique fulfillment. I had dreamed of being a star actress in London and had turned—for a few moments anyway—into an acclaimed director in New York. I began to realize that I had crossed not merely an ocean, but a professional divide. I had learned to look at the stage from the auditorium instead of the auditorium from the stage. I had learned the perspective of London looked at from New York, instead of the other way around; or I thought I had. At the moment we were in mid-ocean and I couldn't see either shore.

I settled into my own little flat again and went to visit Bedford Street. The faithful Frances was installed, complete with cat. I assured her that my parents would be home soon, at least in two or three months; but in my heart I doubted it a little. My mother's star was in the ascendant over California. *Night Must Fall* had been completed, though not yet released; everyone prophesied a great success for her. She was making a second picture and a third was in prospect. Her letters showed signs of homesickness; but at the same time they described the beginnings of a transplanted salon which seemed to be forming around her as she settled down amid the alien corn.

I wrote to her: "Just a line to tell you London has closed in on me. The phone is in full blast, the rain pouring down, the traffic worse than ever, everything the same as before, and I feel as if I'd never been away . . ." But I had, and everything was, in fact, just a little different.

I was offered the direction of a try-out at one of the outlying theatres. Soon I began wrestling with the difficulties and peculiarities I remembered so well. I had brought with me a huge package of American lighting gelatines. The electrician viewed them mistrustfully. My treasured "chocolate" and "bastard amber" evoked satiric comment. I was rather more dictatorial about the lighting than I used to be. The play was good and a rising young actor named Michael Redgrave was good in it; but nothing happened to it.

One of the scripts I had read on the boat turned out to be good too. I succeeded in getting an English star and an American manager for a New York production during the coming season. Letters about this and about the fall tour of *Richard II* thickened across the Atlantic. I felt uneasy and somehow constricted. Maurice asked me to fix a sailing date. I procrastinated and hoped someone in London might give me an acting job, but nobody did.

The long, beautiful June days went by. I hated to see them slip away; but a tremor of excitement stirred in my blood when I thought about New York. I had never seen it except in the winter. Everyone warned me that the heat in August would be terrible. Rehearsal dates were set. I booked my passage.

The day before I left I paid a last visit to Bedford Street. The rooms were empty and full of echoes. I lifted a hand to Old Ben's picture, said goodbye to Frances and walked down the stairs, which was no longer necessary but seemed more fitting. I went through the churchyard and into the church and looked up at the tablet on the wall with Ellen Terry's name on it. I maneuvered my car out of the gates and up the street between the squashed cabbage leaves.

A week later the towers of Lower Manhattan rose from the skyline to meet me, magical as before and full of promise. The Cunard pier seemed like an old friend. A blast of heat practically knocked me over. But I didn't mind. I felt as if I were coming home.

GENEALOGY

INDEX

Webster and Whitty Family Tree

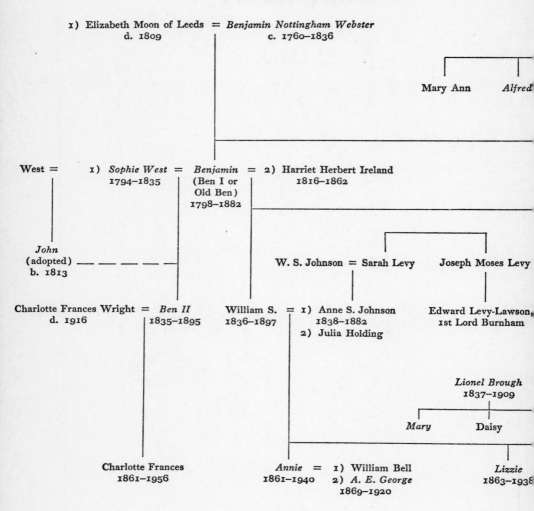

FROM A SHEFFIELD FAMILY

1) Elizabeth Moon of Leeds = *Benjamin Nottingham Webster*
         d. 1809   c. 1760–1836

                                                              Mary Ann   *Alfred*

West =   1) *Sophie West* = *Benjamin* = 2) Harriet Herbert Ireland
                    1794–1835   (Ben I or   1816–1862
                                     Old Ben)
                                     1798–1882

    John   W. S. Johnson = Sarah Levy   Joseph Moses Levy
  (adopted) — — — — — —
   b. 1813

Charlotte Frances Wright = *Ben II*   William S. = 1) Anne S. Johnson   Edward Levy-Lawson,
        d. 1916   1835–1895   1836–1897   1838–1882   1st Lord Burnham
                                                      2) Julia Holding

                                                                        Lionel Brough
                                                                          1837–1909

                                                                      Mary   Daisy

        Charlotte Frances   *Annie* = 1) William Bell   *Lizzie*
           1861–1956   1861–1940   2) *A. E. George*   1863–1938
                                                              1869–1920

Those in italic were actors, dancers, playwrights, or otherwise active in the theatre.

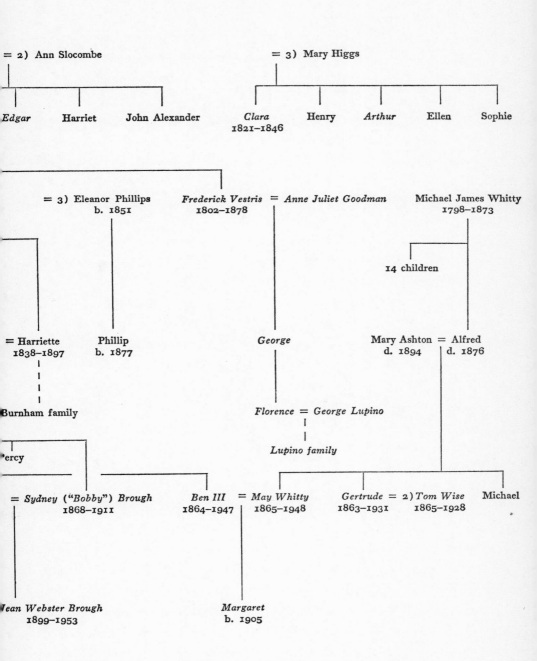

Index of People and Plays

Also of important theatres, organizations, etc. Parts played by Old Ben, Young Ben, May, and Margaret which are mentioned in the text are listed in chronological order.

Abbey Theatre, Dublin, 109, 206, 237
Abraham Lincoln, 289
Achurch, Janet, 148
Ackland, Rodney, 372
Actors' Association, The, 182, 357–9
Actors' Orphanage, 83, 247
Actresses' Franchise League, 249, 251–2
Adams, Maude, 209
Adelphi Theatre, 43, 58, 60, 65, 70–2, 75–81, 84–5, 87–8, 90, 94, 101, 103, 136, 144, 153
Aida, 336, 340
Ainley, Henry, 199, 236, 262, 265, 315
Albery, Sir Bronson, 350
Alexander, Sir George, 125, 143, 154–61, 184, 235
Alexander, Lady, 155
Allen, Viola, 222
Androcles and the Lion, 243, 342
Archer, William, 208, 238, 369
Aria, Eliza, 186, 191
Arms and the Man, 311, 312, 314
Arnott, A., 167, 188
Arts Theatre Club, 305, 330, 345, 350, 367
Asche, Oscar, 236–7, 243
Ashcroft, Dame Peggy, 316, 352, 384, 386
As You Like It, 128, 324, 344

Atkinson, Brooks, 386
Aylmer, Sir Felix, 360

Back to Methuselah, 288
Baddeley, Angela, 291
Baddeley, Hermione, 291
Bainbridge, Captain, 119–21
Bancroft, Sir Squire, 3, 5, 70, 76, 89, 94, 107, 122, 131, 153, 235
Bancroft, Lady (Marie Wilton), 70, 76, 89, 94, 122, 153
Barker, Harley Granville, 201, 207–8, 215–18, 237–44, 295, 329–30, 342, 357
Barrett, Wilson, 122
Barretts of Wimpole Street, The, 354, 362
Barrie, Sir James, 152, 162, 238, 240, 318–19, 334
Barrymore, Ethel, 181–2, 196–201, 209–10, 227
Barrymore, John, 199–200, 297–302, 331, 342, 343
Barrymore, Maurice, 199
Baylis, Lilian, 247, 333, 335–45, 355–7
Bedford, Paul, 78
Beerbohm, Max, 206, 237
Behold, We Live, 355
Belasco, David, 211
Belinda, 270
Ben Nazir, 27

Index of People and Plays

Benson, Sir Frank, 184, 235, 262, 336

Bernhardt, Sarah, 148, 153, 190, 197, 227

Best, Edna, 353

Billington, John, 73

Bill of Divorcement, A, 289

Bing Boys, The, 265

Birmingham Repertory Theatre, 265, 289

Blue Bird, The, 243

Boccaccio, 122

Bohemian Girl, The, 100

Booth, Edwin, 380

Boucicault, Dionysius Lardner, 76, 80–1, 84, 94, 125, 131, 134

Boucicault, Dion (the younger), 125, 241–2, 244, 268–71, 294

Brady, William, 211–14

Braham, John, 26

Braithwaite, Dame Lilian, 252, 254, 264

Brayton, Lily, 236

Bridal, The, 40

British Drama League, 367, 369

Brontë, Charlotte, 4, 54, 362

Brough, Fanny, 145–6, 206

Brough, Jean Webster, ix, 231, 246, 346

Brough, Lizzie: *see* Webster, Eliza

Brough, Lionel, 118, 122, 132, 143, 145, 150

Brough, Robert, 76, 86, 95

Brough, Sydney ("Bobby"), 150, 155, 231

Brough, William, 76, 95

Brough family, ix

Browning, Robert, 40, 125

Buckstone, J. B., 37, 55–7, 61, 63, 66, 70–1, 89

Bulwer-Lytton, Sir Edward, 39, 40, 44–52, 57, 80, 95

Bunn, Alfred, 21, 31, 36, 58, 65

Butt, Dame Clara, 264, 290

Byron, Lord, 20, 44, 49

Campbell, Mrs. Patrick, 158–61, 197, 219–26, 388

Candida, 287, 311, 314

Candidate, The, 135

Captain Brassbound's Conversion, 186

Casson, Sir Lewis, 215, 219, 238, 241, 293–7, 299, 306–9, 315, 335, 347, 360, 369, 371

Caste, 162

Céleste, Mme. (Elliott), 58–62, 65–6, 70, 76–81, 85, 87, 91, 100, 173

Charley's Aunt, 125, 243

Charrington, Margaret, 342

Chekhov, Anton, 95, 215, 316–17, 238, 350

Chekhov, Michael, 370

Cherry Orchard, The, 215, 238, 316–17, 346

Child Born at the Plough, 279

Child of the Wreck, The, 58, 60

Christmas Carol, A, 81

Chu Chin Chow, 237, 266

Church, Esmé, 329, 345–6

Churchill, Winston, 197, 313

City Theatre, Cripplegate, 37

Clancarty, 140, 207

Clandestine Marriage, The, 330–2

Claudel, Paul, 279, 328

Coburg Theatre: *see* Old Vic

Cochran, C. B., 289

Colleen Bawn, The, 76, 81

Collier, Constance, 199, 232–3, 292, 297–8, 300–3, 354

Collins, Wilkie, 72, 85

Colum, Padraic, 109

Comédie Française, 162, 284

Compton, Fay, 297, 300

Confederacy, The, 332–5

Cons, Emma, 13, 247, 337

Cooper, Frank, 168, 176, 181, 183

Cooper, Dame Gladys, 306

Copeau, Jean, 285

Coquelin (Aîné), 93

Cornell, Katharine, 287, 354, 374

Corsican Brothers, The, 165

Index of People and Plays

Count Hannibal, 236
Countess Cathleen, The, 109, 205–6
Court Theatre, London, 214–16, 237–8
Covent Garden, 13, 15, 18–19, 22, 36–40, 44–5, 48, 55, 62, 64, 121
Coward, Noel, 289, 291
Craig, Edith (Ailsa), 162, 168, 171, 174–7, 181, 191, 244, 248–9, 262, 267, 269, 273–81, 333, 355, 383
Craig, E. Gordon, 175, 177–8, 184, 186, 189–91, 280–1
Cricket on the Hearth, The, 81
Criterion Theatre, The, 122, 135, 351, 355
Cruikshank, George, 110
Crystal Palace, 69, 136, 148, 204
Currie, Finlay, 350
Cushman, Charlotte, 66
Cymbeline, 177–8

Daly, Arnold, 209
Daly, Augustin, 148
Dane, Clemence, 193, 278, 289
Dante, 186
Dark Lady of the Sonnets, The, 311, 342
Davenport, E. L., 66, 73
David Garrick, 203
Daviot, Gordon, 366–7
Davis, Richard Harding, 171, 197
Dead Heart, The, 79–80, 90
Dean, Basil, 289
Dear Brutus, 306, 350
De Camp, Victor, 21, 29
Dent, Alan, 219
De Valois, Dame Ninette, 329, 340
Devil's Disciple, The, 311, 347–9
Dickens, Charles, 40, 42, 50, 63–4, 72, 75–83, 85, 115, 148
Diplomacy, 162–3
Doctor's Dilemma, The, 216, 311
Dodd, Henry, 82–3
Doll's House, A, 148, 209, 223
Dorothy, 139, 198

Dowton, William, 25, 46
Drew, John, 199
Drinkwater, John, 289
Drury Lane, Theatre Royal, 13, 15–40, 51–3, 56, 62, 64–5, 81, 88–9, 184, 186, 362, 364
Duke of York's Theatre, 238–42, 364
Du Maurier, Sir Gerald, 70, 152, 163, 197–8, 261, 289, 306, 325, 355
Dunne, Finlay Peter ("Mr. Dooley"), 198, 208, 210
Duse, Eleanora, 148–9, 162, 190, 349

Eadie, Dennis, 238, 240
Eames, Clare, 286–8, 335, 345
East Lynne, 131, 133–4, 184
Edouin, Willie, 145–6
Electra (Hofmannsthal), 221, 223, 225
Elliston, Robert William, 7, 15–16
Elliott, Gertrude (Lady Forbes-Robertson), 199, 263
Elliott, Maxine, 199
Elssler, Fanny, 60
English Nell, 198, 203–4
Embassy Theatre, 305
Enoch Arden, 245
Equity, British Actors', 4, 182, 225, 359–66
Equity, American (AEA), 359, 362–3
Ervine, St. John, 315–16
Esmond, H. V., 162, 198, 200, 209
Esmond, Jill, 309
Espinosa, Edward, 168
Evans, Edith, 336, 361, 372
Evans, Maurice, 292–3, 318, 338, 357, 372–90
Euripides, 207, 215, 294, 296

Fagan, James B., 316–17
Fanatics, The, 289
Fanny's First Play, 242, 311

Index of People and Plays

Farmer's Wife, The, 289
Farren, Nellie, 148
Faucit, Helen, 39, 44, 46, 50, 53, 88
Faust, 166
Faust and Marguerite, 121
Faust Up to Date, 148
Faversham, "Billy", 211, 232–5
Faversham, Julie (Opp), 197, 211, 229, 232–5
Faversham, Philip, 232–5
Faversham, William, 197, 210–11, 232–5
Ffolkes, David, 375–7, 380, 383
Ffrangcon Davies, Gwen, 289, 366–7, 380
Fires of Fate, The, 250
Fisher, Clara, 32
Fiske, Minnie Maddern, 209
Fitzwilliam, Mrs. Fanny, 56, 60–1
Foote, Samuel, 18
Forbes-Robertson, Jean, 317
Forbes-Robertson, Sir Johnston, 69, 162–3, 199, 206, 209, 244, 263
Forster, John, 37, 39, 44–51
Frankau, Pamela, 191
Freaks, The, 269
Frohman, Charles, 211, 238, 240, 242
Full Moon, 319

Galsworthy, John, 152, 215, 289
Garrick Club, 43, 90, 152–3, 248
Gate Theatre, 305
Geisha, The, 201
George, A. E., 207
George, Grace (Mrs. William Brady), 211–14
George V, 232, 250–1, 337
Getting Married, 311
Ghosts, 95
Gielgud, Sir John, 219, 317, 329, 339–45, 350–2, 366–7, 372, 380, 387
Gilbert, Sir W. S., 122, 124
Gillmore, Frank, 363
Girl of the Golden West, The, 211

Girl Unknown, 371–2
Glamorous Night, 364
Godefroi and Yolande, 172–5
Goodner, Carol, 350
Grain of Mustard Seed, The, 289
Green Bushes, The, 66, 87
Green Room Club, 90, 152, 158
Greet, Sir Philip Ben, 129, 321–7, 329, 334, 336, 341, 352, 368
Gregory, Lady, 109, 206
Grein, J. T., 204
Guilbert, Yvette, 197
Guitry, Lucien, 284
Guthrie, Sir Tyrone, 355

Hamlet, 26, 40, 52, 68, 70, 125, 209, 297–303, 309, 339–40, 342–5
Hampden, Walter, 224
Hapgood, Emily, 249–50, 286
Hapgood, Norman, 249–50
Harbour Lights, The, 136, 138
Hardwicke, Sir Cedric, 289, 362
Hare, Sir John, 106, 108, 124, 127–9, 140, 153, 235, 308
Harley, John Pritt, 22
Haymarket, Theatre Royal, 5, 18, 36–7, 40–57, 60–71, 75, 77, 80, 94–5, 122, 247, 297, 334
Hearn, James, 170
Heartbreak House, 288
Hedda Gabler, 215, 221, 225, 287
Henderson, Alexander, 122
Henry IV, 53
Henry V, 44, 139
Henry VIII, 262, 309, 368
High Tor, 384
Hippolytus, 207–8, 294, 299, 303, 308
Hobby-Horse, The, 139
Holcroft, Thomas, 115
Hoodman Blind, 122
Hope, Sir Anthony (Hawkins), 198, 210, 231, 245
Horniman, Miss A. E. F., 237, 247
Hostage, The, 279

Index of People and Plays

House of Temperley, The, 236, 245

Howard, Sidney, 286–7

Howe, Henry H. ("Daddy"), 63, 141, 167–8, 173

How He Lied to Her Husband, 311, 315

Humby, Mrs. Anne, 64

Hunchback, The, 103

Hunt, Martita, 317, 339, 341, 343–4, 355

Ibsen, Henrik, 95, 148, 152, 205, 215, 237, 369

Imaginary Invalid, The, 335, 344

Immortal Hour, The, 289

Importance of Being Earnest, The, 156, 158

Irene Wycherley, 222

Irving, Sir Henry, 70, 88, 99, 105, 122, 125, 131, 140-3, 148, 152, 163–8, 173–91, 357

Irving, H. B., 198

Irving, Laurence, 173, 175, 181, 197

Jackson, Sir Barry, 265, 289

Jane Clegg, 335

Janet Pride, 76

Jefferson, Joseph, 84

Jeffreys, Ellis, 208

Jerrold, Douglas, 42, 63, 85, 95

Jest, The, 297

John Bull's Other Island, 214–18, 311–12

Johnson, W. S., 86, 101, 105

Jolly Roger, The, 361–2

Jones, Henry Arthur, 152

Jones, Robert Edmond, 286, 297

Journey's End, 352

Julius Caesar, 104

Justice, 239, 297

Katerina Ismailova, 370

Kaye-Smith, Sheila, 279

Kean, Charles, 27, 52, 55, 67–70, 76, 82, 94, 105

Kean, Edmund, 10, 11, 15, 20, 22, 25–8, 36–7, 52, 72, 88, 93, 173

Keeley, Mrs. Robert, 75, 88

Keeley, Robert, 74, 75

Keen, Malcolm, 356

Keith, Ian, 383

Kelly, Fanny, 25

Kemble, Charles, 37

Kemble, Fanny, 30, 54, 60

Kendal, Mrs. (afterwards Dame Madge), 118–20, 122, 124–5, 127–8, 131, 137, 152, 308, 323

Kendal, W. H., 108, 119, 122, 124–5, 128, 131, 140, 152, 207, 308

King Arthur, 163, 171

King John, 77

King Lear, 53, 370

Kipling, Rudyard, 201

Kismet, 236–7

Klaw and Erlanger, 212

Knoblock, Edward, 237

Knowles, James Sheridan, 40, 95

Komisarjevsky, T., 316–17, 350, 370

Kotzebue, August von, 68

Lackaye, Wilton, 170

Lacy, Walter, 46–7, 63

Lady from Alfaqueque, The, 329–30

Lady from the Sea, The, 369

Lady of Lyons, The, 44–6, 103

Lady Windermere's Fan, 156–8, 161

Lake, The, 354

Lang, Matheson, 236

Langtry, Lily, 149

Last of Mrs. Cheney, The, 306

La Trobe, Charles, 334

Laughton, Charles, 317, 339

Laurie, John, 356

La Vallière, 39

Index of People and Plays

Lawrence, Gertrude, 291, 354

Lawson, Sir Edward (afterwards Lord Burnham), 90, 100, 105-6

Leah Kleschna, 209

Lee, Auriol, 330-2

Le Gallienne, Eva, 234, 287

Le Gallienne, Julie, 232

Le Gallienne, Richard, 201, 232

Lemon, Mark, 42, 60, 76, 85, 95

Leslie, Fred, 148

Levy, Joseph Moses, 105

Lights o' London, The, 122

Liliom, 346

Lind, Jenny, 60

Linda Grey, 148

Little Minister, The, 209

Litton, Marie, 118, 121

Liverpool Daily Post, The, 111-15

Liverpool Journal, The, 110-11

Livesey, Roger, 350

Loftus, Cecilia (Cissie), 197, 210, 221, 227, 290, 354

London Assurance, 131

London Theatre Council, 364-5

Lonsdale, Frederick, 288, 306

Lord Chamberlain, 18, 45, 51, 76, 204, 304

Lost in London, 144

Louis XI, 164

Loveday, H. J., 167, 179

Love's Labour's Lost, 129, 324

Lunt, Alfred and Lynne (Fontanne), 354

Lupino family, ix

Lyceum Theatre, 79-80, 88, 122, 125, 141, 166-7, 177-82, 185-6, 188

Lyons Mail, The, 164

Macbeth, 53, 104, 141-2, 170, 178, 287, 315, 340, 343-5, 355-7

Macdona, Charles, 310-11, 314

Macdona Players, The, 310-15, 318, 352

Macready, William Charles, 22, 27, 29-33, 36-7, 39-40, 44-57, 63,

Macready (*continued*) 66, 69, 72, 79, 81, 88, 94, 173

Mackenzie, Ronald, 350-1

Madame Sans-Gêne, 180, 183

Madras House, The, 239

Maeterlinck, Maurice, 215, 243

Magda, 221, 226

Major Barbara, 293, 311, 373

Man and Superman, 214-15, 310-12

Man of Destiny, The, 311

Man of Honour, A, 206-7

Mansfield, Richard, 143-4, 170

Marriage of Kitty, The, 241

Marriage of William Asche, The, 211-12

Marshall, Herbert, 353, 355

Marston, Westland, 42, 52, 93, 95

Martin Chuzzlewit, 63, 81

Martin Harvey, Sir John, 80, 164-8, 184, 235, 347-8

Martin Harvey, Lady (N. de Silva), 167-8, 347-8

Martyn, Edward, 205

Mary Rose, 319

Masaniello, 60

Mascotte, La, 122

Masefield, John, 215, 328

Masks and Faces, 69

Massey, Raymond, 360

Master Builder, The, 162, 205, 367

Master Betty (William Henry West), 10

Mathews, Charles J., 55, 74, 79, 88

Maugham, W. Somerset, 152, 206, 288-9

McCarthy, Justin Huntley, 147, 197

Meade, Tom, 168

Medea, 288, 335

Medicine Man, The, 185

Meierhold, V. E., 371

Melba, Dame Nellie, 200

Mellon, Mrs. Alfred (Sarah), 78, 87

Merchant of Venice, The, 68, 105, 269, 274-7, 321-3, 342, 367

Index of People and Plays

Merry Wives of Windsor, The, 186, 323–4

MGM, 374–6, 381

Mice and Men, 198–9

Midsummer Night's Dream, A, 243, 262, 340, 344

Mikhoels, Solomon M., 370

Milne, A. A., 270

Millward, Jessie, 136, 182, 184–5

Milton, Ernest, 174, 279, 337, 361

Miracle, The, 244, 279

Misalliance, 231

Molière, 342, 343

Molnar, Ferenc, 346

Money, 46–51, 57, 69, 89

Montgomery, Robert, 372

Moore, Eva (Mrs. H. V. Esmond), 162, 198, 200, 251, 284, 301

Moore, George, 205–6

Morris, David E., 36

Morris, Margaret, 291

Mountain Sylph, The, 120–1

Mr. Pim Passes By, 270

Mrs. Warren's Profession, 311, 314

Murray, Sir Gilbert, 207–8, 296

Musical Chairs, 350–1, 355, 366

Nazimova, Alla, 223

Ned McCobb's Daughter, 287

Neebe, William, 131–5

Nemirovich-Danchenko, Vladimir, 370

New Theatre, 268–9, 294, 366

New Way to Pay Old Debts, A, 24

Nightingale, Joseph, 116, 118–19, 121

Night Must Fall, 373–4, 389

Notorious Mrs. Ebbsmith, The, 221, 225

Novello, Ivor, 346–7, 364

Octoroon, The, 76, 134, 137

Okhlopkov, N. P., 370

Old Ladies, The, 372

Old Vic (Royal Coburg Theatre), 13, 305, 320–1, 328–9, 335–45, 352, 355–7, 380

Oliver Twist, 154

Olivier, Sir Laurence, 309, 342, 352, 357, 367

Only Way, The, 80, 168, 348

Open Your Eyes, 359

Osbaldiston, D. W., 37–8

Othello, 18, 40, 53, 125, 348, 370

Our Boys, 162

Our Flat, 145–6, 149

Oxberry, John, 56

Oxford Players, The, 316–19, 334

Paolo and Francesca, 199, 203

Paquebot Tenacity (S. S. Tenacity), 285, 345

Parker, Louis N., 263–4

Parnell, Charles Stewart, 147

Parnell, 371, 374

Passing of the Third Floor Back, The, 263

Peg o' My Heart, 265

Percy, S. Esmé, 314

Peter Ibbetson, 297

Peter Pan, 244–5, 294

Peter the Great, 181, 185

Phelps, Samuel, 40, 44, 50, 70, 77, 141

Philanderer, The, 216, 243, 311–12, 318

Phillips, Stephen, 203

Phillips, Watts, 79–80

Pillars of Society, The, 148

Pinero, Sir Arthur Wing, 95, 152, 158–60, 235, 237–8, 240, 269, 288

Pitoëffs, the, 285

Pizarro, 20, 95

Planché, J. R., 95

Playboy of the Western World, The, 237

Poel, William, 241, 295–6, 326, 342

Power, Tyrone, I, 42, 57–8, 66

Power, Tyrone, III, 57

Price, Stephen, 24–5
Prince Consort, 102
Prince Consort, The, 207–9
Prince Karl, 143
Prince of Wales (afterwards Edward VII), 149, 231
Prince of Wales (afterwards Edward VIII), 253, 373
Prisoner of Zenda, The, 156, 170, 198, 265
Proud Maisie, 236
Purgatory, 279
Pygmalion, 310–11

Quality Street, 208, 334–5
Queen Mary, 251–4, 337
Queen of Scots, 367–8
Queen Victoria, 40, 44, 68–9, 77, 82, 103, 165, 185, 201–2
Quid Pro Quo, 64
Quintero brothers, 329

Rachel, Mme., 72
Rain, 289
Rawlings, Margaret, 350
Reade, Charles, 69, 94–5
Redgrave, Sir Michael, 390
Reed, Joseph Verner, 372, 378
Rees, David, 12, 42, 49
Rehan, Ada, 148
Reinhardt, Max, 244
Réjane, Mme., 180
Relph, George, 297, 303
Reunion in Vienna, 354
Rhodes, Harrison, 197, 285–6
Richard II, 343, 374–5, 377–90
Richard III, 10, 11, 29, 43, 143, 179, 297, 331
Richard of Bordeaux, 366–7
Richardson, Sir Ralph, 345
Richelieu, 44, 46
Ricketts, Charles, 293, 309, 315
Rigoletto, 340
Rip Van Winkle, 84, 122
Road to Ruin, 115–16

Robertson, Tom, 95, 124, 127, 238
Robey, George, 261, 361–2
Robson, Dame Flora, 369
Romance, 265
Romeo and Juliet, 66, 103, 342, 372
Rorke, Kate, 292
Rorke, Mary, 168, 174
Royal Dramatic College, The, 82–4, 86
Rupert of Hentzau, 155
Rutherford, Margaret, 350
Ruy Blas, 104

Sacred Flame, The, 288
Sadler's Wells, 18, 70, 77, 141
St. Helena, 372
St. James's Theatre (London), 43, 108, 122, 124–5, 127–9, 131, 136–7, 140, 149, 155–8, 160, 241, 265, 306, 364
St. James Theatre (New York), 378
Saint Joan, 288, 293–5, 297, 307–8, 310, 372
St. John, Christopher, 248, 267
St. Mary's Eve, 60
Salvini, Tomaso, 125
School for Scandal, The, 59, 88, 131, 133, 143, 262
Scrap of Paper, A, 125, 129
Seagull, The, 238
Second Mrs. Tanqueray, The, 158, 160–1
Secret Service, 182
Shakespeare, William, 7, 18, 31, 44, 55, 67, 70, 103, 122, 129, 138, 141, 163, 166, 181, 203, 241–2, 262, 295–6, 305, 321, 326, 335–6, 338–40, 342–3, 345, 357, 368, 379, 381–2, 386–7
Shaw, George Bernard, 95, 152, 178, 186, 201, 205–6, 214–19, 231, 238, 242, 280, 288, 293–4, 308, 310, 314–15, 318, 342–3, 347, 349
Shaw, Glen Byam, 317

Index of People and Plays

She Stoops to Conquer, 131, 143

Sheldon, Suzanne (afterwards Ainley), 181, 196–7, 199, 209, 232–3, 268

Sheridan, Richard Brinsley, 19, 95, 131

Shewing-up of Blanco Posnet, The, 311

Shore Acres, 170

Shubert, Lee and J. J., 212

Siddons, Mrs. Sarah, 19, 142

Silver Cord, The, 287

Sim, Alastair, 356

Simpson, J. Palgrave, 42, 91

Six Characters in Search of an Author, 285

Sothern, E. H., 170, 197

Sothern, Sam, 197, 200

Spanish Curate, The, 370

Squaw Man, The, 211

Stage Guild, The, 359–60

Stanislavsky, Constantin, 215, 370

Star and Garter Hospital, 253–4

Stirling, Mrs. Arthur (Fanny), 66

Stoker, Bram, 167

Story of Waterloo, A, 187–8

Stranger, The, 68

Stratford-on-Avon, 130, 320–1

Strindberg, August, 318–19

Sullivan, Sir Arthur, 124

Sullivan, Barry, 66

Synge, J. M., 237

Tale of Beatrice, The, 279

Tale of Two Cities, A, 79–80

Taming of the Shrew, The, 67, 148, 357

Tandy, Jessica, 350

Taylor, Tom, 69, 79, 95

Tearle, Sir Godfrey, 236, 360

Tempest, The, 323–5, 345

Tempest, Dame Marie, 139, 199, 202–4, 209, 214, 231, 241, 270, 364

Terriss, William, 136, 178, 182, 184–5

Terry, Fred, 162, 235, 262–3

Terry, Ellen, 125, 127, 141–3, 148, 153, 166–84, 186, 189–91, 255, 262–3, 274–81, 342, 355, 390

Terry, Marion, 159, 161, 264

Thackeray, William Makepeace, 72, 82

Theatre Guild, The, 212

Theatrical Ladies' Guild, 246–7

There's Always Juliet, 353, 355

Thomas, Brandon, 125

Thorndike, Dame Sybil, 219, 238, 279, 293–7, 299, 306–9, 315, 335–6, 360, 365–6

Three Arts Club, 290, 347

Three Sisters, The, 317

Toole, J. L., 73, 78, 81

Tree, Sir Herbert Beerbohm, 154, 181, 186, 232, 235, 262, 357

Trelawny of the Wells, 197, 240–3, 268–9

Trevelyan, Hilda, 238, 244, 334

Trilby, 170

Trojan Women, The, 294–7

Trumpet Call, The, 159

Trumpeter's Daughter, The, 61

Twelfth Night, 66, 244, 285, 321–2

Two Foscari, The, 44

Two Gentlemen of Verona, The, 129

Tyler, George, 220, 225

Uncle Vanya, 238, 316–18

Used Up, 66, 68

Valentine, Sydney, 168, 174–5, 240, 358

Vanbrugh, Irene, 156, 238, 241–2, 268, 270, 290, 294

Vanbrugh, Violet, 156, 290

Van Druten, John, 330, 353, 355

Vedrenne, J. E., 214, 216, 238

Vestris, Gaetano, 4

Vestris, Mme. (Eliza), 20, 55–6, 60

Index of People and Plays

Vikings, The, 186
Voysey Inheritance, The, 357

Walker, London, 162
Wall, Alfred M., 357, 359–61
Wallace, Edgar, 288
Wallack, James W. (Sr.), 20, 26, 50
Wallack, J. W. (Jr.), 66, 73
Waller, Lewis, 203, 236
Waring, Florrie, 147, 149
Waring, Herbert, 125, 147, 185, 297
Watson, Henrietta, 206
Webb, Alan, 317
Webster, Alfred, 8, 35
Webster, Annie ("Booey"), 101–6, 108, 125–6, 128–32, 137, 146, 162, 207, 248, 334
Webster, Arthur, 35, 43
Webster, Ben I (Old Ben), ix, x, 109, 118, 121, 132, 141, 153, 173, 184, 362, 390; portraits of, 3–5; birth, x, 7; childhood, 8–9; early struggles, 9–15; marriage to Sophie West, 12; at Drury Lane, 20–8; diary, 25–7; parentage of John, 28–32; at the Haymarket, 36; writes *Highways and Byways, The Golden Farmer,* 39; second marriage, 39; takes over the Haymarket, 40; association with Macready, 39–40, 52–3; production of *Money,* 46–51; Haymarket regime, 55–71; with Mme. Céleste, 60–2; the old Adelphi, 65, 70, 76–8; on Shakespeare, 67; Royal performances, 67–9; letters to, 72–5; the New Adelphi, 78; *Dead Heart* controversy, 79–81; Royal Dramatic College, 82–3; last years at Adelphi, 84–8; farewell benefits, 88–9; third marriage, 89; old age and death, 90–1; summary of career, ix, 92–5; widow and son,

Webster, Ben I (continued)
99–100; children and grandchildren, 86, 100–1

PRINCIPAL PARTS:
Apollo Belvi (*Killing No Murder*), 3
Tartuffe, 3, 41, 93
Triplet (*Masks and Faces*), 3, 41, 69, 93
Harlequin, 9–10, 21
Henry Morland (*The Hier-at-Law*), 15
Almagro (*Pizarro*), 20
Pantaloon, 20–1
Pompey (*Measure for Measure*), 22–3
Erni (*William Tell*), 23
Domingo (*The Boy of Santillane*), 32
Rodrigo (*Othello*), 37
Oswald (*King Lear*), 37
Lancelot Gobbo (*The Merchant of Venice*), 37
Gratiano (*The Merchant of Venice*), 70, 105
Dogberry (*Much Ado About Nothing*), 37
Bob Acres (*The Rivals*), 41, 93
Graves (*Money*), 47–8, 89
Petruchio (*The Taming of the Shrew*), 67, 93
Feste (*Twelfth Night*), 66, 93
Malvolio (*Twelfth Night*), 66
Falstaff (*The Merry Wives of Windsor*), 70
Robert Landry (*The Dead Heart*), 79–80, 93
Joey Ladle (*No Thoroughfare*), 84
Jesuit (*The Wandering Jew*), 88
Webster, Mrs. Ben I: (1) Sophie West, 12, 15, 17, 21, 28–31, 34, 39, 88; (2) Harriet Herbert Ireland, 39, 61, 85, 89; (3) Eleanor Phillips, 89, 99–100

Index of People and Plays

Webster, Ben II, 39, 61–2, 84–5, 100–1

Webster, Mrs. Ben II (Charlotte Frances Wright), 86, 100–1

Webster, Ben III (Young Ben): birth, 86, 102; childhood, 102–7; choice of profession, 107; meets May Whitty, 126; amateur performances, 108, 129, 139; as lawyer, 129, 131, 139; first tour, 129–30; courtship of May, 129, 137; debut, 140; joins Irving in *Macbeth*, 141–3; marries May, ix, 149; describes Hare and Bancroft, 153; with Alexander, 156–61; returns to Irving, 163; American tour, 166–76; with Lyceum company, 177–84; describes Irving, 187–9; Bedford Street home, 193–9; theatre in Nineteen Hundreds, 205–8; second American tour, 208–15; with Shaw and Granville Barker, 214–19; in America with Mrs. Pat Campbell, 165–71; theatre before World War I, 236–8; return to Barker, 242; early films, 245–6; war films, 265; with Irene Vanbrugh, 268–70; end of war, 271; friend of Ellen Terry, 277–8; difficulties in postwar theatre, 288–90; with Ivor Novello, 346; Actors' Ass'n and British Equity, 357–64; as John of Gaunt, 366; in New York, 374–5; to Hollywood, 381; death, x

PRINCIPAL PARTS:
Le Beau (*As You Like It*), 129
Lord Woodstock (*Clancarty*), 140
Malcolm (*Macbeth*), 141
With Alexander: many parts, including Ardale (*The Second Mrs. Tanqueray*), Cecil Graham and Lord Darlington

PRINCIPAL PARTS (continued)
(*Lady Windermere's Fan*), 156–61
Irving repertory: parts included Gratiano, Claudio, Hastings, Guiderius (*Cymbeline*), Lancelot, Valentine (*Faust*), De Neipperg (*Madame Sans-Gêne*), Kikine (*Peter the Great*), 163, 184
De Fauchet (*The Only Way*), 80
With Forbes-Robertson: parts included George Lovell (*Mice and Men*), Cassio (*Othello*), Laertes (*Hamlet*), 199
Simon Dale (*English Nell*), 198
Cashel Byron (*The Admirable Bashville*), 205
Basil Kent (*A Man of Honour*), 207
Hippolytus (*Hippolytus*), 207
Prince Cyril (*The Prince Consort*), 205
Geoffrey Cliffe (*The Marriage of William Asche*), 211
Larry (*John Bull's Other Island*), 215, 217–18
Ridgeon (*The Doctor's Dilemma*), 216
Charteris (*The Philanderer*), 217
Lucas Cleeve (*The Notorious Mrs. Ebbsmith*), 221
Lövborg (*Hedda Gabler*), 221
Von Keller (*Magda*), 221
Orestes (*Electra*), 221
Sir Charles (*The House of Temperley*), 236; as film, 245
The Caliph (*Kismet*), 236
Torvald (*A Doll's House*), 237
The Captain (*Androcles and the Lion*), 243
The Stranger (*The Passing of the Third Floor Back*), 263

Index of People and Plays

PRINCIPAL PARTS (continued)

Tom Wrench (*Trelawny of the Wells*), 268

The Skeleton Man (*The Freaks*), 269

John Tremayne (*Belinda*), 270

George (*Mr. Pim Passes By*), 270

The Judge (*Liliom*), 346

George Parker (*Symphony in Two Flats*), 346

John of Gaunt (*Richard of Bordeaux*), 366

The Judge (*Night Must Fall*), 278

Webster, Mrs. Ben III: *see* May Whitty

Webster, Benjamin Nottingham (of Bath), 6–9, 34–5, 39

Webster, Mrs. Benjamin Nottingham: (1) Elizabeth Moon, 7; (2) Ann Slocombe, 8; (3) Mary Higgs, 8, 34–5

Webster, Charlotte Frances, 100–1

Webster, Clara, 8, 35, 43, 65, 88

Webster, Eliza (Lizzie), 101–6, 108, 128–32, 149–50, 172, 174, 231, 243, 246

Webster, Frederick Vestris, 8, 12, 33, 43, 83, 85

Webster, George, 43

Webster, Harriette, 39, 90, 106–8

Webster, John (West), 29–34, 39, 43, 46, 77

Webster, Margaret (Peggy): meets Old Ben, 3–5; and Mme. Céleste, 58; birth and infancy, 209–11, 228; memory of Mrs. Pat, 219–20; childhood at Chiddingfold and Woolacombe, 232–5, 249–50, 259; early theatregoing, 243–6; memories of World War I, 250–1, 259–63, 268–9; doubtful debut, 263–5; school, 269, 271–3, 283; appearances with Ellen Terry, 273–7; and Edith Craig, 278–80;

Webster, Margaret (*continued*) in Paris and Venice, 283–6; at Etlinger dramatic school, 291–3; debut in *The Trojan Women*, 296–7; in *Hamlet*, 299–303; club and theatre society shows, 304–5, 330–4, 345, 349–52, 367–9; with the Cassons, 307–10, 315, 335; with Macdona Players, 310–15; changes name, 315–16; on Chekhov, 316–17; with Oxford Players, 317–19; "child of famous parents", 320–1; with Ben Greet, 321–7; own theatre enterprises, 332–4, 345–6, 351; at the Old Vic, 335, 339–45, 355–7; success in West End, 350–1; summary of apprentice years, 351–2; with Gielgud, 366–7; British Equity, 360–5; first attempts at directing, 367–9; Moscow Theatre Festival, 369–71; goes to New York, ix, x, 374–6; directs *Richard II*, 377–89; to London and back, 389–91

PRINCIPAL PARTS:

Chorus (*The Trojan Women*), 296–7

Gentlewoman (*Hamlet*), 299

Leader of Chorus (*Hippolytus*), 303

Understudy of Saint Joan, 307–9

With Macdona Players: many parts, including Mrs. Pierce (*Pygmalion*), Violet (*Man and Superman*), Nora (*John Bull's Other Island*), Louka (*Arms and the Man*), Blanche (*Widowers' Houses*), Julia (*The Philanderer*), Lady Brit (*Major Barbara*), Mrs. Dudgeon (*The Devil's Disciple*), 310–15

Gentlewoman (*Macbeth*), 315

With Oxford Players: parts included Sonya (*Uncle Vanya*),

Index of People and Plays

PRINCIPAL PARTS (*continued*)

Anna (*Full Moon*), Phoebe (*Quality Street*), 317–19

Ben Greet Shakespeare Company: parts included Portia, Viola, Rosaline, Rosalind, Mrs. Ford, Hermia, 321–7

Betty (*The Clandestine Marriage*), 330–2

Flippanta (*The Confederacy*), 332–4

Miss Fanny (*Quality Street*), 334

Old Vic repertory: parts included Lady Capulet, Nerissa, Lady Macduff, Audrey, Hermia, Dutchess of York, Toinette (*The Imaginary Invalid*), Megaera (*Androcles and the Lion*), 339–45

Judith (*The Devil's Disciple*), 347–8

Henriette (*Étienne*), 349

Lady Jasper (*A Murder Has Been Arranged*), 349

Mary (*Musical Chairs*), 350

Lady Macbeth (*Macbeth*), 356

Mary Derby (*Richard of Bordeaux*), 366

Mrs. Burbage (*Spring 1600*), 367

Mary Beaton (*Queen of Scots*), 367

Hilda Wangel (*The Master Builder*), 367

Anna Steele (*Parnell*), 372

PLAYS DIRECTED (to 1937):

Henry VIII, Snow in Summer, Love of Women, No Longer Mourn, The Lady from the Sea, Return to Yesterday, Heads I Win . . . !, A Ship Comes Home, Family Hold Back, Richard II, Lovers' Meeting, Three Set Out, Old Music

Webster, Mary Anne, 8

Webster, Philip, 89, 100

Webster, William S., 39, 86, 101–6, 231

Webster, Mrs. William S. (Anne Sarah Johnson), 86, 101

Werner, 49

Whitty, Alfred, 113–16

Whitty, Mrs. Alfred (Mary Louise Ashton), 113–18, 120–4, 129, 132–3, 135–6, 145, 147, 149

Whitty, Anna, 113–14, 130, 248, 254

Whitty, Edward, 112

Whitty, Gertrude (Gretchen; Mrs. Tom Wise), 113–18, 121, 123–4, 129, 132–3, 147, 149–50, 168–9, 176, 199, 208, 214, 223, 228, 265, 319–20, 330–3, 345, 353

Whitty, Dame May, x, xi, 58, 108–9; birth, 113; childhood, 113–18; first appearance, 119–21; comes to London, 121–2; in operetta, 122–4; joins Kendal company, 125; meets Ben, 126; at St. James's, 127–8; tour with Websters, 129–31; in stock, 132–5; tours in melodrama, 136–9; illnesses, 137–9, 148, 176, 198, 210, 229; with Mansfield, 143–4; success in *Our Flat*, 146; river life, 147–9, 200–1; marries Ben, ix, 149; Woolacombe, 150; Forbes-Robertson tour, 162–3; joins Irving, 164–5; in America, 166–76; death of Terriss, 184–5; describes Ellen Terry, 189–90; Bedford Street "salon", 193–9; new century, 201–2; Abbey Theatre begins, 205–6; in America, 208–15; birth of Peggy, 209; describes Mrs. Pat, 220; third American tour, 222–8; Christian Science, 229; prewar years, 230–2; with Granville Barker, 239–42; work for charities, 246, 251, 261, 290; suffrage movement,

Whitty, Dame May (*continued*)
247–9; war work, 251–5;
awarded D.B.E., 255; life in
wartime, 265–71; runs Etlinger
School, 290–3, 306; returns to
stage, 306; social life, 321; in
New York, 353–5; London performances, 355; British Equity,
357–66; *Night Must Fall*, 372,
389; in New York, ix, x, 374–6;
to Hollywood, 381, 389; death, x

PRINCIPAL PARTS:
Chorus in operetta, 119–24
Mary (*A Scrap of Paper*), 125
Neebe repertory: parts included
Lady Teazle, Lydia Languish,
Kate Hardcastle, Lady Isabel
(*East Lynne*), and heroines
of Boucicault melodramas,
132–5
Dora Vane (*The Harbour
Lights*), 136
Lady Sneerwell (*The School for
Scandal*), 143
Constance (*She Stoops to Con-
quer*), 143
Nelly (*Lost in London*), 144
Margery Sylvester (*Our Flat*),
145
Countess Zicka (*Diplomacy*),
162
Irene (*The Profligate*), 162
Irving repertory: parts included
ingenues in *The Corsican
Brothers*, *The Lyons Mail*,
and *Louis XI*, Jessica (*The
Merchant of Venice*), Gentle-
woman (*Macbeth*), 164–76
Edith Varney (*Secret Service*),
182
Miss Susan (*Quality Street*),
208
Carrie (*Irene Wycherley*), 222
Amelia (*The Madras House*),
239

PRINCIPAL PARTS (*con-
tinued*)
Trafalgar Gower (*Trelawny of
the Wells*), 240–1
Mrs. Corsellis (*The Enchanted
Cottage*), 288
Mrs. Ebley (*The Last of Mrs.
Cheney*), 306
Mrs. Coade (*Dear Brutus*), 306
Dame Frances Evers (*Behold,
We Live*), 355
Mildred Surrege (*The Lake*),
355
Mrs. Voysey (*The Voysey In-
heritance*), 357
Mrs. Bramson (*Night Must
Fall*), 373
Whitty, Michael, 113–16, 121, 129,
135, 147, 208
Whitty, Michael James, 109–15
Whitty, Sarah, 113–14, 130, 248,
254
Widowers' Houses, 311–12
Wigan, Mr. and Mrs. Alfred, 79
Wild Duck, The, 162
Wilde, Oscar, 142, 152, 156–8,
165–6, 201
William IV, 40
William Tell, 32–3
Williams, Emlyn, 319, 349, 372
Williams, Harcourt, 335, 339–44
Winston, James, 15
Wise, Tom, 169, 176, 199, 201,
208, 229, 319–20
Wolfit, Sir Donald, 339, 343, 367
Wright, Edward, 79, 86
Wright family, ix
Wyndham, Sir Charles, 70, 122,
135–6, 203, 235
Wyse, John, 328–9, 332–3, 345–6

Yeats, W. B., 109, 205–6, 279
You Never Can Tell, 209, 311
Young Folks' Ways, 108